# The
# Schools
# We Need

## And Why
## We Don't
## Have Them

## Also by E. D. Hirsch, Jr.

Wordsworth and Schelling (1960)

Innocence and Experience: An Introduction to Blake (1964)

Validity in Interpretation (1967)

The Aims of Interpretation (1976)

The Philosophy of Composition (1977)

Cultural Literacy (1987)

The Dictionary of Cultural Literacy, with Joseph Kett and
James Trefil (1988)

A First Dictionary of Cultural Literacy, with William Rowland and
Michael Stanford (1989)


*Editor, The Core Knowledge Series (1991–96)*

What Your Kindergartner Needs to Know (1996)

What Your First Grader Needs to Know (1991)

What Your Second Grader Needs to Know (1991)

What Your Third Grader Needs to Know (1992)

What Your Fourth Grader Needs to Know (1992)

What Your Fifth Grader Needs to Know (1993)

What Your Sixth Grader Needs to Know (1993)

# The Schools We Need

## And Why We Don't Have Them

E. D. Hirsch, Jr.

DOUBLEDAY

New York London Sydney Auckland Toronto

⚓

PUBLISHED BY DOUBLEDAY
a division of Bantam Doubleday Dell Publishing Group, Inc.
1540 Broadway, New York, New York 10036

DOUBLEDAY and the portrayal of an anchor with a dolphin
are trademarks of Doubleday, a division of
Bantam Doubleday Dell Publishing Group, Inc.

*Book design by Claire Naylon Vaccaro*

Library of Congress Cataloging-in-Publication Data

Hirsch, E. D. (Eric Donald), 1928–
The schools we need and why we don't have them / E. D. Hirsch, Jr.—
1st ed.
p.    cm.
Includes bibliographical references.
1. Education—United States—Aims and objectives.   2. Education—
United States—Philosophy.   3. Educational change—United States.
4. Education—Social aspects—United States.   I. Title.
LA210.H57   1996
370'.973—dc20        96-2192
CIP

ISBN 0-385-48457-7

7   9   10   8   6

This Book Is Dedicated

to the Teachers and Principals of Core Knowledge Schools

and

to the Memory of Two Prophets,

William C. Bagley and Antonio Gramsci,

Who Explained in the 1930s

Why the New Educational Ideas

Would Lead to Greater Social Injustice

# Acknowledgments

I am grateful for the encouragement of many friends and educators who have sustained my energy in writing this book.

I ventured to ask the best scholars and scientists I could think of for criticisms of the manuscript, not daring to hope that they would find the time to perform the onerous chore. Each responded with astonishing thoroughness and speed.

Three scholars generously surveyed the entire manuscript. They are Chester E. Finn, Jr., whose general acumen and knowledge of the policy scene are unparalleled, and whose editorial skills are legendary; Diane Ravitch, whose trenchant mind and unequaled knowledge of the history of contemporary American education make her the outstanding educational historian of our day; and Robert Siegler, a cognitive psychologist of great distinction, whom I have never met, but who, because of his profound commitment to improving the education of young children, agreed to vet the scientific side of the book, and who provided a detailed and enormously useful commentary.

Further expert commentary on the manuscript was provided by Carl Bereiter, David Breneman, David Geary, John Holdren, Michael Marshall, Albert Shanker, Herbert Walberg, Clint Wilkinson, and Dan Willingham. Answers to queries on specific points were generously provided by Marilyn J. Adams, John Bishop, Ronald Ferguson, Connie Juel, John Kelleher, Daniel Koretz, Archie LaPointe, John Lloyd, Brenda Loyd, Jean Osborn, Sandra Scarr, Harold Stevenson, and Sara Tarver.

Michael Angell was my cheerful, encouraging, well-informed, and tireless research assistant, who brought me many pounds of Xeroxes and books, thus freeing me for the task of reading them rather than searching for them.

In a special category belongs an astute critic of every word of this book at every stage of its composition—my wife, Polly Hirsch. Patiently tolerant of my obsessions, she has gently led me into paths of sound common sense and toward a charitable understanding of the good intentions behind even the most egregiously failed educational practices.

I am filled with gratitude for all this help, which could only have come from a shared sense of the urgent need for what this book attempts to do. None of these outstanding scholars, educators, and scientists, to whom I owe so much, can be held responsible, however, for any shortcomings in this exposition. The defects are entirely my own.

# Contents

Soon or late, it is ideas, not vested interests, which are dangerous for good or evil.

—JOHN MAYNARD KEYNES,
*The General Theory of Employment,
Interest, and Money* (1936)

The new concept of schooling is in its romantic phase, in which the replacement of "mechanical" by "natural" methods has become unhealthily exaggerated. . . . Previously pupils at least acquired a certain baggage of concrete facts. Now there will no longer be any baggage to put in order. . . . The most paradoxical aspect of it all is that this new type of school is advocated as being democratic, while in fact it is destined not merely to perpetuate social differences but crystallize them in Chinese complexities.

—ANTONIO GRAMSCI,
*Prison Notebooks,*
Quadèrno XXIX (1932)

Blind mouths! that scarce themselves know how to hold
A sheep-hook, or have learned aught else the least
That to the faithful herdman's art belongs!
What recks it them? What need they? They are sped;
And when they list, their lean and flashy songs
Grate on their scrannel pipes of wretched straw;
The hungry sheep look up and are not fed.

—JOHN MILTON,
"Lycidas," ll. 119–25

*Sed quis custodiet ipsos custodes?* (Who will reform the reformers?)

—JUVENAL,
*Satires,* 6, l. 347

# The
# Schools
# We Need

## And Why
## We Don't
## Have Them

# 1.

# Introduction:
# Failed Theories,
# Famished Minds

## 1.
## Continued Educational Failure

Take a young boy or girl from a typical American family who goes to a typical American school, and imagine that child growing up in France or Germany, Japan or Taiwan. Few would choose to make the experiment. Most Americans believe, as do I, that this country, with its traditions of political freedom and its generous optimism, is the greatest country in the world. But the evidence is strong that that very same young child would grow up more competent in those other countries than in the United States—through having learned much, much more at school in the early grades. Although our political traditions and even our universities may be without peer, our K–12 education is among the least effective in the developed world.[1] Its controlling theories, curricular incoherencies, and what I call its "naturalistic fallacies" are positive barriers to a good education. Scholars from abroad who study American schools are astonished that our children, who score very low in international comparisons, are actually as competent as they manage to be.[2] Considering their very American vitality and independent-mindedness, one thinks ruefully of what these children could become under a good, demanding, and fair educational system!

The importance of theories in human affairs was memorably stated by John Maynard Keynes: "Practical men, who believe themselves to be quite exempt from any intellectual influences, are usually the slaves of some defunct economist. . . . It is ideas, not vested interests, that are dangerous for good or evil."[3] Keynes's observation was confirmed on a grand scale by the fall of communism, which consisted less in a failed political arrangement than in a failed socioeconomic theory that did not accord with the realities it claimed to describe and predict. If thousands of Marxist thinkers could have been caught for decades in the grip of a wrong socioeconomic theory, it is not beyond imagination that a cadre of American educational experts could have been captivated by wrong theories over roughly the same period.

For as long as there has been a historical record, educational theories have wavered in emphasis between two opposed but equally important needs in schooling: rigor and flexibility. But despite recent public pressure for school improvement, there has been little movement toward rigor in American educational theories. Although we are a diverse nation, our optimistic educational ideas and slogans tend to be uniform from one education school and reform movement to another. Dressed-up-like-new versions of old ideas still dominate—for sociological and historical reasons that are briefly sketched in later chapters, one of which is called "Critique of a Thoughtworld." This American educational Thoughtworld is a juggernaut that crushes independence of mind.

What chiefly prompts the writing of this book is our national slowness—despite our reputation for practicality—to cast aside these faulty theories. Most current "reforms" are repetitions or rephrasings of long-failed Romantic, antiknowledge proposals that emanated from Teachers College, Columbia University, in the teens, twenties, and thirties of this century. The underlying assumptions of many "break-the-mold" reforms are anything but new. *The Schools We Need* attempts to explain why the slogans promulgated by this monolithic system of ideas have turned out to be positive barriers to school improvement, and why alternative ideas are not readily accepted even in the name of radical reform.

When businesspeople, philanthropists, and parents turn to experts for guidance, they continue to hear the high-sounding, antiknowledge advice that has been offered for more than sixty years—the very prescriptions (now to be facilitated by "technology") that have produced the system's failures. These continually reformulated slogans have led to the total absence of a coherent, knowledge-based curriculum, but are nonetheless presented as novel theories based on the latest research and as remedies for the diseases they themselves have caused. The rhetorical success but educational failure of these slogans bespeaks an intellectual Gresham's law whereunder bad ideas drive out good. In the midst of much expenditure of money and energy, this intellectual stasis largely explains the failure of educational reform efforts to date.

The failure is easily documented. Despite much activity, American school reform has not improved the nation's K–12 education during the decade and more since publication of *A Nation at Risk: The Imperative for Educational Reform* (1983). Among those of developed nations, our public schools still rank near the bottom; and in absolute terms, our children's academic competencies have not risen significantly. One reason for this continued stasis: the difficulty of spreading reform out into the vast system of fifteen thousand independent school districts. But it is doubtful that reform movements have succeeded even within the confines of their own model projects.

Typical is a recent report by the Bruner Foundation stating that an intensive school-improvement effort called the New York State Community Schools Program shows "no evidence of improved academic outcomes for children in New York City Community Schools." The most fully studied reform of all, Head Start, has produced extremely disappointing long-term academic benefits, despite strong evidence from other countries that early-intervention programs (which, unlike Head Start, use knowledge-based curricula) lead to permanent academic improvement. Head Start, by contrast, while it does reduce later dropout rates and assignment to special classes, does not affect educational achievement beyond fourth grade.[4] A beacon of hope in this reform scene is the current effort to create national content standards for different academic subjects. But so far, chaos reigns, and one must adopt a wait-and-see attitude.

Remarkably, the disappointments of reform to date have not led educational experts to question the Romantic principles on which their proposals are based, but rather, to attack the messenger that is bringing the bad news—standardized tests. Whatever the shortcomings of these tests, no one has plausibly denied that they show a consistent positive correlation with real academic competencies. For example, no one has *plausibly* denied (implausible denials have of course been made) that the better one reads, the higher one tends to score on a standardized reading test. If reform efforts of the past decade *were* significantly improving our children's academic competencies, then the standardized tests, however imperfect, would yield some indication of it.

American educational expertise is not educational expertise per se. Very different ideas preside over the more successful systems of Europe and Asia. We need to pick up ideas, and clues to effective practices, wherever we find them. The inherent complexities of mass education and the contradictions and uncertainties of educational research ought to foster openness and pragmatism rather than reliance on hoary slogans. One of my epigraphs—"Who will reform the reformers?"—is adapted from the indignant Roman satirist Juvenal, but I do not intend to dwell on Juvenalian ironies. My purpose is constructive. The proposals in this book derive from mainstream research and from my distress at the social injustice that has resulted from our dominant educational theories. As soon as possible, these theories need to be replaced with better ones.

## 2.
## Growing Social Injustice

It is a bitter irony that the egalitarian rhetoric of American educational orthodoxy has fostered inequality. All recent social observers in the United States have condemned the widening economic gap between rich and poor, and have noted its correlation with a gap in educational achievement. In the period from 1942 to 1966—that is, in the period before the anti-subject-matter theories of the 1920s and '30s metastasized throughout the schools—public education had begun to close the economic gap between races and social classes.[5] But after that period, among students graduating from high school in the mid-1960s—that is, among students who had been taught for all twelve grades of schooling under anti-subject-matter theories—verbal SAT scores began a steep decline. At the same time, the black-white wage gap, which had continually narrowed between 1942 and 1966, suddenly stabilized. This abrupt halt in progress toward wage equity was first detected in the midst of the SAT decline.[6]

Social scientists have been puzzled by this recent halt in progress toward black-white wage equality, despite the advent of new laws and new public attitudes toward employing qualified blacks and other members of minority groups. Until very recently, analyses of black-white wage equality were computed on the basis of educational achievement as determined by the highest grade level completed. And until the late 1960s, grade level had been a roughly adequate measure of educational level, because schools had been performing well enough on average to make a diploma meaningful. The current practice of social promotion had not become endemic. But starting with the sharp educational decline of the late 1960s, and the widespread practice of social promotion, the highest grade that one had nominally completed was no longer an adequate indication of academic achievement, as James Coleman and his colleagues found in their 1966 study of equality of educational opportunity. In the new educational context, despite a slight recent closing of black-white scores on some tests, disadvantaged children, including a disproportionate percentage of blacks, began falling ever further behind their more advantaged peers in actual educational achievement.[7]

Only in very recent years have social scientists begun to refine their analyses of the puzzling halt in black-white wage equality after three decades of progress. It turns out that the disparity (at least 16 percent lower wages for blacks of the same grade level completed) is owing to the fact that blacks have been on average less well educated by the schools. Most of the existing wage disparity, that is, some 12 out of 16 percent, can be explained by *a disparity in actual educational attainment.* After matching black and white earners by their actual educational level rather than by nominal grade level, the black-white wage disparity drops to less than 5 percent, and some of this small remainder can be explained by factors other than direct racial discrimination.[8] This result is simultaneously hopeful and disheartening. It shows that economic class more than race currently determines educational and economic attainment in the United States—a hopeful sign. Yet the lack of true educational and economic mobility in the country must be disheartening to those who believe in equal opportunity and the American Dream.

## 3.
### Premature Polarization

The first step in moving toward greater social justice through education is to avoid the premature polarizations that arise when educational policy is confused with political ideology. In the United States today, the hostile political split between liberals and conservatives has infected the public debate over education—to such an extent that straight thinking is made difficult. Public responses to specific educational proposals are too often correlated with this liberal-conservative division. Newspaper attitudes toward such proposals are too often determined by the political orientation of the editorial page.

Here's an example. Political liberals in the United States advocate greater equality in per-pupil spending among different school districts within a state. Many conservatives oppose shifting funds from one school district to another. Jonathan Kozol's book *Savage Inequalities* (1991) dramatized the injustices inflicted on poor children by the unfair distribution of public resources, and recently courts in Texas, Kentucky, and many other states have ruled that greater equity of funding is indeed required by law. Sadly, some of these rulings have been circumvented by conservative resistance—reflecting the degree to which a sense of community between rich and poor has further declined in the nation and given way to an us-versus-them mentality even with respect to children.

But one's political sympathies with equitable funding have no logical or practical connection with one's views about what ought to be happening inside schools once they are equitably funded. My political sympathies are with those who, like Kozol, advocate greater funding equity. But Kozol, perhaps influenced by his study at education school, expresses many "progressive" educational ideas that I oppose. I would label myself a political liberal and an educational conservative, or perhaps more accurately, an educational pragmatist. Political liberals really ought to oppose progressive educational ideas because they have led to practical failure and greater social inequity. The only practical way to achieve liberalism's aim of greater social justice is to pursue conservative educational policies.

That is not a new idea. In 1932, the Communist intellectual Antonio Gramsci, writing from jail (having been imprisoned by Mussolini), was one of the first to detect the paradoxical consequences of the new "democratic" education, which stressed "life relevance" and other naturalistic approaches over hard work and the transmission of knowledge. Il Duce's educational minister, Giovanni Gentile, was, in contrast to Gramsci, an enthusiastic proponent of the new ideas emanating from Teachers College, Columbia University, in the United States.[9] So prescient were Gramsci's observations that I have used one of them as an opening epigraph to this book:

> The new concept of schooling is in its romantic phase, in which the replacement of "mechanical" by "natural" methods has become unhealthily exaggerated. . . . Previously pupils at least acquired a certain baggage of concrete facts. Now there will no longer be any baggage to put in order. . . . The most paradoxical aspect of it all is that this new type of school is advocated as being democratic, while in fact it is destined not merely to perpetuate social differences but crystallize them in Chinese complexities.[10]

Gramsci saw that to denominate such methods as phonics and memorization of the multiplication table as "conservative," while associating them with the political right, amounted to a serious intellectual error. That was the nub of the standoff between the two most distinguished educational theorists of the political Left—Gramsci and Paulo Freire. Freire, like Gramsci a hero of humanity, devoted himself to the cause of educating the oppressed, particularly in his native Brazil, but his writings have also been influential in the United States. Like other educational progressivists, Freire rejected traditional teaching methods and subject matters, objecting to the "banking theory of schooling," whereby the teacher provides the child with a lot of "rote-learned" information. The consequence of the conservative approach, according to

Freire, is to numb the critical faculties of students and to preserve the oppressor class. He called for a change of both methods and content—new content that would celebrate the culture of the oppressed, and new methods that would encourage intellectual independence and resistance. In short, Freire, like other educational writers since the 1920s, associated political and educational progressivism.

Gramsci took the opposite view. He held that political progressivism demanded educational conservatism. The oppressed class should be taught to master the tools of power and authority—the ability to read, write, and communicate—and to gain enough traditional knowledge to understand the worlds of nature and culture surrounding them. Children, particularly the children of the poor, should not be encouraged to flourish "naturally," which would keep them ignorant and make them slaves of emotion. They should learn the value of hard work, gain the knowledge that leads to understanding, and master the traditional culture in order to command its rhetoric, as Gramsci himself had learned to do. In this debate, history has proved Gramsci to be a better theorist and prophet than Freire. Modern nations that have adopted Gramscian principles have bettered the condition and heightened the political, social, and economic power of oppressed classes of people. By contrast, nations (including our own) that have stuck to the principles of Freire have failed to change the social and economic status quo. Though the Brazilian generals invited Freire to become educational minister of São Paulo, it is not recorded that his methods helped the oppressed of Brazil to any significant degree.

Gramsci was not the only observer to predict the inegalitarian consequences of "naturalistic," "project-oriented," "hands-on," "critical-thinking," and so-called "democratic" education. I focus on Gramsci as a revered theorist of the Left in order to make a strategic point. Ideological polarizations of educational issues tend to be facile and premature. There is not only a practical separation between educational conservatism and political conservatism, but something even stronger. There is an *inverse* relation between educational progressivism and social progressivism. Educational progressivism is a sure means for preserving the social status quo, whereas the best practices of educational conservatism are the only means whereby children from disadvantaged homes can secure the knowledge and skills that will enable them to improve their condition.

The educational standpoint from which this book is written may be accurately described as neither "traditional" nor "progressive." It is pragmatic. Both educational traditionalists and progressivists have tended to be far too dogmatic, polemical, and theory-ridden to be reliable beacons for public policy. The pragmatist tries to avoid simplifications and facile oppositions. This book will argue that the best guide to education on a large scale is observation of practices that have worked well on a large scale, coupled with as exact an understanding as possible of the reasons why those practices have succeeded in many different contexts.

While the ideological terms "conservative" and "progressive" may be two of the most effective labels by which the old educational ideas continue to sustain themselves, the educational community exhibits a further tendency toward terminological polarization and intellectual caricature. Premature polarization of viewpoints is the chief device by which the educational community maintains the intellectual status quo. "Modern" and humane "reform" is pitted against a "traditional" evil empire. The following rhetorical pairings are typical:

- Traditional vs. modern
- Merely verbal vs. hands-on
- Premature vs. developmentally appropriate
- Fragmented vs. integrated
- Boring vs. interesting
- Lockstep vs. individualized

Parents presented with such choices for the education of their children would be unlikely to choose traditional, merely verbal, premature, fragmented, boring, and lockstep instruction over modern, hands-on, developmentally appropriate, integrated, interesting, and individualized instruction. Since this technique of oversimple contrast is so effective, and at the same time so misleading, it may be useful to foreshadow some of the topics this book will examine by providing a prefatory glimpse of the complexities hidden beneath such polarities.

**Traditional vs. Modern Instruction**   Here is a typical progressivist caricature of traditional, knowledge-based education:

> *The emphasis that permeated the traditional school was recitation, memorization, recall, testing, grades, promotion, and failure. And for this kind of education it was necessary that children primarily listen, sit quiet and attentive in seats, try to fix in their minds what the teacher told them, commit to memory the lessons assigned to them, and then, somewhat like a cormorant, be ready at all times to disgorge the intake. . . . This fixed, closed, authoritarian system of education perfectly fitted the needs of a*

*static religion, a static church, a static caste system, a static economic system.*[11]

But the term "traditional," which also covers challenging subject matters taught in a lively, demanding way, is an odd one to use for the knowledge-based approach currently employed in the most advanced nations but eschewed in our own schools for more than half a century. If parents were told that, on the contrary, the so-called "untraditional," or "modern," mode of education so dominant in our schools has coincided with the decline of academic competencies among our students, they might be less eager to embrace the failed techniques characterized as "modern." To the observation that a "reform" has already been tried but has failed, educators usually reply that it was never "properly" tried. But such claims are quite unhistorical. The modern approaches *have* been properly tried. The "never-properly-tried" riposte is, after all, a fail-safe defense for all unsuccessful theories.

**Merely Verbal vs. Hands-On Instruction**  The idea that students will learn better if they see, feel, and touch the subjects they are studying has such obvious merit that it would be quite amazing if traditional education did not make use of multisensory methods of teaching. And, indeed, if one studies the history of educational methods, one finds that every modern nation and traditionalist theorist advocates hands-on methods where they lead to good results.[12] The difficulty with the premature polarization of this issue lies in its disparagement of the verbal as an essential and even dominant focus of schooling. In human beings, an essential residue of understanding is the ability to speak or write about what one has experienced. To disparage an emphasis on learning the words and even the formulas for things and ideas, whether through hands-on instruction or not, bespeaks an antiverbal prejudice which has its roots in the Romantic Era and which has proved especially harmful to children with restricted vocabularies.

**Premature vs. Developmentally Appropriate Instruction**  Suppose for a moment that parents were advised that the opposition of premature vs. developmentally appropriate content has been the means of withholding knowledge from young, disadvantaged children, whereas many advantaged children gain such knowledge at home. Suppose, in addition, parents were informed that young children of comparable ages in other lands were learning such so-called "premature" knowledge with great benefit and no ill effects. And suppose it were shown that the label "developmentally appropriate" is generally applied as a dogmatic gut reaction rather than as an empirically determined fact accepted by the research community. It is hard to believe that parents informed of these complexities would not question the implications of "developmentally appropriate" for their children's education.

**Fragmented vs. Integrated Instruction** Both "traditionalists" and "modernists" ought to prefer integration over fragmentation, and there is no evidence that either party speaking in its own voice defends fragmented over integrated learning. The advantage of truly integrated instruction is that it shows how things fit together, and at the same time helps secure what is being learned by reinforcing it in a variety of contexts. That is the theory, and when it is effectively put into practice, it is accepted by both traditionalists and modernists. Nonetheless, this pseudopolarization has been exploited ever since the teens of this century to disparage the direct teaching of subject matters such as mathematics, spelling, and biology in classes that are specifically devoted to those topics. The whole outdated concept of subject matters was to be replaced by "thematic" or "project-oriented" instruction. The result has been not integration at all but the failure of students to learn the most basic elements of the different subject matters. The result has been a *loss* of intellectual coherence.

**Boring vs. Interesting Instruction** Academic subject matters such as ancient history and science are to be withheld from children in the early grades on the grounds that true education proceeds from the child's interest rather than from an external imposition. Children learn best when new knowledge is built upon what they already know (true), and it is further claimed that the child's interest in a subject will derive from its connection with his or her immediate experiences and home surroundings. Early schooling should therefore teach subjects that have direct relevance to the child's life, such as "my neighborhood" and similar "relevant" topics. Yet every person with enough schooling to be reading these words knows that subject matters by themselves do not repel or attract interest, and that an effective teacher can make almost any subject interesting, and an ineffective one can make almost any subject dull. The presumption that the affairs of one's neighborhood are more interesting than those of faraway times and places is contradicted in every classroom that studies dinosaurs and fairy tales—that is, in just about every early classroom in the nation. The false polarity between "boring" and "interesting" or "relevant" and "irrelevant" really conceals an anti-intellectual, antiacademic bias.

**Lockstep vs. Individualized Instruction** Traditional instruction is said to impose the same content on every student, without taking into account the child's individual strengths, weaknesses, and interests, whereas modern instruction is said to be tailored to each child's individual temperament. Unquestionably, differences in temperament and ability make individualized, one-on-one tutorials the most effective mode of teaching known. Even if all children in a grade need to reach some of the same basic goals in arithmetic, reading, and writing, the best means for leading them to those goals will vary from student to student. This would seem to argue against the teacher's interacting with the whole class and in favor of individualized tutoring. How, then, can we explain the paradox that individuals learn more and better in those lockstep systems of schooling where more emphasis is placed on interactive whole-class instruction than on individualized tutoring?[13] How explain the fact that individual students get more effective *tutorial* attention in those systems, and seem to make more progress when there is greater emphasis on the whole class and less on individual tutorials? The answer lies in simple arithmetic. It is impossible to provide effective one-on-one tutorials to twenty-five students at a time. When one student is being coached individually, twenty-four others are being left to their own devices, usually in silent seatwork. When, on the other hand, the entire group has been given the knowledge that enables them to understand the activities of the whole class, they are all involved in learning much more of the time. The occasional individual help they get is all the more effective. By contrast, classrooms that march under the banner of individual attention often result in individual neglect.[14] If this paradox were explained to parents, would they so readily choose "individualized" instruction?

These examples illustrate some of the characteristics typical of currently polarized educational rhetoric. Its simplified, black-and-white contrast between good guys and bad guys is overdrawn to the point of caricature. While each of its catch phrases usually contains a kernel of truth, that kernel is expressed in a combative, oversimplified form that enables its advocates to skirt underlying complexities. The resulting simplifications have evolved into systems of half-truths that are fully as harmful as total errors, and when they have been confidently acted upon in practice, they have resulted in failure.

4.

## From Cultural Literacy to Core Knowledge

In this Introduction, I should make a few remarks about the connection between this book and an earlier one of mine, *Cultural Literacy* (1987). Some readers might infer a connection in any case. The 1987 book became the subject of intense controversy. If I simply ignored that history, it might be thought that my silence carried hidden significance. So I shall trace in a few words the process that led from *Cultural Literacy* to *The Schools We Need.*

Much as I might relish commenting on the host of pros and cons set down in dozens of reviews of *Cultural Literacy* and in scores of articles, such an exercise would greatly distract from my main purposes. It might also constitute an outdated exercise, since much of the commentary published in the heat of what seemed an important ideological battle would no longer be written or believed today. To take just one example, *Cultural Literacy* was almost invariably identified with Allan Bloom's bestseller *The Closing of the American Mind,* which happened to be published a month before mine. As a result of this chronological contiguity, the two books were inseparably linked as symptomatic of a general cultural phenomenon. But such linkage has now become very rare. Most writers who mention either Bloom's book or my own implicitly agree with a few early reviewers that the two books are not only different but fundamentally opposed. On such matters it is not permissible to judge in one's own case; my more appropriate task is to describe the chain of thought that has led from my earlier book to this one.

This book takes the earlier one as its foundation. The empirical basis of *Cultural Literacy* was widely accepted research in psychology. In recent years, further empirical evidence has supported the basic correctness of the book's inferences, and several researchers have published findings that show the predicted high correlation between general academic and economic proficiency and the knowledge that *Cultural Literacy* identified and indexed. No one would claim that possession of mainstream cultural knowledge is a *sufficient* condition for intellectual ability and financial prosperity, but it may often be a necessary condition for them. Keith Stanovich and his colleagues have shown that, after controlling for IQ, those who score well on cultural literacy tests have more fully developed cognitive abilities than the control group; similarly, Joseph Pentony and others have shown that cultural literacy is highly correlated with academic achievement. Thomas Sticht and his associates have shown that the level of cultural literacy is highly correlated with annual income. These results have led some researchers to conclude that, on present evidence, *Cultural Literacy*'s general argument is confirmed.[15] But in addition to the confidence lent by these findings, the present book is based on much broader firsthand knowledge of the ideas and practices that exist in American schools.

There is no substitute for such direct experience, and for giving me an opportunity to gain it, I owe profound thanks to some very independent-minded principals and teachers. I thank particularly Dr. Constance Jones, the principal of a large, mixed-population public elementary school in Fort Myers, Florida: Three Oaks School, which in 1990 became the first school in the nation to follow the principles of *Cultural Literacy.* The stunning success of Three Oaks then led another principal, Mr. Jeffrey Litt, to introduce the ideas of *Cultural Literacy* to his school, No. 67, the Mohegan School, located in the South Bronx. The Fort Meyers school received a lot of attention, especially in an article in *Life,* but thereafter it was the remarkable results achieved in the South Bronx that drew the attention of network news programs, of *Reader's Digest* and other magazines and newspapers. Public notice for both schools led other elementary schools to make the arduous shift to a solid, knowledge-based curriculum.

Given the atmosphere of controversy surrounding *Cultural Literacy,* this grassroots movement has perforce operated more on ideas than on money. Its nerve center has been a foundation I started in 1986 and first called the Cultural Literacy Foundation. But teachers pointed out that the term "Cultural" raised too many extraneous questions, whereas the term "Core Knowledge" better described the chief aim of the reform, which was to introduce solid knowledge in a coherent way into the elementary curriculum. On their advice, I changed the name to the Core Knowledge Foundation, and the education press now calls our school reform movement the Core Knowledge Movement. It has spread to more than two hundred public schools in thirty-seven states, and there is a much larger, still uncounted number of schools that are successfully using the foundation's principles and materials.

The foundation's activities have brought me into direct contact with hundreds of principals and teachers and thousands of knowledge-thirsty youngsters in schools all over the nation. My continuing contact with these schools has given me a firsthand sense of what I call in this book the "Thoughtworld," the system of ideas that dominates American elementary education. That so many energetic principals and teachers have been willing and even eager to break out of that Thoughtworld has given me the courage and the optimism to write this book. I have now read more widely in the history and sociology of American education to gain a firmer grasp of how and why that Thoughtworld came to monopolize the thinking of the American educational community. Because history discloses the contingencies, extraneous motivations, overhasty conclusions, and empirical vulnerabilities of intellectual movements, historical study lends courage to those who would challenge the status quo. It also helps revive the powerful alternative ideas that flourished before the dominant dispensation quashed them.

Perhaps this book's most significant theoretical advance over *Cultural Literacy* is not any qualification of its argument, which I strongly believe to be true, but rather an *extension* of it. The earlier book explained why economic effectiveness and social justice require all citizens to share an extensive body of school-based background knowledge as a necessary foundation for communication and participation in society. My focus was on the knowledge requirements for full participation by adults, and hence on the breadth of widely shared knowledge that students need to possess by the end of twelfth grade, when many of them enter the economic and political life of the nation. But the logic of that argument entailed a further implication, which I failed fully to recognize.

It was simply this. If shared background knowledge is necessary for full participation in the larger national society, the same reasoning must also hold for full participation in a smaller social group, and most especially that of the classroom itself. If shared knowledge is needed among citizens to understand newspapers as well as one another, then, by the same reasoning, shared knowledge is also needed among class members to understand the teacher and one another. Every classroom is a little society of its own, and *its* effectiveness and fairness depend on the full participation by all *its* members, just as in the larger society. Such universal participation by students cannot occur unless they all share a core of relevant background knowledge. This is easily demonstrated in any classroom group. To the extent that lack of relevant knowledge keeps some students from comprehending today's lesson, it will cause them to fall even further behind in comprehending tomorrow's. Every experienced teacher is implicitly aware of this truth—which is obvious once it is stated. Chapter 1 of this book will concern itself with the educational and social implications of this self-evident, but nonetheless overlooked, feature of schooling.

In emphasizing shared knowledge, *Cultural Literacy* attacked the formalism that currently dominates American educational thought. Educational formalism is based on the idea that inculcating formal skills is much more important than the transmission of knowledge—a widespread doctrine typified by the following observations from an article in a recent issue of an educational journal:

*With knowledge doubling every five years—every 73 days by the year 2020—we can no longer attempt to anticipate future information requirements.*

*Curriculum based on discrete disciplines emerged from a largely male- and western-oriented way of thinking.*

*We must stop valuing right answers and learn how to behave when con-
fronted with paradoxical and ambiguous situations. Doing so requires a
shift from knowledge acquisition to valuing knowledge production.*

*Process is in fact the highest form of content.*[16]

These formalistic assertions have by now attained the status of unques-
tioned fact, mainly by being constantly repeated. Like a number of undocu-
mented doctrines of the educational community, they wither under close scrutiny. This book enters more deeply into the fallacies of such assertions, and
into their historical and intellectual origins. But its central theme, discussed in
detail in Chapters 4 and 5, was only adumbrated in *Cultural Literacy*—the
disastrous consequences of educational naturalism. If formalism was the major
theme of the earlier book, naturalism is the corresponding focus of this one. It
is hard to say which of the two intellectual errors has been the more harmful to
American education. Certainly, each of them deserves a book of its own.

## 5.
## The Nature of the Enemy: Ideas, Not Persons

This book is—of necessity—partly a polemic. American schools need to
be transformed, and to accomplish that, many ideas (including even the
pseudo-idea of "radical transformation") need to be repudiated. But to attack
ideas is not to attack the human participants in what Harriet Tyson Bernstein
has termed "a conspiracy of good intentions." No force is going to remove the
tenured professoriat at education schools or replace the two and a half million
teachers in our public schools. These very diverse persons are not the enemy.
And in any case, the human participants in American education are the participants we shall continue to have. In fact, they are some of the most dedicated
and sympathetic members of our society. No, the enemy is the controlling
system of ideas that currently prevents needed changes from being contem-
plated or understood. It is the enemy within that needs to be defeated.

Hence, this is a book chiefly about ideas. Its central chapters belong as
much to intellectual history as to educational theory. I mention persons only
when they happen to be indissolubly connected with the ideas being discussed. It will be obvious from what I have already said that this book is
emphatically not an indictment of teachers. They have been as ill-served as our
students by the inadequate ideas and impoverished subject-matter instruction
they have been compelled to absorb in order to receive certification. It is

teachers who have, against the odds, raised some of our students to competence, and it is to teachers, particularly the pioneering ones in Core Knowledge schools, that I have dedicated this book.

Some of the things I say have been said before by still unheeded forerunners—not just by my dedicatees William C. Bagley and Antonio Gramsci, but also by Arthur Bestor, Diane Ravitch, and others, most recently Charles Sykes. This book belongs to their tradition. I have added a few conceptions and proposals from my work in the schools, and from recent research, and from the intellectual history of Romanticism. I cherish the hope that these amplifications of the old message may help these earlier writers get a new hearing, now that educational naturalism has for still more tragic decades continued to prove itself an almost total practical failure, and now that its Romantic premises are being noticed and challenged by mainstream cognitive science for the illusions they are.

Ultimately, the success of school reform in the United States will depend upon there being developed in the philanthropic community, the press, the general public, and, above all, the educational community a skeptical, well-informed counterpoise to the monolithic Thoughtworld. In the past, criticisms of that world, in William Bagley's *Education and Emergent Man* (1934) and Arthur Bestor's *Educational Wastelands* (1953), have brought little but vigorous denunciations and discrediting campaigns upon their authors' heads. As I near the age of seventy, and begin to fade away like an old soldier, I am less concerned with the prospect of inevitable denunciation than with the responsibility to bear witness—if there is the slightest chance that doing so will help improve the quality and fairness of our schools.

# Intellectual Capital:
# A Civil Right

## 1.
## Shared Knowledge in Democracies

The need in a democracy to teach children a shared body of knowledge was explained many years ago by Thomas Jefferson when he described his bill "to diffuse knowledge more generally through the mass of the people." A common grade-school education would create a literate and independent citizenry as well as a nesting ground for future leaders. It would be a place where every talent would be given an equal chance to excel, where "every fibre would be eradicated of ancient and future aristocracy; and a foundation laid for a government truly republican."[1] Despite his distrust of central authority, Jefferson encouraged the devising of a common curriculum in order that "the great mass of the people" should be taught not just the elements of reading, writing, and arithmetic, but also that "their memories may here be stored with the most useful facts from Grecian, Roman, European, and American history," as well as "the first elements of morality."

*Of the views of this [education] law, none is more important, none more legitimate, than of rendering the people the safe, as they are the ultimate, guardians of their own liberty. For this purpose, the reading in the first stage [of schooling] where [many] will receive their whole education, is proposed to be chiefly historical. History by apprizing them of the past will enable them to judge of the future. It will avail them of the experience of other times and other nations; it will qualify them as judges of the actions and designs of men; it will enable them to know ambition under every disguise it may assume; and knowing it to defeat its views. In every government on earth is some trace of human weakness, some germ of corruption and degeneracy, which cunning will discover, and wickedness insensibly open, cultivate, and improve. Every government degenerates when trusted to the rulers of the people alone. The people themselves therefore are its only safe depositories. And to render even them safe, their minds must be improved to a certain degree.[2]*

Jefferson's conception was later seconded by Horace Mann, who argued that democracy required a "common school" to provide all children equally with the knowledge and skills that would keep them economically independent and free. Other early prophets of democratic education, such as Louis-Michel Le Peletier, François Guizot, and Jules Ferry in France, propounded similarly inspiring principles of commonalty in early education. In the early years of this century, John Dewey (who said many, sometimes inconsistent things about education) reaffirmed the connections between such common learnings and the goals of community and democracy in *Democracy and Education:*

*Beings who are born not only unaware of but quite indifferent to the aims and habits of the social group have to be rendered cognizant of them and actively interested. Education, and education alone, spans the gap. . . . Men live in a community in virtue of the things which they have in common; and communication is the way in which they come to possess things in common. What they must have in common are aims, beliefs, aspirations, knowledge—a common understanding.[3]*

And from William C. Bagley, a colleague of Dewey's at Columbia University and a profound scholar of education to whom this book is partly dedicated: "A most important function of formal education, especially in a democracy, is to insure as high a level of common culture as possible."[4]

More recently, in 1994, the dependency of the democratic vision on commonly shared knowledge was brought up to date and ratified unanimously by the Parliament of Norway:

*It is a central tenet of popular enlightenment that shared frames of reference must be the common property of all the people—indeed must be an integral part of general education—to escape avoidable differences in competence that can result in social inequality and be abused by undemocratic forces. Those who do not share the background information taken for granted in public discourse will often overlook the point or miss the meaning. Newcomers to a country who are not immersed in its frames of reference often remain outsiders because others cannot take for granted what they know and can do; they are in constant need of extra explanations. Common background knowledge is thus at the core of a national network of communication between members of a democratic community. It makes it possible to fathom complex messages, and to interpret new ideas, situations and challenges. Education plays a leading role in passing on this common background information—the culture everybody must be familiar with if society is to remain democratic and its citizens sovereign.[5]*

In the late industrial era, the need for common learnings has acquired a more than political urgency. The purely economic need for a high level of shared knowledge among workers has led to an unforeseen strengthening of democratic political principles in previously nondemocratic regimes. When the Soviet Union collapsed, the experienced Soviet hand George Kennan was asked in a TV interview whether the new Russian revolution would prove as durable as the former one of 1917. Without hesitation, Kennan predicted that the democratic revolution would prove more lasting than its predecessor: the Soviet state had been forced by economic imperatives to make its people literate, whereas the revolution of 1917 had been carried out by uneducated and therefore malleable peasants.

Because economic imperatives have now been added to political ones, the need to provide effective schooling to all has become more pressing than in any previous era. Politically, citizens must still be educated in order to be protected from their rulers, and, as Jefferson indicated, from themselves. Economically, citizens now require an especially strong schooling to sustain themselves in the workplace. To express the socioeconomic implications of education in the modern world, sociologists have devised the useful concept of "intellectual capital."

"Intellectual capital" has been described by Secretary of Labor Robert Reich as the key to American competitiveness and prosperity. In the popular press, the phrase has been used to denote the knowledge that makes the workers of one country or company more effective than those of another. But the implications of the concept transcend purely economic consequences. And the widening gap between rich and poor is not the only injustice that results from an inequitable distribution of intellectual capital. Sociologists have shown that intellectual capital (i.e., knowledge) operates in almost every sphere of modern society to determine social class, success or failure in school, and even psychological and physical health. The French scholar Pierre

Bourdieu has shown that those who possess a larger share of "cultural capital" tend to acquire much more wealth and status, and to gain more abilities, than those who start out with very little of this precious resource.[6]

Just as it takes money to make money, it takes knowledge to make knowledge. Underlying the implied analogy between money capital and intellectual capital lodges an ancient Biblical paradox (Matthew 13:12): "For whosoever hath, to him shall be given, and he shall have more abundance: but whosoever hath not, from him shall be taken away even that he hath." The paradox holds more inexorably for intellectual than for money capital. Those who are well educated can make money without inherited wealth, but those who lack intellectual capital are left poor indeed. The paradox of Matthew is powerfully at work in the American educational system.[7] Those children who possess intellectual capital when they first arrive at school have the mental scaffolding and Velcro to catch hold of what is going on, and they can turn that new knowledge into still more mental Velcro to gain still more knowledge. But those children who arrive at school lacking the relevant experience and vocabulary—they see not, neither do they understand. They fall further and further behind. The relentless humiliations they experience continue to deplete their energy and motivation to learn. Lack of stimulation has depressed their IQs.[8] The ever-increasing differential in acquired intellectual capital that occurs during the early years ends up creating a permanent gap in such children's acquired abilities, particularly in their abilities to communicate in speech and writing, to learn new things, and to adapt to new challenges. In short, an early inequity in the distribution of intellectual capital may be the single most important source of avoidable injustice in a free society.

Despite claims to the contrary, we know that the initial knowledge deficits of children can be remedied in the early years of preschool and primary school, and that their subsequent learning can be made to proceed at a rate that could guarantee a literate and relatively just society. Other nations in the modern world have shown that this educational achievement is possible even for heterogeneous societies like the United States.[9] One practical advantage in the idea of intellectual capital, therefore, is the direction it gives to educational theory and policy. The implied analogy with money capital suggests the commonsense truth that a child's accumulation of wide-ranging foundational *knowledge* is the key to educational achievement.

The money analogy also suggests a further truth: not just any knowledge will work—only that knowledge which constitutes the shared intellectual currency of the society. Selectivity is critical. To be useful to children, their intellectual capital needs to be broadly shared with others, to enable them to communicate and learn effectively. Confederate or Monopoly money won't work. As democratic theorists from Jefferson to Gudmund Hernes (author of the recent Norwegian Education Act) have argued, the intellectual currency has to be the widely useful and negotiable coin of the realm.[10]

Unfortunately, for several decades the American educational community has operated under a guiding metaphor very different from "intellectual capital." American educational theory has held that the child needs to be given the all-purpose *tools* that are needed for him or her to continue learning and adapting. The particular content used to develop those tools need not be specified. The claim that all-purpose intellectual competencies are independent of the matter out of which they have been formed, if it corresponded to reality, would indeed be an attractive educational idea. For conveniently, in that case, it wouldn't matter greatly what particular things a child learned. The chief aims of education would simply be to ensure that children acquired "love of learning" and gained "critical-thinking" techniques for acquiring and using whatever they would need later—the pliers and wrenches that would permit them to set up shop even on a desert island. But when this tool metaphor has been taken apart and examined for its literal content, its highly exaggerated claims have been powerfully contradicted by research, and after six decades, it has shown itself to be ineffective.[11]

The tool metaphor, with its encouragement of an indifference to specific knowledge, has resulted in social consequences of tragic proportions. It is probably not an exaggeration to say that the broad sway of this theoretical mistake has all but nullified the bright promise of school integration and the civil rights movement. The role that education under a more adequate theory could have played in consolidating social justice after the *Brown* decision can be suggested by two studies—one from 1925, before a process orientation began to dominate in our schools; the other from 1966, after the ascendancy of the tool theory.

In 1966, the Coleman Report found that under the current American educational system the home is, except in the case of extremely good or extremely bad schools, the decisive influence on academic outcomes; our schools on average do little to improve the economic chances of disadvantaged children.[12] Coleman's finding is highly consistent with the idea of the importance of intellectual capital, since under the current process-dominated theory it is the home, by default, and not the school that supplies most of the intellectual capital which enables children to acquire more. When the home is the dominant influence in education, it follows that economically and educationally depressed groups will not be greatly advanced by schooling. This pattern of social determinism found by Coleman in 1966 still persists in the schools of the 1990s.[13]

But history has contributed some very telling contrary results that complement and qualify the research of Coleman and his associates. A 1925 study published by Professor William C. Bagley of Teachers College, Columbia University, powerfully illustrates that researches into the social outcomes of schooling and into the relative influence of the home greatly depend on the educational context in which those researches are conducted. Bagley's *Determinism in Education* analyzed results of the Army Alpha tests given in World War I to some 1,700,000 soldiers.[14] Bagley was interested in correlating the IQ scores of large groups with the states they came from. Some states, such as Oregon and Massachusetts, had good systems of elementary education; others, such as Mississippi, had poor systems. Previously, based on various objective criteria, L. P. Ayres had formed a ranking of the various states according to the quality of their school systems.[15] Bagley wanted to determine whether IQ and competency tests on this vast scale (which tend to balance out innate differences) would correlate with the general quality of schooling as rated independently by Ayres.

Bagley found a high correlation, .72, between the mean IQ of soldiers and the educational quality of their native states during the period when the soldiers would have been in grade school. Interestingly, African-American soldiers from educationally high-ranking states had higher IQs than white soldiers from low-ranking states. Thus, during an era when American schools operated on traditional rather than progressivist principles, excellent schools, even more than the home or the family income (family income of African-Americans in 1900 was not high), made a decisive difference in average IQ and general competence. This striking observation, which is just the reverse of the 1966 findings, supports the theory of intellectual capital over the theory of abstract intellectual tools as the foundation of intellectual competence. Indeed, as I shall be concerned to show in Chapter 5, intellectual capital is *itself* the great all-purpose tool of adaptation in the modern world.

## 2.
## Dependency of Learning upon Shared Knowledge

Why is shared knowledge among students essential to an effective classroom? Anyone who has ever taught a class knows that explaining a new subject will induce smiles of recognition in some students but looks of puzzlement in others. Every teacher who reads exams has said or thought, "Well, I *taught* them that, even if some of them didn't *learn* it." What makes the click of understanding occur in some students but not in others?

Psychological research has shown that the ability to learn something new depends on an ability to accommodate the new thing to the already known. When the automobile first came on the scene, people called it a "horseless carriage," thus accommodating the new to the old. When a teacher tells a class that electrons go around the nucleus of an atom as the planets go around the sun, that analogy may be helpful for students who already know about the solar system, but not for students who don't. Relevant background knowledge can be conceived as a stock of potential analogies that enable new ideas to be assimilated. Experts in any field learn new things faster than novices do, because their rich, highly accessible background knowledge gives them a greater variety of means for capturing the new ideas. This enabling function of relevant prior knowledge is essential at every stage of learning.

When a child "gets" what is being offered in a classroom, it is like someone getting a joke. A click occurs. People with the requisite background knowledge will get the joke, but those who lack it will be puzzled until somebody explains the background knowledge that was assumed in telling the joke. A classroom of twenty-five to thirty children cannot move forward as a group until all students have gained the taken-for-granted knowledge necessary for "getting" the next step in learning. If the class must pause too often while its lagging members are given background knowledge they should have gained in earlier grades, the progress of the class is bound to be excruciatingly slow for better-prepared students. If, on the other hand, instead of slowing down the class for laggards, the teacher presses ahead, the less-prepared students are bound to be left further and further behind. In the American context, this familiar problem is not adequately overcome by placing students in different "ability" tracks, because the basic structural problem has little to do with ability. Even smart people don't always get jokes.

That all first graders should enter school "ready to learn" was the number-one principle enunciated by President Bush and forty-nine governors at the education summit of 1989, and confirmed by Congress in 1993. Implicit in the ready-to-learn principle is the (true) assumption that children cannot keep up in first grade unless they arrive there with the knowledge and vocabulary that will enable them to participate actively in the class. They must be able to talk to the teacher and to other children, and they must in turn be able to understand what the teacher and other children are saying to them. In short, being "ready to learn" means, at a minimum, sharing critical skills, elements of knowledge, and vocabulary with other members of the first-grade community.

This special focus on first graders is understandable if one assumes that an initial readiness to learn will provide the momentum necessary to carry the child through subsequent grades. Otherwise, it would be hard to justify such preferential emphasis on first graders. But since the underlying assumption of continued momentum for all is demonstrably false in our current educational system, logical consistency would require that we extend the readiness-to-learn principle to second graders and third graders, and so on. For it is a fundamental requirement of democratic education that every student who enters a class at the beginning of the year should be vouchsafed the academic preparation needed to gain the knowledge and skills to be taught in that year. The readiness-to-learn principle cries out for generalization: In a democracy, all students should enter a grade ready to learn. True, the requisite skills, background knowledge, and vocabulary for such readiness are very unequally provided by the children's home environments. But precisely for that reason, it is the duty of schools to provide each child with the knowledge and skills requisite for academic progress—regardless of home background.

For effective classroom learning to take place, class members need to share enough common reference points to enable all students to learn steadily, albeit at differing rates and in response to varied approaches. Harold Stevenson and James Stigler in their important book, *The Learning Gap,* show that when this requisite commonality of preparation is lacking, as it is in most American classrooms today, the progress of learning will be slow compared with that of educational systems which do achieve commonality of academic preparation within the classroom. It is arguable that this structural difference between American classrooms and those of more effective systems is an important cause of the poor showing of American students in international comparisons. Stevenson and Stigler make the following shrewd observation about the "error" of attributing our classroom incoherence to the much-discussed "diversity" of American students as compared with that of children in more "homogeneous" nations:

> *The error . . . is the assumption that it is the diversity in children's social and cultural backgrounds that poses the greatest problem for teaching. In fact, a far greater problem is variability in children's educational background, and thus in their levels of preparation for learning the academic curriculum.*[16]

The learning gap that Stevenson and Stigler describe is a gap in academic performance between American and Asian students. Subsequent work by Stevenson and his colleagues has shown that this gap grows wider over time, putting American students much further behind their Asian peers by eleventh grade than they were in sixth.[17] The funnel shape of this widening international gap has an eerie similarity to the funnel shape of the widening gap *inside*

American schools between advantaged and disadvantaged students as they progress through the grades.[18] A plausible explanation for the widening in both cases is that a lack of academic commonality in the American classroom not only slows down the class as a whole, thus making us lag behind other countries, but also creates an increasing discrepancy between students who are lucky enough to have gained the needed background knowledge at home and those who have to depend mainly on what they get sporadically in school. The learning of luckier students snowballs upon their initial advantage, while that of the less fortunate ones, dependent on what the incoherent American school offers, never even begins to gather momentum. The lack of shared knowledge among American students not only holds back their average progress, creating a national excellence gap, but, more drastically, holds back disadvantaged students, thus creating a fairness gap as well.

These gaps in excellence and fairness explain why the most consistent problems of misbehavior occur among students at the top and at the bottom of the academic range, the one group antagonized by boredom, the other by boredom compounded with humiliation—emotions that are induced and exacerbated by lack of shared knowledge in the classroom. Constance Jones has found that when American grade-schoolers are offered schooling that provides them with needed background preparation, there is a sharp decline in absenteeism and disciplinary problems.[19] In Britain, research by Dennis O'Keeffe has similarly concluded that if students are "equipped with the requisite intellectual tools, levels of truancy are less." He concludes that "the pathology is mostly in the intellectual transmission and not in the children."[20]

Reduction of truancy and misbehavior is just one advantage that accrues when all students are made ready to learn. More positively, giving young children enabling knowledge is inherently motivational; it liberates their natural eagerness to learn. Steven Pinker has shown that children are born with a "language instinct."[21] It is arguable, and indeed it has been argued since Aristotle, that the language instinct is part of a more general instinct to learn, which impels youngsters toward becoming members of the adult community. A human child is biologically so helpless and vulnerable in its early years, so dependent upon the wider community for survival, that in the course of human evolution, children who lacked the learning instinct would not have been likely to survive.[22] Their natural curiosity and eagerness are inborn instincts that have to be systematically *thwarted* in order to make the children bored or indifferent.

The positive effects of giving children enabling knowledge thus accomplishes a lot more than just making them better behaved. They are better behaved mainly because they are absorbed in learning. In the first year during which a coherent, content-oriented curriculum is introduced into an American elementary school, library use rises typically by 70 percent. This suggests that the "Velcro hooks" image of enabling knowledge is inadequate to describe the phenomenon. The metaphor explains the click effect of enabling knowledge, but it doesn't convey the active curiosity that it encourages in young children. "Velcro hooks" make learning seem a passive occupation, like waiting to hook a fish. But a child's intellectual fishing is highly active, as the increase in library use indicates. Giving children enabling knowledge gives them not just passive hooks but also active tentacles. I owe this image to the distinguished child psychologist Sandra Scarr, who provided the following example. A child walks into the school library and sees a book called *Exploring the Nile.* She says to herself, "I've already learned something about the Nile. Let's see what this book has to say." By contrast, a child who doesn't know anything about the Nile, not even the name, will often just pass the book by. Among advantaged children, wide knowledge nourishes an active curiosity to learn still more, and more, so that the ever-active tentacles create still more tentacles. There is no insuperable reason why American schools cannot make all children more advantaged in this respect.

## 3.
## The Myth of the Existing Curriculum

The curricular chaos of the American elementary school is a feature of our public education that few people are even remotely aware of. We know, of course, that there exists no national curriculum, but we assume, quite reasonably, that agreement has been reached locally regarding what shall be taught to children at each grade level—if not within the whole district, then certainly within an individual school. After all, the stated reason for preserving the principle of local control of education is that the *localities* ought to determine what our children shall learn. But despite the democratic virtue of that principle, the idea that there exists a coherent plan for teaching content within the local district, or even within the individual school, is a gravely misleading myth.

That the idea is a myth is not a darkly kept secret. Rather, the idea that there is a local curriculum is accepted as truth by experts within the school system. Recently, a district superintendent told me that for twenty years he had mistakenly assumed each of his schools was determining what would be taught to children at each grade level, but was shocked to find that assumption entirely false; he discovered that no principal in his district could tell him what minimal content each child in a grade was expected to learn. He was not surprised when I told him I had received a letter from a distraught mother of identical twins in which she complained that her children had been placed in different classes at the same school and were learning totally different things. Anyone who wishes to conduct an experiment to confirm the proposition that the existence of the local curriculum is a myth can easily do so. Simply ask the principal of your nearest elementary school for a description of the minimal specific content that all children at a grade level are supposed to learn. Those who have tried this experiment have come away empty-handed.

Perhaps "empty-handed" is the wrong word. The principal might hand you a big sheaf of papers. Many states and local districts have produced thick documents called "curriculum guides," which, for all their thickness, do not answer the simple question "What specific content are all children at a grade level required to learn?" Or, in addition to the guidelines, your principal might hand you a list of textbooks that each teacher at a grade level is supposed to use. But a list of textbooks does not provide an answer to the question about minimal content any more than does a thick pile of district guidelines. Consider the following research regarding textbook use in American schools:

> *Daunted by the length of most textbooks and knowing that the children's future teachers will be likely to return to the material, American teachers often omit some topics. Different topics are omitted by different teachers, thereby making it impossible for the children's later teachers to know what has been covered at earlier grades—they cannot be sure what their students know and do not know.*[23]

Four years ago, I had a vivid confirmation of the mythical nature of the local curriculum. A Core Knowledge school had started up the year before, which meant its teachers at each grade level had agreed to teach content far more specifically defined than that in official district "curricula." Now the school was announcing a big rise in test scores and a decline in discipline problems. A *Wall Street Journal* reporter, preparing an article about the school, asked the principal, "What has the school given up from the old curriculum to adopt the new one?" The principal kept replying that the school had not given up anything; the teachers were still following the same district guidelines. The skeptical reporter insistently repeated the question; he could not understand how two different curricula could occupy the same space at the same time. But of course the principal was right. The district guidelines were so vague that they and the more specific curriculum could both be followed at the same time.

Such lack of specificity in district guidelines explains why principals cannot state with confidence what children in a grade are learning within their schools. In fact, the children are learning quite different things. I emphasize in this context the importance of defining content for a particular grade level, since the school year is the critical unit for curricular planning. The normal pattern is: a new year, a new teacher. Guidelines developed in multiyear units are ineffective in practice because students change teachers in successive years. Vague, multiyear goals make neither the student nor the teacher responsible for gaps; a gap is always something that should have been filled in some other year! Close monitoring becomes impossible. Accountability cannot be maintained for either students or teachers.

It might be wondered how it is possible for states and localities to produce lengthy curricular guides that, for all their bulk, fail to define specific knowledge for specific grade levels. Here are some typical instructions (they pertain to first-grade social studies): "The child shall be able to identify and explain the significance of national symbols, major holidays, historical figures and events. Identify beliefs and value systems of specific groups. Recognize the effects of science and technology on yesterday's and today's societies."

These words disclose a characteristic reluctance on the part of district guides to impinge upon the teachers' prerogatives—in this case, by not stating *which* national symbols, major holidays, historical figures, and historical events the local curriculum makers have in view. But, in the absence of specifics, is there any reason to believe that different teachers will respond to these directions in similar ways? When children from diverse first-grade classes that follow these instructions enter second grade, what shared knowledge can the second-grade teacher take for granted among them? What are the "specific" groups the students became acquainted with in studying the "beliefs and value systems of specific groups"? The word "specific" in such a context carries an unintended irony.

I have found a tiny number of district curricula that are much more specific than the typical guidelines just quoted—particularly in science and social studies. Let me therefore examine the very best one I have found so far, since it will, with fairness, illustrate the sort of problem that leads even in the best of cases to our curricular incoherence. The first-grade science instructions in this superior local guide admirably state that the child shall "use the term 'decay' to describe the breakdown of organic material." In social studies, the guide states (again admirably) that the child shall "locate North and South Poles, the

Equator and oceans bordering North America on map/globe." That is exactly the sort of guidance such documents ought to provide.

But even in this best of guides there is grave unevenness in specificity and coherence. Take, for example, the subject of plants and seeds in the science section:

- Grade one: "Describe seeds and grow plants from seeds. State three requirements for seed germination and plant growth."
- Grade two: "Arrange illustrations of plants in various stages of development in order from seed to adult."
- Grade four: "Plant seeds and identify and determine the environmental factors responsible for the success and failure of plant development."
- Grade five: "Identify and plot the growth of the seed parts and infer that the cotyledon is food for the living embryo."

The theory behind this sort of repetition is one of deepening through "spiraling." But it is universally experienced by students as boring repetition, as in the oft-heard complaint from those who have been made to read *Charlotte's Web* three times in six grades.

The spiraling method of forming local curriculum frameworks proceeds as follows: One first defines a few highly general "objectives," and one then carries them through several grades. In this particular local district, science in each grade follows general objectives such as: "Illustrate interrelationships of organisms and their interaction with the environment." Since this "objective" or "strand" is one of the four main principles for science through the first five elementary grades, it is not surprising that the district curriculum repeats themes grade after grade. In this case, the repetition is seeds. But here's another of the four science objectives: "Describe the interactions of physical features and their effects on planet Earth." Given that objective, it isn't surprising that we find units on the *sun* repeated in grades one, two, four, and five; units on the *Earth* repeated in grades one, two, three, four, and five; units on *planets* repeated in grades one, two, and four; units on the *moon* repeated in grades one, two, three, and four.

If repetition and boredom are dangers in the "strand" approach, a corollary danger is the creation of *gaps* that open up in the spaces between the strands. Frequent repetitions and gaps are the besetting weaknesses of local curricula, and they are made inevitable when the strand approach is compounded with vagueness. Huge gaps are bound to arise. There was no indication even in this topflight local curriculum that children were to be introduced to the basic character of photosynthesis, nor that they were to be made aware of simple tools and how they work, nor that they would know how to measure physical things in inches, feet, pounds, kilograms, grams, quarts, pints, and cubic centimeters. It might be assumed that the individual teacher would fill in these gaps. But experience has shown this to be an unwarranted assumption. Major gaps in the local guidelines become major gaps in students' minds.

How did we achieve this degree of curricular ineptitude, unique in the developed world? Beginning in the 1930s as part of the advance of progessive education in the public schools and the colleges of education, there were curriculum-revision movements across the land.[24] Over the past six decades, such vague, gap-ridden "conceptual" curricula have been developed as a reaction to earlier, content-oriented approaches to forming a curriculum. The new curricula have attempted to get beyond the "rote learning" of "mere facts," and to gain unity and conceptual depth by following broad and deep instructional aims. But the examples just cited illustrate the kinds of defects that result from curricula which rely primarily on processes, "objectives" and "strands." Even the best local guides of this type have fundamental weaknesses.

The first inherent weakness is the arbitrariness of the large-scale conceptual schemes and classifications that make up all such curricular "strands" or "objectives." Such schemes may appear to be deep and comprehensive, but most of them are indeed quite arbitrary. The conceptual objectives in each district tend to be different from one another, with each district preferring its own. Equally striking is the arbitrariness of the various conceptual schemes recently produced by curricular experts for the American Association for the Advancement of Science, the National Council of Teachers of Science, and the National Academy of Sciences. These documents all follow different conceptual schemes.

There is another inherent shortcoming in the overreliance on large-scale abstract objectives (as opposed to "mere" content) as a means of determining a curriculum. These general objectives do not compel either a definite or a coherent sequence of instruction. That is because the large conceptual scheme and its concrete expressions (through particular contents) have a very tenuous and uncertain relationship to each other. A big scheme is just too general to guide the teacher in the selection of particulars. For instance, one multigrade science objective in our superior local district states, "Understand interactions of matter and energy." This is operationally equivalent to saying, "Understand physics, chemistry, and biology." The teachers who must decide what to include under such "objectives" are given little practical help.

Apart from a misplaced reliance in local curricula on arbitrary conceptual schemes, the main source of their repetitions and gaps continues to be their lack of content specificity. At first glance, my superior district is something of a puzzle in this respect. Its social science guide is splendidly specific in places. First graders must "distinguish between a globe, political, and relief maps." Second graders must "label a compass rose correctly" and "tell the meaning of 'the stars and stripes.'" By the time students get to grade six, they are to identify the Hwang, Yangtze, and Hsi rivers; the Himalaya Mountains, the Tlin Ling Mountains, the Central Mountains of Japan, and Mount Fuji; the Gobi Desert, the East China Plains, and the Manchurian Plain; Hong Kong, Taiwan, and Yokohama; the Pacific Ocean, the Sea of Japan, and the Yellow Sea. There are similarly explicit geographical specifications for Southeast Asia, India, and Africa! One is surprised and happy to see this untypical focus on concrete geographical knowledge, and this useful guidance to the teacher regarding which of the innumerable geographical features are the essential ones to know.

How, then, may we explain the absence of similar specific guidance to the most important geographical features of the United States? No rivers, not the Mississippi, the Missouri, the Snake, the Rio Grande, or the James; no mountains, not the Alleghenies, the Rockies, or the Cascades; no mention of the Great Plains or the Great Lakes; no city (except that in the school district itself) and no state (except for that of the district). Yet all the foregoing geographical detail about Asia and Africa is presented as essential knowledge. Does the teacher need no guidance about key elements of U.S. geography that should be learned in the early grades? The textbooks themselves contain far too much detail to be useful in that regard. Why is there no specific decision about the essential elements of U.S. geography when there are such definite decisions about the Mekong, the Irrawaddy, and the Salween?

Let me offer an explanation for this highly typical omission which may help explain the unevenness in American curricular specificity. To select Asian geographical features is a noncontroversial activity. To select geographical features within the United States may be considered a highly controversial act. What cities shall *not* be mentioned? Akron, Ohio? But that city is very important for rubber manufacture; shouldn't kids know that tires come from Akron? Heavens! Once you start down that road, where will you stop? There are ninety U.S. cities as big as or bigger than Akron. Are we going to make kids learn ninety cities? And who is to determine the cutoff for U.S. rivers? Hadn't we better leave the whole question of specific U.S. geographical features alone? Such decisions are best left up to the individual teacher. Except for decisions about Asia and Africa, which no one will challenge, we'll just explain how to use an atlas and read a map.

Nowhere is this unhelpful vagueness more apparent than in language arts curricula throughout the United States. While the specificity of some district curricula in science and social studies may be admirable in places, the same cannot be said for any local language arts framework I know of. The only specific book, story, or poem I could find in the district curriculum I have been describing was in grade seven: *The Reader's Guide to Periodical Literature.*

The following is the first broad "objective" to be found in the district's language arts curriculum, and like the other language arts objectives, it spirals through each of the first six grades:

- Grade one: "Develop and apply a word attack system independently using appropriate contextual, phonetic, structural and reference clues."
- Grade two: "Develop and apply a word attack system independently using appropriate contextual, phonetic, structural and reference clues."
- Grade three: "Develop and apply a word attack system independently using appropriate contextual, phonetic, structural and reference clues."
- Grade four: "Develop and apply a word attack system independently using appropriate contextual, phonetic, structural and reference clues."
- Grade five: "Develop and apply a word attack system independently using appropriate contextual, phonetic, structural and reference clues."
- Grade six: "Develop and apply a word attack system independently using appropriate contextual, phonetic, structural and reference clues."

Then, through all six grades, the teacher is instructed to engage the students in formal operations that are subsumed under "contextual clues," "phonetic clues," "structural clues," "reference clues."

While these elements of literacy do need to be taught, this purely formal approach to teaching them, lacking as it does any guidance to specific writings through which they might be taught, is psychologically unsound, according to the research community.[25] It seems almost calculated to be repetitive, deadening, and boring. Its sharp focus on process, as well as its neglect of particular books, stories, and essays as means of teaching literacy skills, not only fails to guide teachers but misses an opportunity to teach both skills and important traditional knowledge simultaneously to children. It is precisely the sort of vague framework that leads to multiple readings of *Charlotte's Web,* and to disadvantaged children's lack of acquaintance with knowledge that advantaged children pick up at home.

Adequately detailed guidelines help teachers by discriminating between knowledge that is required and knowledge that is merely desirable. The selection of particular important facts actually reduces the total amount of specific information that a teacher needs to consider essential. Such guidelines encourage greater depth and coherence in teaching. It's true that they also tend to generate disagreement—which partly explains why our school districts continue to issue vague guidelines: why be specific when vagueness will avoid controversy? On the other hand, without specifics, disadvantaged students and their teachers play a Kafkaesque game whose rules are never clearly defined. Soon the unlucky are consigned to slow tracks and never enter the mainstream of learning and society.

## 4.
## Our Migrant Children

What chiefly makes our schools unfair, then, even for children who remain in the same school year after year, is that some students are learning less than others not because of their innate lack of academic ability or their lack of willingness to learn but because of inherent shortcomings in curricular organization. A systemic failure to teach all children the knowledge they need in order to understand what the next grade has to offer is *the* major source of avoidable injustice in our schools. It is impossible for a teacher to reach all children when some of them lack the necessary building blocks of learning. Under these circumstances, the most important single task of an individual school is to ensure that all children within that school gain the prior knowledge they will need at the next grade level. Since our system currently leaves that supremely important task to the vagaries of individual classrooms, the result is a systemically imposed unfairness even for students who remain in the same school. Such inherent unfairness is greatly exacerbated for children who must change schools, sometimes in the middle of the year.

Consider the plight of Jane, who enters second grade in a new school. Her former first-grade teacher deferred all world history to a later grade, but in her new school many first graders have already learned about ancient Egypt. The new teacher's references to the Nile River, the Pyramids, and hieroglyphics simply mystify Jane, and fail to convey to her the new information that the allusions were meant to impart. Multiply that incomprehension by many others in Jane's new environment, and then multiply those by further comprehension failures which accrue because of the initial failures of uptake, and we begin to see why Jane is not flourishing academically in her new school. Add to these academic handicaps the emotional devastation of not understanding what other children are understanding, and add to avoidable academic problems the *un*avoidable ones of adjusting to a new group, and it is not hard to understand why newcomers fail to flourish in American schools. Then add to all of these drawbacks the fact that the social group with the greatest percentage of school changers is made up of low-income families who move for economic reasons, and one understands more fully why disadvantaged children suffer disproportionately from the curricular incoherence of the American educational system.

It is often said that we are a nation of immigrants. We are also a people that continues to migrate within the nation's borders. According to the United States General Accounting Office, about one fifth of all Americans relocate every year: "The United States has one of the highest mobility rates of all developed countries; annually, about one-fifth of all Americans move. Elementary school children who move frequently face disruption to their lives, including their schooling."[26] Few young families are able to time their moves to coincide with the beginning and end of the school year.[27] In a typical community, the average rate at which students transfer in and out of schools during the school year is nearly one third: "The average rate for Milwaukee public elementary schools is around 30 percent."[28] And among the parents who move, it is those in the lowest income brackets who move most frequently— much more often than middle- and high-income families.[29] This high mobility among low-income parents guarantees that the disadvantaged children who will be most severely affected by the educational handicaps of changing schools are the very ones who move most often. In a typical inner-city school, only about half the students who start in September are still there in May.[30] The myth of the local curriculum can be matched by the myth of the local school—if one means by that term not just a building and a staff but also the students who attend it during the year.

Like most Americans, I was ignorant of the huge dimensions of this little-publicized problem. Student mobility is rarely mentioned in discussions of school reform—which says more about the self-imposed restrictions on our educational thinking than about the urgencies of our educational problems. Any challenge to the principle of an autonomous local curriculum is considered taboo. Hence all the problems exacerbated by that taboo, including the deleterious effects of student mobility, receive far less public attention than they deserve. I was first alerted to the magnitude of the mobility problem in 1992 when I began receiving official reports from Core Knowledge Schools. The first one I saw was from Public School No. 179, in San Antonio, Texas, the Hawthorne School. On the first page of the report, under the rubric "Students," was a box with the following data:

Grade levels served:                   PK–5

Membership:                            522

| Ethnicity: | Asian | 2.5% |
|---|---|---|
| | Black | 4.8% |
| | Hispanic | 83.2% |
| | White | 9.5% |

| Transfers: | In | 108 |
|---|---|---|
| | Out | 176 |

Percent of membership
transferred:                      54.4%

The term of art for the percentages of transferred students is "mobility rate." The average mobility rates for the inner city lie routinely between 45 and 80 percent, with many suburban rates between 25 and 40 percent. Some inner-city schools in New York City and elsewhere have mobility rates of over 100 percent. That is to say, the total number of students moving in and out during the year exceeds the total number of students attending the school. "In some of the nation's most transient districts where some slots turn over several times, schools have mobility rates of more than 100 percent."[31]

A recent report from the General Accounting Office stated that one sixth of all third graders attend at least three schools between first and third grade. A quarter of low-income third graders have attended at least three different schools, a figure that rises to over a third among those with limited English proficiency.[32] The adverse effects of these moves on educational achievement contribute significantly to the low achievement of our system as a whole. The General Accounting Office found that many more migrating third graders were reading below grade level, compared with those who had not yet changed schools.[33] Given the curricular incoherence faced even by those who stay at the same school, the fragmentation of the education provided to frequently moving students approaches the unthinkable.

The adverse effects of such social and academic incoherence are powerful even among nonpoverty students, and are greatly intensified when parents have low educational levels and when compensatory education is not available in the home. Dr. David Wood and his associates have analyzed the effects of mobility on 9,915 children. With this large group, the researchers were able to factor out the influences of poverty, race, single-parent households, and lack of parental education in order to isolate just the effects of school changing alone. Even with these adverse influences factored out, children who changed school often were much more likely to exhibit behavioral problems and to fail a grade—which is difficult to do in current American schools. In an interview, Dr. Wood summarized his findings by saying that mobility alone "is as potent a predictor [of poor school performance] as having parents who are not well educated, or parents who are poor."[34]

It is important, however, not to regard these authoritative findings as inevitable consequences of student mobility. The findings describe, rather, the consequences of mobility within the American system as it is currently constituted. Just as with the 1966 Coleman Report, which disclosed the decisive importance of the home, the Wood results of 1993 should be placed in their particular historical, cultural, and educational contexts rather than conceived of as timeless and inevitable. There is strong evidence that the adverse educational effects of student mobility are much greater in the United States than in countries that use a nationwide core curriculum. In a summary of research, Herbert Walberg, citing the work of Bruce C. Straits, states that "common learning goals, curriculum, and assessment within states (or within an entire nation), moreover, also alleviate the grave learning disabilities faced by children, especially poorly achieving children who move from one district to another with different curricula, assessment, and goals."[35]

Before I learned the extent of the student-mobility problem in the United States, I already suspected that the issue had been inadequately dealt with for children of migrant farm workers, who must change schools several times in the course of the year as their parents move northward to gather crops. The adverse consequence of this degree of curricular instability are easily imagined. One would have thought, therefore, that at least in this special case a core curriculum could be devised in order to provide for more educational coherence and stability. Indeed, in 1989 a group of educational researchers ventured to suggest that perhaps a nationwide core curriculum (confined of course to migrant children) might be desirable. The November 29, 1989, issue of *Education Week* contained an article about this study and reactions to it:

> In an interview last week, Mr. Trotter, one of the authors, elaborated on two of the boldest suggestions to emerge from the study: the establishment of a national curriculum and diploma tailored to the needs of migrant children. "In talking to the kids there were incredible levels of frustration," he said. "They almost were being pushed out of school by the whiplash effect of changing curriculum as they changed schools." . . . Officials at the Pennsylvania and U.S. Education Departments have already distanced themselves from those recommendations. Mr. Ledebur, who oversees the state's education programs for migrant workers, last

*week stressed that all the recommendations represent the views of the*
*authors, and not the state. . . . "Even though there are serious problems*
*regarding the education of migrant children," he said, "a [migrant] na-*
*tional curriculum may not be the best way to deal with those problems."*
*. . . And Francis V. Corrigan, acting director of migrant education for*
*the federal department, said, . . . "In spite of their merits in terms of*
*the needs of migrant students, we also have some state and local responsi-*
*bilities to consider here."*

Though the problem of high mobility rates has grown more pressing and
acute, it is hardly a new problem in the United States. In the 1930s, William
Bagley, with his customary courage, had this to say:

*The notion that each community must have a curriculum all its own is not*
*only silly, but tragic. It neglects two important needs. The first, as we*
*have already seen, is the need of a democracy for many common elements*
*in the culture of all the people, to the end that the people may discuss*
*collective problems in terms that will convey common meanings. The*
*second need is extremely practical. It is the need of recognizing the fact*
*that American people simply will not "stay put." They are the most*
*mobile people in the world. . . . Under these conditions, failure to have*
*a goodly measure of uniformity in school subjects and grade placement is a*
*gross injustice to at least ten million school children at the present time.*[36]

While few would be likely to follow Bagley in courageously calling the
principle of the local curriculum "silly," many researchers would agree that
Bagley was right to call its consequences "tragic." Even those experts who
hold strongly to the principle of local control of curriculum might well concede the need for a voluntary agreement about a common sequence in the
curriculum—at least in those areas like math and science and the basic facts of
history and geography, which, unlike sex education, are not and should not be
subjects of controversy. The principle of the local curriculum is desirable in a
democracy, so long as schooling is effective and fair. But against the principle
of local autonomy must be weighed the paramount principles of educational
excellence and social fairness. Democratic principles sometimes conflict with
one another; none is absolute. In any case, a strong majority of the American
public shares Bagley's view. According to a 1991 Gallup Poll, that majority
clearly recognizes the desirability of curricular coherence and commonality as
a necessary precondition of excellence and fairness in education, and favors it
by a very wide margin.[37] How long before the clear will of the majority is

accepted by the ruling experts, who continue to view curricular particularism as an absolute and inviolable principle?

## 5.
## International Research on Shared Knowledge

I n view of the strong theoretical and practical reasons for providing common intellectual capital in early grades, one would predict that the advantages of a core curriculum would show up in comparisons between national systems which do and those which do not use core curricula. Such comparisons ought to be especially informative with subjects, like math and science, for which similar achievement goals are set in all national systems. I am not making the argument that a core curriculum alone is necessary and sufficient to produce uniformly good results but, rather, that it is a *necessary* condition for producing them, to which must be added other factors like strong support in the general culture. The prediction that a core curriculum is necessary to greater excellence and fairness is strongly confirmed by analyzing such comparisons. The following graph traces student math achievement in a core system (Japan) and in a noncore system (United States). In conducting this crossnational comparison, Harold Stevenson and his colleagues made sure that the test accurately reflected the knowledge and skills which eleventh graders in both nations were mandated to learn, and that the socioeconomic sampling of students was exactly comparable. Other factors, such as the time of the school year when the data were collected and the conditions under which the tests were taken, were carefully controlled.

The graph shows that much larger percentages of U.S. students are performing at very low levels. If we assume that innate math ability is normally distributed, outcomes under a fair educational system should reflect that normal distribution. Children with high math abilities should be enabled to realize their talents, while the far greater number of children with middling abilities should achieve at a respectable level, and children with low abilities should be brought to an acceptable minimal competence. That pattern of equity and excellence is precisely the pattern illustrated in the Japanese results. By contrast, the U.S. curve is abnormally populous on the left, low side of the scores, showing that large percentages of students who began with a normal diversity of math abilities have been hindered from achieving their potentials; a percentage of students, presumably with low abilities, made scores of zero and slightly above, while top students did not perform as well as their foreign counterparts. The U.S. system produces an inequitable distribution of scores,

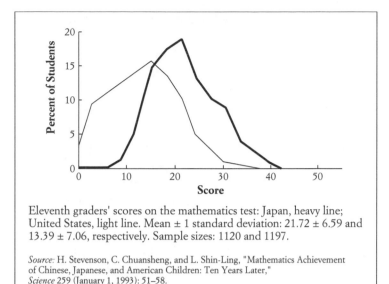

Eleventh graders' scores on the mathematics test: Japan, heavy line; United States, light line. Mean ± 1 standard deviation: 21.72 ± 6.59 and 13.39 ± 7.06, respectively. Sample sizes: 1120 and 1197.

*Source:* H. Stevenson, C. Chuansheng, and L. Shin-Ling, "Mathematics Achievement of Chinese, Japanese, and American Children: Ten Years Later," *Science* 259 (January 1, 1993): 51–58.

a low average performance, and a large amount of mathematical incompetence.

Such contrasts are so dramatic that every conceivable mode of defense has been deployed to call them in question and explain them away. Comparative international research can always be challenged on the ground that apples and oranges are being compared. Such a defense falls on sympathetic ears in the United States. A long tradition of American exceptionalism assumes that the United States will always be an apple, while other nations will always be oranges. But there are two considerations (besides common sense) that tell against the peremptory dismissal of the growing number of international comparisons that show unfavorable results for the United States. The first is the evidence of an absolute educational decline in the United States in the period 1966–80 using U.S. data alone. The second is the evidence of a relative decline vis-à-vis other nations during that same period using identical modes of comparison over time.

It is often stated that the reason for the sharp decline in verbal SAT scores in the United States between 1966 and 1980 was the democratization of the test-taking population. But, as I documented in 1987, this defense does not explain the 64 percent decline in the *absolute number* of high-achieving students—those who had formerly been scoring above 600 on the verbal SAT.[38] No one believes or argues that the population from which this group comes— that is, the absolute number of top students taking the SAT—has declined. From the decline at the top, and the large drop in the overall mean, one can reasonably infer a decline in the educational quality of the system for all students, including those at the top.

As to the apples-vs.-oranges objection to international studies, it might apply to a single-shot comparison but not to identical comparisons over time. Whatever apple-orange inappropriatenesses existed in the first study would also exist in the second, making the *direction* of results highly informative. If a comparison done in 1985 (and published in 1988) showed a relative decline from a similar one done in 1970, the change would reliably indicate the direction of American educational quality as compared to that of other nations. In 1970, the International Association for the Evaluation of Educational Achievement (IEA) conducted a multinational study of science achievement, and then in the 1980s repeated the study. In the 1970 study, the United States ranked seventh out of seventeen countries; in the 1980s it ranked fifteenth out of seventeen—third from the bottom, a drop that was considered worthy of special mention in the executive summary of the 1988 IEA report.[39]

In contemplating such results from the IEA and other sources, it's important to keep in mind why they carry so much weight. Every modern nation educates over 98 percent of its children in the early grades, so the data are not unfairly slanted against a country like the United States, which "educates everybody." Also, because the comparative data are derived from the entire range of abilities in the population, they indicate the *inherent* effectiveness of the systems producing the results. The special value of large-scale comparative research is that it washes out many of the variables which cannot be controlled for in the small scale. International comparisons take large, representative samples from educational systems which have been operating for many years with millions of children and whose average results can be known. Hence, the conclusions derived from these large populations of students in diverse cultural contexts are far more reliable than the results, however dramatic, of more confined research that cannot factor out cultural and historical variables. Only when an educational arrangement succeeds on a large scale over a long period in diverse contexts can one confidently accept its claim to general application.

It is true that most educational programs, national and local, including those performing badly, are based on genuine, if sometimes partial, insights into the nature of children and learning. Few school reforms have been tried that haven't worked reasonably well on a small scale. Yet the primary cause of an initial success may not have been the innovation itself but other factors, such as the enthusiasm of the participants. This false positive is known among sociologists as the "Hawthorne effect," and its workings are often invoked when a school reform that one *doesn't* like appears to be successful. Education is such a slow-moving and multifaceted enterprise that no innovation can be securely evaluated right away, any more than a new drug can be confidently evaluated on the basis of small clinical trials. The efficacy of either new drugs or new educational policies may not be known until they have been used over many years by many thousands of people—as both the thalidomide affair and U.S. education since the late 1960s have dramatically illustrated.

In determining the relative efficacy of core-curriculum policies, the decade-long separation of the two IEA studies allows us to observe that between the 1970s and the 1980s the rank order of science achievement in core-curriculum nations rose or stayed stable, while the rank order in noncore countries declined. What counts here is relative movement. One would expect the core countries to stay stable with respect to one another and—since most countries in the sample do use core curricula—not to shift much in rankings. One would expect the noncore countries to show a relative decline. That is what happened. Among the three noncore countries, England dropped from ninth to eleventh, Australia from third to tenth, and the United States from seventh to fifteenth. Among the core nations, Sweden remained at sixth, Finland rose from seventh to fifth (the United States having vacated seventh place), while Japan and Hungary traded second and first place.[40]

Another effect of using core curricula shows up in the IEA comparisons. The 1988 report evaluated national systems according to the equality of educational opportunity they provided children—a fairness rating for each system. This was a measure of the extent to which a nation educates children at all schools to an appropriate average level of achievement, regardless of location or social class. Strikingly, the systems that ranked high in fairness also ranked high in excellence; the best-performing systems were also the most equitable ones. For instance, among Finnish schools, only 2 percent of schools showed below-standard average achievement; in Japan, it was 1 percent; in Korea, 5 percent; in Sweden, 1 percent; and in Hungary, 0 percent. Among the noncore countries, the percentages of schools below par were: Australia, 8 percent; the Netherlands, 16 percent; England, 19 percent; and the United States, 30 percent.[41]

One fairness score was anomalous—that of the Netherlands. Whereas Holland placed third of seventeen in average science achievement, its fairness score (16 percent of schools below par) was a distant last among the countries of northern continental Europe. Britain did even worse, with 19 percent of schools below par. One cause of these results was probably that Holland and Britain, in contrast to their European neighbors, lacked a common core curriculum. When the results were analyzed, the British had not yet adopted their national curriculum. Any private school in the Netherlands that met certain basic standards for plant and faculty was eligible to receive public funding.

That 16 percent of Dutch schools fell below par was probably owing to the fact that in the Netherlands there are many schools doing their own thing—a theory strongly supported by the similar results from Britain, the other non-core-curriculum nation of Northern Europe.

A country that lacks nationwide curricular standards can produce high average results when each of its schools has a good common curriculum and when mobility rates between schools are low, keeping the student body stable, so that each child receives a coherent education. Switzerland, for example, which did not participate in the IEA study but which has top scores for excellence and fairness according to other studies, uses a different core curriculum within each small canton. But since the Swiss do not move very often, the result is a coherent curriculum for each child.[42] If the students at good Dutch schools performed superbly, that would explain how average achievement could remain high even though scores were low at 16 percent of Dutch schools. All the more reason to conclude that, in the Dutch context, students at these inferior schools were being cheated. In the Netherlands, the absence of a core curriculum has permitted spots of unfairness even within a generally excellent system. The Dutch result is very useful, therefore, as an apparent exception that confirms the rule.

Support for this generalization about core curricula comes from France, which did not participate in the 1988 IEA study. The French have been keeping educational data on a national scale for many decades and can justly pride themselves on having greatly diminished the socially induced learning gap between advantaged and disadvantaged children. Remarkably, in France the initial gap between advantaged and disadvantaged students, instead of widening steadily as in the United States, decreases with each school grade. By the end of seventh grade, the child of a North African immigrant who has attended two years of French preschool (*école maternelle*) will on average have narrowed the socially induced learning gap.[43] Such success in achieving fairness is explained at least in part by the fact that national systems which have core curricula are able to provide a school-based education which relies relatively less on the undependable home curriculum to supply the prior knowledge needed for learning in each grade.

## 6.
## The New Civil Rights Frontier

I n the 1960s and '70s, when the legal foundations of social justice were getting firmer, public schools across the United States were getting worse. Bad schools hold back disadvantaged children disproportionately because disadvantaged homes are typically less able than advantaged ones to compensate for the knowledge gaps left by the schools. An overall decline in the quality of schooling will thus have an uneven social effect. All children, including those of the middle class, will be poorly educated, but the negative effects will be strongest among the least privileged. As they go through the grades, disadvantaged students will accumulate relatively less intellectual capital than they would have under a more demanding system. Educational injustice will grow—whether or not the schools are racially integrated. Since inferior education is today the primary cause of social and economic injustice, the struggle for equality of educational opportunity is in effect the new civil rights frontier.[44] This new struggle is more subtle and complex than the earlier one of sit-ins and freedom rides. In this struggle, it is harder to tell good from evil, true from false.

The basic explanation for the strong correlation between equality of educational opportunity and use of a core curriculum has been given. A core curriculum induces grade readiness for all children and thus enables all members of a classroom to learn. When all children possess the prior knowledge they need for understanding new material, the teacher will spend far less time in boring reviews and in special coaching of those who are behind. Everybody will be more stimulated, more accountable, and will learn more. In the preceding section, I showed that all national systems rated fair by the IEA standard use this core-curriculum approach, and I showed, moreover, that *no* noncore system cited in the report has managed to achieve fairness.[45]

Since some children are apter and harder-working than others, equality of educational opportunity does not mean that all students will make very high test scores. Yet overall school scores are indicative. It is of course true that good schools in the inner city can never *entirely* equalize educational opportunity compared with schools in the suburbs, because the home is also a school, where students spend more time than in the official one. Other things being equal, students from good-home schools will always have an educational advantage over students from less-good-home schools. Nonetheless, basic gaps in knowledge can be compensated for in the classroom, as the international data prove. It follows that a moderately high average achievement in all schools is a roughly accurate index to national educational fairness, whether the schools are in the inner city or the suburbs.

In the United States, our schools' inequitable distribution of intellectual capital causes the gap between academic haves and have-nots to grow wider in each successive early grade until, by fourth grade, it is usually unbridgeable. This tragic process currently seems inexorable. The longitudinal researches of Walter Loban in the 1960s tracked the acquired learning abilities of disadvantaged and advantaged students as they moved from grade one to grade four and beyond, with results that the following graph vividly indicates. Note that some crucial data are not directly represented, namely, that one group showed low oral skills in kindergarten, the other high oral skills before either group learned to read.

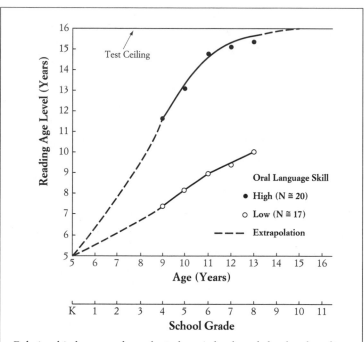

Relationship between chronological-age/school-grade level and median reading ability for students rated high or low in oral language skills in kindergarten.

*Source:* Constructed by T. G. Sticht et al., *Auding and Reading: A Developmental Model* (Alexandria, Va.: Human Resources Organization, 1974), from data presented in W. Loban, *Language Ability: Grades Seven, Eight, and Nine* (Berkeley, Calif.: University of California, 1964), Table 16, page 117.

Later researches by Jeanne Chall duplicated this result, as did the Coleman Report of 1966. One observation by Coleman and his colleagues has important implications for explaining and overcoming the widening gap. It is the finding that good schools have stronger positive effects and poor schools stronger negative ones on disadvantaged students. This may be denominated "Coleman's Law."[46] Since our public school system as a whole is not very good, a small educational disadvantage in kindergarten normally widens to a big learning gap by grade four—a result that unfortunately applies even to graduates of Head Start.

Head Start is politically popular as a tool for achieving equal educational opportunity. Many believe that the program should be extended to all disadvantaged children. Despite occasional political setbacks and temporary damage to its reputation by research impugning its efficacy, Head Start has managed to emerge as a Great Society program that still enjoys the protection of both political parties. But just how complex the search for equal educational opportunity has become may be gauged from the fact that Head Start does not achieve educational *improvement,* much less educational equity.

That is the well-documented conclusion of the Department of Health and Human Services, which in 1985 published a review of all existing research on the effects of Head Start. It stated that "in the long run, cognitive and socioemotional test scores of former Head Start students do not remain superior to those of disadvantaged students who did not attend Head Start."[47] Why does this astonishing fade-out occur? Edward Zigler, Sterling Professor of Psychology at Yale and one of the founders of Head Start, gives an unintended clue in an anecdote about his time as director of the Office of Child Development. He was presiding at a meeting of

> *the department's power structure, including the HEW [Department of Health Education and Welfare] deputy secretary. They were impressed with "Sesame Street" and dwelled on the fact that it was so inexpensive. "We can get 'Sesame Street' to reach poor kids by spending sixty-five cents per child," they said. "Why should we spend over a thousand dollars per child on Head Start?" . . . Finally, as they kept pressing I said I would give Head Start money to "Sesame Street" if they could answer this question: How long would a poor child have to watch "Sesame Street" to get his or her teeth filled? When nobody could answer, that was the end of the meeting.[48]*

From its inception in the 1960s, Zigler and his cofounders conceived of Head Start as much more than an educational program. The health, nutrition, motivation, and self-confidence of poor children were deemed to be at least as important to their future well-being as their academic learning. Another feature present from the beginning was Head Start's rule that parents be involved in running each local program. A rationale for that principle: building parents' self-esteem would help develop their children's. In short, Head Start has not been primarily an *academic* program. Though momentary academic benefits have sometimes been measured, they are not securely fixed and they quickly fade.

Researchers have sought further explanations for this academic fade-out. The team of scientists who wrote the 1985 review of Head Start research offered the following: "The educational environment in elementary schools does not support and stimulate the children as effectively as Head Start did. This suggests that more innovative arrangements designed to sustain the early developmental benefits of Head Start would be desirable."[49] The researchers imply that while Head Start may have yielded momentary benefits, later schooling erases them. Children fortunate enough to attend Head Start must enter a public school system that is incoherent and fragmented. But this explanation of fade-out is only half the story. Head Start is not a single, academically describable program. Its academics vary greatly from place to place. While it is usually beneficial for a time, it tends to lack academic coherence and is rarely accountable for specific academic outcomes. When its graduates subsequently enter a program that also lacks academic coherence and is also unaccountable for specific academic outcomes, the children have left the frying pan for the fire. This is implicitly an argument for extending Head Start while at the same time improving its academic rigor and that of the schooling which follows.

Preschool programs elsewhere in the world *do* achieve long-term academic benefits for disadvantaged students. In France, early schooling permanently boosts educational achievements of children of low-paid workers and immigrants from North Africa.[50] What, then, makes the academic benefits of early education endure in some countries but fade in our own? A few contrasts: Head Start lasts three hours, is staffed by nonprofessionals, and is nonacademic. The *école maternelle* (attended by over 90 percent of French three- and four-year-olds) lasts all day and goes twelve months a year, is staffed by professionals, and has well-defined academic goals. Children then enter a grade-school system that also has a well-defined academic and cognitive core.

American experts have developed astonishingly resourceful techniques for denying the desirability of an academic core curriculum. In effect, they say:

- We have educated children reasonably well in the past without using a core of universal content standards.
- We already have an informal core-knowledge system in the United States, determined by the widespread use of just a few textbooks.
- We do not need to emphasize particular content: knowledge is changing and increasing so rapidly that the best approach is to teach children *how* to learn.
- There is a danger that standardization of content would be imposed by the federal government and would open the way to federal control of education.
- It is illegitimate to compare the United States with other countries, which are in every case far less diverse than we are.
- A canned, lockstep curriculum would obliterate the distinctive characteristics of American localities and make schools into cookie cutters that turn out the same product everywhere.

In the preceding pages, I have tried to expose these stand-pat positions for the evasions they are. Indeed, if the foregoing analyses are right, a diverse, nomadic nation like ours has a greater need for a grade-by-grade core curriculum than do countries that are less migratory and diverse, just as a nomadic, disadvantaged child has a greater need for academic coherence than does an advantaged child. Head Start, especially, needs an agreed-on cognitive core of basic knowledge and vocabulary. Extreme localism, coupled with vagueness, seems increasingly outmoded at a time when children must change schools a lot and when the educational needs of young children have become very much the same throughout the world.

It is a fundamental injustice that what American children are enabled to learn in school should be determined by what their homes have already given them. Although this chapter has focused on this injustice, nothing said here should be construed to imply that our *advantaged* children are on the whole receiving an adequate education. They are not. The public schools of a democracy have a duty to educate all students to their potential. A child's initial lack of intellectual capital is not an immutable given that our schools are powerless to change; rather, it is a challenge that schools can meet by overcoming their academic incoherence. Throughout the world, just one way has been devised to meet the double challenge of educational excellence and fairness: to teach definite skills and a solid core of content appropriate in an effective manner in each year of preschool and grade-school education.

# 3.

# An
# Impregnable
# Fortress

## 1.
## Orthodoxy Masquerading as Reform

Historians date the present era of American education from the publication in 1918 of *Cardinal Principles of Secondary Education.* Written by the Commission on the Reorganization of Secondary Education, and published by the Bureau of Education of the U.S. Department of the Interior, it was an official document that represented mainstream educational thought. Like most subsequent pronouncements of the educational community, it was a reform-minded document that challenged an emphasis on subject matter. In 1918, of course, schools were still strongly focused on academic subject matter, including Latin. But with ever greater numbers of students coming to school and an ever-growing immigrant population, the time had come, these educators believed, to place a countervailing emphasis on health, vocation, family membership, ethical character, and the worthy use of leisure—topics specially singled out in *Cardinal Principles.* That manifesto could thus be viewed as recommending a balanced approach to the nation's needs—a concern for the whole student rather than just his or her intellectual side, and a desire to democratize public education by accommodating teaching to children's "individual differences in capacities and aptitudes." But already discernible were the anti-intellectual, progressive attitudes that were thenceforward to prevail in the educational community. The first draft of *Cardinal Principles* failed even to include the phrase "command of fundamental processes" (i.e., reading, writing, and arithmetic), which in the final version was the only allusion to academic goals.

This hostility to academic subject matter has been the continued focus of educational "reform" ever since *Cardinal Principles*—a tradition that needs to be kept in mind when current reformers attack "mere facts" and "rote learning." Subject-matter education in elementary schools has been under relentless and successful siege for more than seventy years. But lest it be thought that members of the educational community knowingly pretend to be reformers while they are really status quo traditionalists voicing age-old slogans, it must be conceded that the deception is not deliberate. Their reform proposals continue to be based on a sincere but quite inaccurate belief that a fact-oriented classroom prevails in American public schools today, whereas, in reality, the most striking feature of our elementary schools is that the anti-rote-learning reforms being advocated are already firmly in place. The anti-subject-matter viewpoint of *Cardinal Principles* has dominated the training and certification of teachers in our teacher-training schools since the 1930s, that is, during the entire working lives of all persons now teaching in our schools. This historical reality seems not to have affected the educationist worldview or its reform prescriptions. Education professors continue to make proposals which assume that our elementary schools are still in the grip of drill-and-practice and subject-matter-driven education.

Education professors continue to assume that teachers are still giving lectures to docile classes lined up in rows, are still forcing children to engage in "rote learning," and are still insisting on the mere accumulation of facts. Yet a visit to any of our public elementary schools will disclose that these denounced practices are rare. One finds few monologic lectures but a great many project-oriented, hands-on activities. The little rote learning to be observed consistently is the recitation of the Pledge of Allegiance. A daring teacher will occasionally ask pupils to learn poems or songs by heart, or even state capitals and foreign vocabulary words, but such practices are frowned upon. The scarcity of memorization is hardly surprising. A vigorous attack on rote learning has dominated education schools, professional journals, and teacher's lounges for many decades. The continued beating of this dead horse illustrates the extreme disconnection between the stated evils that are said to need reforming and the actual practices of American elementary schools.

Since the publication in 1964 of Lawrence Cremin's pathbreaking *The Transformation of the School,* it has been known that by the 1930s the anti-subject-matter principles of progressive education had become the established tenets taught to elementary teachers throughout the nation. Yet, after many decades of progressivist intellectual dominance, reformers still recommend these doctrines as "innovations" that are necessary to improve our schools. Post-Cremin historians of American education like Larry Cuban and Arthur

Zilversmit concede that progressive ideology has indeed long dominated our schools of education, but they argue that this intellectual monopoly has not significantly affected school practice. For Cuban, the movements of ideas in American education are like waves on the surface of the sea, scarcely affecting the depths below. In the same vein, Zilversmit points out that although modern schools have unbolted students' desks from the floor, schools are continually reverting to the practice of putting them back in orderly rows.[1] Teachers and schools just can't seem to overcome traditional habits.

That is, however, just one of the two possible explanations: 1) either the progressive dogmas have not been properly put into practice, or 2) they have been put into practice but are themselves defective. If the teachers, the human vessels, are at fault, with schools remaining just too institutionalized and hidebound to change despite the progressive dogmas they openly enunciate, then we must work ever harder to reform the human vessels. If, on the other hand, the dogmas themselves are faulty, that would require a very considerable change in what is being taught in education schools and advocated in reforms. Given the stark option of changing one's cherished doctrines or changing other people's practices, education professors have tended to prefer the second choice.

In this conflict of historical interpretations, I believe that Cremin provides the more comprehensive and accurate view. Progressivism has dominated the schools for so long that small rebellions against it, such as realigning the children's desks, are less a measure of its lack of influence than its lack of practicality. The critical evidence for gauging the influence of progressivism is not a series of snapshots of specific classroom practices, which are highly variable, but a longitudinal view of the decline of subject-matter learning during the last six or seven decades. The anti-subject-matter principles of progressivism have demonstrably triumphed in American schools.

To take an example, one basic tenet of antitraditional, progressivist "reform" from 1918 to the 1990s has been an insistence on the superiority of naturalistic, hands-on teaching of cognitive skills over the lecture-and-drill-and-practice teaching of a defined body of knowledge. Learning should be holistic and natural, presented in projects, not fragmented into isolated academic subjects. The project method claims to raise student interest, fix learnings vividly in students' memories, induce love of learning, and stimulate students' creativity and individuality. The traditional method is supposed to fragment knowledge, bore students, turn them into passive dependents, make them hate learning, and stifle their individuality and creativity.

(One thing the traditional method of teaching did accomplish was to cause children to actually learn the subjects they were being directly taught and drilled in and then rigorously tested on. Pragmatists like me reject the polar opposition between naturalistic and artificial modes of teaching, and prefer a mixture of naturalistic and more direct instructional methods.[2] The great drawback of the naturalistic method, which critics of progressive "reforms" [including Dewey] long ago pointed out, is that indirection doesn't always work. No invisible hand guarantees that lively, absorbing school activities will eventuate in the desired learnings and competencies. On the evidence of history, that objection has proved to be well founded.)

The disorienting lack of fit between the reformer-drawn but unwarranted picture of drill and practice in today's schools and the project-centered teaching activities that are everywhere pursued in them is reinforced by the tendency to connect this naturalistic teaching with cybernetic futurology. The computer is conceived as a hands-on, "interactive" learning environment that supports the antipathy to bookish learning. We are moving, it is predicted, toward the bookless classroom or even toward an abandonment of the classroom entirely. The school as we currently know it will be a thing of the past. Such radical, "break-the-mold" thinking disarms the criticism that the "project method" has been tried for many decades with generally poor results. While we wait for the bookless and brickless classroom to arrive, futuristic enthusiasm for computers serves mainly to divert attention from past failures and perpetuate progressivist thought and practice.

Another example of the dominance of progressivist ideas: *Cardinal Principles,* besides reducing the emphasis on academic subject matters, advocated another change that is still being promoted as reform in the 1990s: schools must pay more attention to the "individual differences" of children. Their varying abilities and "learning styles" must not be submerged under a single, lockstep system of academic standards and teaching methods. During the past ten years, I have visited dozens of elementary schools without finding a single one in which sensitivity to the different individual talents and needs of children was not a concern of teachers and principals. This idea is just as firmly established, and as long victorious, as the repudiation of "rote learning." Nonetheless, a stress upon different learning styles and other individual differences continues to be presented as a highly promising reform novelty.

The most widely distributed educational pamphlet of the teens and twenties of this century was William Heard Kilpatrick's *The Project Method* (1918), which sold over sixty thousand copies. In 1993, *Education Week* caught the irony of implying that current reform proposals are new in the following headline about the New American Schools Development Corporation, a reform group seeking to create what it calls "break-the-mold" schools. The headline ran, PROGRESSIVE-ERA CONCEPT NOW BREAKS MOLD: NASDC SCHOOLS EXPLORE "PROJECT LEARNING", and the article (by Lynn Olson) went on to state:

> "project-based learning" organizes knowledge from a number of disciplines around a big idea or common principle, instead of around more traditional subjects. "Students plan and carry out a project that forces them to engage in meaningful learning experiences. . . . Too often we don't really engage [students], . . . We chop everything up into little pieces. We compartmentalize everything. And then, somehow, they don't remember it very well."[3]

Kilpatrick could hardly have stated his idea better than these reformers of the 1990s. That is not surprising, since Kilpatrick's method, under various names, has long been securely in place. (The name Kilpatrick will appear as a leitmotif in this book. It is a name that should be better known. Although the progressive movement in American education is often associated with John Dewey or with Harold Rugg, author of *The Child-Centered School* [1928], the most influential introducer of progressive ideas into American schools of education was William Heard Kilpatrick, whose books and articles were used as key educational texts and who, at Teachers College, Columbia University, directly trained a large number of future education professors in the formative years 1918–40.)

Also unbroken is the reform tradition of teaching the whole child, not just the intellectual side:

> The hallmarks of the new school are freedom, activity, and creative self-expression. The old school is described as "the listening regime," a place of "fears, restraints, and long, weary hours of suppression," whose philosophy is based on outmoded allegiance to discipline and subject matter. The new school is devoted to "self-expression" and "maximum child growth," a place where children are eager to go to school because . . . "they model in clay and sand; they draw and paint, read and write, make up stories and dramatize them; they work in the garden; they churn and weave and cook"; its philosophy is "the concept of Self." . . . The whole child is to be educated. Hence the materials of education are as broad and interrelated as life itself. For experience is not only an intellectual matter; it is physical, rhythmic, emotional.[4]

The book from which the above recommendations (in quotation marks) were excerpted is *The Child-Centered School,* published in 1928. Today, it would be hard to find an elementary school in the United States, or for that matter in most nations of Asia or Europe, that does not put into practice at least some of these conceptions. Yet similar ideas continue to be advocated as changes that our schools must introduce so that humane and effective education can at last begin to occur. That our schools are neither better nor more equitable, even though these practices have been in place for many years, is a paradox that our educational experts can scarcely admit into contemplation.

Another example: Reformers still ask schools to create an "active" learning environment where children effectively take charge of their own learning instead of "passively" taking in what adults force upon them. In the 1990s, schools are still being advised to place an

> *emphasis on students' active engagement in making and critiquing their own classmates' knowledge. At root, such activities violate the paradigm that sanctifies knowledge as something the teacher possesses at the beginning, which students acquire during the course, and then demonstrate as their own private possession on a test. To credit students' knowledge, and their capacity to construct and critique knowledge, is to empower students in a way that violates the unspoken norms of most classrooms.*[5]

The following complaint against too much emphasis on content and too little on process in the schools is the focus of an entirely typical article in *Education Week:*

> *Adding subject matter to the curriculum offers the illusion of school reform. . . . New policies promise students will learn more, but they have to wend their way through the official, taught, learned, and tested curricula. They seldom reach students' heads as intended. They are magicians' tricks. . . . Lopsided school-reform in the 1980's concentrated on content, not teaching, and rejected the practical knowledge of parents, teachers, and informed observers. Will the mindless prejudice against pedagogy continue into the 1990's?*[6]

There is, in short, little in the current literature of school reform that does not yield a powerful sense of déjà vu to anyone who has read the Romantic, progressive literature of the teens, twenties, and thirties of this century, as well as the standard textbooks used in education schools. There have been vocabulary changes. "Projects" have become "thematic learnings" or "multi-disciplinary" activities. "Training the mind" (which used to be mocked by early reformers) has become "critical-thinking skill." "Lived experience" has become "hands-on activity" or "deep understanding." "Group participation" has become "cooperative learning." But except for such cosmetic variations, and an attempt to integrate computers into the mix, the reforms being advocated have long dominated the schools. The repudiation of the supposedly deleterious "overemphasis" on subject matter is a reform that has already been victorious for half a century. The most radical reform that schools could possibly undertake—a focus on well-defined and challenging subject matter in the traditional disciplines—is rarely recommended. Traditional subject matter is taken to be the very thing that needs to be eradicated.

## 2.
## The Pervasiveness of Antiknowledge Views

The deep aversion to and contempt for factual knowledge that pervade the thinking of American educators was at first so paradoxical and difficult for an outsider like me to understand or believe that it took me many years to appreciate it. It is not too much to say that an antiknowledge attitude is the defining element in the worldview of many early-childhood educators and reformers. Only gradually have I come to realize that this deep-dyed sentiment has been a powerful cause of our educational failings—as serious in its ultimate effects as any other single cause. Because it has taken me more than a decade to become persuaded of this paradox, I must expect my readers to be as skeptical of the proposition as I first was. Let me briefly narrate a few of the numerous firsthand experiences that brought me to my present understanding.

Until a few years ago, I had interpreted these antiknowledge sentiments as stratagems for resisting change—in this case, the factual strengthening of the elementary curriculum. I believed that, deep down, educators did not hold knowledge in contempt. My thought was: "Most people dislike change. These scornful-sounding dismissals of factual knowledge, calling it 'trivial pursuit' and 'rote learning,' are effective rhetorical devices for keeping things the same." By vigorously holding on to this theory, I was able to interpret the statements I was hearing as strategic defense mechanisms rather than as expressions of fundamental belief.

Three summers ago, I agreed to speak to three large groups of educators, each group consisting of 150 to 250 school principals and administrators from all parts of the country. These gatherings, administered by an organization called IDEA, take place during the summer on college campuses in such places as Denver, Appleton, Wisconsin, and Los Angeles. Since IDEA conferees come from every region, the gatherings are excellent occasions for getting to know the culture of education firsthand in an informal setting.

In my first small-group session, an educator asked me what sorts of things I thought first graders should know. I mentioned, as they occurred to me, several examples of what first graders were learning in Core Knowledge schools: some fables of Aesop; some facts about Egypt, including mummies and the Nile; some elements of geography, like being able to find north, south, east, and west both out of doors and on globes and maps, as well as being able to identify the Atlantic and Pacific oceans and the seven continents. Immediately, one of the participants asked me if I really thought it was of any use whatever to a first grader to learn the seven continents? No one at the meeting was willing to defend the idea of teaching such facts to young children. Even if some might have privately favored doing so, no one dared to speak out. If dissenters were present, they were being powerfully inhibited by social constraints.

An hour or so later, in a plenary meeting, I was asked by a curious teacher, intrigued by the idea of teaching solid substance in early grades (for some did seem interested in the general idea), whether I had *enjoyed* editing resource books for the early grades. I said, yes indeed, that I had learned a great deal. Next question: What had I learned that was most interesting? I pondered. Well, perhaps, the most exciting thing for me was at last to understand the relations between the earth and the sun during a year's orbit, and why, at the equator, spring and fall are the hottest seasons. Then, from another quarter, a dash of cold water was thrown on this momentary enthusiasm when an educator asked me if I thought that tidbit of information had made me a better person. Again, no one spoke up to defend teaching factual knowledge.

The comment about the uselessness of factual knowledge for becoming a "better person" was soon followed by a remark from someone who identified herself as an elementary-school principal: Was I aware that it was developmentally inappropriate to expose first graders to the Eiffel Tower—as the Core Knowledge materials recommended? I was too astounded by the assertion to respond effectively. I had no notion how this confident statement was arrived at, and I was too polite in an old-style Southern way to challenge directly the questioner's professional authority in such a matter. Also, I didn't dare mention as relevant the fact that troops of French preschoolers continually visit the Eiffel Tower without harmful psychological effects, because I had already learned that any mention of French children (or those of other nations) would bring the reproach that *we* are not French. In fact, I don't remember what I said at that moment. But I do remember that no one in the audience offered to defend the teaching of solid factual content to young children.

During the next several days, I traveled to two more IDEA campuses where large numbers of educational administrators were gathered, representing a good sampling of the thinking of school officials across the nation. On each campus, I encountered similar attitudes regarding the uselessness of factual knowledge and the undesirability of asking students to learn it. It was almost universally assumed that the teaching and learning of facts must occur in a fragmented, dry, and inhumane way, and that teaching such information as the names and shapes of the seven continents could only be accomplished by memorizing meaningless items disconnected from a child's interest and experience.

It was at these IDEA meetings that I also realized the degree to which these antifact prejudices are currently being reinforced by an enthusiasm for the "new world of technology." The decades-old antipathy to bookish knowledge in the educational community has now been made to seem up to date and even avant-garde by conjuring up the promise of electronics. The "new world of technology," I discovered, confers a number of benefits on the antifact point of view. Several IDEA participants told me that current knowledge, no matter what sort, quickly becomes outmoded. A "knowledge explosion" has occurred that makes the teaching of "today's facts" irrelevant, since they are sure to be gone tomorrow. So great a quantity of information is being produced in this new information age that it is fruitless to try to cover it in school. The universal availability of technology has now rendered obsolete "old-fashioned" techniques such as learning the multiplication table by heart. Instead of taking the view that the information age requires everyone to have *more* intellectual capital, these experts viewed technology as a means for reinforcing rather than reducing their antagonism to teaching factual knowledge.

In the IDEA discussions, facts and information were invariably referred to as "mere," in contrast to something better called "true knowledge." In these educators' minds, there existed a polarity between exciting, practically useful, morally beneficial teaching on the one hand and memorization of meaningless facts through dry, dull teaching on the other. At IDEA, I had entered an either-or world that had the flavor of a medieval morality play, in which good was set against evil. The possibility that factually rich and demanding learning of subject matter could, while requiring hard work, also be interesting, even captivating—not to mention morally beneficial and skill-enhancing—was not a concept that IDEA participants brought under discussion.

These hundreds of participants did not consider themselves to be enemies of knowledge, and might well have thought it outrageous that anyone would so describe them. On the contrary, they thought of themselves as friends of "true knowledge" as distinct from "mere facts." When I asked what they meant by "true knowledge," some participants said that it consisted in knowing "the interrelations of things," but they did not explain how things can be related without first being known. They also assumed that any really important factual knowledge is picked up automatically in the course of experience. (That it is *not* automatically picked up by American students is by now well documented.[7])

In sum, these educators saw themselves as foes not of knowledge itself but only of "disconnected" facts, which they considered to be insignificant when compared to "meaningful" knowledge. They assumed that our students' ignorance is a condition created by "the larger culture" rather than a condition created by schooling itself. There was no sense of a connection between educators' own antiknowledge attitudes and the current academic incompetence of our students as measured by world standards. There was no thought of a possible causal relation between lack of factual knowledge and lack of ability to read, write, and solve math problems. The IDEA participants saw themselves as doing *more* than imparting mere information. As a Westport, Connecticut, superintendent recently told parents who complained of great gaps in their children's learning, the schools were imparting more than facts:

> *Knowing what subject matter to teach is a problem because of the information explosion, said Dr. Kelleher. The school situation today is different from what it was when they went to school, he told the parents. The Westport system tries to achieve "knowledge plus," he said.[8]*

Recently, a news article announced the selection of the 1994 Teacher of the Year. This able professional was asked what tips she would give her fellow teachers. Among her words of advice, which included respecting children and finding creative ways to interest them, was the following comment about teachers' responsibilities: "They're not there to teach subject matter, they're there to teach children." One knows what she means, of course. In the 1920s and '30s, she might have said, "Teach the child, not the subject," the slogan of "child-centered schooling." Such phrases can be understood benignly, not as opposed to knowledge but simply as expressing a kind of emphasis in the way knowledge is imparted. The practical consequence of these hoary slogans, however, are anything but benign, and their continued dominance shows the degree to which even the ablest educators have been captivated by polarities that date back seventy or eighty years. In fact, the sloganized oppositions go back even further, as the following remark by John Dewey attests:

*[We must] get rid of the prejudicial notion that there is some gap in kind (as distinct from degree) between the child's experience and the various forms of subject-matter that make up the course of study. From the side of the child it is a question of seeing how his experience already contains within itself elements—facts and truths—of just the same sort as those entering into the formulated study; and what is of more importance, how it contains within itself the attitudes, the motives and the interests which have operated in developing and organizing the subject-matter to the plane which it now occupies.[9]*

Dewey's words, disposing of the polarity between child-centered and subject-matter-centered education, were published in 1902! Clearly, Dewey did not succeed in laying the oversimplifications to rest. On the contrary, they continue to be promulgated by education schools, continue to corrupt the common sense of even some of our ablest teachers and administrators, and continue to be advocated by experts under the banner of "reform."

## 3.
## Why America's Universities Are Better Than Its Schools

The influence of the intellectual orthodoxy that controls our public schooling and its reformers may partly be gauged by contrasting our K–12 system with an educational domain *not* controlled by the educationist point of view—our public colleges and universities. There is wide agreement in the international community that the United States has created the best public universities and the worst public schools of the developed world.[10] Foreign students arrive by the thousands to study at American colleges and universities, but well-informed foreign parents are rarely willing to send their children to our public elementary schools if the children can learn English well in any other way. One of my friends, a Swiss, is a medical researcher at the University of Virginia, a job he esteems and could not easily duplicate in Switzerland. But so distressed are he and his wife by the education offered to their two young children in the public schools that they are sadly debating whether to return to Switzerland.

What causes this startling contrast in quality between American schools and American universities? It is not inevitable that a nation must fail to achieve educational excellence in both spheres. In fact, it is *easier* to create a good K–12 system than a good university system, the evidence being that many nations have created better elementary schools than ours but few or none have created better universities.

Perhaps American culture is friendly to first-rate universities (I don't mean to imply that all of them are first-rate, or that their faculties are uniformly admirable) because of our tradition of free speech and our consequent toleration, even encouragement, of dissent. Open discussion and iconoclasm create the sort of atmosphere in which intellectual excellence can flourish. Over a portal of the University of Virginia's Cabell Hall are Jefferson's words about the kind of university he wished to create: "This institution will be based on the illimitable freedom of the human mind. For here we are not afraid to follow truth wherever it may lead, nor to tolerate any error so long as reason is left free to combat it." That conception is a universe away from the intolerant, conformist atmosphere of the educational community.

But there is another difference, in addition to their openness and competitiveness, that distinguishes our universities from our schools, and I think it may be the most critical difference of all. Our colleges and universities, and the scholars who control their destinies, place great value on depth, breadth, and accuracy of knowledge, as well as on independence of thought. But depth, breadth, and accuracy of knowledge are the very things that our K–12 system tends to disparage as belonging to the "banking theory of schooling." Knowledge is considered less desirable than more "practical" all-purpose goals such as "higher-order skills," "self-esteem," "metacognitive skills," and "critical-thinking skills." "Mere facts" are conceived to be indissolubly connected to "rote learning," which may be the most disparaging phrase in the educationists' glossary.

It is unclear how long our best universities can maintain their excellence when the students who enter them and who will subsequently staff them are ill-prepared. Since 1965, for example, there has been a 75 percent decline in the absolute number of students who score above 650 in verbal and math college-entrance tests, proving that the decline of our best students is not owing simply to the inclusion of a greater number of minority students. Helping to maintain quality against this tide of ill-preparedness has been an influx of well-educated foreigners into our research universities. Many of these postgraduate students stay in the United States, but many do not. The Japanese high-technology industry, for example, has strong intellectual roots in American universities, with more than 13,000 Japanese students in the United States (compared with about 700 American students in Japan).

Despite this influx of intellectual capital from abroad, which parallels the influx of financial capital, we cannot permanently maintain a K–12 intellectual deficit any more than we can permanently maintain a negative trade balance. All of our most-difficult-to-enter universities must now maintain remedial centers for writing and mathematics, and in some cases for reading. It is disconcerting to see these centers pop up everywhere. No doubt many of the students who use them are foreign students or affirmative action students, but their clientele is definitely not limited entirely to minority and disadvantaged students. It is an inherently unstable situation and must lead to a decline of standards at all American universities, and probably has already done so.

If an emphasis on knowledge and dissent has led to high quality in a remarkable number of our universities, while an emphasis on process and conformity has led to low quality in most of our schools, common sense suggests that giving knowledge and dissent an energetic trial may carry practical benefits. The very existence of this quality gap is presumptive evidence that the slogans dominating our K–12 system and the efforts to reform it are defective and do not deserve the benefit of the doubt. The controlling theories and the people who propound them have, with the best of intentions, served the nation ill. It is not mainly our schools that need "restructuring," but the ideas of those who would restructure them.

## 4.
## Charter and Choice: Yes, but What Choice?

Would-be school reformers who are not members of the educational community have become used to defeat. Parents, politicians, business executives, and other outsiders have knocked at the gate of a huge Castle, as in a Kafka story, only to be turned aside or caught in the web of powerful slogans like "critical thinking," "individualized instruction," "new technology," "authentic assessment," "higher-order thinking skills," and various other reformulated versions of Romantic progressivism that have been grafted on to content-neutral organizational changes such as "school restructuring" and "site-based decision making." Philanthropists and capitalists have spent large sums to design "break-the-mold" schools. States and municipalities, alarmed by a lack of school improvement, have tried to circumvent the Castle by turning public schools over to private companies. But each hopeful "innovation" echoes the familiar content-neglectful phrases: "critical thinking," and so on. No force has been able to resist this intellectual orthodoxy.

As a consequence of their frustration, numerous Americans have come to support charter schools, where parents themselves make the important decisions, and "school choice"—the structural change that would allow parents to select the public school their child will attend. These ideas are based on the sound theory that parent empowerment would moderate the evils of institutional monopoly through the power of competition. Charter and choice advocates argue that a lack of competition among public schools has meant a lack of incentive for schools to improve, and they predict that the benefits of competitiveness in the economic sphere can be duplicated in public education.

I agree with this idea in theory, but in practice there may be a flaw in assuming that competition alone can greatly improve schools under present circumstances. The implicit analogy with economic competition is imperfect. In the economic sphere, customers tend to know what they want. Consumer preference in schooling, by contrast, is not easily determined by the consumers themselves. For one thing, the results of schooling take a long time to show themselves. Even when parents know what they want to be achieved in the long run, they rarely have a clear conception of what they wish schools to be doing day by day in order to achieve it. This mixture of long-term clarity with short-term uncertainty explains a paradoxical finding: American parents think that our schools are failing in general (because they know that the nationwide results are poor), whereas they think that their *own* child's school (a clean, well-lighted place where lots of activity is going on) is performing well.

The available evidence shows that parental choice has not greatly improved student achievement in the United States to date—a result consistent with international evidence showing that choice by itself is not an adequate principle of reform. The Dutch instituted publicly financed school choice many years ago, and today the Netherlands exhibits the least consistent school quality in northern continental Europe. Today, some 16 percent of Dutch schools perform below par, compared with 1 to 5 percent of below-par schools in the *non*choice systems of Sweden, Denmark, Japan, and South Korea. This evidence by no means warrants *opposition* to public-school choice and charter schools, and in fact I favor these structural changes in the hope that they will lead to substantive changes. However, it is unlikely that any structural reform can leverage our whole educational system until the current intellectual monopoly is broken.[11]

The basic problem with parental choice: it introduces competition under monopolistic conditions that may cancel out its utility. Other things being equal, parents prefer to send their children to the closest school. A better one that is five miles further away needs to be *much* better before parents have sufficient incentive to travel the extra distance. Since they rarely have a principled way of judging the comparative quality of the close vs. the distant school, they will usually keep their child in place. It is difficult even for experts to judge comparative school quality without knowing a great deal about the schools being compared. That difficulty is further compounded for parents by the likelihood that there will be some good teachers in bad schools and some bad teachers in good ones. A parent must ask, "Which sort of teacher will my child get when I choose a school?"

Overshadowing all of these difficulties is another formidable impediment to informed parental choice: the near impossibility of choosing between schools, even those that adopt special themes, when all of them espouse the same general "philosophy" of education—the same concern for "the individual child and his or her needs," for "critical thinking," "self-esteem," "joy in learning," "respect for others"; and the same pledge by the school staff to use the latest research-based pedagogical methods, such as "site-based decision making," "cooperative learning," "child-centered pedagogy." With such similarity of rhetoric among schools, it is a discerning parent indeed who can make a wise choice.

At this point, I wish to present a positive foil to the educational outlook I shall be criticizing in this book. For my aim in challenging inadequate theories is to leave space for better ones. Let us suppose that among the schools from which a parent could choose was one that subscribed to the following philosophy:

*All teachers at our school have not only pedagogical training but also a detailed knowledge of the subject matter that they teach. We instill in all children an ethic of toleration, civility, orderliness, responsibility, and hard work. Our staff has agreed on a definite core of knowledge and skill that all children will attain in each grade. We make sure that every child learns this core, and gains the specific knowledge and skill needed to prosper at the next grade level, thus enabling knowledge to build upon knowledge. Our teachers continually confer with their colleagues about effective ways of stimulating children to learn and integrate this specific knowledge and skill. The specificity of our goals enables us to monitor children, and give focused attention where necessary. To this end, we provide parents with a detailed outline of the* specific *knowledge and skill goals for each grade, and we stay in constant touch with them regarding the child's progress. Through this knowledge-based approach, we make sure that* all *normal children perform at grade level, while, in addition, the most talented children are challenged to excel. Attaining this specific and well-integrated knowledge and skill gives our students pleasure in learning, as well as self-respect, and it ensures that they will enter the next grade ready and eager to learn more.*

When American parents are offered *that* kind of choice, there is evidence that they will send their children long distances to attend such a school.

Unfortunately, the choice I have just described is not available to most parents within the United States. Although such a philosophy guides the best-performing school systems of Europe and Asia, any attempt in present-day America to create a public school that focuses on knowledge is usually met with disparagement and fierce resistance. In 1992, for example, a group of parents in Fort Collins, Colorado, tried to start an elementary school on the principles described above. The educational community fought bitterly at every step, threatening to retaliate against teachers who wished to cooperate, and going so far as to hire lawyers to help restrain parents from promulgating such heresy. Fortunately, the savvy parents managed to carry the day, and their public school, the Washington Core Knowledge School, is flourishing—evidence that the principle of choice combined with independence of the intellectual monopoly can effect change. The school has an enthusiastic student body and a long waiting list, which includes a disproportionately large number of children of minority parents, who see such rigorous education as the foundation of their children's economic autonomy.[12]

## 5.
## An Intellectual Monopoly

Critics have long complained that public education in the United States is an institutional and intellectual monopoly. We owe to Arthur Bestor the phrase "interlocking public school directorate" to describe the coordinated groups of people who control the institutions of the education world:

> *The members of these committees and commissions, the men and women actively engaged in questionnaire making, curriculum outlining, and propagandizing are drawn almost exclusively from three interrelated professional groups. First of all, there are professors of education in universities, colleges, and normal schools. Second, there are superintendents, principals, and other local public school administrators and supervisors. Third, there are officials, "experts," and other bureaucrats in the state departments of public instruction and the federal Office of Education. These three groups, collectively known as professional educationists, have drawn together in recent years into what amounts to an interlocking public school directorate.[13]*

The control exercised by this monopoly is sustained by its power to certify teachers. Education schools and their allies in state departments of education perpetuate themselves by requiring a prospective teacher to take a specified number of courses in an education school in order to be credentialed as a public-school teacher. The millions of teachers who pass through this certification process become a captive audience for indoctrination. A few years before Bestor's vigorous exposé, Mortimer Smith, observing the similarity between educational thought and the dogmas of a religious sect, had written to much the same effect:

> *If anyone will take the trouble to investigate, it will be found that those who make up the staffs of the schools and colleges of education, and the administrators and teachers whom they train to run the system have a truly amazing uniformity of opinion regarding the aims, the content, and the methods of education. They constitute a cohesive body of believers with a clearly formulated set of dogmas and doctrines, and they are perpetuating the faith by seeing to it through state laws and the rules of state departments of education, that only those teachers and administrators are certified who have been trained in correct dogma.[14]*

Like any guild that determines who can and cannot enter a profession, the citadel of education has developed powerful techniques for preventing outside interference, not least of which is mastery of slogan. That some teachers are able in their later life to transcend this initial indoctrination is a credit to their independence, for which I am continually grateful when I visit schools.

To the groups mentioned by Smith in 1949 and Bestor in 1953 must now be added the National Education Association and program officers of powerful foundations. Too often, members of these groups have themselves been trained in education schools and have internalized the Thoughtworld. As a result, the antiknowledge ideology that Bestor warned against in 1953 has become even more powerful since he wrote.

The co-opting of much of the foundation world by this system of ideas has been an especially grave handicap to knowledge-based school reform. The time seems to be past when program officers are independent scholars and vigorous critics of the Thoughtworld, such as James Koerner at the Sloan Foundation, author of *The Miseducation of American Teachers* (1963). The special advantage of private philanthropy is its ability to *oppose* received opinion and resist the dominant tide. Today, the educational community has succeeded in peopling much of the foundation world with its own graduates or allies, and in persuading that world that its antiknowledge views coincide with ethical and social right-thinking. The old guard has brilliantly succeeded in portraying its failed ideas as new, research-based, and conducive to social justice, although they are none of these.

Bestor caught the flavor of these strategies well. It is sad to think that there is nothing outdated in his 1953 description of the educational community's resistance to internal or external disagreement:

*One of the most shocking facts about the field of education is the almost complete absence of rigorous criticism from within. The paean of praise that greets every novel proposal, the closing of ranks that occurs whenever a word of criticism is spoken from the outside and . . . the extreme unwillingness of professional educationists to submit their proposals to free public discussion and honest criticism frequently assumes the even uglier form of showering critics, no matter how upright and well-informed, with vituperation and personal abuse.*[15]

When such pressure for intellectual conformity is combined with administrative control over employment and the dispensation of a great deal of foundation money, it is not surprising that the citadel should become an institutional monopoly.

Yet institutional monopoly alone is not the source of the system's failure. Public schooling is under monopolistic control in almost every modern nation, and quality does not necessarily suffer as a result. Japan's elementary schools are among the best and fairest in the world, yet Japan's schools are under the tight control of Monbusho, the all-powerful ministry of education. The benign aim of that and similar educational ministries in other liberal democracies is to ensure quality and fairness in education rather than to resist intellectual challenge and change. Powerful as they are, these ministries are answerable to legislatures, and are peopled by wide-ranging scholars who are open to criticism and new ideas. The educational ministry of Norway is a distinguished case in point. In education, there are monopolies and monopolies.

The intellectual uniformity of the American educational community was not inevitable. It was a consequence and an accident of history. From Teachers College, Columbia University, there occurred a quasi-biological propagation of ideas through which the intellectual DNA of the parent institution in New York was implanted in daughter institutions, and thereafter continued to be replicated from one education school to another. By now, most education professors, and most students taught by them, are the intellectual children, grandchildren, or great-grandchildren of Teachers College, Columbia University.[16]

Our American experience demonstrates that an intellectual monopoly which requires conformity of ideas is more stultifying than a merely institutional one. Despite the myth of local control, the intellectual monopoly ruling American K–12 education is more pervasive and harmful than the merely bureaucratic control exercised in other liberal democracies. Its prevailing ideas are more extreme and process-dominated than those found in systems that are more successful than our own.

## 6.
## Needed: Vigorous Challenge from Within and Without

W ho will challenge this intellectual monopoly? How can parents, politicians, and philanthropists be expected to perceive that the slogans of educational experts are misleading polarizations and simplifications? Who, unwarned of their seductions, would wish to *oppose* "critical and creative thinking" or "self-esteem" or "attention to the individuality of the child," or would deliberately wish to impose "developmentally inappropriate" tasks upon young children? How can ordinary citizens be expected to know that these phrases, applied as they currently are, produce the opposite of what they are supposed to achieve? Consider the following paradoxes, which I shall be explaining in subsequent pages:

- To stress critical thinking while de-emphasizing knowledge *reduces* a student's capacity to think critically.
- Giving a child constant praise to bolster self-esteem regardless of academic achievement breeds complacency, or skepticism, or both, and, ultimately, a *decline* in self-esteem.
- For a teacher to pay significant attention to each individual child in a class of twenty to forty students means individual *neglect* for most children most of the time.
- Schoolwork that has been called "developmentally inappropriate" has proved to be highly appropriate to millions of students the world over, while the infantile pabulum now fed to American children *is* developmentally inappropriate (in a downward direction) and often bores them.

Inundated by high-sounding slogans, parents, politicians, and philanthropists cannot be expected to exercise skepticism unless they are provided access to well-established alternative expertise—the chief requisite for true reform. One barrier to developing such expertise has been the politicization of educational issues that are at bottom technical rather than political. For example, finding the most effective methods for teaching young children how to read is a technical rather than an ideological matter. Yet the "phonics approach" to reading instruction is identified with "conservative," "hickory stick" Republicans, while the "whole-language approach" is identified with "liberal," "wishy-washy" Democrats.

In the heat of this battle, few have wished to heed researchers like Jeanne Chall and Marilyn Jager Adams, who found that a middle-of-the-road approach which includes both phonics and a whole-language approach is the most effective teaching method. But what rancorous attacks from both sides these researchers have endured, what cynicism about their "hidden agendas!" Indeed, because Adams's work was sponsored by research grants from the U.S. Department of Education, two education professors from Teachers College, Columbia University, insisted upon inserting in her book a more "liberal," pro-whole-language "Afterword," adding to the public confusion.

In this case, the confusion over reading methods might abate if the participants or members of the public asked research psychologists how they view this dispute about phonics vs. whole language. In mainline departments of psychology (as distinct from education-school departments of psychology), among those who have studied the subject there is consensus supporting the Chall-Adams middle-of-the-road conclusion. Still, mainline research findings are simply ignored in favor of polarization. It is assumed that any challenge to progressive educational orthodoxy must be a politically conservative challenge. This tactic has been quite effective in silencing criticism and avoiding changes in practice.[17]

One must look to the mainline press for public criticism of these bankrupt ideas, but so far the outlook for an effective challenge from this quarter has proved to be bleak. Despite the social and economic significance of schooling, reporters tend to consider the education beat the way they do agricultural reporting in the hinterlands—of enormous importance but dull. Education is usually assigned to a junior reporter, who, just as he or she has gained useful knowledge and skepticism, is elevated to another beat. If only our education reporting came close to the shrewdness, skepticism, and probing of our political reporting, we might see plenty of informed criticism in the press, and thereafter in the foundation world and the general public.

I recently received from a well-informed parent a long, exasperated letter, which quoted the following press comment on education from a local paper:

> *On our wish list for graduates the first item would be the ability to read at least moderately complex material with comprehension, and to clearly*

*express oneself. Also at the top of the list would be reasoning and prob-*
*lem-solving ability. With these two tools graduates would be prepared for*
*a reality they may not expect: that learning does not end with school. Few*
*jobs today are done exactly the way they were a decade or two ago.*
*Workers have had to learn new skills, new technologies just to keep their*
*jobs, let alone move up. Increasingly, workers who cannot learn will fall*
*behind . . . so schools will need to prepare students for a lifetime of*
*learning.*[18]

The parent then proceeded to point out that (amid the truisms about modern employment) the newspaper was advancing the same fallacies promulgated by educators and reformers: 1) that it is possible to teach abstract reading ability; 2) that it is possible to teach abstract problem-solving ability; and 3) that once provided with these abstract abilities, students would be able to pursue a "lifetime of learning." As our parent pointed out, each of these three assumptions is a half-truth whose limitations the reporter or editor obviously knew nothing of.

The press is the best agency for challenging the intellectual status quo and for bringing issues out into the daylight. It would be of great benefit to the general public if reporters turned to two neglected sources of scientific and technical expertise—educational specialists in Europe and Asia, and American researchers who work outside the educational community. Education reporters rarely interview researchers in departments of psychology. If they did, they would learn that the mainstream scientific community gives little credence to many of the psychological presuppositions of the educational community, such as the assumption that children can be taught generalized critical-thinking and problem-solving skills.

The public needs to be offered choice of ideas even more than choice of schools. The educational community, operating behind a web of slogans and brooking no internal dissent, resists the scrutiny and the rough-and-tumble of scientific criticism that characterizes subject-matter disciplines. A well-informed press might begin to induce dissent where it is most needed—within the American educational community itself. I know from direct experience that there are many people in that community who would break out of enforced intellectual conformity if given the chance to do so.

## 4.

# Critique
# of a
# Thoughtworld

## 1.
## Introduction

In previous chapters I showed that many of the school "reforms" now being advocated are the very practices which have put American education at risk. To an uncommitted mind, that raises the following question: Why do educators persist in advocating the very antifact, anti-rote-learning, antiverbal practices that have led to poor results—persist in urging them, indeed, even more intensively than before?

The basic answer is this: Within the educational community, there is currently no *thinkable* alternative. Part of essential American educational doctrine has consisted of the disparagement of so-called "traditional" education. The long dominance of antitraditional rhetoric in our teacher-training institutions has ensured that competing, nonprogressive principles are not readily available within their walls. No professor at an American education school is going to advocate *pro*-rote-learning, *pro*fact, or *pro*verbal pedagogy. Since there is only one true belief, expressed in one constantly repeated catechism, the heretical suggestion that the creed itself might be faulty cannot be uttered. To question progressive doctrine would be to put in doubt the identity of the education profession itself. Its foundational premise is that progressive principles are right. Being right, *they* cannot possibly be the cause of educational ineffectiveness. There must be other, better explanations for the ineffectiveness of our schools. Among the "better" explanations are:

- To deny that our schools really are ineffective. There is no real crisis in the schools, which are basically fine—better than they ever were, considering demographic changes. (A subcategory of this position is the denial of test results: the tests are not assessing true outcomes in the schools and are, in fact, inhibiting true education.)
- To deny the current dominance of progressivism. The real problem is that progressivism never actually caught hold. Teachers in our schools are to be blamed for persisting in their traditional, nonprogressive practices.
- To deny that progressivism, even where it has been followed, has been *authentically* followed. Teachers who accept the progressive creed are to be blamed for improperly executing it. Since progressive principles are correct, they must lead to good results when properly followed. Since the results are not good, the principles cannot have been properly executed.
- To invoke insuperable external conditions that prevent the adequate expression of progressivism. Shortcomings are to be attributed not to faulty doctrine but to overwhelming social problems, like broken families, the culture of violence, a multiethnic student population, and the demand for schools to do too many different things. These larger problems are so pervasive in the culture that they affect educational results even at affluent suburban schools.

In sum, since progressive doctrine cannot be at fault, the only proper cure for our ailing schools is homeopathic "reform," that is, even stronger doses of progressive principles administered even more intensively.

To break the cycle of doctrinal dependency, it will be essential to bring progressive doctrine itself into question—to bring even education professors to think the unthinkable. Historical description is probably the best way to initiate such "break-the-mold" thinking. Perhaps an understanding of the historical origins of progressive ideas might begin to help overthrow their feckless tyranny. This chapter will try to achieve three main goals: 1) to understand the American educational Thoughtworld by tracing its historical origins and probing beneath the technical terms that tend to obscure its essential features; 2) to demystify that same Thoughtworld by showing how the technical overlay has disguised its nontechnical character; and 3) (both here and in the next chapter) to refute the quasi-scientific pretenses of the technical overlay. In his book *Psychology of Worldviews,* Karl Jaspers observed that one cannot well understand a thoughtworld without being motivated by attraction or repudiation.

But he shrewdly added that either approach can lead to accurate understanding and insight.[1]

My principal reliance in this chapter, as elsewhere, is on mainstream historical and scientific research. Some of my criticisms of the Thoughtworld are technical ones based on accepted research findings that are in conflict with dogmas of the educational world. But mere conclusions from research are not likely to change dearly held beliefs. "Research tells us" is one of the favorite phrases of the educational community. What that "research tells us" tends to be highly comforting to established educational dogma. But what about what historical and psychological research tells me? Isn't that going to be comforting to my point of view? No one can be confident that preselection is not driving his or her own interpretation of scientific research. Yet when there is a clear conflict between widely accepted mainstream science and the science cited by educational experts, it seems reasonable to conclude that mainstream science, being more diversified and disinterested, is more likely to be correct.

The human disposition to preselect research results is sometimes called an "ideology," a word implying that beliefs are chosen primarily to promote self-interest or class interests. It is true that American educational ideas are not completely free from self-interested ideology, particularly in their self-aggrandizing stress on process. But I shall avoid the word "ideology". Much more than institutional ideology has been at work in forming dominant American educational ideas, many of which belong to our culture generally. Views about early childhood, book learning, creativity, independent-mindedness, and school control belong both to the educational community and to received American culture. Deep-rooted national attitudes have caused certain educational doctrines to take hold in the United States much more persistently than elsewhere. I shall discuss some of these broadly shared attitudes before turning at the end of the chapter to the more professionally oriented elements of American educational thought.

# 2.
## Romanticism

At Teachers College, Columbia University, high on the frieze of the Horace Mann building facing Broadway, are names expressing the educational ideals that inspired the founders of the institution—nine great educators from the sixteenth to the nineteenth century: Loyola, Melanchthon,

Sturm, Comenius, Pestalozzi, Herbart, Froebel, Horace Mann, and Thomas
Arnold. One would like to know what deliberations or debates went into the
selection of the names. Clearly, the frieze was meant to celebrate the noble
calling of educator. That might explain the absence of Thomas Jefferson, who
was the most significant early thinker about public education in the United
States, but was not a schoolmaster. On the other hand, Herbart was not a
schoolmaster either, yet more than Jefferson, alas, he did greatly influence the
direction taken by modern American education.

The frieze seems to say: "Let other sides of the building celebrate the
names of poets and philosophers. Here at Teachers College the frieze facing
Broadway will celebrate thinkers who changed *modern* education, whether by
new theories (like Herbart) or by putting theory and action together for the
education of the young." The selection is admirable for its emphasis on elementary schooling, listing Friedrich Froebel, the inventor of kindergarten; Johann Herbart, a philosopher-psychologist of early education, as well as ep-
onym of the Herbart Society, which fostered "child-centered education"; and
Johann Pestalozzi, who advocated bringing education into harmony with the
natural development of the child. It is not a mere coincidence that these men
should have been contemporaries who knew one another: Pestalozzi was born
in 1746, Herbart in 1776, and Froebel in 1782. They flourished in Switzerland
and Germany during the height of the Romantic Movement. It was European
Romanticism that created the new conception of the child which came to
dominate American educational theory.

Before the Romantic Movement, the underlying conception of education,
and one that has never altogether disappeared in any society, assumed that a
child is a still-to-be-formed creature whose instinctual impulses need less to be
encouraged than to be molded to the ways of the society in which it is growing
up. That is still the dominant conception of education in most societies of Asia
and Africa, and it continued to be so in the West up to the late eighteenth
century.

Plato, for instance, attached high importance to education because he was
convinced that a good life and a just society required the special training and
encouragement of the rational parts of human nature so they would dominate
and control its instinctive, emotional aspects. For Plato, the root of evil would
be an education that allowed instinct and emotion to dominate over reason.
The recently popular motto "Follow your bliss," where "bliss" means whatever your instinctive preferences happen to be, would have seemed to Plato a
moral blasphemy. Likewise, the Judeo-Christian theory of education, while
stressing rationality less than Plato did, discloses a similar distrust of human nature and of its instinctive emotions. One of the most celebrated pas-

sages in St. Augustine's *Confessions* describes the following childhood escapade.[2]

He and some other young boys decided to steal some pears from a farmer's tree. It was not the stealing of the pears that caused Augustine to regard the incident as exemplary of human nature; after all, he and his unsocialized friends may have been hungry, and they wanted to eat pears. More significant to Augustine was the fact that they picked many more pears than they could possibly eat, perversely carrying them away to throw to pigs. The only explanation for such a nihilistic and destructive act, Augustine thought, was that even in the young child, or especially in the young child, there are an evil and a perversity explainable only by the doctrine of original sin. The pear tree episode said to Augustine that human nature is corrupt from birth. The aim of education is not to follow human nature but to correct it, to set it on a path of virtue that is often contrary to its natural development. To give one's fallen natural instincts free rein would beget a life of greed, selfishness, and crime.

Although the thinkers of the Enlightenment broke with sectarian religion and the idea of original sin, most of them did not break with the molding and civilizing principles of education that had animated societies through history. The founders of the United States—Enlightenment figures like Madison and Jefferson (and emphatically their colleague Hamilton, memorialized on the Teachers College frieze)—took a skeptical and suspicious view of human nature. Their suspicion underlies the protections afforded individuals against the tyranny of the majority; the reliance on a Senate to avoid the dangers of purely representative government; and the doctrine of separation of powers, which erects a structural protection against power-seeking and greed. The Constitution they framed does not imply trust in the innate goodness of human nature when allowed to follow its bliss.

In Jefferson's writings on public education, which are the fullest we have from the Founding Fathers, the stress on cultivating an aristocracy of talent and virtue, as well as the stringent rules for moral education, does not disclose a confidence that human nature should be encouraged to follow its natural development. The study of history (not nature) was to be the main subject of education for the people:

> [It] *will qualify them as judges of the actions and designs of men; it will enable them to know ambition under every disguise it may assume; and knowing it to defeat its views. In every government on earth is some trace of human weakness, some germ of corruption and degeneracy, which cunning will discover, and wickedness insensibly open, cultivate, and improve.*[3]

But starting in the later eighteenth century, a new intellectual movement, European Romanticism, introduced two epochal conceptions that challenged these unsentimental traditions. First, Romanticism believed that human nature is innately good, and should therefore be encouraged to take its natural course, unspoiled by the artificial impositions of social prejudice and convention. Second, Romanticism concluded that the child is neither a scaled-down, ignorant version of the adult nor a formless piece of clay in need of molding, rather, the child is a special being in its own right with unique, trustworthy—indeed holy—impulses that should be allowed to develop and run their course.

Behind this momentous shift in attitude toward the trustworthiness of human nature lay the quasi-religious faith that Romantic thinkers placed in everything "natural." Ever since Rousseau's *Émile* (1762), such optimistic, quasi-religious ideas had been attached to theories of education. Later, they became translated into prestigious philosophical systems by German Romantic philosophers like Hegel (b. 1770) and Schelling (b. 1775). In his *Naturphilosophie,* Schelling stated explicitly that the God-infused natural world and human nature were both emanations of the same divine substance. This was the explicit statement of the implicit ideas that underlay the new, Romantic conception of the child and the Romantic antipathy to the trammeling conventions of society. How could truly natural development go wrong so long as it was unthwarted? After all, natural instincts come from a divine source. It is only the separation from that source through the artificial impositions of human culture and society which can lead the child astray.

Here are some pronouncements to that effect from the European father of American early education, Friedrich Froebel:

> *To young plants and animals we give space, and time, and rest, knowing that they will unfold to beauty by laws working in each. We avoid acting upon them by force, for we know that such intrusion upon their natural growth could only injure their development. Yet man treats the young human being as though it were a piece of wax, a lump of clay out of which he can mould what he will! . . . Education and instruction should from the very first be passive, observant, protective, rather than prescribing, determining, interfering. . . . All training and instruction which prescribes and fixes, that is interferes with Nature, must tend to limit and injure.*[4]

Johann Pestalozzi similarly warns against hurrying children into purely conventional learning:

*Any method of opening up man's powers which claims to be natural must
be open and easy. . . . Parents should not hurry their children into
working at things remote from their immediate interests. By anticipating
the ordinary course, they diminish the powers of their children, and dis-
turb profoundly the equilibrium of their nature.*[5]

Schiller celebrated such unification with nature in his "Ode to Joy" (1785),
as many will remember from the last movement of Beethoven's Ninth Sym-
phony, where "joy" expresses the reunion with that nature from which we
have been separated by social convention—*"Was die Mode streng geteilt"*
("What fashion has torn apart"). In the same vein, William Blake in his *Songs
of Innocence* (1789) celebrated childhood for its closeness to the divine, and
was an early enthusiast for Wordsworth's "Ode: Intimations of Immortality
from Recollections of Early Childhood" (1804), which contains these lines:

*Thou little Child, yet glorious in the might
Of heaven-born freedom on thy being's height,
Why with such earnest pains dost thou provoke
The years to bring the inevitable yoke,
Thus blindly with thy blessedness at strife?
Full soon thy Soul shall have her earthly freight,
And custom lie upon thee with a weight,
Heavy as frost, and deep almost as life!*[6]

From the sentiment that social "custom" and "fashion" (*die Mode*) deaden
and corrupt, it is not a far step to the idea that it is unhealthy, unnatural, and
harmful to press book learning upon young children prematurely. Full soon
the child's soul will have its earthly freight, no need to rush the inevitable
corruption.

The idea that civilization has a corrupting rather than a benign, uplifting,
virtue-enhancing effect on the young child is a distinct contribution of European Romanticism to American thought. The contrast between the instinctive
holiness of the child and the corrupting principle of custom and civilization is
a conception for which Romanticism deserves full credit. It is an educational
view that can glide easily into disparagement of book learning and into anti-
intellectualism.

In the United States, our intellectual traditions include on the one side
Cotton Mather, Jefferson, Madison, and Hamilton, with their suspicions of
instinctive human nature, and on the other, Emerson, Thoreau, and Whitman,
with their trust in the "holiness of the heart's affections." For Emerson's

friend Bronson Alcott, the father of Louisa May, neither Pestalozzi nor Wordsworth expressed radically enough his own sense of the infallible divinity of the child:

> *Not Wordsworth's genius, Pestalozzi's love*
> *The stream have sounded of clear infancy.*
> *Baptismal waters from the Head above*
> *These babes I foster daily are to me;*
> *I dip my pitcher in these living springs*
> *And draw, from depths below, sincerity;*
> *Unsealed, mine eyes behold all outward things*
> *Arrayed in splendors of divinity.*[7]

The great progenitor of progressive education in the United States, Colonel Francis Parker, inspired his fellow teachers by telling them:

> *The spontaneous tendencies of the child are the records of inborn divinity.*
> *We are here, my fellow teachers, for one purpose, and that purpose is to*
> *understand these tendencies and continue them in all these directions,*
> *following nature.*[8]

It is by now a very deeply rooted sentiment in American education to think that what is natural works automatically for the good. Everything done naturally has an inner necessity and rightness. Americans have tended to be optimistic that things left to their own devices will tend to work out in the end—which is to say that Romanticism is deep-dyed in our culture.

In education, this optimistic cast of mind induces trust in the child's natural development, and suspicion of harsh discipline, bookish hard work, and other forms of artificial stimulation and constraint. The chief begetter of contemporary American educational thought, William Heard Kilpatrick, believed that, as disciples of Dewey, he and his colleagues had moved beyond such European Romantics as Pestalozzi, Herbart, and Froebel. But in fact Kilpatrick simply translated Romantic optimism about human nature and natural development into secular, scientific language. The technical translation was verbal; behind it lay the Romantic faith that things will work out better in education if the child's development is allowed to run its untrammeled course in a naturalistic setting. From time to time, even the very term "nature" creeps into Kilpatrick's language:

*A well-managed regime of purposeful activity, freed from artificial and external demands of subject matter requirements, promises not only the best preventive of personality maladjustment but often furnishes an indispensable part of any adequate remedial treatment. To learn to pursue worthy ends with honest study and appropriate action is nature's road to mental health.[9]*

Natural beings, left alone to follow their instincts, will in the end produce the mutual good. Evil lies in the separation from nature caused by unnatural constraint, such as seating children in straight rows and forcing their unique individual natures into conformity. As a result of this Romantic cast of mind, the placement of school desks in the classroom became a defining issue in American educational culture. Placing the desks in semicircles or helter-skelter symbolized the triumph of good, free, modern education over inhumane, artificial, constraining traditional education. Many schools still proudly announce that *they* do not arrange their seats in rows.

History, including the recent history of American education, shows that human affairs are rarely brought right by letting them take their natural course. Human nature, to the extent that it can be known, should not be left to its own devices. We humans have contradictory impulses, and the choices we make about which ones to develop and make dominant should not be left to accident and chance. True enough, we cannot defeat human nature, but we can try to bring out the best and thwart the worst. The aim of civilization, and by consequence of education, is less to follow nature than to guide it toward humane and worthy ends. This is of course an antique principle, but not just a Western one. It reflects the accumulated wisdom of many cultures in many lands. In the annals of recorded thought, European Romanticism, with its (alas) powerful influence on American culture and education, has been a post-Enlightenment aberration, a mistake we need to correct.

Although the United States was born in the Enlightenment, it was bred in Romanticism. The conflict in American culture between the two traditions is wonderfully memorialized in *Huckleberry Finn* in the standoff between Aunt Sally, who belongs to the school of Plato and St. Augustine, and Huck Finn, who is a Wordsworthian:

*. . . if I'd 'a' knowed what a trouble it was to make a book I wouldn't 'a' tackled it, and ain't a-going to no more. But I reckon I got to light out for the Territory ahead of the rest, because Aunt Sally she's going to adopt me and sivilize me, and I can't stand it. I been there before.[10]*

Huck is confident that he will maintain his happiness and virtue better out in the Territory, close to nature, than he will in town, near civilization and Aunt Sally. But there is little in human history to justify his Romantic faith.

The conflict between our Enlightenment and our Romantic views of human nature continues unabated in American culture today. Lately, there has perhaps occurred a tempering of our optimism about the beneficence of things natural and the innate goodness of human nature—the tragedy of the Vietnam War, the halt in continually rising prosperity, the omnipresent television scenes of genocidal conflict throughout the world, the violence among children in our schools—this drumbeat of tragic experience has tended to qualify our anti-tragic, Romantic faith in the inherent goodness and dependability of the human child when allowed to follow its own development. Increasingly, there has been a questioning of the belief that all will be well if the child is encouraged to grow naturally like a tree, and there has been a renewed interest in the idea of moral education—a kind of symbolic reinstatement of Aunt Sally.

But many Americans still have faith that things natural must be better than things artificial, just as naturally arranged school desks must be better than desks in a row. The underlying tenets of the Romantic Movement have proved highly durable in the United States; almost all our dominant ideas and phrases pertaining to early education are traceable to it. The idea of developing a child's creativity and imagination originated with Romanticism. The ideal of educating not just the intellect but the "whole child," including the imagination, derives initially from Romantic pantheistic faith in the unerring goodness of whatever comes forth from the child without artificial hindrance. Samuel Taylor Coleridge spoke of the "synthetic and magical power to which we have exclusively appropriated the name of imagination," which "brings the whole soul of man into activity."[11] The change in the early childhood curriculum from the moral tales of the McGuffey Readers to the myths, fairy tales, and stories of the present day has marked a shift in emphasis from molding the child's moral sense to bringing out the child's creativity and imagination. Possibly a majority of Americans still believe that an early education which follows the child's natural development *must* be more beneficial than the Jeffersonian ideal of instilling knowledge and virtue at an early age.

But the complete dominance of the Romantic view did not occur until several decades after education schools had been converted to progressivism in the 1920s and '30s. From these cells, the doctrine emerged victorious in the public schools in the 1950s, when growing numbers of traditional educators retired and progressives moved in as principals and superintendents. Thereafter, it took a full generation of progressive students, extending from preschool to high school, before the full effects of Romantic progressivism manifested themselves in the graduating seniors of the 1960s—the time of the dramatic decline in SAT scores.

A great deal hinges on whether we continue to accept uncritically the Romantic beliefs of progressivism, which are still the dominant beliefs of the educational community. Any challenge to them is regarded as heretical and is resisted by that community with an almost religious fervor; that is not surprising, considering their quasi-religious origins. But it can be argued that Romantic developmental ideas (which I shall focus on in the next section) are, of all the ideas in the Thoughtworld, the ones which have been most damaging to the quality and, above all, to the equity of our public education.

## 3.
## Developmentalism and Other Naturalistic Fallacies

From Romanticism the American educational community inherited the faith that early childhood is a time of innocence and naturalness, a time for *being* a child. "Shades of the prison house" begin to close all too quickly around the young child. It is wrong to spoil the one time of life when children can develop in tune with the order of things. It is wrong to be parents who live out their own unfulfilled ambitions by rushing their children, creating unseasonable pressure, and ruining their lives. Self-evidently, premature book learning goes against nature. According to the educational community, "research has shown" that untimely interventions and constraints are "developmentally inappropriate" and create a hothouse, forced-feeding atmosphere.

Images of forced feeding (like the cruel exploitation of a Strasbourg goose) and hothouses (where plants are unseasonably forced into artificial maturity) are recurrent images in the antiacademic literature of early childhood education. This Romantic point of view has encouraged an extremely negative attitude toward teaching very young children letters and phonics, arithmetic, and factual information. Popular books with titles like David Elkind's *The Hurried Child: Growing Up Too Fast Too Soon* and *Miseducation: Preschoolers at Risk* tell many Americans what they are already disposed to hear.

Such expert attacks against early book learning intensify the already powerful Romanticism in American culture. Many parents wistfully regret that school should impose discipline and hard work on very young children. Many parents have internalized the either-or polarity between joyful, nonacademic, "developmentally appropriate" education and joyless, unnatural academics. They identify school learning with cramped abstraction and artificiality, and link "developmentally appropriate" learning with concrete and creative play that engages all the senses and teaches as nature commands, at a slow but sure pace. That challenging subject matter can be combined with joyful and concrete activities which engage all the senses is not imagined as a possibility. "There will be time later for all that" is a recurrent theme of parents. Americans have breathed in developmentalism from the ambient air ever since the time of Emerson and Alcott. Few have to be persuaded.

If the debate in our society were between children's happiness and unhappiness, or between forced seatwork on the one side and multisensory play on the other, any humane person would side with the Romantic developmentalists. But what is the weight of evidence regarding the mental health and creativity of young children who have undergone an academically challenging early education?

The principal large-scale evidence comes from France, which has been operating *écoles maternelles* (preschools) for a hundred years, and which, since World War II, has been providing academic education to more than 80 percent of three-year-olds, more than 95 percent of four-year-olds, and 99 percent of five-year-olds. These are real schools. The French distinguish between American-style day care centers (*crèches*) and genuine schools (*écoles*) for very young children. Recently, French social scientists completed longitudinal studies of some four thousand children on the long-term effects of *écoles maternelles* on the more than 30 percent of French *two*-year-olds who now attend these preschools. The results are striking. Those who attend school at a younger age are more effective academically and, by all indirect measures, better adjusted and happier for having had early exposure to challenging and stimulating early academic experiences.[12]

The French results are even more compelling from the standpoint of social justice. When disadvantaged children attend *écoles maternelles* at age two, their academic performance by grade six or seven equals that of highly advantaged children who have not attended preschool until age four. If advantaged children also attend preschool at age two, they continue to retain their academic lead in later grades, but in that case all students are performing at a very high level. The French experience shows that a good, academically focused preschool can overcome the egregious academic differences that currently develop between social classes in American schools. In Chapter 1, I suggested that the disappointing results of Head Start probably have more to do with the lack of a coherent approach to content (a hallmark of developmentalism) than with any unique problems in modern American society.

The contrast between the American and French results with Head Start–style programs amounts almost to a controlled experiment in which the critical differences between the programs lie more in the philosophy behind early schooling than in the sociology of the young pupils. The populations of *écoles maternelles* in the suburbs of Paris and Marseilles are as racially and ethnically diverse as those of school districts in the United States. French educational professionals as a group have never been Romantic developmentalists. Rousseau may have written *Émile* in the suburbs of Paris, but his greatest influence on educational philosophy has been outside France, on such Romantic thinkers as Pestalozzi, Herbart, and Froebel and, through them, American educational professionals. The French themselves have always challenged Rousseau's idea that humans are naturally good but corrupted by civilization. French early-childhood specialists with whom I have talked are just as deeply concerned as American specialists with creating a preschool atmosphere that is joyful and multisensory, but they also have very clear ideas about the academic goals that all normal children should reach.

Because of American culture's long-standing Romantic notions about early childhood, the professional version of developmentalism does not have to be argued very forcefully. Research leading to a different conclusion is given short shrift. Studies by Harvard's Jerome Bruner once led him to say that "any subject can be taught effectively in some intellectually honest form to any child at any stage of development."[13] This famous remark is usually quoted in order to be dismissed. Yet Bruner's assertion represents the thinking of many psychologists who work outside education schools. If one also brings in studies from neurobiology, the claim that early education requires extreme gradualness and hands-off spontaneity is refuted by research that has determined what "nature" is actually telling us about the brain's development. The following is from a recent popular article on advances in neurobiology:

> "It's crazy," says Pasko Rakic, a Yale neurobiologist. "Americans think kids should not be asked to do difficult things with their brains while they are young: 'Let them play; they'll study at the university.' The problem is, if you don't train them early, it's much harder."
>
> It is never too early for a child to exercise his mind. Some of the benefits of early brain workouts have been known for centuries. Teachers of music, gymnastics and chess, for example, have long insisted that practicing begin early. Linguists have marveled that children can learn a new language without an accent, while adults cannot. "In order to pronounce certain words, you have to put the vocal cord in a certain tension," Rakic says. "To do that you have to contract throat muscles. Control of these muscles is in the synapses that were formed before puberty."
>
> There is, says Rakic, a fairly simple scientific explanation: Children's brains can make far more synaptic connections than can adults'. Shortly

*after birth the brain makes connections at an incredible pace. As puberty approaches the number tapers off. Then two processes begin—functional validation, in which the connections the brain finds useful are made permanent, and selective elimination, in which those that are not continually used are eliminated. Says Rakic: "We chisel our brain from the larger stone, so to speak." The greatest chiseling is accomplished between the ages of two and 11.*

*"Of course," Rakic adds, "this doesn't mean you cannot learn in later life. You can learn tremendously. But in childhood there is an ability to learn quickly which is unparalleled."[14]*

Contrast that statement from an expert outside the educational community with the following advice, taken from "Guidelines for Appropriate Curriculum Content and Assessment in Programs Serving Children Ages 3 Through 8," the "Position Statement" put out by the National Association for the Education of Young Children and the National Association of Early Childhood Specialists in State Departments of Education:

*Children should not be expected to comprehend abstract/symbolic concepts or master skills or content that can be acquired more easily later on. To some extent, this guideline addresses the issue of efficiency in teaching and learning. For instance, first, second, and third grade teachers all report that children cannot comprehend place value: teachers spend hours trying to teach this abstract concept, and children either become frustrated or resort to memorizing meaningless tricks.[15]*

To follow this advice would put off a lot of basic mathematical learning until fourth grade—about age ten. It is doubtful that such a policy would contribute to "efficiency in teaching and learning." In France and Japan and other developed nations, children at the end of first grade perform written operations with two-digit numbers and have an at least implicit understanding of place value to two places. By the end of second grade, these children know the multiplication table through 9 times 9, and can add and subtract three-digit numbers, meaning that they can borrow and carry, thus demonstrating an operational understanding of place value. By the end of third grade, they can add and subtract five-digit numbers, can write numbers through 99,000, can create a number that is 10 times or 100 times bigger than a given number, and can write down one tenth of a given number—all without great strain on them or their teachers and without any known harmful psychological effects.[16]

The reported difficulty that American children under age ten have in understanding place value is very likely owing to their lack of consistent instruction and practice in arithmetic. For millions of children in Europe and Asia, constant familiarity with numbers and frequent manipulation of them bring first implicit and then, by second grade, explicit understanding of place value. There is vivid evidence that the process is painless, and even fun.[17] To follow the advice given here would defer for several years learnings that, even in the United States, with its low scores in mathematics, are ostensibly scheduled to be taught in the first three grades. Early-education experts in countries where children *are* easily learning place value in early grades would not likely agree with the above position statement. Nonetheless, the statement was supported by the following American professional associations:

Association for Supervision and Curriculum Development
National Association of State Boards of Education
National Council of Teachers of Mathematics
National Council for Social Studies
Association for Childhood Education International
Southern Early Childhood Association
American Association of Physical Education, Health, Recreation, and
    Dance
International Reading Association
National Black Child Development Institute
National Science Teachers Association

For a nonspecialist like me to challenge an official position taken by the top professional organizations in early-childhood education ought to raise feelings such as Dr. Samuel Johnson expressed after he had challenged the two thousand-year-old doctrine of the dramatic unities: "I am almost frightened at my own temerity; and when I estimate the fame and the strength of those that maintain the contrary opinion, am ready to sink down in reverential silence." But good empiricist that he was, Dr. Johnson also stated that he did not "think the present question one of those that are to be decided by mere authority."[18] The same empirical principle applies to the question of when it is best to teach place value.

How did we arrive at a situation in which the American professional associations are setting forth what would be considered by most overseas experts and by mainstream American psychologists to be impractical and misleading advice? To understand how such views came to be held with greater confidence in the United States than elsewhere, one has to refer to the powerful historical influence of Romanticism, traced in the previous section. Romanticism's quasi-religious views of early childhood took hold more firmly in the United States than anywhere else in the world, with the possible exception of Germany.

Of course, one reason Romantic doctrines about childhood initially took hold was that they did express partial truths. The Romantic Movement marked a genuine advance in early education, and many principles taught by Pestalozzi, Herbart, and Froebel are consistent with principles that have proved to be effective in practice and are supported by psychological research. For instance, the Romantic emphasis on the importance of play in early education is accepted by educational systems throughout the world, as well as by mainstream psychological research. But other Romantic ideas, such as the importance of delaying book learning, when they are carried too far or accepted uncritically, conflict with effective practice and research. In short, not all naturalistic principles are fallacies; they become so when they are applied uncritically.

Two doctrines of educational naturalism that have become fallacies by being taken to extremes are 1) the doctrine of developmentalism, or *natural tempo,* which holds that there is a natural age (usually after age eight) for introducing bookish content (as in the position statement above); 2) the doctrine of holistic learning, or *natural pedagogy,* which holds that natural (lifelike, project-like, thematic) methods of instruction are always the most effective teaching methods.

The two views are summarized by William Heard Kilpatrick in his introduction to writings of Pestalozzi:

> *Pestalozzi said that "life itself is the true basis of teaching and education" and still further that "life shapes us and the life that shapes us is not a matter of words, but of action." And our most modern education holds that, since the child will learn what he lives, the school must be a place of living. . . . In this way does Pestalozzi seem to anticipate the modern school that we now most acclaim.*[19]

About the principle of natural tempo, Pestalozzi had this to say:

> *Nature has enclosed man's higher aptitudes as in a shell; if you break the shell before it opens on its own, you will find only a budding pearl. You will have destroyed the treasure you should have preserved for your child.*[20]

And thus Froebel:

*Behold the Plant—you call it Weed: when grown under Pressure and Constraint you scarcely guess its natural Life and Purpose. But in open Ground see what regularity it shows, how its inward life becomes manifest. . . . If you early force on [children] Form and Work that are unsuited to their Nature, they will grow stunted and misshapen.[21]*

The credibility of the doctrine of natural tempo was enhanced by Jean Piaget's observation that every normal child seems to follow a natural sequence of conceptual development. Since Piaget, the doctrine has been couched in scientific terms, as in the official, "scientific" advice to defer the teaching of place value. But its ultimate source is Romantic faith in the holiness of natural growth. Such doctrine claims to be based on research, especially that of Piaget, but research does not confirm this. Indeed, Piaget himself (not to mention later researchers who have qualified his views) cautioned his uncritical adherents against a purely naturalistic approach, observing

*that environment can play a decisive role in the development of the mind; that the thought content of the stages and the ages at which they occur are not immutably fixed; that sound methods can therefore increase the students' efficiency and even accelerate their spiritual growth without making it any the less sound.[22]*

Similar cautions are in order regarding the doctrine of natural pedagogy, which holds that it is better to learn things naturally in a lifelike, thematic, holistic context than in a lecture or a drill-and-practice format. Thus Pestalozzi and Froebel:

*The forces of Nature, although they lead infallibly to their end (which is truth), show no stiffness or difficulties in their working. The nightingale's song vibrates through the darkness, and all natural objects move in thrilling freedom—not a sign of intrusive compulsion anywhere. [Pestalozzi][23]*

*Therefore education and instruction should from the very first be passive, observant, protective, rather than prescribing, determining, interfering. [Froebel]*

In more technical terms, the same principle is expressed in the "Guidelines for Appropriate Curriculum Content and Assessment in Programs Serving Children Ages 3 Through 8," which advise deferring place value:

> *Conceptual organizers such as themes, units, or projects give children something meaningful and substantive to engage their minds. It is difficult for children to make sense of abstract concepts such as colors, mathematical symbols, or letter sounds when they are presented at random or devoid of any meaningful context.*[24]

Surely there is much to be said for this approach to teaching young children. But whether such modes of instruction are *always* superior is a matter to be determined empirically for specific subjects and groups of children. It's true that any mode of instruction that engages children's interest and pleasure is to be preferred if it consistently yields good practical results. It's true that showing is by itself more engaging than telling—in teaching as in writing. But a combination of showing and telling yields the fastest and securest results in both writing and teaching. For most subjects, a pedagogy that mixes indirect, lifelike methods with direct, focused ones will yield the highest student interest and attainment.[25] The inherent superiority of holistic, project instruction is not a self-evident truth, and only seems so because of our unquestioning Romantic faith in the superiority of the "natural" over the "artificial." Constantly to create a lifelike, "meaningful context" is not the principle that is followed in teaching young children ballet, or piano playing, or downfield blocking, where some admixture of specialized drill and practice is thought to be essential.

The doctrine of natural pedagogy makes assumptions that are just as untrue and harmful as those underlying the doctrine of natural tempo. It assumes that the proper way of learning involves lifelike, holistic projects which intrinsically motivate children and coincidentally teach them how to work together and use knowledge. That is nature's preferred way of teaching. But it turns out to be a very insecure way of learning such things as standard grammar, spelling, phonics, and the multiplication table. How does it happen, then, that some children do learn all these things through holistic, thematic, and project-oriented schooling, while other children do not? Most often the correct answer is that the children who do learn grammar, and phonics, and so on, come from educated homes where they receive additional drill and practice in those skills. But that commonsense answer is inconsistent with the premise of natural pedagogy, which spurns drill and practice (no matter where undertaken) as deadening and unnecessary. So, on the naturalistic premises of the educational community, there must be some other explanation for the very different results of schooling with different students.

The explanation is usually conveyed by phrases like "lack of self-esteem" or "individual differences in abilities and learning styles." In other words, natural pedagogy works differently with nonlearning students because, for social or innate reasons, their natures are different. The result of such an explanation shifts the cause away from the actual procedures of schooling to something that is beyond the ability of schools to remedy. Low self-esteem, for example, is caused by larger forces in society such as broken families and racism. Variations in ability are caused by individual differences that are innate, hence natural, and beyond real remedy. The doctrine of natural pedagogy thus encourages a tendency already strong in American culture—to connect academic achievement more with social determinism and natural talent than with focused hard work.

The resulting overemphasis on innate ability really amounts to an empirical mistake. No matter how much musical ability a person has, he or she will not learn to play the piano well without a lot of drill and practice. No matter how much innate math ability a child has, he or she will not learn the multiplication table effectively by osmosis. One finding of neurobiology is that all learnings require effort—first of all, the effort of attention; in addition, many learnings require repeated efforts ("distributed practice") to forge and fix new neural networks.[26] For these learnings, there is no way around repeated and sometimes hard work. If the efforts can be made "effortless" and fun, so much the better. But unless they are directed and monitored—a primary responsibility of the teacher—secure learning will not occur. The fallacy of natural pedagogy thus breeds the further fallacy that innate ability is the royal road to all learning, that nonlearning children are being held back by lack of such ability rather than by lack of hard, directed work. It is inconceivable to people who hold this point of view that these children have been held back by a history of educational neglect, caused by an undemanding naturalistic pedagogy.

To understand the extent to which naturalistic views are fallacies, it is helpful to place them in the context of recent psychological work that has deepened our understanding of what is natural in learning. If a learning follows a definite sequence in all cultures and circumstances, it is assumed to be developmentally inherent. Such universal patterns of natural development are thought to be based on (though not limited to) primary processes that have been determined by human evolution and are found even across species. Play, for example, is universal in children and also many kinds of animals. The play instinct helps develop basic cognitive activities into more integrated and complex cognitions involving orientation in space, physical manipulation of objects, representation of objects, social relations, speaking, listening, and elementary counting.

These primary learnings (a concept introduced by David Geary) do seem to follow a definite and universal sequence, and therefore to support the Pestalozzi-Piaget model. The model has also been gaining a lot of empirical support from transcultural studies of language development; language growth in every culture apparently follows an invariant pattern. The same seems to be true of developing fine motor skills, and of basic conceptual development. In sum, language development, psychomotor development, and (to a more variable degree) basic conceptual development do appear to follow a temporal sequence that can reasonably be called "natural" because it is a sequence that has been shown to be transcultural and universal.[27]

But beyond these developmental universals, there are secondary learnings that, while necessary to particular cultures, are not universal. Among these nonnatural learnings are reading, writing, certain basic arithmetical operations, and concepts such as the base-ten system of counting, multicolumn addition and subtraction, carrying and borrowing, multiplication and division. These secondary learnings do *not* fit the Pestalozzi-Piaget scheme of automatic development.[28] It is quite misleading to think of them in developmental terms on the analogy of an acorn developing into an oak. The learnings do not develop at all unless they are taught—a self-evident inference from their nonuniversality across cultures. The implication of research along these lines is that while the normal tempo of psychomotor and conceptual development makes it inefficient to teach certain aspects of reading, writing, and arithmetic too early (before, say, age four), there is *no* age when a child is developmentally ready by nature for learning reading, writing, and arithmetic.

The inherent nonnaturalness of these learnings raises a practical question. Is there, on average, a best time vs. a premature or belated time to introduce certain learnings? Psychomotor development is a natural and primary process. If a child's slowness in developing fine motor skills makes that child unable to write prettily, is it better to avoid forcing penmanship on the child and simply wait? What has been concluded by the teachers at the *écoles maternelles,* who have more collective experience with the two-to-five age group than any other single body of professionals in the world? They avoid dogmatism in either direction on questions of timing. Long experience has shown them that it is good practice psychologically and academically to use gentle social pressure in encouraging slow developers to move ahead, and that it is equally important not to press too hard.[29] That's not a surprising conclusion, but it is less individualistic than the aforementioned "Position Statement" of American early-childhood specialists, which advises that "decisions about when knowledge and skills are introduced and/or expected to be accomplished are based on knowledge of prior experiences of individual children."[30]

Since reading and place value are nonnatural learnings, it is unlikely that children are ever *naturally* ready to learn them. Children's readiness for secondary processes such as reading and arithmetic is not simply a matter of natural development but also one of *prior relevant learning.* Learning builds on learning. Other things being equal—that is, given the same extent of prior relevant learning—the plasticity of the young mind makes most learnings easier and more durable at early ages.[31]

Thus the most urgent educational question in the crucial early years from three to seven is not a quasi-religious one concerning the inviolability of young childhood and the possibility of spiritual damage, but a practical question about what other learnings must be sacrificed in pursuing one kind of learning too intensively. To try to rush a child who lacks fine motor skills to write in a clear hand is futile, potentially frustrating, and, what is worse, excessively time-consuming. Better to devote only moderate time to that very demanding task while spending more time in practicing drawing or other more enjoyable fine motor activities. That is the kernel of wisdom implicit in the official American "Position Statement." But by the early school grades—that is, after age six or seven—the occasions where inherent slowness of primary development places powerful limitations on secondary learning are few. If the prime example is place value, then the true developmental constraints must be very few indeed.[32]

While there is no natural way to learn nonnatural, secondary processes, many American experts would still insist on the Romantic doctrine that having a young child learn nonnatural processes through "drill and kill" or reward and punishment does psychological harm. Consistent pressure on young children is of course harmful and will backfire, but enticement and a little pressure are no bad thing. The idea that stress avoidance is the sum of wisdom in early education assumes that what is natural is also what is painless. But some pain, like pleasure, is an unavoidable part of the educative process, and the one is not less natural than the other. Effort and persistence are needed for almost all secondary learning. Even the idea of avoiding stress in children can be overdone. Experimental animals given "stress experiences as infants performed better on learning tasks after they were adults than did nonstressed controls."[33]

Developmentalism holds that each child develops at his or her naturally ordained pace, which should never be forced lest the child be harmed or perverted. What has been the practical effect of this view on American education? One effect has been to repudiate as unnatural the significant effort that *all* learning requires, whether it is painful or joyful. If one child learns more slowly than another, developmentalism says that the slower child should not be pushed, but should be allowed to progress naturally. Thus Kilpatrick: "Our old-type school, with its formal subject matter, remote from life, made us think of the learning process as laborious and repellent. But . . . life's inherent learning comes in fact without effort, comes in fact automatically and stays with us."[34]

Yet a guiding principle of more successful educational systems holds that slower children should be encouraged to work all the longer and more intensively. Children, parents, and teachers in such systems are made explicitly aware of the minimal knowledge and skills the children are required to attain at each grade, and everyone cooperates in putting forth the effort needed to reach that goal. Usually it *is* reached, but even when it is not, children approach it more closely by putting forth extra effort, and they do so without harmful psychological effect.[35]

Extremely deleterious social consequences follow upon developmentalism's overemphasis on natural (i.e., genetically determined) talent and its assumption that speed of learning is innate. The assumption is very often wrong. In the United States, there demonstrably exists a too-neat parallelism between "innate" academic talent and social class—a parallelism that is far greater than in France and far greater than statistical variation could justify. It might be the case that children of poor, ill-educated parents in a particular school might have a somewhat lower mean academic talent than children of well-off, educated parents. But it is not biologically believable that almost *all* such children would be innately slow. On the contrary, it is a near certainty that there will be a lot of variance of innate talent within both social groups, and that some disadvantaged children will be more talented academically than some advantaged ones. In the United States, the all-too-consistent correlation between low academic performance and low economic status shows that something more than innate talent is determining the results.

It is probable that developmentalism itself is a significant cause of the inequity. Learning builds cumulatively on learning. By encouraging an early education that is free of "unnatural" bookish knowledge and of "inappropriate" pressure to exert hard effort, developmentalism virtually ensures that children from well-educated homes who happen to be primed with academically relevant background knowledge, which they bring with them to school, will learn faster than disadvantaged children who do not bring such knowledge with them and do not receive it at school. Developmentalism withholds academic knowledge on principle. But in the current social context it withholds it differentially, according to social class. The home-provided background knowledge of advantaged students helps make them quicker and more academically advanced than their less-advantaged classmates—not because they have uniformly superior innate talent but because they have uniformly greater intellectual capital. Under such circumstances the "innate" pace of development that is "natural" for each child would be very difficult to ascertain, and has little to do with the actual speed with which American schoolchildren are currently able to learn.

It is therefore cause for great concern that developmentalists have drawn upon the latent Romanticism in American culture to persuade state legislatures to mandate an unproved practice called "multiaged education," in which children of different ages are placed in classes according to their "readiness" for a subject. Supposedly, this innovation will mean that all children will learn at the "natural" pace appropriate to them, and not have imposed on them an artificial and, for some, unreachable standard. But the practical effect of the law will be to make children, teachers, and schools unaccountable for improving the present inequitable state of affairs. Slower students will be placed in their "developmentally appropriate" group, regardless of their age and, in fact, regardless of their "innate abilities," which the schools are not equipped to determine.

To pass such legislation when the principle of multiage education has not been tested on a large scale, or tested at all with proper controls, is radical and unwise legislation that could only have been enacted because the majority of the population is already convinced that "allowing each child to progress at his or her own pace" is self-evidently the natural and right thing to do. To those steeped in Romantic developmentalism, the principle appears to be so obviously true that it does not require clear evidence of its effectiveness or fairness; it is enough that a majority of educational experts support this "reform," which resonates with the culturally inherited predisposition of the public and the legislature. It would be hard to imagine a clearer example of the powerful influence of Romantic developmentalism than its success in persuading state legislatures to mandate an inadequately tested and socially deleterious inheritance from the age of Alcott and Emerson.

4.

American Exceptionalism and Localism

E arlier in this book, I cited unambiguous evidence that showed a relative
decline in American schooling during the past two decades as compared
with the results achieved by other developed nations.³⁶ But I felt uneasy in
doing so. I did not want the reader to close the book in disgust. When citing
such data at educational colloquia, I have often experienced responses indicating that international comparisons seem to many Americans irrelevant, inadequate, and even downright un-American. The topic tends to bring a resigned
glaze over the eyes of educators, a sad boredom with anyone who would think
that other nations' situations are comparable to our own. By contrast, vigorous
approval from such an audience can always be aroused by a participant who
rises to say, "It's all very well to talk about homogeneous countries like France
or Korea, but what has that got to do with my school? I've got kids from
seventeen nations. Some of their parents don't speak English. I've got kids
who are severely learning-disabled, kids who come to school with marks of
abuse on their bodies. Please don't talk to me about France or Korea." (Vigorous applause.)

In such a climate of feeling, I have long since decided that it is better not to
mention international comparisons at all in public forums. But here, in the
cooler context of print, it is worth noting that American students are *not*
always ethnically and economically more diverse than students in the schools
of other nations. It is true that many U.S. classes have to deal with children
whose first language is not English and whose families may be nonfunctional,
and that those problems do impose enormous difficulties on our schools. But
those difficulties do not excuse or foreordain the low achievement scores of
the children. With my own eyes I have seen schools in the suburbs of Paris
where the ethnic and social diversity is equal to that of the Bronx and Miami.
Currently, in the Paris region, the total percentage of nonnaturalized, non-
French students is 23.2 percent of the school population. (The percentages are
of course much higher in certain suburbs.) The groups represented include
North African, West African, Spanish, Portuguese, Italian, and Southeast
Asian, and there are smaller percentages of students from almost every nation
in the world.³⁷

In 1992, Professor Harold Stevenson, a distinguished psychologist at the
University of Michigan, published with his former student James Stigler a
book called *The Learning Gap.* It is potentially one of the most important
books for American education published in the past fifty years. I say "poten-

tially" because a book cannot have practical importance if it is not read or heeded, and this work of science has been left stranded on the shoals of the invincibly complacent Americanism of the educational community. Written for the general public, *The Learning Gap* is a distillation of comparative studies of education in different countries conducted over a ten-year period by the authors and their numerous colleagues in Taiwan, Japan, and the United States. The book's findings are stunning and, reinforced by data from other countries, tell us a great deal about apparently universal characteristics of successful systems of elementary education. The research reports on which the book is based were published in refereed scientific journals. From a scientific standpoint, the data and analyses are beyond reproach, and no scientist of standing has challenged them.

Yet Professor Stevenson has suffered the indignity of having his professional competence challenged with distortive and dismissive pseudoarguments by members of the educational community who have made careers of dismissing international comparisons. These nonrefereed "researchers" find ready publication in educational journals by preserving the intellectual comfort of their readers. The flavor of their dismissals can be illustrated in the statement "the students are not comparable, the curricula are not comparable, the schools are not comparable, and the tests are not comparable. The comparisons are so flawed as to be meaningless."[38] And if even those inevitable "flaws" were overcome, there would still remain the consideration of our special Americanism. We would not wish to emulate the practices of other nations. Our system, unlike theirs, has "distinctive characteristics which promote the American values of egalitarianism, utilitarianism, and individualism, which have given educational objectives other than maximum achievement higher priority than they have enjoyed in much of the rest of the industrialized world"[39]

These writers play a role in the educational community that demands to be filled. What Voltaire said of God applies to such anticomparative apologists: if they did not exist, it would be necessary to invent them. But their comforting messages would be much less likely to be believed inside and outside the educational community if there were not throughout American culture a strong predisposition that finds it inappropriate to compare our institutions with those of other nations. This is the sentiment historians call "American exceptionalism"—a widespread set of attitudes that claim "distinctive characteristics" for our country and its institutions, making us so entirely different from other countries that we have little or nothing to learn from them, and ought not to be compared with them.

American exceptionalism holds that we as a people are not only different from but better than other peoples, and that our problems are unique. As Michael Kammen says, the theme is "as old as the nation itself and, equally important, has played an integral part in the society's sense of its own identity."[40] Although our current textbooks teach the past shortcomings of the United States, the unanimous teachings of earlier schoolbooks have brought American exceptionalism into our orally transmitted culture. One of the first great American educators, Noah Webster, was a vigorous exceptionalist who insisted that even our spelling should reflect our uniqueness. Ruth Elson, in her study of the books used in our schools from 1790 to 1900, showed that they unanimously contrasted virtuous and natural Americans with corrupt and decadent Europeans.[41] Michael Kammen summarizes:

> *Throughout the nineteenth century, imaginative writers and historians, popular orators and clergy joined a chorus that continually chanted an ode to the nation's special mission and readiness to fulfill it. . . . The American Revolution contributed significantly to a strong sense of exceptionalism, one that became pervasive in our popular culture.*[42]

By 1865, with the Civil War just over, the Boston Brahmin poet James Russell Lowell delivered at the Harvard commencement a "Commemoration Ode" for the fallen leader, Abraham Lincoln. His ultimate praise was for Lincoln's unique Americanness, to achieve which nature had had to form a completely new "mould":

> *Nature they say doth dote*
> *And cannot make a man*
> *Save on some worn-out plan,*
> *Repeating as by rote:*
> *For him her Old-World moulds aside she threw,*
> *And choosing sweet clay from the breast*
> *Of the unexhausted West,*
> *With stuff untainted shaped a hero new,*
> *Wise, steadfast in the strength of God, and true.*
> ·  ·  ·  ·  ·  ·  ·  ·  ·  ·  ·  ·  ·  ·  ·  ·
> *Our children shall behold his fame,*
> *The kindly, earnest, brave foreseeing man,*
> *Sagacious, patient, dreading praise not blame,*
> *New birth of our soil, the first American.*[43]

The "stuff untainted" of our Western soil meant that we were free from the burden of the past—even free, by implication, from original sin. Freedom from a tainted past, celebration of the vast pure landscape, and a derogation of traditions and books—all were very American, very exceptionalist versions of Romanticism. We of the "Virgin Land" were freer, more independent, more innocent, and more vigorously diverse than sinful Europe. Everything here was bigger—our virtues and our vices, our energies and our obstacles. We were destined to lead and redeem other nations, not vice versa. We were set on earth to teach them, not to learn from them.

The *educational* version of American exceptionalism was given its definitive form by that codifier of American educational thought William Heard Kilpatrick. The kind of education we needed, he argued, had to be as different from other nations' as we ourselves were different. Those other countries were undemocratic, hierarchical, and static. They had a "fixed, closed, authoritarian system of education perfectly fitted to the needs of a static religion, a static church, a static caste system, a static economic system."[44] We, by contrast, were democratic, diverse, and dynamic. In his book *Education for a Changing Civilization,* Kilpatrick made a central theme out of an argument he had already made in his earlier *Foundations of Method*—that America required an unfixed, dynamic approach as befitted our unique nation and the new, changeable era we were entering. The subject matter of the American curriculum could never be set in advance: "If people face a rapidly shifting and changing world, changing in unexpected ways and in unexpected directions, then what? Why, their education would stress thinking and methods of attack."[45]

In the fullness of time, the exceptionalist sentiments Kilpatrick transmitted to the educational community became dogmas that are still repeated in endless variations. It is no longer said, of course, that America must lead the rapidly changing industrial era by emptying our education of "fixed" and "static" content. There has been a small adjustment. Now we must avoid fixed and static content in order to enter the *information age.* Kilpatrickism is brought up to date by saying that what he called the "rapidly shifting and changing world, changing in unexpected ways and in unexpected directions," has been caused not by the industrial but by the computer revolution. But the goal which that new condition implies for American education is still said to be what Kilpatrick said it was in 1925: to ignore content (which is quickly outmoded) and to "stress thinking and methods of attack." Despite their up-to-date sound, these misguided doctrines continue to be promulgated as they were in the 1920s.

The educational influence of American exceptionalism may be gauged by contrasting contemporary British educational reform with our own. Until recently, the British educational community was dominated by anti-subject-matter progressivism almost as vigorously as ours has been, particularly after World War II, when all things American were held in high regard. The two educational communities reinforced each other. Some of our own most confident anti-subject-matter movements after the war were inspired by *Summerhill* (1960), written by the British schoolmaster A. S. Neill. The book contained statements like "All that any child needs is the three R's; the rest should be tools and clay and sports and theater and paint and freedom." By 1969, according to Diane Ravitch, *Summerhill* was selling in the United States at a rate of more than two hundred thousand copies a year.[46] There were other examples of the transatlantic dominance of progressivism, including the Anglo-American Dartmouth Conferences, which ratified the idea of turning language arts instruction in a process-oriented direction.

But time has not been kind to educational progressivism in Britain. Because of Britain's closeness to the Continent, as well as its economic dependence on the European Community, it became widely known to the British public that France, Sweden, and other nations on the Continent were achieving much better educational results than Britain—results clearly associated with a more coherent emphasis on content. British educational experts were widely criticized in the press for defending an extreme anti-subject-matter, pro-process stance. In due course, they were compelled to modify their position and to accept a coherent approach to content. But before the 1980s, there was not a large difference between the pro-process attitudes of the British and the American educational communities.

But the free fall into process was halted by the British Parliament in 1987, when, against the resistance of educational professionals, it voted to introduce a national curriculum into the schools. Britons had been constantly traveling to the Continent. Being less isolated from external influences than we in the United States, and perhaps less afflicted by so extreme a sense of national uniqueness, they gained firsthand acquaintance with other school systems. This direct knowledge gradually led British public opinion to support the idea of grade-by-grade school content. By 1987, it had become crystal clear to a majority of Britons that school systems which used national curricula were performing much better than the British school system. Proud as Britons are of their special national character, they have a more tempered sense of their uniqueness than we do of ours. Their willingness to learn from international experience sets a good example for us. Moderating our American exceptionalism in the educational sphere is going to be a high priority for achieving educational improvement in the United States.

Besides the themes of innocence, bigness, and diversity that contribute to our sense of uniqueness, the exceptionalist theme of localism is of special significance in American educational thought. Unlike other peoples, we Americans reject the principle that a distant authority can dictate what we shall teach our children. Our conflict between central and local authority goes back to the first days of the Republic. Hamilton and others advocated a relatively strong central authority, while Jefferson and his party, ever sensitive to the slightest possibility of tyranny, wanted to keep as much power as possible in local hands. Protection from despotic control was the primary idea of localism in the early years. Later on, it was extended to resist another kind of tyranny— that of bureaucratic mindlessness, indifference, and inefficiency. Modern localism says, Don't even try to get something done through the central government or, for that matter, through the state government. Head-office bureaucrats have no sense of the complexities of the local situation, or any knowledge of the persons involved.

But the practicalities of historical change in the twentieth century have required a reexamination of American localism in some obvious domains. We have chosen to abandon local currencies printed by individual banks in favor of a national currency. We have adopted standard-gauge railroads. We set our watches by translocal time zones rather than by local sun time. In most nations of the modern world, people have also recognized that educational quality and equity require a measure of translocal commonality in the content of early schooling. Nonetheless, it is quixotic to resist educational localism in the United States, where there is no plausible mechanism for replacing this sanctified arrangement. Hence, local control of education must be taken as a starting point for policy.

But granting the inevitability of localism in the United States, a chief aim of educational policy ought to be to compensate for its most egregious shortcomings. When the American occupation of Japan was coming to an end after World War II, and Japan was taking control of its own affairs, American authorities recommended that the Japanese school system be placed under American-style local governance. Americans argued that it would be a means of ensuring democracy and resistance to centralized thought-control. The Japanese replied in effect, "We intend to follow your principles of government, but localism in education is not a protection against anything. It mainly leads to unfairness to students, because it does not provide any means for insuring that all children receive a quality education."[47]

Other democracies have drawn exactly the same conclusion. On a visit to Denmark, a colleague of mine was taken on a tour by one of that country's most distinguished scholars. The Dane pointed to the school he had attended, and mentioned other notable scientists and scholars who had graduated from the same school. "Gee," my friend said, "that must be a specially good school." "No," replied his host, "here in Denmark, we make sure that all the schools are equally good." The importance for democracy of moderating a purely local approach to schooling has been widely understood throughout the world. The extreme mobility figures in the United States, cited in Chapter 2, make a tempering of our localism even more imperative.

In the face of the obvious drawbacks of localism, American educators have banked on our exceptionalist traditions to argue against even voluntary commonality of content across localities, on the grounds that a decision to devote part of classroom time to common content is an infringement on the American teacher's autonomy and professional judgment—a canard that has been promulgated by education schools since William Heard Kilpatrick enunciated it in the 1920s.[48] Proof of the irrelevance of content commonality to professional status is that it exists in just those nations where teachers have the most prestige and are paid the highest salaries. These teachers enjoy a great deal of freedom in the classroom, as well as the benefit of cooperation with their colleagues, based on the common goals they share.

Extreme localism has proved itself to be a formula for failure and inequity. Present-day reformers invoke the sanctity of local control of education, even to the point of priding themselves on not making any curricular decisions and not giving any curricular advice. But this is to abandon fundamental responsibilities of educational leadership. Always leaving content up to somebody else is a pedagogical and political irresponsibility, not a democratic virtue. Extreme localism has failed not only American children but also the teachers themselves, who, to do their job properly, need agreed-on goals and the benefit of cooperation with their colleagues.

Of course, there are some tenets of American exceptionalism to which most of us continue to subscribe. We are justifiably proud of the degree to which our children are encouraged to think for themselves, to be independent-minded and critical of received ideas. The popularity in the United States of the "critical thinking" movement, as well as the anxiety expressed about "lockstep education," attests to the value that Americans attach to independent-mindedness. But there is evidence from as early on as Tocqueville that this independent, skeptical element in our culture has always been strong, that it has always been nurtured in our literature, our homes, and our schools. Independent-mindedness used to be sustained just as diligently in the nineteenth century, when our schools stressed subject matter, as it is now, when they stress "critical thinking." It is a fallacy to believe that independent-mindedness can be sustained by disparaging factual knowledge. On the contrary, there has never been an effective independent thinker who did not thoroughly master the received views against which he or she rebeled.

The danger created by American exceptionalism is that until its irrational complacencies are neutralized, it may be impossible to introduce educational change based on pragmatic or rational principles. To a public indoctrinated with exceptionalism, it does not seem odd that typical proposals for educational improvement should be based on homegrown American "break-the-mold" experiments that have never been tried on a large scale—as if it were irrelevant that there already exists a body of knowledge regarding what does and does not work elsewhere. So long as educationists and the general public believe that our culture and our children are incomparable, American exceptionalism will continue to be exploited as an effective means of resisting real change.

# 5.
## Individualism

Individualism is as American as pecan pie. No one is going to give it up or wants to. But it comes in varieties and degrees. When this native theme plays out in the schools, there are significant contrasts between the rhetoric and the reality of individualism. Barry Shain, following in the steps of Vernon Parrington and Octavius Frothingham, has shown in *The Myth of American Individualism* that our present ideas of individualism are quite different from those current in the United States before 1850. Our present-day emphasis on the absolute worth and uniqueness of each child came to the American scene late, arriving only after European Romanticism had been transported to New England, whence it emerged victorious in the nineteenth century. Thus Shain:

> *As Vernon Parrington saw it, Romantic thought, finally free from both the communal and rational constraints of the 18th century, was a "glorification of the ideal of individualism." Fundamental to this movement, he argues, was "an assertion of the inalienable worth of man; theoretically it was an assertion of the divinity in instinct, the transference of supernatural attributes to the natural constitution of mankind."*[49]

The individualism that dominates in our schools ultimately derives from this Romantic faith in the holiness of the natural. Like developmentalism, it springs from the quasi-religious "transference of supernatural attributes to the natural constitution of mankind." Romantic individualism holds that each person has a natural and uniquely divine spark, which, if nurtured, cannot go wrong. The scientific and social terms with which we celebrate "individual differences" are mainly technical masks for the robust Romanticism of Pestalozzi and Froebel. Various writers of the nineteenth century, including William Hazlitt and Alexis de Tocqueville, made shrewd connections between the egalitarianism of the American and French revolutions and pantheistic faith in the equal divinity of all persons. Tocqueville went so far as to claim that pantheism was implicit in the very idea of universal equality, and thus in democracy itself.

The school phenomenon that is currently called "grade inflation" is a perhaps inevitable consequence of Romantic individualism. I once heard a superintendent of schools say on TV that each child has a special "genius." He probably did not realize that his sentiment descended from the father of all grade inflation, Edward Young, who said as early as 1759 that all writers have innate genius. Young made his observation in the midst of the great eighteenth-century debate over whether the modern writers could ever equal the ancient ones. Of course they can, Young answered: each original composition "rises spontaneously from the vital root of genius; it grows, it is not made." "Genius," he wrote, "is that god within. Genius can set us right in composition without the rules of the learned."[50]

Since in American schools every child is unique and of equal worth with every other child, academic competition, which subverts this egalitarian and individualist creed, must be discouraged. Emphasis is to be placed on the child's unique imagination and creativity, not on the lockstep learning of predetermined and inert traditions. Such individualism leads, it is said, to that independent-mindedness which has made America great. If students are to be graded at all, which subverts the principle of equal worth, the implication is clear: each child deserves to pass. Each child's paper, drawing, or variety of spelling expresses his or her uniqueness. What has been called "grade inflation" is perhaps more accurately called "grade egalitarianism" or "grade individualism." If followed to its logical extreme, each child's unique spark, being divine, would deserve an A; but since that principle would not be publicly accepted, a policy of nongrading is currently preferred in many schools.

Many in the educational community have sought and found "scientific" justification for nongrading and for universal social promotion to the next grade. "Research has shown" that holding a child back a grade adversely affects attitudes and learning, while low grades adversely affect self-esteem. But as the distinguished psychologist Robin Dawes has observed, this emphasis on self-esteem has little empirical justification. Dawes has shown the lack of correlation (.17) between academic self-esteem and academic accomplishment.

While self-contempt may indeed lead to idleness, the only consistent correlative of academic achievement is effort, which is not well correlated with self-esteem.[51]

Moreover, the compensatory, racial overtones of the self-esteem movement should be exposed for what they are. For beneath the brave words about individualism, self-esteem, and intrinsic worth, there are often unspoken racial implications in the practice of compensatory grading. Although grades may have become more equal, schools have made little or no progress in equalizing the actual academic achievements of social, ethnic, and racial groups. Despite recent progress in narrowing the achievement gap between racial groups, each summer brings similar disappointing news about test scores, with similar socially and racially correlated divergences. A kind of desperation has set in that expresses itself either by scapegoating rhetoric about racism or by attempts to abolish the educational gap between groups by decree. This latter tactic, the achieving of equality by fiat, is accomplished at schools and colleges by interpreting standardized test scores differentially according to race and social class, or by simply rejecting the validity of the tests and the "false" message that their scores send.

The salvaging of individual worth and self-esteem by artificially raising grades when schooling has failed to raise achievement was exemplified in the recent decision by the College Board simply to lift SAT scores. This was accomplished by a "non-linear transformation" of the verbal SAT mean from 425 to 500—the score which in earlier years had been the actual mean but which had fallen by some 75 points. In explaining its action, the Board stated that the mean has fallen because many more "minority" students are now taking the SAT tests.

This kind of artificial pat on the back is just the sort of racially condescending action advocated by Richard Herrnstein and Charles Murray in *The Bell Curve,* a book that abandons the attempt to raise the competencies of ethnic and social groups with "innately" deficient IQs.[52] While it is certainly true that scores by minority students have helped to lower the SAT mean, the implicit assumption of the College Board that this fact will always be true masks a condescension which is closely related to grade inflation, IQ determinism, and the self-esteem movement. A much better decision would have been to announce that the College Board would never artificially raise the numerical mean of the SAT tests, and would look forward to a time when the mean would rise to a point much above even the earlier mark. Instead of keeping the existing standard in place to stimulate students and schools to greater effort, the College Board action invites complacency about the achievements of students and of American education. It is as though the College Board had turned the illusionist therapy the educational community practices on students upon itself in order to preserve its own self-esteem.

The actions of the College Board and the self-esteem movement compellingly reveal that the education world is long on the rhetoric of Romantic individualism but short on ideas and hope. Passing students by fiat is therapy by illusion. It is analogous to the belief that psychological and social improvement can come from unearned gold stars and ubiquitous smiley faces awarded to whatever work students happen to perform. But the therapy of illusion simply delays the time of reckoning. Students who have been praised for their innate excellence and unique inner worth later find that they cannot hold down good jobs. Meanwhile, they have been taught by the schools not to blame the schools (which seem not to grasp the close affinity between condescension and racism) but to blame instead the society beyond the schools for failing to give them a fair shake.

Some of the most widely noted recent reforms in the public schools have been implicitly directed less to individualism than to social inequity based on ethnicity or race. The enthusiastic but disorganized introduction of "multicultural" elements into the curriculum; the adoption of "Afrocentric" curricula in predominantly African-American schools; the efforts to induce self-esteem and motivation among students who lack it because of their ethnicity or race; the attempt to remove "cultural bias" from textbooks and tests; the silent introduction of compensatory grading—all are among these reforms. When acquaintances hear that I am writing a book about the current educational scene, one of the things they ask is whether I am going to deal with "multiculturalism." The term has joined "phonics" and "outcomes-based education" as another casus belli between conservatives and liberals.

When done well, introducing multicultural elements into the early curriculum has been useful to American children because it has recognized real achievements and contributions by minorities. Its effect has been to encourage group self-respect on the part of minorities, as well as general respect for all groups. Although continued educational inequity in schools where multiculturalism has been introduced demonstrates that this curricular shift is not sufficient by itself to make much difference in achievement levels, it is a shift that no one has argued *against* with any cogency when it has been done with balance. The mistake is to endow this beneficial change with quasi-magical effects on achievement and self-esteem that it cannot possibly have.

A good antidote to the implicit despair and determinism to which Romantic individualism has currently led is to heed Orlando Patterson's contrast between the educational achievements of blacks in Jamaica and in the United States. Both groups come from the same racial stock and language groups of West Africa. Both were transported to the United States and the West Indies during the same historical era. Given their similar cultural and genetic origins, and their similar historical degradation in slavery, why is the educational attainment of West Indian blacks significantly higher than that of U.S. blacks, and why does it produce a statistically remarkable number of distinguished African-Americans of Caribbean origin such as Colin Powell (whose parents came from the Caribbean) and Patterson himself?

Patterson's analysis makes it overwhelmingly clear that the chief explanation must be cultural rather than individual and genetic. While the differences in historical-cultural-psychological factors are complex, one very clear difference that Patterson points out is a contrast in educational practices and attitudes between Jamaica and the United States:

> *A comparison of the two school systems suggests that attitudes are much more critical than the material resources of the schools or the homes of the students. In objective material terms, the poorest Black American is materially much better off than the average West Indian peasant. The poverty of Harlem does not begin to compare to the poverty of a shanty town in Kingston or any rural village in Jamaica. Educational facilities are usually far more inadequate in Jamaica than in the United States. School success does not seem to depend on the physical condition of the home or of the school; it is more profoundly related to attitudes towards the dominant culture on the part of the parents, the students, and the teachers. Attitudes are critical. The fundamental assumption in the Caribbean on the part of those Black teachers who taught me throughout elementary school—in classes that averaged eighty-six students in one-room schoolhouses, sometimes several hundred students in a large room—was that we were teachable. "I did it, so can you." No one doubted for a moment that the students could be taught: not the students, their parents or teachers. If we wanted to succeed, we had to acquire this thing; if we didn't, well, it was up to us.*[53]

Some of the efforts to help minorities, such as the introduction of multicultural curricular elements, may be socially and psychologically useful; others, such as condescending attempts to praise or to grade children into self-esteem, are harmful. These amateur psychological efforts fail because they lie to children about their achievements. The falsehood and the implicit condescension are ultimately picked up by children, who, for all their enforced ignorance, are natively smart. Their resulting skepticism leads to further erosion of their self-esteem. The only sure method of making children self-confident about their work in schools (which will help their general self-esteem) is, as Patterson and Dawes suggest, to nurture the hard work that will lead to actual academic achievement.

In recent years, a new "scientific" validation of Romantic individualism has generated a lot of interest in the schools—the "individual learning styles" movement, together with its most recent variant, the "multiple intelligences" movement. "Research has shown" that there are seven intelligences. If you aren't innately smart in one intelligence, you are bound to be smart in one or more of the other six. The basic principle is that of compensatory intelligence, which makes everybody smart in something. This scientific account is consonant with the already existing faith in an equally divine spark in all. The movement holds that schools have placed too much emphasis on the logical and verbal kinds of intelligence. (This sentiment agrees with the antiverbal tradition of Romanticism that I discuss below under "Anti-Intellectualism.") Henceforth, schools will need to give equal recognition to different learning styles and to "nonacademic" intelligences such as musical and athletic abilities. No longer will every child be locked into the narrow verbal-logical mode of merely academic subjects. At last the era of the universal A may be at hand, thanks to recent research.

The enthusiasm for the doctrines of individual learning styles and multiple intelligences, as new, scientized versions of Romantic individualism exemplifies the consistent and troublesome tendency of the educational community to elevate ideologically pleasing but nonconsensus scientific findings over ideologically troublesome ones that *have* achieved scientific consensus. This is a recipe for continued practical failure in our schools.

In the short run, a lack of consensus in scientific research is untroublesome and even necessary to intellectual progress. Research at the frontier is almost always in dispute. But at the same time, nonconsensus findings are also highly likely to be incorrect. As consensus in science increases, so does the likelihood of correctness. Everybody now agrees that the chemical formula for water is $H_2O$. The fact of that consensus does not guarantee its absolute truth, but it does guarantee its high degree of reliability. If you are engaged in a practical activity like schooling, you need to bank on consensus science because, even in those rare cases where it is slightly wrong, it reflects highly consistent practical success. To adopt nonconsensus science as the basis of school policy is to conduct very perilous human experimentation on a large scale without a license and with little hope of practical success. In a conflict between ideology and reality, reality always trumps. That is the larger point illustrated by the current acceptance of the theories of multiple learning styles and multiple intelligences.

Every educational theorist has recognized at least to some degree the importance of individual differences among students. Every good teacher tries to nurture students' talents and strengthen their weaknesses. This widely accepted principle, coupled with the failure of schools to bring minority students to academic proficiency, may explain the enthusiasm that greeted the emphasis on nonacademic proficiencies and alternative learning styles in Howard Gardner's book *Frames of Mind* (1983). Gardner, a distinguished professor at the Harvard Graduate School of Education and an engaging writer, has been a voice for balance in many domains of education reform, and has recently advocated the focused teaching of subject matters. His support of multiple learning styles has been less sound and beneficial. In *Frames of Mind,* Gardner argued that there are seven independent intelligences, which different students possess in different proportions.

After Gardner's book appeared, a number of public schools adopted the "multiple intelligences" approach, confident that they were not just fulfilling the social desiderata of individualism and equality but also applying the latest scientific findings. But neither the multiple intelligences theory nor the similar multiple learning styles theory is well accepted in the scientific community. While researchers agree that different styles and intelligences do exist, no one is sure what their traits and neurophysiological foundations are.

A comment by the distinguished psychologist George A. Miller in a December 1983 *New York Times Book Review* summarizes the scientific consensus regarding multiple learning styles and intelligences: "It is probable, therefore, that Mr. Gardner's catalogue of intelligences is wrong. In the absence of an explanatory theory, the chance of accidentally making the right observations—describing the right phenomena, creating the right categories, making the right measurements—is small to the vanishing point." And Miller then gets to the heart of the policy issues raised by the current interest in multiple intelligences and learning styles when he adds:

> *Since none of the work has been done that would have to be done before a single-value assessment of intelligence could be replaced by a seven-value assessment, the discussion is all hunch and opinion. It is true that, if such profiles were available, an educator might be better able to match the materials and modes of instruction to an individual student. But since nobody knows whether the educator should play to the student's strengths or bolster the student's weaknesses (or both), the new psychometrics does not seem to advance practical matters much beyond present psychometrics.*

Professor Miller here identifies a basic issue that must be confronted by anyone who places an emphasis on individuality in education. Should schools develop a student's special talent and style of learning at the expense of developing standard academic competencies such as reading, speaking, mathematics, and general knowledge? Research cannot answer that question. Should everyone get an A for something? That is a question of social policy that does not find an answer in research. Equity, however, clearly requires that schools give all children the knowledge and skills they need to become politically functional, economically successful, and autonomous citizens. If schools do not define with some particularity what those attainments are, and if they do not cause every student to reach them, no amount of overt concern for individuality can enable each student to develop his or her potential as a participant in the larger society.

## 6.
## Anti-Intellectualism

As I sit here writing about anti-intellectualism in American education, a debate is raging in my state, Virginia, over a proposal to "raise standards of learning" by mandating knowledge standards for each grade. The factual knowledge that is specified in the Virginia draft is far more explicit than in any currently existing state guidelines. But prospects for approval in any but watered-down form are dim. According to the *Washington Post* (March 29, 1995), the draft guidelines "have provoked scathing criticism from teachers' groups, superintendents, parent organizations, education professors, and legislators, both Republican and Democrat. Some say the goals are unrealistically ambitious for the lower grades, [and] promote rote memorization over critical thinking." (Now, at a later date, as I revise this text, I can report that a watered-down compromise was reached.)

That American professors of education are more hostile to the teaching of factual knowledge than education professors elsewhere in the world offers another point of entry into the American educational Thoughtworld. But, as the report from the *Washington Post* indicates, it is not just education professors who express hostility to "rote memorization." That attitude also rallies Republicans and Democrats, parents and legislators, and, as I infer from the tenor of the *Post* article, newspaper reporters as well. There is widespread antiknowledge sentiment in American thought that Richard Hofstadter has labeled "anti-intellectualism."[54]

It is a convenient term, but I wonder whether Hofstadter's definition of it does adequate justice to its attractions for a wide spectrum of Americans. Hofstadter defines anti-intellectualism as contempt for "knowledge for its own sake." This definition perhaps misses something essential, namely, that the knowledge most often scorned by Americans tends to be academic knowledge connected with scientific lore and past traditions—the kind taught in lecture halls and recorded mostly in books. Disinterested curiosity is not in itself scorned by Americans—only disinterested curiosity about the contents of lectures and books.

Of course, Hofstadter is right that interested, as distinct from disinterested, practicality is a persistent American trait. We are fondest of knowledge that has utility for economic and moral improvement, a preference I happen to share. Befitting our early image of ourselves as giving mankind a new, Edenic start in history, Americans have valued knowledge that comes directly from experience more than knowledge that comes from books. "Critical thinking" about one's own direct experience is to be preferred to "rote memorization" of the writings of others. Huck Finn is an archetypal American antibook figure. He is going to get *his* education by critically thinking about what he discovers on the river and in the Territory. Nature and experience will be his teachers. Huck's attitudes are not very different from those of Walt Whitman:

> *When I heard the learn'd astronomer;*
> *When the proofs, the figures, were ranged in columns before me;*
> *When I was shown the charts and the diagrams, to add, divide, and*
>     *measure them;*
> *When I, sitting, heard the astronomer, where he lectured with much*
>     *applause in the lecture-room,*
> *How soon, unaccountable, I became tired and sick;*
> *Till rising and gliding out, I wander'd off by myself,*
> *In the mystical moist night-air, and from time to time,*
> *Look'd up in perfect silence at the stars.*[55]

Whitman wrote those lines in 1865. American thought has been conflicted about the value of book learning since the mid-nineteenth century. With one part of our minds we have remained loyal to the Jeffersonian and Enlightenment faith in the utility of scholarship, research, and ever-advancing knowledge. So strong was our faith in the economic, political, and social efficacy of universal education that this Enlightenment trait of American thinking was salient enough to be noted by Tocqueville: "They [the Americans] have all a lively faith in the perfectibility of man, they judge the diffusion of knowledge [also Jefferson's phrase] must necessarily be advantageous, and the consequences of ignorance fatal."[56]

But since the mid-nineteenth century, American distrust of book learning has been equally strong. Books became associated with a corrupt tradition and sinful Europe. Americans are people who look forward, not back. "The eyes of man are set in his forehead, not his hindhead" (Emerson). "History is bunk" (Henry Ford). A much deeper and better education is to be gained from direct, practical experience than from listening to lectures in lecture rooms. One becomes truly educated not by reading but by interacting with people and things in the vast American landscape. Thus arose a conflict between our Enlightenment tradition, which connected democracy with book learning, and our Romantic tradition, which disparaged culture and books. The two conflicting traditions were personified in nineteenth-century Boston by Horace Mann on the one hand and Ralph Waldo Emerson on the other. After listening to Mann expatiate on the importance of the common school to American democracy, Emerson made the following disdainful comment in his journal:

> *Yesterday Mr Mann's address on Education. It was full of the modern gloomy view of our democratical institutions, and hence the inference to the importance of Schools. . . . Education! . . . We are shut up in schools and college recitation rooms for ten or fifteen years & come out at last with a bellyfull of words & do not know a thing. We cannot use our hands or our legs or our eyes or our arms. We do not know an edible root in the woods. We cannot tell our course by the stars nor the hour of the day by the sun. It is well if we can swim & skate. We are afraid of a horse, of a cow, of a dog, of a cat, of a spider. Far better was the Roman rule to teach a boy nothing that he could not learn standing. . . . The farm, the farm is the right school. The reason of my deep respect for the farmer is that he is a realist and not a dictionary. The farm is a piece of the world, the School house is not. The farm by training the physical rectifies and invigorates the metaphysical & moral nature.[57]*

Anti-intellectualism and individualism came together in Emerson's fear that books can corrupt the unique spark of divinity in each human soul:

> *I had better never see a book than be warped by its attraction clean out of my own orbit, and made a satellite instead of a system. The one thing in the world of value is the active soul—the soul, free, sovereign, active. This every man is entitled to; this every man contains within him, although in almost all men obstructed and as yet unborn.[58]*

Born in the Enlightenment but bred in Romanticism, our nation has retained a curious ambivalence about education and book learning, nurturing both Enlightenment hope that they can bring us nearer social justice (as in Mann) and Romantic fear that they can hinder individualism, understanding, and independence of mind (as in Emerson). Americans are still fond of encouraging their children to work part-time in the "real" world while in school. We still have the Emersonian image of the bookish nerd as a pale, unhealthy weakling, ignorant of the real world and out of touch with his or her own best nature. Faith in nature, and scornful repudiation of the baggage of the past, come together in the educationist idea that "hands-on" knowledge is more useful than verbal knowledge. There is a direct line of descent from Emerson's antibookish writings of the 1830s to the insistence on practical skills in the *Cardinal Principles* of 1918. By that date, antiacademic sentiment, while simply an element of general American thought, had become the dominant principle taught in education schools.

The focus in *Cardinal Principles* on such nonacademic goals as health, vocation, citizenship, worthy use of leisure, and the like has remained stable through various permutations of educational vocabulary from 1918 to the present. The superiority of doing over knowing, the stress on vocationalism and social utility, the hostility to traditional subject matters—all became central to curriculum revision in the 1920s and '30s. The following statements come from Kilpatrick's *Foundations of Method* (1925):

> *We are properly concerned first with children that they shall grow, and only secondarily with subject matter that it be learned. . . . Subject matter is good only and because it furnishes a better way-of-behaving. . . . The separate school subjects. Shall we not have to give them up if the ideas of purposeful activity and intrinsic subject-matter be adopted? As hitherto conceived and taught, yes; separate subjects for children would have to go.*[59]

In 1939, Charles Prosser, an influential opponent of bookishness, stated in parallel clauses—which displayed a knowledge of rhetoric he would withhold from most of his students—that

> *business arithmetic is superior to plane or solid geometry; learning ways of keeping physically fit, to the study of French; learning the technique of selecting an occupation, to the study of algebra; simple science of everyday life, to geology; simple business English, to Elizabethan classics.*[60]

Echoing Prosser, a new version of *Cardinal Principles* called *Education for All American Youth* (1944) stated that "there is no aristocracy of subjects. . . . Mathematics and mechanics, art and agriculture, history and homemaking are all peers."[61] In practice, this leveling of educational hierarchies resulted in the suppression of traditional subject categories in favor of nontraditional, nonacademic ones like home economics, consumer practices, and personal adjustment. Emerson's playful claim that practical know-how should be elevated above school learning was now becoming well established as the primary aim of school itself. By the 1940s, according to Diane Ravitch, these utilitarian ideas and practices had become widespread in public schools:

> *Their common features were: centering the curriculum around basic areas of human activity, instead of traditional subject matter; incorporating subject matter only insofar as it was useful in everyday situations; stressing functional values such as behavior, attitudes, skills, and know-how, rather than bookish or abstract knowledge; reorienting studies to the immediate needs and interests of students.*[62]

These anti-intellectual traditions have not proved viable or useful in the contemporary world. Today, it is no longer possible to assert that learning algebra is inferior to learning how to select an occupation. With the nature of jobs shifting every few years, it has become obvious that algebra is in fact the more practical study. A recent popular movie, *Stand and Deliver* (1987), was premised on the idea that learning mathematics is the road out of the barrio. With jobs having become highly changeable, no one knows how to teach for specific occupations. In the present, ever-shifting economic scene, the student needs the ability to learn *new* occupations. Hence, a general ability to learn, based on broad general knowledge and vocabulary, is a more practical tool than direct vocational training.

Under these circumstances, the Romantic attack on the "merely" verbal has had fateful consequences for modern American education. Emerson complained that school provides only "a bellyfull of words," and praised the farmer for being "a realist and not a dictionary." But celebrating what is "real" above what is "verbal" has almost no practical relevance to modern education. The prejudice against the verbal is itself a cultural and verbal tradition that has no firm connection to reality. Every decent job available in a modern economy is dependent upon communication and learning—two activities that take place primarily through the medium of words.

Words stand for things. Verbal understanding is not "merely" verbal. Words are the indispensable human tools for understanding realities. One of the fundamental aims of an adequate education is to gain a large vocabulary—to become what Emerson disparagingly calls "a dictionary." This is not the only important aim, of course. Understanding the best traditions of one's culture, learning the fundamentals of many fields of knowledge, acquiring habits of private virtue and public-spiritedness, are certainly of equal or greater importance. But, especially today, an educated person is enabled by knowing words to learn a variety of new skills and new jobs. Gaining a broad knowledge of words, and therefore also a knowledge of the things to which words refer, must be among the most practical and significant educational goals in our time.

We don't think of a child's learning of words as "rote memorization." The remarkable learning rate of eight new words a day is far from being a merely receptive activity. As psychologists have shown, learning words requires complex trial-and-error guesses. Young children constantly try to make sense of what they hear on the basis of a bare minimum of relevant background knowledge. Recently in my hearing, an adult said to a five-year-old, "How is Your Highness this morning?" There was a pause of some seconds. The child replied, "I'm a *little* taller; I grow some every night—in my sleep." This child had managed to make some sense out of "Your Highness," even if it wasn't the sense that was meant—by dint of the hypothesis-making that goes on in even the simplest communication. But sometimes when a child does not know enough context, he or she cannot at that moment be an active participant in the class, no matter how resourceful the child or teacher may be. When classes are exceptionally heterogeneous in academic preparation and knowledge of words, as they often are in the United States, universally effective whole-class instruction is impossible. Sometimes, therefore, as Isabel Beck has shown, disadvantaged children can only catch up in their vocabulary by a direct targeting of the words that need to be learned.[63]

But whether a word is learned by targeted practice or by the contextual method of enriched language use, its actual meaning is, for the most part, just a brute fact. In a sense, all words are learned by rote. There is rarely a comprehensible connection between a word and a thing, only a cultural connection that has to be memorized, not "understood." What's to understand when a child learns that the name "bee" identifies a certain kind of flying thing? We Americans understand the words "chair" or "table" by rote, just as the Germans have to learn *Stuhl* and *Tisch,* the French *chaise* and *table*—all by rote. Such an apparently mindless daily performance as making first graders recite the (to them) meaningless sounds of the Pledge of Allegiance encourages trial-and-error inferences that result in many children understanding the meaning of the Pledge by fifth grade.

Pestalozzi, like other Romantics, was an enemy of what he called "verbalism," but he was also a pragmatist who followed a mixture of methods rather than an ideologue who dismissed drill and practice. He conceded the great power of verbal rote memorization as a means of gaining understanding and critical thought:

*[The children] accomplished feats which seemed to me impossible for their years. . . . I taught them to read whole charts of geography printed with the most difficult abbreviations, some of the most unfamiliar words being indicated by only a few letters, at an age when they could hardly read print. You have seen the unwavering accuracy with which they deciphered these charts, and the evident ease with which they learned them by rote. I even attempted at times to make some of the older children master very difficult scientific propositions which they did not understand. They committed the sentences to memory by reading aloud and by repetition. So also with the questions that explained them. It was at first, like all catechizing, merely a parrot-like reproduction of meaningless words. But the sharp separation of individual ideas, the definite order in this separation, together with the fact that the words themselves impressed light and meaning, in the midst of the darkness, indelibly upon their minds, gradually awakened insight into the subject matter, and transformed the darkness into the clear light of day.*[64]

One need not go as far as Pestalozzi did in following such practices, of course. But one reason that the early Romantic innovations in education— from Pestalozzi to Colonel Parker's school in Quincy, Massachusetts, or Dewey's Lab School in Chicago—were so successful was that these early versions of progressivism retained definite knowledge goals and *mixed* traditional with untraditional practices. Pestalozzi was wiser and more flexible than most of his disciples in advocating what he called a "systematic treatment of vocabulary":

*An extensive vocabulary is an inestimable advantage to children. Familiarity with the name enables them to fix the object whenever it enters their consciousness, and a logical and correct series of names develops and maintains in them a consciousness of the vital relation of things to each other. Nor is this all. We should never imagine, because a child does not understand everything about an object, that what he knows is useless to him. When a child has systematically mastered a scientific vocabulary, at any rate, he enjoys the same advantage as the child of a merchant who in his earliest years, and in his own home, learns the names of innumerable objects of commerce.*[65]

Like many educational reformers, Pestalozzi was interested in social justice, and thought that children of peasants could gain the same knowledge as children of merchants if that knowledge was taught intensively and systematically. In the comment quoted above, Pestalozzi implies one of the fundamental arguments being made in this book, that in order to enhance the knowledge of those who come from underprivileged homes, it is necessary to teach all students in a focused and direct way the knowledge which the children of privilege gain indirectly by constant exposure and repetition at home. The unfairness of an antibookish or developmentalist approach to schooling lies in its assumption that knowledge can be equally withheld from the children of merchants and the children of peasants to achieve the same results. Much to the distress of some of his fellow Romantics, who occasionally criticized his methods, Pestalozzi was flexible enough to use common sense in the service of social justice.

Dare it be said? In the tradition of Emerson, for all his greatness, there is a lot of foolishness. How could he be blind to the fact that if children did not gain "a bellyfull of words" in school, they would never be able to understand the words he was writing down? Emerson was the elitist, Horace Mann the true democrat. Romantic anti-intellectualism and developmentalism, as Gramsci understood, are luxuries of the merchant class that the poor cannot afford. For that matter, neither can the contemporary middle class in the United States. Today, the Enlightenment view of the value of knowledge is the only view we can afford. When the eighteenth-century Encyclopedists attempted to systematize human knowledge in a set of books, they were placing their hope for progress in the ever-growing experience of humankind, as made available by the invention of writing. They thought it foolish for each person to attempt to reinvent the wheel. Instead of finding a conflict between book learning and utility, they insisted upon the superior practicality of books over unlettered experience, and the greater utility of knowledge over ignorance.

There were implicit ironies in the anti-intellectualism of the American educational community as it moved from "home economics" and "shop" in the 1920s to "critical thinking" and "problem-solving skills" in the 1990s. Earlier, the proponents of traditional, subject-matter education had claimed that the study of Latin, classical literature, and mathematics had not only direct benefits but also indirect ones in inculcating general "mental discipline." Hard subjects, it was said, "trained the mind." Traditional study supposedly taught the student both Latin and critical thinking. But in the early years of this century, educationist opponents of Latin and other traditional subjects, using the research of Edward Lee Thorndike as a battering ram, rejected mental discipline as scientifically disproved. Thorndike had shown that skills are *not* transferred from one domain to another. Learning Latin did *not* "teach you to think," it just taught you Latin.

Today, anti-subject-matter educationists profess faith in general, "critical-thinking" skills much as traditionalists did, but with just as little scientific justification. Although "critical thinking" has replaced the vocationalism of earlier decades as an aim that is superior to mere book learning, the same anti-intellectual, anti-subject-matter, and supposedly anti-elitist bias lies at its root. It was assumed that teaching all children "practical know-how" would have a socially leveling effect; that children from all sorts of families and with all sorts of abilities would meet on the common ground of citizenship; that unac-ademic, practical schooling would be highly democratic in its teachings and effects. But what in fact occurred and still occurs is a widening of the academic and economic gap between haves and have-nots. Teaching "practical," an-tibookish skills such as critical thinking has turned out to be highly impractical and inequitable.

The absurd notion that inner-city children lack critical-thinking skills whereas suburban children, who happen to have big vocabularies, possess them is an assumption that cannot stand up to scrutiny. Street-smart children can think very critically in situations that would stump their suburban peers. If their critical-thinking skills *could* be massively transferred from the street to the classroom, special training in this area would be quite unnecessary. The incapacity of the critical-thinking movement to make a dent in the academic gap between haves and have-nots is strong evidence that this version of anti-intellectualism lacks a basis in reality. Edward Thorndike, whose work repudi-ated the idea that skills can be massively transferred from one domain to another, was, sixty years ago, the chief scientific authority for anti-intellectual-ism. Now the heirs of his early disciples have forgotten his basic premise. An emphasis on general mind-training skills at the expense of book learning has resulted, as developmentalism has, in depriving disadvantaged children of needed knowledge. As Gramsci prophesied, all versions of anti-intellectualism in education have highly inequitable and undemocratic practical conse-quences.

7.
## Professional Separatism

W hile most teachers are educated in nonresearch institutions, the guiding ideas and attitudes at teacher-training schools throughout the nation have originated in the education schools of research universities. Both critics and defenders of education schools agree that professors of education in these institutions are held in low esteem as a group by their colleagues. Even their defenders, like Geraldine J. Clifford and James W. Guthrie, authors of *Ed School: A Brief for Professional Education,* speak of "their multifaceted and chronic status deprivation."[66] Derek Bok, as president of Harvard, campaigned to raise the prestige of education schools, but found that renewed interest in school reform "had failed to raise the campus status of schools of education in research universities."[67] One purpose of the following section will be to trace some of the causes and effects of this sociological deprivation, which, because of its fateful consequences, is as much to be deplored by outsiders as by educationists themselves.

"The widest street in the world" is one witty description of the street that separates the campus of Teachers College from the rest of Columbia University. The current sentiment at research universities that professors of education are "lesser breeds without the law" is one that has been expressed since the beginning of the century. In 1916, Abraham Flexner wrote that education schools had "lost their heads" when they called for the removal of important knowledge as well as trivia from the school curriculum. He complained of their unwarranted devotion to technique, as well as of the "absurdities and trivialities" of their course offerings and dissertation topics.[68] In 1929, Irving Babbitt of Harvard observed that professors of pedagogy "are held in almost universal suspicion in academic circles, and are not infrequently looked upon by their colleagues as downright charlatans." Not long thereafter, in 1933, the retiring president of Harvard, Lawrence Lowell, told the Board of Overseers that Harvard's school of education was "a kitten that ought to be drowned." During the downsizing of more recent decades, education schools continue to be among the first place universities look for belt-tightening, and in some places, notably Johns Hopkins, Yale, and Duke, such schools have disappeared.[69]

But the plight of education schools in the universities is counterbalanced by their enormous importance in the sphere of teacher certification and by their huge ideological influence in the nation's schools. It is never a healthy circumstance when people who are held in low esteem exercise dominant influence in an important sphere. The conjunction of power with resentment is deadly. The educational community's identification of knowledge with "elitism"—a theme that long antedated the recent addition of "Eurocentrism" to the antiknowledge armory—is a strategy born more of hostility than of rational principle. Professors of education, surrounded in the university by prestigious colleagues whose strong suit is thought to be knowledge, have translated resentment against this elite cadre into resentment against the knowledge from which it draws its prestige. This displaced antagonism has expressed itself rhetorically as populist antielitism, which, added to endemic anti-intellectualism, further derogates traditional book learning.

Years ago, on the frontier, education schools were the dominant institutions in their localities, a good example being the teacher-training institute that later became UCLA. These early "normal schools," or teacher-training colleges, were instituted by the states or local communities to ensure that schools were staffed by people with qualifications to teach in them. Having no local rivals, these normal schools were oriented mainly to subject matter, on the assumption that competency in teaching depended primarily on mastery of the material to be taught and secondarily on the best methods for teaching it. Since these mission-oriented institutions were entirely devoted to teacher training, there was little invidious rivalry between departments.

Subsequent discontent was germinated not in the normal schools themselves but in the rivalry between normal schools and the developing universities. The Los Angeles State Normal School had been founded in 1882 to train elementary-school teachers.[70] Until the 1920s, it remained a two-year certificate-granting (rather than a four-year B.A.-granting) institution. By then, however, Los Angeles had grown to be the fifth largest city in the United States; the Normal School had grown accordingly and was eager to gain the status of a B.A.-granting institution, to transform itself into a more prestigious knowledge-oriented university like Berkeley. In due course, it became a four-year university, and in 1927 its name was changed from the Los Angeles State Normal School to the University of California at Los Angeles.

The nation's gain was a serious loss to the prestige of the teacher-training unit that had been the raison d'être of the original institution. With its change in title, the new university came under the charge of the central administration at Berkeley, some members of which felt that the mere training of teachers was not an activity appropriate for a true university. At UCLA, there also arose uncertainty within the teacher-training unit about whether it should remain an integral part of the institution.[71] Thus did the child (the new university, UCLA) spit upon its parent (the Normal School). And thus did the parent, having formed its progeny for its own glorification, slink away in wounded isolation, consoling itself with the nobility of its vocation, and attempting to give itself compensatory academic standing by high-sounding process terms borrowed from Columbia University's Teachers College and other education schools that had experienced a similar history.

As with many another episode in intellectual history, this one is marked by paradox. The search for professional identity and status by finding subject matters unique to education did not prove very successful. As James Koerner has observed, "Whatever disciplines the school of education might incorporate in educational studies were already the province of other academics. This left them only pedagogy as a unique possession."[72] Thus the search for identity and status led to an emphasis on process, which entailed a reduction of both intellectual content and intellectual interaction with the rest of the university. Whence the paradox: the decline in intellectual substance, which was instituted to create a special, separate discipline, thereby defeated the very goals being aimed at—institutional prestige and an imposing institutional identity.[73]

Horace Mann recognized as early as 1839 that teacher-training institutions were inevitably exposed to such tensions and temptations, because professors tended to be more interested in their subjects and their prestige than in their social missions. He wanted no part of Harvard and its distractions from the purposes at hand. "The business of the normal school," he said, "is to possess the whole ground; to engross the whole attention of all the instructors and all the pupils; to have no rival of any kind, no incidental or collateral purposes, and the very existence of the school will be staked on its success."[74] In the 1890s, John Dewey took a different approach, with the same end in view. He persuaded the president of the University of Chicago to form a separate department of pedagogy, with himself as chairman. (He was already chairman of the philosophy department.) The idea was *not* to subordinate pedagogy to philosophy, but vice versa, to put knowledge in the service of the mission-oriented enterprise of education. In a notable letter to his wife, he wrote in 1894: "I sometimes think I will drop teaching philosophy directly, and teach it via *pedagogy*."[75]

Two features are especially notable about these early ideals of Mann and Dewey. First, they had not the slightest doubt about priorities. The pragmatic was primary; theory and scholarship in education departments were valuable only as they contributed to educational improvement and to the democratic ideals that education was to serve. *Every* child in a democracy, Dewey argued, must have "training in science, in art, in history; command of the fundamental methods of inquiry and the fundamental tools of intercourse and communication . . . habits of industry, perseverance, and, above all, habits of serviceableness."[76] Everything in teacher training must be directed to those very concrete goals of knowledge and moral habit. Second, the dominance of the practical over the theoretical having been established, there was to be no internecine warfare between theory and practice, knowledge and method. The principle of accommodation between pedagogy and subject-matter disciplines was self-evident and assumed. It was simply unthinkable that there could be rivalrous antagonism between a teacher of teachers and a scholar of history or a scientist. The knowledge to be taught was to be the best, the truest knowledge currently available from scholars in the field.

With expansion of the need for ever more teacher-training colleges, those ideals changed. What Matthew Arnold observed about the necessary conditions for creating literary works holds true for creating intellectual movements. "Two powers," Arnold said, "must concur, the power of the man and the power of the moment." By the 1920s, with the decline of earlier ideals of service, historical conditions had determined that the moment had arrived for the educational community to assert itself socially and intellectually. Eighty-eight state normal schools had become teachers colleges between 1910 and 1930.[77] The growth of these college-level schools and departments of education required a large increase in the numbers of professors of education, which, in turn, intensified the demand for a distinct intellectual system for that professoriat—new journals, new professional associations, and, above all, distinctive principles of thought. To fill that demand, it was reasonable to look toward the mother of American teacher-training institutions: Teachers College in New York City, founded in 1889 and incorporated into Columbia University in 1898—the institution that trained more professors of education than any other in the fateful period between 1910 and 1930.

Although John Dewey, who happened to move to Columbia in 1904 after a dispute with the president of the University of Chicago, is often credited with formulating the ideas that came to dominate the modern American educational community, historians have shown that Dewey's name was given to a rather distorted version of his ideas by the direct leader of the new movement, William Heard Kilpatrick.[78] The few education students who actually heard Dewey did not readily understand him, whereas Kilpatrick's lectures attracted six hundred students at a time, standing room only. Kilpatrick is said to have trained some thirty-five thousand students during his career at Teachers College, at just the period when the new schools and colleges of education were beginning to be staffed. His professorial disciples subsequently perpetuated his ideas by training still more and more professors of education throughout the nation. This lineage helps explain the relative uniformity of current American educational doctrine.

Kilpatrick was a vessel for ideas that his acolytes were hungry to hear—ideas that gave the new profession a status, a mission, and a distinctive identity. I mention his name frequently in this book because although he was not the only important figure to develop the current ideas of the American educational community, he was the charismatic codifier of them. His article "Project Method," of 1918, which recommended project activities rather than traditional subject-matter education, was among the most influential documents in the history of American education. A good many of the principles still animating the current educational scene are to be found in Kilpatrick's enormously influential book, *Foundations of Method* (1925). It is in that book and in his articles and lectures, rather than in Dewey's diversified and difficult writings, where one needs to look to find the direct origins of the educational ideas traced in this chapter.

Starting with its title, which placed an emphasis on method, one can find most of the major themes of present-day pedagogical "reform" in Kilpatrick's book: the identification of correct pedagogy with liberal, democratic American ideals; the dubious claim that it was basing itself on the most advanced scientific research; the insistence upon the individuality of the child and the autonomy of the teacher; the disparagement of mere subject matter and of other nations' educational methods; the admonition to teach children rather than subjects; the claim that knowledge is changing so fast that no specific subject matter should be required in the curriculum; the attack on rote learning; the attack on tests and even report cards; the claim that following the project method would develop critical-thinking skills. Kilpatrick's book even celebrated the whole-language over the phonics approach to reading instruction. Above all, what won general acceptance in the educational community was the idea that a new method free from the trammels of traditional knowledge could encompass the whole sphere of education by merging subject matter into the process of pedagogy. It was this process-over-all concept that helped give the newly emerging professoriat its claim to an independent and separate existence.

When Kilpatrick was given a chance to design his own experimental class, the first thing he did was replace screwed-down desks with movable tables and chairs. Then, "for this class he laid down one principle: He wanted children to engage in 'activity leading to further activity without badness.' "[79]

*At first those in charge of the school were taken aback when I proposed that the class have absolutely no set curriculum; that the teacher was to be perfectly free to do what she thought wise; that the children were to be free to think and to act. The children were not to be required to learn reading, to master prescribed arithmetic or spelling: there were to be no examinations. They were not to be marked or graded in terms of a prescribed curriculum. I laid down only one principle: "activity leading to further activity without badness."[80]*

Despite its influence and resounding title, *Foundations of Method* is remarkably disappointing as an intellectual performance. It is cast in the form of a conversation, but the only ideas developed with any semblance of sustained argument and evidence are the opening ones concerning abstract "laws of thought," and scientific-sounding terms like "neurones," "synapses," "mental set," "stimulus-response," and so on. Whatever the enduring soundness of these highly generalized psychological principles, their connection to a specific pedagogical method of the sort Kilpatrick advocates is not, and cannot be, effectively argued. Kilpatrick does not seem to notice that the very generality of such principles can be used to justify *any* effective pedagogical method, since every pedagogy which works must by that very fact apply laws of thought which are by definition universal. This is a logical difficulty that continues to plague, or ought to plague, the new scientistic proponents of psychological "constructivism." In the end, it is concrete results by which pedagogical methods are to be judged. For all Kilpatrick's stress on the individuality of the student and the autonomy of the teacher, one misses in his exposition any appreciation of the subtle ways in which general psychological laws need to be mediated in hugely diverse ways by the diverse cultures of particular classrooms and teachers.

What guaranteed Kilpatrick's success as a prophet was his self-aware tone as the leader of a new institutional dispensation. Science and American democracy together required a new mode of teaching and thinking—one which had been revealed by Dewey and Thorndike to insiders who were specialists in the new method, but which remained unknown to outsiders and hidebound traditionalists. This pugnacious tone of scientific certitude, combined with a message of professional identity (which the members of the newly forming profession very much wanted to hear), carried all before it.

In his institutional influence, then, Kilpatrick stood for militant separatism—the separation of education from other disciplines, the separation of subject matter from pedagogy, and the separation of forward-thinking social thinkers from reactionary (implicitly antidemocratic) traditionalists. Teachers of pedagogy, once despised, could now claim a superiority of understanding, based on the most advanced insights into scientific psychology (Thorndike) and on morally superior social principles (Dewey). The new professorial army had the strength of ten because its principles were the best ones—socially, scientifically, and philosophically. The aggressive tone of the prophecy was well suited to its historical function of developing an identity for the profession, and this tone of self-righteous militancy is still evident today. Historically, it may have been almost inevitable for such an uncompromising separatism to emerge victorious as the dominant attitude of the new profession. Any more conciliatory approach might jeopardize its professional distinctiveness and prestige.

But in historical perspective this militancy was a new departure for educational thinking in the United States. The noble ideals under which Teachers College was founded were continuations of the communitarian spirit of Horace Mann and, indirectly, of Jefferson. The training of teachers was to be integral to the promise of American democracy, and a perpetuation of its best principles. Kilpatrick certainly shared these broad social goals in the abstract, but he did so in a highly unaccommodating spirit in which the very idea of transmitting the best in the American tradition was made to seem old-fashioned and outmoded. Kilpatrick explicitly rejected the ideal of education as transmission and social perpetuation. Such an aim he associated with older, "static" civilizations. By contrast, modern America represented a "dynamic" civilization in which children were not to be slaves of the past, but made into independent thinkers who, unburdened by earlier customs and prejudices, would stand ready to face the future.[81]

This was a far more individualized and rootless view of education than Dewey, whom Kilpatrick continually invoked, had proposed. Dewey was not a separatist either in pedagogy or with respect to past tradition. Indeed, the opening pages of *Democracy and Education* identifies the foundational aim of education as the

> *renewing of the social group. . . . Education in its broadest sense is the means of this social continuity of life. . . . Beings who are born not only unaware of but quite indifferent to the aims and habits of the group have to be rendered cognizant of them and actively interested. Education and education alone spans the gap. . . . Unless pains are taken to see that genuine and thorough transmission takes place, the most civilized group will relapse into barbarism and then into savagery.*[82]

"Though Dewey rarely named names in his criticisms of progressive reform," writes Robert Westbrook in his distinguished biography of Dewey,

> *one of his principal targets was William H. Kilpatrick, his colleague at Columbia University, whose "project method" was perhaps the single*

*most influential practical curricular reform to emerge from child-centered progressivism. The* Teachers College Record *distributed some sixty thousand reprints of the 1918 article in which Kilpatrick first described the project method, and by the twenties Kilpatrick was the dominant figure at the leading school of education in the country. . . . Kilpatrick thought of himself as Dewey's disciple. . . . But [Dewey] insisted that projects must have as one of their goals the child's mastery of organized subjects. . . . [M]uch of what critics then (and now) attacked as aimless, contentless "Deweyism" was in fact aimless, contentless "Kilpatrickism."*[83]

Dewey, and indeed all the profoundest thinkers in the American educational tradition, have been integrationists, not separatists. First, they have been integrationists with respect to the past, acknowledging the centrality of transmission and continuity in education. Second, they have been integrationists with respect to fields of knowledge, never advocating the idea that training the mind by a vague, future-oriented method directed to "critical thinking" can replace either subject-matter knowledge or the common learnings that constitute the life of the community.

In this light, the true continuer of what was best and deepest in the Horace Mann tradition was not Kilpatrick but his less influential colleague at Teachers College, William Bagley. That Kilpatrick rather than Bagley won the minds and hearts of future education professors was a grave misfortune for the nation. Besides strongly opposing the newly fashionable disparagement of subject matter, Bagley passionately identified the need for the schools in a democracy to share a community of knowledge:

*A most important function of formal education, especially in a democracy, is to insure as high a level of common culture as possible—meanings, understandings, standards, and aspirations common to a large proportion of the democratic group, to the end that the collective thinking and the collective decisions of the group may be done and made on the highest possible plane. This obviously calls for a goodly measure of common elements in the school programs throughout the country.*[84]

The failure of Bagley's accommodating, communitarian vision to win over his colleagues was mainly owing to its integrationism and lack of professional distinctiveness. So confident was Kilpatrick of his prophetic mission that when Bagley died in 1946, he wrote in his diary: "He has long been a hurtful reactionary, the most respectable [and] vocal of all. . . . His going marks the end of an era. No one who professes to know education will henceforth stand forth in opposition as he did." Unfortunately, the prophecy was accurate. Bagley's work was defeated by the new professional context in which it had appeared. Being right was not enough; his writings simply did not obey the institutional imperative to form a distinctive and identifiable pedagogical discipline. Instead of an autonomous, process-oriented expertise and a jargon vocabulary that made guild specialists of educators (in the way Kilpatrick's proposals did), Bagley offered his colleagues a more complex vision that entailed a life of learning and service to the community, of cooperation with other domains of study. It was a profounder and more practical vision, and in the end it would have been much more conducive to the prestige of the educational profession itself.

For, in the end, it has been the fundamental unsoundness of the Kilpatrick approach that has generated the suspicion—often mixed with contempt—with which education professors and experts are often regarded by their colleagues and, increasingly, by the general public. The history of educational ideas in the United States offers a good illustration of the way in which collective professional and institutional motivations are all too often opposed to the best understandings and instincts of the individual members of a profession. It illustrates Reinhold Niebuhr's profoundly observed contrast between highly moral individuals and immoral social groups. The group can be a great beast that pulls individuals in the wrong direction against their own best sentiments. For, outside of their professional context, few educators privately retain the hostility to knowledge and community that their profession has taught them to enunciate.

That ideals of accommodation and integration still remain viable for mission-oriented enterprises is demonstrated by professional training schools that are in a healthy state, such as those for engineering, law, and medicine— prestigious fields with which departments of education like to compare themselves. But, unlike education schools, the ones just mentioned have in common a collegial and cooperative relationship with the subject-matter disciplines to which they are related. They constantly engage in joint programs of instruction and in informal study groups. Law nowadays is in constant interchange with philosophy, economics, sociology, and even literature; medicine, with philosophy, sociology, biology, and chemistry. Engineering schools are necessarily in constant touch with basic science departments. In many universities, these professional schools thrive on the intellectual ferment of cross-fertilization and joint appointments between departments.

Contrast that condition of cooperation with the glum and resentful isolation of education schools. The idea of joint appointments with other departments is looked upon as a threat that must be resisted with all vigor. The move is interpreted in entirely sociological terms as a threat to autonomy and self-esteem, and as a matter of academic politics, with no intellectual justification or interest:

> *In recent years deans have tried to stretch the mantle of prestige and legitimacy from a high-status department over a school of education by the sharing of a faculty member. . . . Education is alleged to be a rather hollow intellectual vessel which can be filled only by injecting knowledge generated in "real" disciplines. . . . That joint appointments are problematic is clear to any awake academic. If the faculty member is recruited to the joint position from a doctoral program in the cognate field, he or she has likely been well socialized to the academic and status norms of the particular discipline. . . . Education thus finds itself having its low status confirmed while being deprived of a partial faculty position.[85]*

That such beleaguered attitudes are unhealthy and unpromising both for the nation and for education schools themselves is self-evident to an outsider. The idea that subject-matter disciplines are governed by "academic and status norms" rather than by advancing knowledge is a view that healthy professional schools like law and medicine simply do not accept. They believe that advances in their own missions depend on advances in knowledge in related fields. On the whole, this belief has proved itself to be justified. The contrary idea in education schools that, for example, educational psychology is separate from and independent of the general field of psychology is dangerous nonsense which holds back the progress of the educational mission itself.

The obvious antidote to such emotion-ridden, resentment-bound ideas is to elevate the prestige of education schools and educational experts, as Derek Bok recommended. To work such a change, however, it will be necessary to improve not only the public perceptions that have led to low prestige but also the realities behind those perceptions. The task cannot be accomplished by public relations alone. The urgency of the task can be stated bluntly. There is no possibility of adequate improvement in the quality of schooling so long as these influential experts continue to hold both their current ideas and their influential positions as trainers of teachers and administrators. Since there is no chance of dismissing en masse the professors and bureaucrats who control the destiny of our schools, our best hope lies in changing their separatist and antiknowledge ideas.

The integrationist tradition represented by Dewey, Bagley, and others was the finest and soundest tradition of pedagogical thinking in the United States. The best hope for creating a first-rate educational system is to ground it in ideas from the most reliable sources, namely the subject-matter disciplines. The practical superiority of integrationism over separatism in education is due mainly to its inherent intellectual superiority. Its ideas, which emerged from the rough-and-tumble of free exchange and scientific criticism, are not only more likely to be the truest ideas but are more likely than defective ones to work.

I have traced the origins of those defective ideas back to American exceptionalism and European Romanticism, and to the professional and institutional imperatives that caused them to drive out better ideas from the education schools. In understanding the main outlines of that story, one may glimpse the possibility of other and better intellectual and institutional arrangements. No constructive purpose is served by criticizing our already beset educational experts unless we can offer some hope of education schools becoming more effective and prestigious places. The outline of that better picture can be discerned in the high ideals with which those schools began, and in the wisdom of earlier scholars like William C. Bagley, who resisted the Romantic, antiknowledge ideas that became dominant within their walls. These forgotten heroes are historical proof that to be a professor of education is not automatically to be a professor of process.

# 8.
## Summary

From the foregoing sketch, the reader should be familiar with the main sources of the antiknowledge ideas that have plagued our educational system and our recent, unsuccessful attempts to reform it. From the powerful historical and social forces that I've called American exceptionalism, Romanticism, and professional separatism, and from their subcategories, have arisen almost all the misleading ideas of the Thoughtworld.

It was not inevitable, however, that the inadequate ideas of the educational community should have taken the particular form they did. Certain slogans undoubtedly came into existence by historical accident. For instance, the fatuous claim that knowledge is changing so fast that specific subject matter need not be a critical component of education seems to have been invented by Kilpatrick in the 1920s. While his slogan was not a necessary inference from either Romanticism or professional separatism, it coincided with the impulses of both. It fit educational Romanticism by emphasizing individual growth above conventional knowledge, and it fit separatism by derogating the subject-matter knowledge to which other, noneducational experts had a more credible claim. It even fit American exceptionalism by contrasting merely factual, slavish European education with independent-minded, critical-thinking American education, appropriate for a free people. It was thus a professionally useful slogan. Yet if Kilpatrick had not invented that particular slogan, it might not have gained any more currency in the United States than it did elsewhere in the world.

If we judge ideas by their consequences, it is reasonable to conclude that the three leading intellectual impulses of the Thoughtworld have been as wrong as they have been deleterious. The psychological and ethical assumptions of Romanticism have not worked out the way their originators had hoped and predicted. Romanticism may have created some of the greatest poetry in our language, but its theories of education have been wrong theories. American exceptionalism does have some basis in reality in that our democratic political traditions and our habits of intellectual independence are special in world history; but exceptionalism can become mere complacency that evades the challenge of learning from the experiences of other peoples. Professionalism in the noblest sense denotes both heightened pride in one's work and a heightened sense of responsibility; but extreme professionalism becomes narrow and separatist. It results in a sense of group grievance and in a self-protective mentality that evades responsibility.

In short, educationist ideas have been carried too far. The self-aggrandizing Thoughtworld that established itself in the teens and twenties of this century was too much concerned with its status and self-identity, and too little concerned with the high democratic ideals of service and practicality that originally held sway over the education profession in the United States. The tradition of Horace Mann got submerged in the tradition of William Heard Kilpatrick. Idealistic practicality gave way to a militant separatism that expanded its half-truths to cover the whole educational landscape. Any idea carried too far loses the element of truth it once possessed. Now, after six decades of antiknowledge extremism, it is unclear whether the public needs to oppose this defective tradition with a countervailing extremism that repudiates process in favor of knowledge, or whether it might be possible to reintroduce a tradition of accommodation whose hallmarks are skepticism, openness, and practicality. The second approach would be preferable, but either approach would result in an education system far better than the one we now have.

# 5.

# Reality's Revenge:
# Education and
# Mainstream Research

## 1.
### The Virtues of Mainstream Research

I have already suggested that the uses made by the educational community of scientific-sounding terms like "developmentally appropriate" are not really sanctioned by scientific research. The first part of this chapter will explore how the educational community invokes research very selectively to preserve the intellectual status quo of the Thoughtworld. Then, the chapter will turn to some aspects of mainstream research that can provide reliable guidance to educational improvement.

Reliable guidance depends on reliable research. A lot of technical issues in education have been prematurely transformed into material for ideological warfare, the most notable example being the ongoing battle over phonics vs. whole-language teaching in elementary reading instruction. Many combatants in this and other educational disputes assume cynically, and often correctly, that research is being cited as a rhetorical weapon to sustain a sectarian position. This is a deplorable development. Ideology and research should be disentangled as much as humanly possible. Research findings that are accurate and reliable must transcend partisanship, and must be seen to do so. When research is cited with misleading selectivity, or when it is second-rate and unreliable, it ceases, after a time, to be useful even as rhetoric.

My discussion of educational research in this chapter will trek through a certain amount of technical detail. The trip is worth taking because of the practical benefits that solid, mainstream research can yield. High-quality, refereed research summarizes the most reliable accumulated educational experience available to us. Its intelligent applications usually work much better in the classroom than mere hunches, because the conclusions of good, replicated research are far more often right than wrong. Good research represents the reality principle in education.

But, since much educational research is concentrated in such "soft" subjects as history, sociology, and psychology, it necessarily contains unknown factors, uncontrolled variables, and ineradicable uncertainties. There *is* consensus on certain important matters, however, and in this chapter I shall be focusing on the most widely agreed-upon and disinterested conclusions.

By "disinterested" I refer to a cast of mind, not to a lack of concern. Because educational research is applied research, the topics studied will have been generated by direct, practical goals, but a good researcher's preferences will not have predetermined the results. In good medical research, too, practical aims decide what questions get asked and what money gets allocated, but the answers and the results of this applied research are dictated by the realities, not by preferences.

The questions we ask of educational research sometimes reflect conflicted aims, such as: How can we educate everyone to a fairly high competence without holding back our ablest and most motivated students? Research can describe and quantify the trade-offs involved in such questions, but it cannot evaluate how to act upon them. Such evaluation is a matter of policy, and in a democracy, educational policy should be decided openly and with the most accurate knowledge available. Research is the servant of policy, not its master.

But in another sense, good research *is* a kind of master, exhibiting a certain finality. Although it cannot decide policy, it can at least connect us with reality. A subthesis of this book is that our failures in precollegiate education have been caused by the lack of fit between our dominant theories and the realities they have claimed to represent. Our educational failures reflect reality's revenge over inadequate ideas. The history of American education since the 1930s has been the stubborn persistence of illusion in the face of reality. Illusion has not been defeated. But since reality cannot be defeated either, and since it determines what actually happens in the world, the result has been educational decline.

## 2.
## Selective Use of Research I: Constructivism

The goal of present-day educational reformers is to produce students with "higher-order skills" who are able to think independently about the unfamiliar problems they will encounter in the information age, who have become "problem solvers" and have "learned how to learn," and who are on their way to becoming "critical thinkers" and "lifelong learners." The method advocated for achieving these "higher-order skills" is "discovery learning," by which students solve problems and make decisions on their own through "inquiry" and "independent analysis" of "real-world" projects. What Kilpatrick in the 1920s called the "project method" is now called "discovery learning." The goals and methods are summarized in a 1993 textbook on teaching in elementary school. The purpose of the school is

> *to provide the means for the learner to develop the intellectual skills related to critical thinking and problem solving. If thinking is to be the central purpose of American education, as many believe it should be, then ways must be devised to help individuals develop that capability. Inquiry is intended to do this by focusing on the development of such mental processes as identifying and analyzing problems, stating hypotheses, collecting and classifying relevant data, testing hypotheses, and coming to conclusions. It seeks to develop independence. Children are encouraged to find things out for themselves by applying the scientific method of inquiry. Through inquiry, they should* learn how to learn. *Inquiry stresses discovering things for oneself.*[1]

This attractive picture is implicitly contrasted with traditional "factory-model" schools, which produce students who think as they are told to think and merely parrot back precooked ideas or rote-memorized facts without understanding them, and who are unable to cope with new situations and new knowledge.

This consensus among present-day reformers is well summarized by Zemelman, Daniels, and Hyde in their 1993 book, *Best Practice:*

> *In virtually every school subject, we now have recent summary reports, meta-analyses of instructional research, bulletins from pilot classrooms, and landmark sets of professional recommendations. Today there is a strong consensus definition of Best Practice, of state-of-the-art teaching in*

*every critical field. . . . Whether the recommendations come from the
National Council of Teachers of Mathematics, the Center for the Study of
Reading, the National Writing Project, the National Council for the Social
Studies, the American Association for the Advancement of Science, the
National Council of Teachers of English, the National Association for the
Education of Young Children, or the International Reading Association,
the fundamental insights into teaching and learning are remarkably con-
gruent. Indeed on many key issues, the recommendations from these di-
verse organizations are unanimous.*

Zemelman, Daniels, and Hyde then list twenty-five "LESS" and "MORE"
admonitions on which all these organizations agree. Among them are the following:

*LESS whole-class teacher-directed instruction*
*LESS student passivity, sitting, listening, receiving*
*LESS student time reading textbooks*
*LESS attempts by teachers to cover large amounts of material*
*LESS rote memorization of facts and details*
*LESS stress on competition and grades*
*LESS use of and reliance on standardized tests*

*MORE experiential, inductive, hands-on learning*
*MORE active learning with all the attendant noise of students doing,
     talking, collaborating*
*MORE deep study of a smaller number of topics*
*MORE responsibility transferred to students for their work: goal-setting,
     record-keeping, monitoring, evaluation*
*MORE choice for students; e.g., picking their own books, etc.*
*MORE attention to affective needs and varying cognitive styles of stu-
     dents*
*MORE cooperative, collaborative activity*
*MORE reliance on descriptive evaluations of student growth*

The authors praise the current consensus on these "child-centered" principles
for being "progressive, developmentally appropriate, research based, and eminently teachable."[2]

Alternatives to these "research-based" recommendations are dismissed
with the scornful remark that they don't "go along with what research is telling
us about how students learn." Such dismissals are conversation stoppers, be-

ing clothed in the authority of science. But the findings of research emphatically do not accord with the "reforms" currently being recommended by the educational community. In fact, many reformers have neglected mainstream research in favor of nonconsensus theories (like "multiple intelligences") that happen to support progressivist goals and methods. Later sections of this chapter will describe some actual findings of mainstream research. The purpose of this section and the next will be to arm readers with informed skepticism when they are told that some age-old, proven practice which appeals to common sense goes against "what research is telling us about how students learn."

Those characteristic words of dismissal were uttered by Mary Lindquist, president of the National Council of Teachers of Mathematics (NCTM), when she denounced some mathematics textbooks written by John Saxon.[3] Saxon is a maverick ex–Air Force pilot who in his earlier days flew fifty-five missions in Korea and subsequently taught electrical engineering at the Air Force Academy. In reaction against the progressivist methods that had failed to teach his students the fundamentals of math, he decided to mortgage his house and start a textbook publishing company to challenge the dominant discovery-learning trend. Saxon is definitely an independent-minded critical thinker—just the sort of person educational reformers say they are hoping to produce. But nonetheless, he and his books have been vigorously denounced by reformers in the math establishment—especially by the NCTM:

> *NCTM President Mary Lindquist accuses Saxon of "using techniques that have been used for years. There's no great revelation in what he's doing." She believes his books are "too prescriptive. There's no one right way to teach math," she says. "I can't imagine a curriculum working for every student in every situation." Saxon's program, she adds [the clincher], "certainly doesn't go along with what research is telling us about how students learn."*[4]

But in fact, Saxon's approach is reasonably close to what research *is* telling us about how students learn—much closer, as I shall show in Section 6 of this chapter, than are the progressive methods advocated by the NCTM.[5] Saxon's mainly commonsense techniques have been working well enough to persuade hundreds of schools to buck the math establishment and buy his books. He is now a multimillionaire, with book sales and market share increasing every year. He has shaken up not only members of the math establishment but also mainstream publishers who kowtow to it. While no independent evaluations of his program have been reported in the research literature (apparently nobody wants to undertake them), most teachers who use his books say that their children are far better at math than their predecessors were.[6] Saxon is a true American type—and a hopeful symbol that, in time, American pragmatism and independent thinking can make inroads against progressivist orthodoxy.

In mathematics, that orthodoxy recommends that instead of making students rote-learn the multiplication table and solve a lot of workbook problems, schools should encourage them to work on "real-life" problems and "shift toward mathematical reasoning—away from an emphasis on mechanistic answer finding."[7] While no sensible person would dissent from the goal of developing students' mathematical reasoning skills, he or she might very well question the claim that the failure of American grade schools to teach math competently stems from their use of traditional practices such as rote memorization of addition and subtraction facts. One of the complaints parents make is that their children are not mastering such facts. Is it possible that the ideas recommended by the NCTM are the very ideas that *already* pervade the schools they are supposed to transform?

Such a hypothesis is reinforced by the teaching methods that the NCTM and other reform groups advocate for achieving higher-order thinking skills. These "new" methods include attention to individual needs and learning styles, discovery learning, and thematic learning. But these teaching techniques are essentially the project-oriented, child-centered methods that have long dominated American educational thought and have prevailed for decades in our schools.

Loyalists to earlier times rightly complain of ingratitude to early progressivists such as Kilpatrick and Rugg when current reformers imply that they are advocating novel techniques based on the latest research. J. A. Beane, and M. W. Apple complain as follows:

> *How could our collective memory have failed so easily?* Thematic unit teaching *and* curriculum integration *have become buzz words in educational circles, but have we forgotten that both concepts have their roots in the problem-centered "core" approaches advocated by earlier social reconstructionists? Are "developmentally appropriate" practices a recent invention, or do they stretch back to the progressive child-centered schools created early in this century? When we speak of cooperative learning today, shall we simply ignore the cooperative group process work done in schools and communities as part of democratic movements since the 1920s? How can we seem puzzled by ways to connect schools to their communities when so many stories of significant service projects can be found in the professional literature of at least the past sixty years? . . .*

*Many of our most trusted and powerful ideas about schooling are the hard-won gains of long and courageous efforts to make our schools more democratic (see, for example, Rugg 1939). We are the beneficiaries of those efforts.*[8]

That these remarks happen to come from two advocates of the child-centered tradition doesn't compromise their historical accuracy. The authors rightly question the claim that the "new" reform ideas are fundamentally different from the progressivist pedagogy already in place, and they challenge the idea that the "buzz words" originate in pure, disinterested science. On the contrary, the child-centered, antifact goals and methods came first. Then the most convenient current theories were enlisted and adapted to support them.

Chief among these is a psychological theory called "constructivism." This theory holds that students are not passive vessels for receiving knowledge but active participants who construct knowledge for themselves. This theory is said to support "learner-centered" teaching, hands-on learning, discovery learning, and the rest. Constructivism is a psychological theory about memory and learning. In its broadest outlines and most cautious elaborations, the theory is widely accepted in mainstream psychology. As early as the 1930s, F. C. Bartlett, in a seminal book on memory, showed that human remembering is rarely a perfect retrieval of something stored in our minds but, rather, a reconstruction that in some details may be quite different from the original experience. Since schooling is based upon remembered learning, and since meaningful memory is not a purely passive record but an active construct, it follows that learning, too, is not passively received but actively constructed.

This basic insight of constructivism has been confirmed many times. Starting in the 1960s, a series of experiments showed that what we chiefly remember from reading or hearing speech is not the actual sequence of words but, rather, their gist. We don't simply retrieve the words verbatim, we partly reconstruct them, usually on the basis of the knowledge and expectations that we held before encountering them. Often, we cannot tell the difference between what was actually said and some version of what was said that we think means the same thing. This creative-constructive activity of memory characterizes all meaningful, connected learnings.

On the other hand, if we learn and repeat a nonmeaningful series of monosyllables like *puv, loa, rix,* we are not likely to retrieve something constructed and re-created. Thus, it is reasonable for educators to draw a rough distinction between meaningful, constructed learning and meaningless, rote-learned recall that is nonconstructed. Constructed learning is therefore on the whole a good thing—better for most educational purposes than pure photographic or phonographic recall. The psychological literature is replete with idiots savants who exhibit verbatim recall but lack comprehension. If we want our schools to produce competent persons, then constructed, meaningful learning is best.

But constructivism is not only desirable, it is also universal. It characterizes *all* meaningful learning no matter how derived. The nature of one's constructed understanding is normally irrelevant to the means by which one constructed it. Once a person has constructed the meaning of $5 + 2 = 7$, the procedure by which he or she gained that understanding becomes a matter of complete indifference. The confusion of a destination with the means used to get there is a logical confusion that has even been given a name: "the genetic fallacy." The leap from the general theory of constructivism to advocacy of the particular practice of discovery learning is overhasty and logically illegitimate. *Any* learning that involves the meaningful use of language is self-evidently constructed learning—unless one believes in thought transference or mental telepathy. The only way a student can understand what a teacher or anyone else is saying is through a complex, sometimes strenuous activity of constructing meaning from words. Hearing a lecture—in the event that one is understanding it—requires an active construction of meaning. Listening, like reading, is far from being a passive, purely receptive activity.

But the very universality of constructivism implies certain drawbacks for the practical application of the theory. Since most learning activity, including listening to a lecture, is constructivist, constructivism is an uncertain guide to teaching practice. Regardless of teaching method, the amount of constructive activity students engage in can vary for different students under the same classroom circumstances. Sometimes their construction is an active misconstruction, as when first graders pledge allegiance to the "Republic of Richard Stands." There is no necessary relation between the mode of instruction offered by the teacher and the amount of active meaning-construction engaged in by the student. In fact, as I shall show later on, the amount of *useful* construction and learning that occur depends chiefly on the amount of relevant background knowledge the student already possesses rather than on the mode of instruction.

It is true, on the other hand, that self-generated student-constructed learning (discovery learning) is sometimes better retained and more readily accessible than constructed learning that is teacher-induced. But if discovery learning is well retained, it also has drawbacks. It takes more time and is sometimes insecure in its results—insecure not in the durability of what is remembered but in the content of what is remembered. Students "discover" all sorts of things, some of them irrelevant to the purposes at hand and some of them wrong. To choose the discovery technique over another is to choose one application of constructivism over another. Such choices are practical ones to be determined on each occasion by educational goals and results, not by special sanction from neutral psychological theory. Discovery learning must, in the end, be justified by its observed effectiveness, and on that score, the results emphatically do not justify an extreme or exclusive reliance on what is currently called "constructivist" practice. Educators are too hasty in concluding that constructivism justifies "MORE experiential, inductive, hands-on learning, MORE active learning with all the attendant noise of students doing, talking, collaborating," and so on. This faulty inference is based on the assumption that other forms of learning involve mere "transmission" and "reception" instead of the active construction of knowledge. But all meaningful learnings, induced by any and all methods, entail such active construction.

In short, the term "constructivism" has become a kind of magical incantation used to defend discovery learning, which is no more sanctioned by psychological theory than any other form of constructed learning. To pretend that it is so sanctioned illustrates what I mean by the "selective use of research." Despite the enthusiastic invocations of the term "constructivism," neither discovery learning nor any other form of pedagogy is specially singled out and sanctioned by modern psychology.

# 3.
## Selective Use of Research II: "Thinking Skills"

An equally selective use of research characterizes the current enthusiasm for teaching "higher-order thinking skills"—an omnium term that comprises "critical-thinking skills," "problem-solving skills," and "metacognitive strategies," all of which are said to be superior to teaching specific content or mere fact. It will be useful to summarize mainstream research into the effectiveness of teaching such abstract skills. The results of that research should affect the credibility of the claim, universally expounded in our schools of education, that the teaching of process, attitude, and strategy is far more valuable than the teaching of mere information.

The early advocates of critical thinking encouraged students to exercise skepticism, probe beneath surfaces, and follow the canons of formal or informal logic. Students were exhorted to avoid logical fallacies such as *post hoc, ergo propter hoc,* overhasty conclusions from inadequate samples, and the imputing of causal significance to mere correlations. More recently, however, the critical-thinking movement has expanded beyond a narrow focus on logical coherence, and claims, in its commercial advertisements, to embrace almost everything that "current research" has shown to be desirable, whether or not the various desiderata have any connection with each other or with critical thought:

> *Critical thinking is at the heart of effective reading, writing, speaking, and listening. It enables us to link together mastery of content with such diverse goals as self-esteem, self-discipline, multi-culturalism, effective co-operative learning, and problem solving. It enables all students to learn to assess their own learning. It enables all instructors and administrators to raise the level of their own teaching and thinking.*[9]

In addition, critical thinking is said to yield "methods for engaging students in active learning" and to play a "key role as the foundation for the design of higher order teaching, learning and assessment."[10]

More modest hopes are entertained by those who favor the direct teaching of so-called "metacognitive skills." Researchers have observed that one of the consistent differences between experts and novices is that experts self-consciously monitor and evaluate some of their mental strategies as they deploy them.[11] If novices could be taught to monitor *their* strategies, then perhaps their performance might begin to approximate that of experts. Students are encouraged to monitor their own thought processes to improve their competencies in reading, writing, and problem solving. They are asked to self-monitor how to read for the main idea, how to compute by the most efficient means, and how to assess their progress in the various subtasks of expository writing.[12] Insofar as self-monitoring makes students more thoughtful readers, writers, and problem solvers, such metacognitive instruction clearly ought to be encouraged.

But whether such direct instruction in critical thinking or in self-monitoring *does* in fact improve performance is a subject of debate in the research community. For instance, the evidence regarding critical thinking is not reassuring. Instruction in critical thinking has been going on in several countries for over a hundred years. Yet researchers found that students from nations as varied as Israel, Germany, Austria, the Philippines, and the United States, including those who have been taught critical thinking, continue to fall into logical fallacies.[13] My own informal observation confirms that finding. Colleagues who are logicians by profession are not by reason of their specialty immune from sloppy and hasty judgments when they pronounce upon public policy and other complex subjects they know little about. Usually, it isn't the logical structure of people's inferences that chiefly causes uncritical thinking but, rather, the uninformed or misinformed faultiness of their premises.

The practical ineffectualness of general training in critical thinking has been confirmed in controlled experiments. People who have just finished a one-semester course in logic are only marginally more logical than people who have never taken logic. Other experiments show that training in abstract "higher-order skills" does not much improve thinking.[14] A good deal of relevant data has been gathered on a problem called the "Wason Card selection problem," which shows that despite being given hints and rules, people are rarely able to apply procedural rules in appropriate ways to unfamiliar problems that belong to different domains.[15] Thus, a key subject of debate in the research community is whether direct instruction in thinking works sufficiently well to justify spending a lot of classroom time in consciously inculcating either abstract logical principles or general self-monitoring strategies.

Of course, no one challenges the wisdom of including specific tips on procedural strategies as an integral part of subject-matter instruction. Most teachers do so as a matter of course—and to good effect. All good writing teachers give strategic, self-monitoring tips concerning the writing process; good math teachers do the same with regard to problem-solving strategies; and there is some evidence that instilling comprehension strategies works in the teaching of reading.

But although giving *specific* metacognitive tips within subject-matter instruction is known to be a useful teaching practice, one may question the current claim that teaching general "higher-order skills" is an *improvement* over subject-matter study. The enthusiasm for metaskills could easily become an updated, "research based" version of the progressivist antisubject-matter tradition that has already caused our schools to decline. The recent disproportionate emphasis on metacognition at the expense of content was epitomized by the Connecticut superintendent who said that his students were learning something better than subject matter, which he called "knowledge plus."[16] When metacognition usurps cognition, we had better start looking very closely at what research really says about the effectiveness of teaching these "higher-order skills."

In the case of critical thinking, it has been shown that direct instruction does lead to moderately improved performance on the Cornell Critical-Thinking Test.[17] That is hardly surprising. Direct instruction in any domain usually leads to some degree of improvement on tests in that domain. Informal logic is, after all, a subject matter in its own right. The still-unsettled research debate concerns whether instruction in critical thinking translates into improved real-world critical thinking. If such transfer of training were shown to take place, the expenditure of extra instructional time might be justified. But the evidence is not encouraging. The study of transfer of training still yields, after a hundred years of research, weak and ambiguous results. That means, minimally, that the minor transfer effects of instruction in critical thinking are probably not worth the expenditure of significant extra instructional time.[18]

There is somewhat more support in research for teaching metacognitive or self-monitoring strategies specifically targeted to improved performance in reading, writing, and mathematical problem solving. Such instruction tries to make students self-consciously aware of techniques that will improve their performance on domain-specific operations. For instance, teaching multiplication to children by making them aware of the technique of skip counting as a self-checking or self-monitoring device has proved to be a useful problem-solving skill. You can multiply 5 times 3 by skip counting by fives three times or by skip counting by threes five times. It's fun; it's a good way to check on results; and it's a good way to learn the concept of multiplication. Similarly, in the teaching of reading, metacognitive techniques called "question asking" and "reciprocal teaching" are mildly effective for improving comprehension. Teaching these domain-specific metacognitive strategies has proved to be more useful to problem solving than teaching broad problem-solving strategies in the hope of encouraging spontaneous reconceptualizations of diverse problem types.[19]

Another severe constraint on the efficacy of directly teaching "higher-order skills" is much discussed in the research literature. A key skill in expert performance is to know both a strategy and also *when* it will be useful to apply it.[20] That aspect of metacognitive knowledge is gained only after a great deal of practice and experience, and has proved not to be reliably teachable by isolated instruction.[21] Strategies that apply to specific and replicated circumstances and activities such as addition and subtraction have therefore turned out to be the most useful strategies for students—strategies taught within a domain, not general strategies for learning and thinking. Teaching a strategy that lies between the general and the domain-specific (i.e., the teaching of comprehension skills in reading) yields an in-between practical result, a positive but modest improvement in reading skill compared to control groups.[22]

Some very good work in analyzing the nature and effectiveness of metacognitive strategies in children has been conducted by Robert S. Siegler, whom the American Psychological Association selected to write the final chapter of its 1993 book, *The Challenge in Mathematics and Science Education: Psychology's Response.* Siegler has shown that children's untaught strategies are highly adaptive to their level of familiarity with subject matters. He also found that the direct teaching of "efficient" metacognitive strategies, and the deliberate suppression of less efficient ones such as counting on one's fingers, may actually slow down the achieving of expert mathematical skill! Siegler uses the term "associative knowledge" for the adaptive procedural knowledge of students, and avoids the term "higher-order thinking skills." This seems wise, since some sort of procedural knowledge is always associated with learning, and it is not clear why this procedural knowledge is of a "higher order" (and therefore by implication better) than the content knowledge with which it is associated.[23]

Siegler is concerned that the teaching of self-monitoring strategies to slow or disadvantaged children might hinder rather than help their progress in learning. Although the rationale behind teaching self-monitoring strategies is to speed up learning in the most efficient possible way, research has not yet shown that large doses of metacognitive teaching succeed in doing so. In fact, there are good grounds for suspecting that a strong emphasis on metacognitive instruction can sometimes hinder student progress, particularly among slow or disadvantaged children. Possible drawbacks of an Emphasis on Metacognition (EOM):

- EOM may interfere with the orderly development of adaptive problem-solving strategies
- EOM may carry severe opportunity costs by usurping subject-matter instruction
- EOM may overload working memory and thus impair rather than help learning
- All of these potential drawbacks may have the most adverse effects on slow or disadvantaged students[24]

**EOM May Interfere with the Orderly Development of Adaptive Problem-Solving Strategies**   One reason for this is that consciously learning the abstract principle behind a strategy may be much harder than implicitly learning the strategy itself, so that teaching the abstract principle may slow down first graders' progress. For instance, teaching students the strategy of *consciously and systematically* asking questions about the text they are reading may be harder and less productive than focusing the same mental energy on implicit understanding, and on asking explicit questions only as real questions arise. Metacognitive instruction can even interfere with the orderly development of adaptive procedural knowledge. Siegler interviewed first-grade teachers to find out why some of them forbade children to count on their fingers as a "backup strategy." Some teachers reasoned that since skillful children retrieved addition facts mentally from memory, slower students would become more expert if they were *required* to use the expert strategy. On that reasoning, children were forbidden to use finger counting. Siegler comments: "When children know correct answers sufficiently well to retrieve them, they do so spontaneously. Preventing them from using backup strategies when they do not know the answers leads to a great deal of incorrect performance. It is hard to see how this approach can aid learning."[25]

**EOM May Carry Severe Opportunity Costs by Usurping Subject-Matter Instruction**   Annemarie Palinscar and Ann Brown, who have done excellent work on teaching comprehension skills, report that a number of "40-minute training sessions" are spent on informal logic or metacognitive reading instruction, during which students are taught procedures designed to focus on the gist of material, to integrate information throughout the passage, to generate questions and evaluate them, to answer these questions, and to help them pay attention to structure while reading. Since this kind of approach has been reported to be effective in the teaching of reading, the main danger is the current uncritical application of metacognitive instruction. While abstract (and rather difficult) procedural instruction is going on, the extensive metacognitive sessions might sometimes be spent more fruitfully on, for example, better understanding of the subject matter and the vocabulary that would be used in the upcoming reading, or on background information regarding various topics in the reading, knowledge of which might make the task more engaging and accessible to students. Such content-oriented use of instructional time is not necessarily superior in all cases, but it is well to remember that trade-offs are involved in isolating strategy instruction or emphasizing it over content instruction.

My caveats against the overuse of metacognitive strategies are less vigorous, however, than my warnings against overreliance on the teaching of critical thinking and other abstract skills. Teaching students specific metacognitive strategies for reading comprehension has proved highly helpful to them; those students who have been trained in such methods read better than those who have not been so trained. Students, for instance, who have been taught to formulate questions when reading and to set definite comprehension goals for themselves do in fact master content more readily than students who have not been so taught.[26]

**EOM May Overload Short-Term Memory and Thus Impair Rather Than Help Learning**   For beginners in reading, mathematics, and writing, there is not much room in working memory for anything beyond the fundamental elements of the task. Decoding and word recognition tax beginning readers to the limit.[27] The early stages of mathematical operations are intensely demanding. In writing, it is difficult just to master letter formation and spelling. Even at later grades of elementary school, these tasks are far from trivial. If in addition to performing them we also ask children to monitor their own performances metacognitively, there is a likelihood that such demands will further tax working memory and even degrade performance rather than improve it. This problem becomes particularly acute with beginning or ill-prepared students.

The basic argument for teaching metacognition seems to be that since experts monitor their own performances and engage in conscious and unconscious strategies regarding the task itself, novices will take a shortcut to becoming more like experts if they do the same thing. But this is a version of the mistake that Siegler identified among first-grade teachers who wanted students to use expert strategies instead of counting on their fingers. Enthusiasts for expert-style metacognition may overlook the critical fact that experts in any skill have so automated the basic components of their tasks that they have plenty of room in working memory to engage in self-monitoring. Jill Larkin and others have noted that experts think about very different aspects of problems than do novices, who are quite wrapped up in thinking about basic operations. When novices try to think about expert-level aspects and neglect the prerequisites, they perform even worse than before.[28]

Alfred North Whitehead made a shrewd remark on this score in his *Introduction to Mathematics:*

> *It is a profoundly erroneous truism repeated by all copybooks, and by eminent people when they are making speeches, that we should cultivate the habit of thinking of what we are doing. The precise opposite is the case. Civilization advances by extending the number of operations which we can perform without thinking about them. Operations of thought are like cavalry charges in a battle—they are strictly limited in number, they require fresh horses, and must only be made at decisive moments.*[29]

**All of These Potential Drawbacks of EOM May Have the Most Adverse Effects on Slow or Disadvantaged Students**  If Whitehead is right (and much work in cognitive psychology suggests that he is), a chief aim in the elementary grades is to help students automate the maximum number of basic processes in reading, writing, and mathematics. An extra burden of self-conscious monitoring is much heavier for slower students than it is for students who have already automated many processes. So while teachers' enthusiasm for metacognition may hinder and slow down all elementary students, it can be especially burdensome for slower ones, and is likely to slow them down disproportionately. Instead of asking such students to monitor themselves like experts, we should perhaps help them "extend the number of operations they can perform without thinking about them." Research into effective teaching shows that enabling students to take small, easy steps is the fastest way to help them become experts.

Keeping in mind the research I have sketched so far in this chapter, it may be helpful to remind the reader why I have thought it important to enter into some of these details. We need to bring informed skepticism to bear on the pro-process, antifact claims and dismissals that one constantly hears from American educators. This morning, April 25, 1995, I find the following letter in the *Washington Post:*

> *Let's face it. No teacher can teach everything in an academic discipline. The real underlying question is whether teachers teach students or content; students after all are not vessels waiting for a teacher to fill them. The more important task is for teachers to help students learn how to make the best use of their individual learning styles and potentials in articulating and solving problems germane to their world. . . . The blowout of potential information on the information superhighway is an indication of the implausibility of a factoid-based approach to curriculum. Students have to be challenged to articulate the questions that need attention in the solution of problems. This critical thinking is essential to the service/information-based postindustrial society we are rapidly becoming. Education is now a life-long process, and the facts of today will hardly serve to answer the needs of tomorrow. Students don't need to be drilled in isolated facts; they need the intellectual space to develop skills for asking pertinent questions and for knowing where and how to find the needed data. There are only so many minutes in a school day; to the extent that students are forced to memorize pieces of data to the exclusion of the skills that can turn that data into information, those precious minutes—not to mention student energy—are wasted.*[30]

Journalists could stimulate a great advance in public awareness if they began to view such antifact statements with a grain of salt and an ounce of skepticism. The problem with these all-too-familiar sentiments is not that they fail to make sense but that their premises are deeply flawed. It is true that students can and should be taught to ask questions like "How does he know that?" about a wide range of claims. But it is misleading to suggest that, absent a great deal of solid knowledge, children can be taught abstract generalized skills for "articulating and solving problems germane to their world." If this learning-to-learn principle were supported by mainstream research and by real-world results, how fortunate we would all be. But the teaching of general accessing, metacognitive, and thinking skills has proved to be a premature panacea—a continually repeated slogan without a consistent basis in reality. The present era demands an education that is very different from the illusory one proposed in the above-quoted letter. The next section will devote itself to sketching what mainstream research has disclosed about the *real* nature of competency in the information age.

## 4.
## The Structure of Real-World Competency

The oft-repeated goal of the educational community—to inculcate general thinking skills—is not, then, soundly based in research. And that is stating the point too mildly. The idea that school can inculcate abstract, generalized skills for thinking, "accessing," and problem solving, and that these skills can be readily applied to the real world is, bluntly, a mirage. So also is the hope that a thinking skill in one domain can be readily and reliably transferred to other domains. Yet broad-gauged thinking abilities do exist. Most of us know well-educated people, even some not very bright ones, who have high general competence, can think critically about diverse subjects, can communicate well, can solve a diversity of problems, and are ready to tackle unfamiliar challenges. The belief that our schools should regularly produce such people appeals to both experience and common sense. If the goal didn't make apparent sense, it could hardly have retained its attractiveness to the educational community and the general public. Rightly understood, then, the goal of general competence *does* define one important aim of modern education. The task is not to change that goal but to interpret it accurately so that it corresponds to the nature of real-world competency and can actually be achieved.

In Section 2 of the present chapter, this is how I summarized the standard account of modern educational aims, using the standard language of current reform movements:

> *The goal of present-day educational reformers is to produce students with "higher-order skills" who are able to think independently about the unfamiliar problems they will encounter in the "information age," who have become "problem solvers" and have "learned how to learn," and who are on their way to becoming "critical thinkers" and "lifelong learners."*

This is precisely right. What is wrong is the inaccurate, abstract model of what such skills consist of, and the misconceived attack by the educational community on mere "factoids," on the mistaken assumption that the wished-for "higher-order skills" are independent of a broad grounding in specific facts and information. There is a great deal of evidence, indeed a consensus in cognitive psychology, that people who are able to think independently about unfamiliar problems and who are broad-gauged problem solvers, critical thinkers, and lifelong learners are, without exception, well-informed people. There is also a lot of evidence that many students who have recently graduated from our schools are *not* well-informed, that they are deficient in higher-order general skills, and that their schooling has long been dominated by the antifact theories which are being advocated as "reforms" for the information age. To attain the desired goal, what we need is a more accurate understanding of what being a critical thinker and lifelong learner actually entails.

In Chapter 2, I argued that we need to replace the educational metaphor of tools with the more accurate metaphor of intellectual capital. I said that intellectual capital is the tool of tools, the real-world foundation for the various abstract skills that are being recommended by teaching manuals which call on schools to

> *provide the means for the learner to develop the intellectual skills related to critical thinking and problem solving. If thinking is to be the central purpose of American education, as many believe it should be, then ways must be devised to help individuals develop that capability.*[31]

The nature of these real-world competencies is highly complex. It would be misleading to pretend that cognitive psychologists and neurobiologists have come to agreement about the most accurate description of them. Even some of the most widely accepted models, such as the one labeled "schema," have been challenged. The descriptive details and even the broad outlines of higher-level mental functions are still subjects of controversy. Moreover, from what is already known, we can expect a picture that will grow even more complicated and multilayered as time goes on, and will probably not be captured in simple models or slogans.

But there are functional shortcuts to describing and understanding some key characteristics of real-world skills in the modern era. It is safe to say, for example, that none of these skills are available to a person with limited communication skills and a highly restricted vocabulary. Communication skills are needed simply to understand problems and perforce to solve them. One cannot "learn to learn" without having learned to understand what one is being taught. Let's start from there. There are no real-world examples of adults with information age competencies who are functioning with a fourth-grade vocabulary. Even if the possession of a broad vocabulary does not in itself guarantee the possession of critical-thinking skills, lack of intellectual capital is a sure index to the lack of such skills.

The correlation of vocabulary level with intellectual skill applies not only to adults but also to children in preschool, elementary school, and middle school. Only children who possess the communication skills to participate fully in the classroom community at their level are in a position to learn diverse new things within that community. For their level, they have *already* learned how to learn, and are in a position to learn still more. Their readiness to learn new things in a domain is sensitively dependent on what they already know in that domain, as indicated by possession of a relevant vocabulary.[32] Jerome Kagan has well observed that one of the chief learning abilities of children is their aptitude for capturing a range of experiences by the symbolizing function of the mind, a function that most often manifests itself in words.[33] A great many (of course not all) of the intellectual skills of normal children and adults are correlated with their use of words.

The connection of learning-to-learn skills with language mastery does *not* imply that schooling should devote itself to teaching students word lists, or that many other kinds of talents and masteries should not be encouraged, or that children who are more visual or tactile than verbal in orientation should not be accommodated by diversified teaching methods. I make this obvious point without delay to forestall misunderstanding or caricature of what I am saying. That is only prudent. Among the several criticisms of *Cultural Literacy,* the most dull-minded was that it advised educators to teach disconnected, rote-memorized words and facts. That interpretation made the book's argument seem at once impractical and stupid, which may have been the polemical intent of those who so interpreted it.

So, let me say as explicitly as I can that to want children to possess a broad vocabulary is not to advocate a mechanical or inept manner of achieving that goal. Any challenge to current ideas, such as this book is compelled to be, is likely to be discredited as impractical or ill-informed. But overfacile dismissals ought to be cut off at the pass, if only to compel more complexity and ingenuity in the discussion. Just as *Cultural Literacy* did not recommend that its index to shared knowledge be memorized as a list, neither does the present argument for a broad vocabulary imply the rote memorization of word lists. I shall be dealing with methods of pedagogy in a later section of this chapter.

My insistence that schooling should arm children with a broad vocabulary is logically required by the goal of inculcating problem-solving skills. These real-world competencies depend on communication/learning abilities, which in turn depend upon a broad vocabulary. The linguistic prerequisite is a foundation for a whole range of competencies in domains such as mathematics, art, history, ethics, politics, and science. Even if these linguistic skills are not identical with other competencies, they are prerequisites for them. A general look at how these linguistic skills develop will exemplify the stage-by-stage process by which most other thinking and learning skills are attained.

In a TV interview, Marilyn Jager Adams, the author of an authoritative book on beginning reading, estimated that children who leave first grade without being able to read at grade level have a very poor outlook for later success in school and economic life.[34] It was a startling and memorable statement, one that no doubt requires a lot of statistical qualification. Yet it touches on a profound truth about the cumulative nature of language skills—namely, that they build up rapidly and decisively in the early years, and that it is difficult to compensate for very early deficits. Since linguistic skills are critical for mastery in other subject matters and skills, it is worth examining the basic reasons for the dependence of later language skills on the earlier stages of their acquisition.

The critical importance of initial conditions recalls "chaos theory," which holds that the flapping of a butterfly's wings in Brazil can set off a long chain of causal factors that will determine the path of a thunderstorm six months later in Atlanta. Small incremental changes in early language learning can produce enormous consequences later on. Young children who arrive at preschool with a very small vocabulary, and a correspondingly limited knowledge base, *can* fortunately be brought to an age-adequate vocabulary by intelligent, focused help, and from that base they can continue to perform at grade level. But evidence from a variety of sources indicates that when this language and knowledge deficit is not compensated for early, it is nearly impossible to reach grade-level skills in later grades, despite intensive remediation.[35] The policy implication of these findings is that, given academically effective early intervention, a lot of remedial money should gradually be shifted to preschool-kindergarten programs and to sustaining programs in the early grades (though that move would be unwise so long as Romantic doctrines of developmentalism continue to prevent preschool-kindergarten programs from being academically effective).

So far, I have mentioned the importance of early oral language masteries as the basis for the gradual attainment of communication/learning skills, which will form the basis of many other skills. I have not yet mentioned reading and writing. That is because speaking and listening competencies are primary. There is a linguistic law that deserves to be called "Sticht's Law," having been disclosed by some excellent research by Thomas Sticht.[36] He found that reading ability in nondeaf children cannot exceed their listening ability. While this principle cannot be extended automatically to highly advanced readers and difficult texts, it does hold for the early stages of reading. Sticht showed that, for most children, by seventh grade the ability to read with speed and comprehension and the ability to listen had become identical. Oral-aural communication skills are primary, and they place a definite limit on a person's reading-writing skills.

This principle is foundational because the decoding aspects of reading, that is, the ability to turn the black marks on paper into words, although it is a skill that rightly receives a lot of emphasis in early grades, does not represent the true upper limit on reading ability, once decoding skills have been mastered. While the process of decoding from letters to language is the foundation of reading, it isn't the essence of reading, which is the *comprehension* of written language. Sticht's Law holds that for nondeaf persons, the comprehension of written language cannot exceed the comprehension of oral language, that oral speech is the foundation of written speech. If children's oral-aural vocabulary and their oral-aural comprehension abilities are not well developed, neither will their reading abilities be. But if children's oral-aural communication abilities *are* well developed, the only barrier to their becoming good readers is lack of fluency and accuracy in their decoding skills.

The child's original acquisition of oral-aural speech is an evolutionarily based, natural process, universal in all human groups. But the acquisition of literacy is a nonnatural culture-specific process that is not universal.[37] Math learning similarly starts from the natural, evolution-determined number sense, which we share with some other animals, and we build on that base to gain the culture-specific conventions of base-ten mathematics.[38] The process of learning in young childhood is to move from the natural to the cultural, from the oral-language base as the foundation for reading. If a young child's speaking and listening skills have been impoverished by growing up in a limited linguistic environment, no effort should be spared to enhance those foundational oral-aural skills as a prerequisite for further literacy skills.

If that compensatory and preparatory work is done, and if decoding fluency has also been achieved, a reverse influence begins to make itself felt in later elementary school, after second or third grade. Although reading skill cannot exceed listening skill, reading can and usually does become a source of language experience that greatly enhances listening and speaking skills. Once a child learns to read with facility and comprehension, reading and being read to help the learning of new words and the gaining of corollary new knowledge. Thenceforth, a feedback system between oral and written speech enriches the child's language and learning experience, and adds opportunities to gain ever broader knowledge and vocabulary.

This means that a child with a good oral-aural start in life but without early facility in decoding skills is cut off from a range of further language and learning experiences that children with more decoding facility are gaining. That handicap will not only slow down the child's skill in reading but also diminish the total amount of his or her language and learning experience. Children who arrive at school with less varied oral-aural language experience are usually also children who have received less home instruction in phonics and experience in listening to reading. In comparison with more fortunate students, they continue to be impoverished linguistically, with less rich language experiences at home, less comprehension of oral speech in school, and, because of deficiencies in decoding, less access to written speech. With focused, expert teaching in preschool through first grade, these inequities can be greatly diminished. Every normal child can and should be reading at grade level by the end of first or second grade, and also at the end of every grade thereafter. *Because of the sensitivity of academic progress to early conditions, the achievement of this single, attainable goal—every child reading at grade level by the end of first or second grade—would do more than any other single reform to improve the quality and equity of American schooling.*

But what does "reading at grade level" mean? If we assume that a school's language arts instruction in first grade has given all children such necessities as phonological awareness, accurate letter and word recognition, and other decoding skills, then "reading at grade level" must be limited by speaking and listening at grade level. To have grade-level skill means that the child has gained an understanding of certain conventions and expectations of language use and genre—for instance, that readings which start out saying "Once upon a time" are going to be stories. It means that certain repeated conventions of grammar and syntax have been mastered, allowing expression and comprehension of more complex sentence forms.

But not all children gain the skill of reading at grade level, even when they have been given lots of successfully focused instruction in decoding and have mastered that foundational skill. Something more is needed to read at grade level. That something more is an understanding of an ever-growing number of word meanings as used in context. Word meanings are not formal structures like grammar and syntax. They are symbols that represent ranges of knowledge and experience. They cannot be gained without learning what educators disparagingly call "factoids," for they include words such as "birthday," "George Washington," "tree," "1492," "gravity," and "Kwaanza."[39]

The reading tests that currently determine whether children are reading at grade level sample not only decoding fluency and syntactic ability but also word comprehension. And since the sampled words stand for concepts and schemas—that is, for knowledge—to read at grade level also means mastery of words that represent knowledge. There is no accurate way to describe reading ability as a purely formal skill, or to remove from it the information-based knowledge disparaged as "factoids." As the child moves up the grades, and as decoding and syntactic skills become mature and automatic, vocabulary becomes an ever more critical determinant of whether the child is reading at grade level. In short, the key element—the one that grows ever more important for the acquisition of communication/learning skills—is the child's knowledge/vocabulary base. The notion that reading is a mechanical skill divorced from domain-specific knowledge is as great a mirage as the idea of formal "thinking" skills.

These considerations mean that the teaching of communication/learning skills, while completely dependent on the mastery of decoding processes, should never be exclusively focused on those processes. Whenever trade-offs are made in allocating time to language skills in early grades, Sticht's Law should be kept firmly in mind. Reading skill cannot exceed listening skill. It is at least as important to advance a child's oral-aural fluency and comprehension as to practice the mechanics of reading. Both must be done. Children should not fall behind in either sort of learning. An unthinking identification of communication/learning skills with the mechanics of literacy, and a consequent neglect of knowledge and vocabulary, is in the end a grave handicap to advancement in communication/learning skills. A preoccupation with the mechanics of reading (necessary as they are) is a very good illustration of the inferiority of the tool metaphor as compared with the metaphor of intellectual capital. Decoding tools, once mastered, are a mere platform. Their upper potential is quite insignificant compared with that of comprehension skills that are conferred by knowledge and a broad vocabulary.

What are these general oral-aural comprehension skills? I have suggested that they are limited by one's vocabulary, which is a self-evident fact to most people. But it is well to recall that vocabulary alone isn't a sufficient key to comprehension skill, as we know from the anecdote about the person who went to hear a lecture by Einstein and complained afterward that he knew all the words, it was just the way they were put together that baffled him. The profound meaning of the anecdote is that the skill of comprehending or learning to learn requires not just a broad range of words but also a broad range of knowledge in specific domains.[40] This point has been illustrated so often in psycholinguistic studies that it is astonishing to know that quite sophisticated people still hold to the belief that generalized learning skills do not require a broad liberal knowledge or, to use my preferred phrase, a rich endowment of intellectual capital.

I should make one final point about early language skills before turning to other real-world competencies. The aim in early education is not only to achieve a high level of oral-aural communication skills but to make the child's decoding skills approach the oral-aural limit as rapidly as possible. This can be accomplished only when decoding skills are well practiced and grow ever more unconscious and automatic. This point needs stressing because it is exemplary for most other intellectual skills. Basic processes need to be made unconscious and automatic as early as possible in order to free the mind for critical thinking and problem solving. In the 1950s, George Miller estimated that the human mind could consciously cope with only five to seven different things at a time; he called this limited sphere of mental activity "short-term memory."[41] The currently preferred term is "working memory," and it is now thought that the limitation is not so much the absolute number of items as the absolute amount of time that items can be functionally active in mind at one time. Clearly, if few or none of the operations of decoding need to be held consciously in mind, if they are so well grooved as to be automatic, then the child has more room in conscious working memory to think critically and creatively about comprehension and problem solving.

The development of real-world language skill results, then, in functional masteries which are extremely complex in their interactions but which can be schematized for convenience into three aspects: 1) mastery of the continually repeated formal elements of language to the point of automaticity, 2) the gaining of a content-rich knowledge base represented by particular word meanings and cultural conventions, and 3) the successful active deployment of these elements in comprehension and problem solving. This general pattern holds not just for speaking and listening but also for reading, where the mastery of decoding skills belongs to the realm of continually repeated formal elements that need to become unconscious and automatic.[42] The same three-part pattern holds for penmanship and composition, where a great deal of effort is required to habituate the learner to the continually repeated formal elements of making letters and words, so that level-one letter formation becomes sufficiently automatic so as not to interfere with the conscious deployment of written words to convey meaning.[43] Because of the limitations of working memory, the more these formal and foundational processes are automatic, the more effectively the comprehension, expression, and problem-solving aspects of any intellectual skill can be deployed. Higher-level skills critically depend upon the automatic mastery of repeated lower-level activities.

The pattern that holds for reading and writing holds also for mathematics.

In math, what correspond to the repeated elements of grammar, syntax, spelling, and letter formation are the rules that govern operations used in solving problems. These include basic addition, subtraction, and multiplication activities, as well as operations on equations. But mathematics also contains elements corresponding to particular vocabulary meanings, such as the basic number facts of addition, subtraction, and multiplication, as well as the special conventions of different problem types. Psychologists have called the repeated grammar-like operations of mathematics "rules," and the more vocabulary-like, content-oriented aspects "schemas." They argue that

> *the development of problem-solving skills in algebra involves schema acquisition and rule automation. The processes underlying the acquisition of these two skills, as well as the amount of experience needed for skill development, appear to be independent. Rule automation concerns the ease of use of basic algebraic procedures, such as subtracting or adding variables to each side of an equation. More specifically,* automation *refers to the automatic execution of a procedure without having to think about the rules governing the use of that procedure. One of the benefits of rule automation is a reduction in the working-memory demands associated with using the procedure. The freeing of working-memory resources makes the processing of other features of the problem easier and less error-prone. . . . Once the rules have been memorized and automatically executed for one set of problems, they are readily used to solve different types of algebra problems. Before this point, however, rules learned in the context of one algebra problem are not readily transferred—that is, these rules are not readily used to solve other types of algebra problems. In all, rule automation not only reduces working-memory requirements of the problem but also leads to the use of these rules for solving other forms of algebra problems. Rule automation, however, appears to occur only with extensive practice. Schema acquisition, on the other hand, appears to occur rather quickly, that is, with very little practice.*[44]

The similarity of this description of the development of math skills with the pattern for the development of communication/learning skills suggests that we have hit upon a general structure for real-world problem-solving and critical-thinking skills. First, expertness in the skill depends upon the automation, through a great deal of practice, of the repeated, formal elements of the skill, thus freeing the conscious mind for critical thought. Secondly, expertness depends upon the acquisition of the relevant vocabulary, conventions, and schemas that form the relevant knowledge base for the skill. Proficiency in the formal operations is gained only after a lot of practice, whereas the long-term retention of relevant knowledge, which is equally necessary for effective higher-order thinking, can occur somewhat faster, with fewer exposures. The research that has disclosed these general characteristics of real-world intellectual skills has implications for educational policy that I shall go on to discuss in the next section.

## 5.
## What Is Higher-Order Thinking?

Two traditions in cognitive psychology are useful for understanding the nature of the critical-thinking, problem-solving skills that we wish to develop in our students. One tradition has studied the characteristic differences between expert and novice thinking, sometimes with the practical goal of making novices think more like experts as fast as possible.[45] Another tradition has investigated the differences between accurate and inaccurate thinking of the everyday newspaper-reading, bargain-hunting sort that all of us must engage in as nonexperts.[46] Both sorts of study converge on the conclusion that, once basic underlying skills have been automated, the almost universal feature of reliable higher-order thinking about any subject or problem is the possession of a broad, well-integrated base of background knowledge relevant to the subject. This sounds suspiciously like plain common sense (i.e., accurate everyday thinking), but the findings entail certain illuminating complexities and details that are worth contemplating. Moreover, since the findings run counter to the prevailing fact-disparaging slogans of educational reform, it will be strategically useful to sketch briefly what research has disclosed about the knowledge-based character of higher-order thinking.

The argument used by educators to disparage "merely" factual knowledge and to elevate abstract, formal principles of thought consists in the claim that knowledge is changing so rapidly that specific information is outmoded almost as soon as it has been learned. This claim goes back at least as far as Kilpatrick's *Foundations of Method* (1925). It gains its apparent plausibility from the observation that science and technology have advanced at a great rate in this century, making scientific and technological obsolescence a common feature of modern life. The argument assumes that there is an analogy between technological and intellectual obsolescence. Educators in this tradition shore up that analogy with the further claim that factual knowledge has become a futility because of the ever-growing quantity of new facts. The great cascade of information now flowing over the information highway makes it pointless to accumulate odd bits of data. How, after all, do you know which bits are going to endure? It is much more efficient for students to spend time acquiring techniques for organizing, analyzing, and accessing this perpetual Niagara of information.

Like the tool metaphor for education, the model of acquiring processing techniques that would be permanently useful—as contrasted with acquiring mere facts that are soon obsolete—would be highly attractive if it happened to be workable and true. But the picture of higher thinking skills as consisting of all-purpose processing and accessing techniques is not just a *partly* inadequate metaphor—it is a totally misleading model of the way higher-order thinking actually works. Higher thought does not apply formal techniques to looked-up data; rather, it deploys diverse relevant cues, estimates, and analyses from preexisting knowledge. The method of applying formal techniques to looked-up data is precisely the inept and unreliable problem-solving device used by novices. As a model of real-world higher-order thinking, the picture is not simply inaccurate—it reverses the realities. It describes the lower-order thinking of novices, not the higher-order thinking of experts.

A useful illustration of the point is presented by Jill Larkin and Ruth Chabay in a study of the ways in which novices and experts go about solving a simple physics problem.[47] The problem Larkin and Chabay set up is (in simple terms) to find out how much friction there is between a sled and the snow-covered ground when a girl is pulling her little brother through the snow at a constant rate. The brother and the sled together weigh 50 pounds. The sister is pulling with a force of 10 pounds, and she pulls the rope at an angle of 30 degrees from the horizontal. What is the coefficient of friction? The typical novice tries to solve the problem by applying formal equations that can be looked up in a book, thus dutifully following the tool principle of problem solving. The student finds that the applicable formula is $f = {}_uN$, where f is force, N is the "normal force" (which is usually equal to weight), and ${}_u$ is the coefficient of friction, which is the quantity to be solved. The novice sees that $f = {}_u \times 50$. The student assumes that $f = 10$, the force exerted by the girl. So $10 = {}_u \times 50$ and ${}_u = {}^{10}/_{50}$, which equals .2. The answer is wrong, not because the equation or the math is wrong but because the novice doesn't know enough about real-world physics to know how to connect the formula to the problem. The novice's procedure illustrates not just the inappropriateness of the formalistic model but also the bankruptcy of the claim that students need only learn how to look things up—so-called "accessing skills." In this typical case, the skill of looking things up simply lends spurious exactitude to the student's misconceptions.

The expert physicist goes about the problem differently. He or she analyzes the critical components of the situation before looking up equations, and makes two critical observations before even bothering with numbers. The first observation is that the sled is going at a constant speed, so that, in effect, there is no net residue of forces acting on the sled; there is an exact balance between the force exerted horizontally by the girl's pull and the force exerted against that pull by friction. If there had been some difference in the two forces, then the sled would speed up or slow down. So the answer has got to be that the friction is exactly equal to the horizontal component of the force exerted by the girl. The physicist also sees that since the rope is pulled at 30 degrees, part of the girl's 10 pounds of force is vertical. The answer is going to be that the friction equals the *horizontal* force of the girl's pull, which is going to be the 10 pounds minus its vertical component. The structure of the answer is solved on the basis of multiple cues and relevant knowledge, before any formulas are looked up and applied. Larkin and Chabay make the following comment (which is much more to our purpose than the details of the physics involved):

> *Scientists' problem solving starts with redescribing the problem in terms of the powerful concepts of their discipline.* Because the concepts are richly connected with each other, the redescribed problem allows cross checking among inferences to avoid errors. *[My emphasis.]*[48]

An important feature of higher-order thinking is this "cross checking among inferences," based on a number of "richly connected" concepts. In higher-order thinking, we situate a problem in mental space on analogy with the way we situate ourselves in physical space—through a process of cross-checking or triangulation among relevant guideposts in our landscape of pre-existing knowledge. If we look at a problem from a couple of different angles, using a couple of different cues, and if our different estimates converge, we gain confidence in our analysis and can proceed with confidence. If, on the other hand, there is some dissonance or conflict between our cues, then warning signals go up and we figure out which approach is more probable or fruitful. The procedure is clearly a very different and far more reliable mode of thinking than the error-prone method of applying formal techniques to looked-up data.

The example also illustrates the implausibility of the claim that school-based information quickly grows outdated. How outmoded will the knowledge used to solve the sled problem become? A philosopher of science, Nicholas Rescher, once observed that the latest science is in a sense the least reliable science, because, being on the frontier, it is always in dispute with other, rival theories—any of which may emerge victorious. Accordingly, reasoned

Rescher, the most reliable physics is "stone-age physics": if you throw the rock up, it is going to come down. For most problems that require critical thought by the ordinary person regarding ethics, politics, history, and even technology, the most needed knowledge is usually rather basic, long-lived, and slow to change. True, just as physics is under revision at the frontier, so American history before the Civil War is constantly under revision in certain details (e.g., did Abraham Lincoln have an affair with Ann Rutledge?). But behind the ever-changing front lines, there is a body of reliable knowledge which has not changed, and will not change very much, and which serves very well as a landscape to orient us in mental space. It is true that, over time, the content of the most significant and useful background knowledge for today's world does change. But I have never seen a carefully reasoned defense of the repeated assertion that, in the new age, factual knowledge is changing so fast as to make the learning of significant information useless. Probably, no carefully reasoned defense of this mindless claim could be mounted.

The physics example from Larkin and Chabay, if viewed in isolation, might be taken to show that higher-order thinking depends on abstract concepts rather than on factual details. But most research indicates that while the thinking activities through which we reach conclusions and solve problems are not crowded with literally remembered facts, neither are they made up of abstract concepts alone.[49] The models, cues, and schemas through which we think critically are neither pure concepts nor a literal recall of data but a complex and varied combination of concepts, estimates, and factual examples. The key trait to remember about higher-order thinking is its mixed character, consisting of operational facility and domain-specific knowledge.

Some of the most useful studies of higher-order thinking have been concerned with improving our ability to make intelligent and accurate estimates on which to base decisions in our ethical, economic, and civic lives.[50] Since most of us cannot remember, and do not want to take the time to learn, all the details of the U.S. budget deficit and similar matters, we follow political and economic debates with a degree of impressionism that leaves many of us open to slogans and demagoguery. What kind of critical thinking can improve our ability to reach accurate conclusions on such issues? How can we protect ourselves and our students from oversimplifications, lies, and scapegoating conspiracy theories?

It is hard to see why a generalized skepticism, unsupported by accurate knowledge, is superior to a generalized credulity, similarly unsupported. Indeed, uninformed, generalized skepticism expresses itself as a form of credulity, despite our inclination to call I'm-from-Missouri postures "critical thinking." Our best hope for intelligent civic thought lies in our ability to make good ballpark estimates that are close enough to truth to make our decisions well-informed and sound. But life is too short, and learning too arduous, for all citizens to memorize a lot of economic and demographic data. Our current yearly government budget deficit—is it around $30, $300, or $3,000 per American family? Sure, we could look it up, but few of us will. If we can't make an intelligent estimate from the knowledge we already have, we usually won't make an intelligent estimate at all. A lot of higher-order thinking involves our ability to make these sorts of estimates, and to make them well. How do some people manage to do it? And how can we all learn how to do it? From answers to those questions, what implications can be deduced for the K–12 curriculum?

The best research on this subject shows that neither fact-filled memorization nor large conceptual generalizations are effective modes of education for higher-order thinking about the complexities of the modern world. On the other hand, it has been shown that accurate factual estimates are necessary for understanding many issues. Norman Brown and Robert Siegler summarize the underlying problem for modern education:

> Faced with the issue of how to inculcate such information, educators have oscillated between two approaches. One has been to require students to memorize large numbers of quantitative facts. The other has been to deemphasize dates, magnitudes, and other quantities, and to focus on understanding of qualitative relations. Each of these approaches has major drawbacks, however. . . . There are just too many such facts for anyone to memorize a high percentage of them. On the other hand, it is difficult if not impossible to acquire more than a superficial understanding of a domain without some degree of quantitative sophistication about it.[51]

The breadth-depth issue will always be with us, and will always require compromises and common sense. The particular compromise one makes will depend upon subject matter and goals. In practice, an appropriate compromise has been reached by self-taught, well-informed people and by the fortunate students of particularly able teachers. One well-tested teaching method, already followed by many good books and teachers, provides students with a carefully chosen but generous sampling of factual data that are set forth in a meaningful web of inferences and generalizations about the larger domain. Researchers have shown that such generously selective factual instruction leads to accurate inferences not directly deducible from the literal facts that were taught. The mechanisms by which we are able to use these selective exemplifications in order to make remarkably accurate factual guesses about untaught domains are a subject of vigorous current research.

Whatever the underlying psychological mechanisms prove to be, research has demonstrated that the teaching of a generous number of carefully chosen exemplary facts within a meaningful explanatory context is a better method for inducing insightful thinking than is any proposed alternative. These alternatives include 1) the teaching of the whole factual domain, 2) the teaching of the general principles only, and 3) the teaching of a single example in great depth (the less-is-more theory). None of these methods is as effective for inducing effective real-world thinking as sampling well-selected and consistent facts in a carefully prepared explanatory context.[52] This careful-sampling method works well even when (as usually happens) the literal details of the taught facts are not memorized by students, and cannot be retrieved accurately from memory after a period of several months. Nonetheless, a strong improvement in accurate thinking persists if students have once been taught a carefully chosen sample of the factual data.

This finding has strong implications for curriculum making. The conclusion from cognitive research shows that there is an unavoidable interdependence between relational and factual knowledge, and that teaching a broad range of factual knowledge is essential to effective thinking both within domains and among domains. Despite the popularity of the antifact motif in our progressive education tradition, and despite its faith in the power of a few "real-world" projects to educate students "holistically" for the modern world, no state board or school district has yet abandoned the principle of requiring a broad range of different subject matters in elementary school. Across the land, there are still universal requirements for mathematics, science, language arts, and social studies.

Is this curricular conservatism a mere residue of traditional thinking, or does it indicate that common sense has not been defeated by Romantic theory? I favor the latter hypothesis. Despite the vagueness of state and district guidelines, their continued parceling out of schooling into different subject matters, against continued pleas for a more "integrated" and holistic approach, shows an implicit understanding that breadth of knowledge is an essential element of higher-order thinking. School boards have rightly assumed that the mental landscape needs to be broadly surveyed and mapped in order to enable future citizens to cope with a large variety of judgments. No effective system of schooling in the world has abandoned this principle of subject-matter breadth in early schooling.

For later schooling, however, a good deal of evidence—marshaled in the superb research of John Bishop of Cornell—shows that in the last two years of high school, and later on, the balance of utility shifts in favor of deeper and more narrowly specialized training as the best education for the modern world.[53] This finding means that breadth in earlier schooling is all the more essential to developing adequate higher-order thinking and living skills in our citizens-to-be. If schooling is going to become more and more specialized in later life, it is ever more important to map out the wider intellectual landscape accurately and well in the earlier years. Otherwise, we shall produce not critical thinkers but narrow, ignorant ones, subject to delusion and rhetoric. This danger was uppermost in Jefferson's mind when he advocated teaching of human history in early years. In our age, the same argument holds for the domains connected with mathematics, science, technology, and communication skills. A wide range of knowledge and a broad vocabulary supply entry wedges into unfamiliar domains, thus truly enabling "lifelong learning," as well as the attainment of new knowledge and greater depth as needed. The unmistakable implication for modern education is that, instead of constantly deferring the introduction of challenging and extensive knowledge, we need to be taking the opposite tack by increasing both the challenge and the breadth of early education.

Understanding the importance of breadth in early schooling reinforces the practical need to reach agreement about the grade-by-grade sequence in which wide knowledge is taught. In Chapter 2, I described in some detail how the neglect of intellectual capital in favor of intellectual tools has produced curriculum guidelines of such vagueness that they guarantee significant gaps and repetitions in the knowledge that our students receive, even when they stay in the same school. The adverse consequences of this curriculum defect on higher-order thinking are serious in the extreme. Gaps and repetitions mean ignorance and narrowness; they mean huge opportunities lost. If modern education increasingly demands deep and narrow specialization in later grades, these lost early opportunities will never be made up. Cognitive science has shown that higher-order thinking requires both breadth of factual knowledge and points of depth as well. The best tool for higher-order thinking is intellectual capital—that is, to know a lot, not just facts but also the domain-appropriate procedures and strategies for dealing with them. The research findings regarding critical thinking and learning to learn point to an inference about factual knowledge that is completely different from the one usually drawn.

## 6.
## Consensus Research on Pedagogy

A consensus regarding the most effective teaching methods has emerged from three independent sources whose findings converge on the same pedagogical principles. This pattern of independent convergence (a kind of intellectual triangulation) is, along with accurate prediction, one of the most powerful, confidence-building patterns in scientific research. There are few or no examples in the history of science (none that I know of) when the same result, reached by three or more truly independent means, has been overturned.

A wonderful example of this convergence was described by Abraham Pais in his biography of Albert Einstein. At the end of the nineteenth century, the existence of atoms and molecules was still a matter of debate among scientists. In 1811, a physics profesor, Amedeo Avogadro, put forth the hypothesis that the same volume of any gas under the same temperature and pressure must contain the same number of molecules. If molecules exist, then a mole—that is, the molecular weight in grams of any substance—must contain the same number of molecules, no matter what the substance. This number, N, is still called "Avogadro's number." In the early 1900s, Einstein reasoned that if totally different experimental ways of determining N converged on the same result, then molecules must exist. In March 1905, he submitted a paper computing N on the basis of blackbody radiation. In April 1905, his Ph.D. thesis described a new theoretical method for determining N from data on sugar solutions. In May 1905, Einstein submitted an article computing N on the basis of Brownian motion (the zigzag movements of tiny particles suspended in a liquid). Later, in 1910, Einstein submitted a paper on "critical opalescence," which explained why the sky is blue, and derived still another, independent way of determining N. All of these different mathematical/empirical inferences converged on the same magnitude. Pais states:

> *The debate on molecular reality came to a close only as a result of developments in the first decade of the twentieth century. This was not just because of Einstein's first paper on Brownian motion or of any single good determination of N. Rather, the issue was settled once and for all because of the extraordinary agreement in the values of N obtained by many different methods. Matters were clinched not by a determination of N but by an overdetermination of N. From subjects as diverse as radioactivity,*

*Brownian motion, and the blue in the sky, it was possible to state, by
1909, that a dozen independent ways of measuring N yielded results all of
which lay between 6 and 9 × 10²³* [54]

The independent convergence on the fundamentals of effective pedagogy
that exists today is less mathematical but nonetheless compelling. The same
findings have been derived from three quite different and entirely independent
sources: 1) small-scale pairings of different teaching methods; 2) basic research
in cognition, learning, memory, psycholinguistics, and other areas of cognitive
psychology; and 3) large-scale international comparative studies. The findings
from all three sources are highly consistent with each other regarding the most
effective pedagogical principles. Because real-world classroom observations
are so complexly affected by so many uncontrolled variables, the most persuasive aspect of the current picture is the congruence of the classroom-based
observations with cognitive psychology—which is currently our best and most
reliable source of insight into the processes of learning.

In presenting these findings, my strategy will be briefly to go through some
of the classroom studies and summarize their points of agreement. Then, I will
relate those points to findings in cognitive psychology. Finally, I will comment
on their congruence with the results of international comparisons. Not all
readers may be interested in these research details, which are included for
purposes of documentation, and may wish to turn to the summary conclusions
at the end of this section. First, then, the classroom studies.

**New Zealand Studies**   In a series of "process-outcome" studies between 1970
and 1973, researchers from the University of Canterbury in New Zealand
found that time spent focused on content and the amount of content taught
were more important factors than the teacher behaviors that were used to
teach the content. With seventh graders, it did not matter whether the teacher
used questions and student responses or gave straight lectures. But younger
students, for example, third graders, learned better with the question-and-
answer mode. The researchers found that the questions asked needed to be
narrow in focus, clear, and easily answered. High expectations and occasional
praise were more effective than indifference or matter-of-factness. Whether
the lecture or the question format was used, careful structuring of content by
the teacher, followed by summary reviews, was the most effective teaching
method.[55]

**"Follow Through" Studies**   Jane Stallings and her colleagues observed and
evaluated results from 108 first-grade classes and 58 third-grade classes taught

by different methods. Programs having strong academic focus rather than programs using the project-method approach produced the highest gains in reading and math. Brophy and Good summarize the Stallings findings as follows: "Almost anything connected with the classical recitation pattern of teacher questioning (particularly direct factual questions rather than more open questions) followed by student response, followed by teacher feedback, correlated positively with achievement." As in the New Zealand studies, students who spent most of their time being instructed or guided by their teachers did much better than students who did projects or were expected to learn on their own.[56]

**Brophy-Evertson Studies**   Between 1973 and 1979, Brophy and his colleagues conducted a series of studies in which they first determined that some teachers got consistently good results over the years, and others consistently bad ones. They made close observations of the teacher behaviors associated, respectively, with good and bad academic outcomes. Teachers who produced the most achievement were focused on academics. They were warm but businesslike. Teachers who produced the least achievement used a "heavily affective" approach and were more concerned with the child's self-esteem and psychic well-being than with academics. They emphasized warmth, used student ideas, employed a democratic style, and encouraged student-student interaction. The researchers further found that learning proceeded best when the material was somewhat new and challenging, but could also be assimilated relatively easily into what students already knew. The biggest contrast was not between modes of academic instruction but between all such instruction and "learner-centered" "discovery learning," which was ineffective. Paradoxically, the students were more motivated and engaged by academic-centered instruction than by student-centered instruction.

In 1982, Brophy and his colleagues summarized some their later findings on the effective teaching of beginning reading. These were the most salient points:

1. Sustained focus on content.
2. All students involved (whole-class instruction dominates).
3. Brisk pace, with easy enough tasks for consistent student success.
4. Students reading aloud often and getting consistent feedback.
5. Decoding skills mastered to the point of overlearning (automaticity).
6. In the course of time, each child asked to perform and getting immediate, nonjudgmental feedback.[57]

**Good-Grouws Studies**   For over a decade, Good and Grouws pursued process-outcome studies that support the Brophy-Evertson findings. Their 1977 summary contained the following points:

1. The best teachers were clearer.
2. They introduced more new concepts, engaged in less review.
3. They asked fewer questions.
4. Their feedback to the students was quick and nonevaluative.
5. They used whole-class instruction most of the time.
6. They were demanding and conveyed high expectations.[58]

**The Gage Studies**   N. L. Gage and his colleagues at Stanford University have produced a series of process-outcome studies from the 1960s to the 1980s. These results, consistent with the above, are summarized in the following points of advice to teachers:

1. Introduce material with an overview or analogy.
2. Use review and repetition.
3. Praise or repeat student answers.
4. Be patient in waiting for responses.
5. Integrate the responses into the lesson.
6. Give assignments that offer practice and variety.
7. Be sure questions and assignments are new and challenging, yet easy enough to allow success with reasonable effort.[59]

**Other Studies**   In 1986, Rosenshine and Stevens listed five other "particularly praiseworthy" studies of effective teaching modes, all of which came to similar conclusions. They summarize these conclusions as follows:

1. Review prerequisite learning.
2. Start with a brief statement of goals.
3. Introduce new material in small steps.
4. Maintain clarity and detail in presentation.
5. Achieve a high level of active practice.
6. Obtain response and check for understanding (CFU).
7. Guide student practice initially.
8. Give systematic, continual feedback.
9. Monitor and give specific advice during seatwork.[60]

**The Brophy-Good Summary** In their final summation of research in this area, Brophy and Good make a comment worth quoting directly. They draw two chief conclusions from reviewing all of this research:

> *One is that academic learning is influenced by the amount of time students spend in appropriate academic tasks. The second is that students learn more efficiently when their teachers first structure new information for them and help them relate it to what they already know, and then monitor their performance and provide corrective feedback during recitation, drill, practice, or application activities. . . . There are no shortcuts to successful attainment of higher-level learning objectives. Such success will not be achieved with relative ease through discovery learning by the student. Instead, it will require considerable instruction from the teacher, as well as thorough mastery of basic knowledge and skills which must be integrated and applied in the process of "higher-level" performance. Development of basic knowledge and skills to the level of automatic and errorless performance will require a great deal of drill and practice. Thus drill and practice activities should not be slighted as "low level." They appear to be just as essential to complex and creative intellectual performance as they are to the performance of a virtuoso violinist.*[61]

Before I go on to discuss correlations between these findings and research in cognitive psychology, I will digress to make an observation connecting these results to student motivation. While common sense might have predicted the *academic* superiority of structured, whole-class instruction over less academically focused, learner-centered instruction, it was unexpected that these studies should have demonstrated the *motivational* superiority of instruction centered on content rather than on students. Why is academically focused instruction more engaging and motivating to young learners than learner-centered instruction?

I know of no research that explains this finding, but I shall hazard the guess that individualized, learner-centered instruction must be extremely boring to most students most of the time, since, by mathematical necessity, they are not receiving individualized attention most of the time. It may also be the case that the slow pace and progress of less structured teaching may fail to engage and motivate students. A teacher must be extraordinarily talented to know just how to interact engagingly with each individual child. Given the strong motivation of young children to learn about the adult world, the best way to engage them is by a dramatic, interactive, and clear presentation that incidentally brings out the inherent satisfaction in skill mastery and interest in subject matter.

I have already explained the basis in cognitive psychology for the finding that students should be taught procedural skills to the point of "overlearning." (See Section 4 of this chapter for a discussion of the structure of real-world competency.) "Overlearning" is a rather unfortunate term of art, since intuitively it seems a bad idea to overdo anything. But the term simply means that students should become able to supply the right answer or to follow the right procedure very fast, without hesitation. Through practice, they become so habituated to a procedure that they no longer have to think or struggle to perform it. This leaves their highly limited working memory free to focus on other aspects of the task at hand. The classroom research cited above simply reported that teachers who followed the principle of overlearning produced much better results. Cognitive psychology explains why. Students who have mastered word recognition through structured practice of that procedural task, for example, are much better able to comprehend what they are reading. One of the best ways of overlearning word recognition is by "repeated readings": students read a selection over and over again until they can read it with facility. Research shows that by using the repeated-reading method,

> *students not only improved in fluency on each passage, they also showed a transfer-of-training effect in that the first reading of each new passage was faster than the previous initial reading had been, and the number of readings to reach criterion decreased.* **The most important finding was that there was improvement in comprehension.** *[My emphasis.]*[62]

Automating word recognition leaves the mind free to focus on comprehension. This is precisely what studies of working memory in cognitive psychology would lead one to predict.

The classroom studies also stressed the importance of teaching new content in small incremental steps. This is likewise explained by the limitations of working memory, since the mind can handle only a small number of new things at one time. A new thing has to become integrated with prior knowledge before the mind can give it meaning, store it in memory, and attend to something else. New learnings should not be introduced until feedback from students indicates that they have mastered the old learnings quite well, though not, as in the case of procedural skills, to the point of overlearning. Research into long-term memory shows why this slow-but-sure method of feedback and review works best. "Once is not enough" should be the motto of long-term memory, though nonmeaningful review and boring repetition are *not* good techniques. The classroom research cited above indicated that the best teachers did not engage in incessant review. Memory studies suggest that the best approach to achieving retention in long-term memory is "distributed practice." Ideally, lessons should spread a topic over several days, with repetitions occurring at moderately distant intervals. Thus Bahrick:

> *Students learned and relearned 50 English-Spanish word pairs seven times to the same criterion. They were tested for recall and recognition 8 years later. The original relearning sessions were spaced either at 30-day intervals, at 1-day intervals, or all on the same day. Eight years later, participants who were trained at 30-day intervals recalled about twice as many words as those trained at 1-day intervals, and both of these groups retained more than the subjects who were trained and retrained on the same day.[63]*

It would follow that a two-day interval is better than one-day for introducing reviews. This feature of learning explains the importance of a deliberate pace of instruction, as all the classroom studies showed. Whatever practical arrangements are chosen for classroom learning, the principle of content rehearsal is absolutely essential for fixing content in long-term memory. Until that fixation occurs, content learning cannot be said to have happened.

That receiving continual feedback from the students is essential to good teaching is a robust finding in all the studies, and also gets support from research into both short-term and long-term memory. Feedback indicates whether the material has been learned well enough to free short-term (i.e., working) memory for new tasks. Moreover, the process of engaging in question-answer and other feedback practices constitutes content rehearsal, which also helps achieve secure learning in memory. Good teachers seem to be implicitly aware of this double function of question asking—that is, simultaneous monitoring and rehearsing.

Finally, research in cognitive psychology supports the finding that classes should often begin with a review or an analogy which connects the new topic with knowledge students already have. Psycholinguistic studies have shown that verbal comprehension powerfully depends on students' relevant background knowledge and particularly on their ability to apply that knowledge to something new.[64] Meaningful understanding seems to be equivalent to joining the new knowledge to something already known. Other psycholinguistic studies show that comprehension is enhanced when clues are offered at the beginning of a written passage indicating the overall character and direction of the passage. One needs to have a sense of the whole in order to predict the character of the parts and the way they fit with each other. Just as holistic, generic clues are important for the reader's comprehension of a written passage, such clues are similarly important for the student's understanding in the classroom. This psycholinguistic principle shows why a summary at the beginning of a class can give students the right "mindset" for assimilating the new material.[65]

These few principles concerning working memory, long-term memory, and the best prior conditions for meaningful learning explain the effectiveness of almost all the practices that were found to be effective in the classroom studies. Their congruence with mainstream psychology was well observed by Rosenshine and Stevens when they stated that research in cognitive psychology

> *helps explain why students taught with structured curricula generally do better than those taught with either more individualized or discovery learning approaches. It also explains why young students who receive their instruction from a teacher usually achieve more than those who are expected to learn new materials and skills on their own or from each other. When young children are expected to learn on their own, particularly in the early stages, the students run the danger of not attending to the right cues, or not processing important points, and of proceeding on to later points before they have done sufficient elaboration and practice.[66]*

Now I shall turn to some data from international studies on classroom practice. The fullest such research has been conducted by Harold Stevenson and his several colleagues in the United States, China, Japan, and Taiwan, who observed 324 Asian and American mathematics classrooms divided between first grade and fifth grade. Each classroom was studied for over twenty hours by trained observers who took voluminous notes. There can be little doubt of the accuracy of the resulting generalizations regarding classroom practice in Asia and the United States. Nor can there be any doubt of the differences in mathematical achievement between the Asian and American classrooms. In international comparative studies of math achievement among developed nations, Asian countries rank at the top, the United States at the bottom. Hence, this international research by Stevenson and his colleagues can be interpreted as a process-outcome study on a grand scale, one in which the different classroom processes that yield dramatically different outcomes are fully and accurately described.

Classroom practice is not of course the only factor that has caused this huge difference in outcomes. Chinese and Japanese adults value mathematics; they are well educated in the subject, are able to teach math to their children outside of school. Nonetheless, classroom practice is a highly important factor in determining these results. (In their book *The Learning Gap,* Stevenson and Stigler effectively dispose of the argument that our inferior classroom results are owing to our greater "diversity."[67]) In light of the contrast in outcomes, it is no surprise that the activities which typically occur in Asian classrooms follow the effective pedagogical principles deduced from small-scale American studies and from cognitive psychology. By contrast, the activities that typically occur in American classrooms run counter to those research findings. Lest these contrasts seem to deprecate *all* American teachers, however, it should be remembered that it was the work of first-rate American teachers which originally determined the results of the research into effective pedagogical principles. Unfortunately, as comparative studies show, such superior pedagogy is not at all typical in the United States.

To illustrate the agreement between the small-scale intranational studies and the international studies, I shall first summarize the small-scale research findings in each category, then the corresponding findings from the international studies.

### SOCIAL ATMOSPHERE

*Small-scale, intranational studies:*

In the best classrooms, the social atmosphere was warm and supportive, but at the same time businesslike and focused on the job at hand. By contrast, the worst-performing classrooms were "heavily affective," with a lot of verbal praise and self-esteem talk. In the best classes, the teacher was respectful to students but demanded good discipline as well as hard work. In the worst, the atmosphere was less ordered and disciplined.

*International studies:*

The most frequent form of evaluation used by American teachers was praise, a technique that is rarely used in either Taiwan or Japan. Praise cuts off discussion and highlights the teacher's role as the authority. It also encourages students to be satisfied with their performance rather than informing them about where they need improvement. Chinese and Japanese teachers have a low tolerance for errors, and when they occur, they seldom ignore them. Discussing errors helps to clarify misunderstandings, encourage argument and justification, and involve students in the exciting quest of assessing the strengths and weaknesses of the various alternative solutions that have been proposed.[68]

INITIAL ORIENTATION

*Small-scale, intranational studies:*

The teacher first reviews the knowledge prerequisite to the new learning and orients the class to what is in store. One good way is to introduce the material with an overview or analogy connecting it with previous knowledge and to present a brief statement of goals for the day's class.

*International studies:*

The Asian teacher stands in front of the class as a cue that the lesson will soon start. The room quiets. "Let us begin," says the teacher in Sendai. After brief reciprocal bows between pupils and teacher, the teacher opens the class with a description of what will be accomplished during the class period. From that point until the teacher summarizes the day's lesson, and announces "We are through," the Japanese elementary school class—like those in Taiwan and China—consists of teacher and students working together toward the goals described at the beginning of the class. Contrast this scene with a fifth-grade American mathematics classroom that we recently visited. Immediately after getting the students' attention, the teacher pointed out that today was Tuesday, "band day," and that all students in the band should go to the band room. "Those of you doing the news report today should meet over there in the corner," he continued. He then began the mathematics class with the remaining students by reviewing the solution to a computation problem that had been included in the previous day's homework. After this brief review, the teacher directed the students' attention to the blackboard where the day's assignment had been written. The teacher then spent most of the rest of the period walking about the room monitoring the children's work, talking to individual children about questions or errors, and uttering "shush" whenever the students began talking among themselves. This example is typical.[69]

PACE

*Small-scale, intranational studies:*

The best teachers introduce new material in small, easily mastered steps, setting a deliberate but brisk pace, not moving ahead until students show that they understand. Better results come from teachers who move forward with new concepts, have higher expectations, and provide review, but not "incessant review."

*International studies:*

The pace is slow, but the outcome is impressive. Japanese teachers want their students to be reflective and to gain a deep understanding of mathematics. Each concept and skill is taught with great thoroughness, thereby eliminating the need to teach the concept again later. Covering only a few problems does not mean that the lesson turns out to be short on content. In the United States curriculum planners, textbook publishers, and teachers themselves seem to believe that students learn more effectively if they solve a large number of problems rather than if they concentrate their attention on only a few.[70]

## CLARITY

*Small-scale, intranational studies:*

The most effective teachers were not just clearer but more focused on the content or skill goal, asked questions but fewer of them, and kept the focus by continually integrating student responses into the lesson. A useful tool for clarity in presentation: an end-of-class summary review indicating where the lesson went and what it did.

*International studies:*

Irrelevant interruptions often add to children's difficulty in perceiving lessons as a coherent whole. In American observations, the teacher interrupted the flow of the lesson with irrelevant comments, or the class was interrupted by someone else in 20 percent of all first-grade lessons and 47 percent of all fifth-grade lessons. In Sendai, Taipei, and Beijing, interruptions occurred less than 10 percent of the time at both grade levels. Coherence is also disrupted by frequent shifting from one topic to another within a single lesson. Twenty-one percent of the shifts within American lessons were to different topics (rather than to different materials or activities), compared with only 5 percent in the Japanese lessons. Before ending the lesson the Asian teacher reviews what has been learned, and relates it to the problem she posed at the beginning of the lesson. American teachers are much less likely than Asian teachers to end lessons in this way. For example, we found that fifth-grade teachers in Beijing spent eight times as long at the end of the class period summarizing the lessons as did those in Chicago.[71]

## MANAGING AND MONITORING

*Small-scale, intranational studies:*

In the most effective teaching, whole-class instruction is used most of the time. The teacher obtains responses and checks for understanding for each student, ensuring that each child gets some feedback and that all students stay involved. While feedback to the students is frequent, it is not incessant. The teacher is patient in waiting for responses. Student answers are often repeated for the class. Many effective teachers make constructive, nonevaluative use of student errors, working through how they were made. Students are more engaged and motivated in these classrooms than in student-centered ones.

*International studies:*

Chinese and Japanese teachers rely on students to generate ideas and evaluate the correctness of the ideas. The possibility that they will be called upon to state their own solution keeps Asian students alert, but this technique has two other important functions. First, it engages students in the lesson, increasing their motivation by making them feel they are participants in a group process. Second, it conveys a more realistic impression of how knowledge is acquired. American teachers are less likely to give students opportunities to respond at such length. Although a great deal of interaction appears to occur in American classrooms—with students and teachers posing questions and giving answers—American teachers generally ask questions that are answerable with a yes or a no or a short phrase. They seek a correct answer and continue calling on students until one produces it.[72]

## DRILL AND PRACTICE

*Small-scale, intranational studies:*

Two kinds of practice are needed, corresponding to two objects of learning—content and skills. For content, new concepts are discussed and reviewed until secure in the memory. Procedural skills are mastered to the point of overlearning (automaticity). Guided practice should be part of whole-class instruction before seatwork occurs. Small-group seatwork generally works better than individual seatwork, but seatwork per se is used rather sparingly for both content and skills. Supervision and feedback are provided during seatwork.

*International studies:*

When children must work alone for long periods of time without guidance or reaction from the teacher, they begin to lose focus on the purpose of their activity. Asian teachers assign less seatwork than American teachers; further-more, they use seatwork differently. Asian teachers tend to use short, frequent periods of seatwork, alternating between discussing problems and allowing children to work problems on their own. When seatwork is embedded within the lesson, instruction and practice are tightly woven into a coherent whole. Teachers can gauge children's understanding of the preceding part of the lesson by observing how they solve practice problems. Interspersing seatwork with instruction in this way helps the teacher assess how rapidly she can proceed through the lesson. American teachers, on the other hand, tend to relegate seatwork to one long period at the end of the class, where it becomes little more than a time for repetitious practice. In Chicago, 59 percent of all fifth-grade lessons ended with a period of seatwork, compared with 23 percent in Sendai and 14 percent in Taipei. American teachers often do not discuss the work or its connection to the goal of the lesson, or publicly evaluate its accu-racy. Seatwork was never evaluated or discussed during 48 percent of all American fifth-grade lessons observed, compared to less than 3 percent of Japanese classes and 6 percent of Taiwan classes.[73]

Since it was predominantly research into effective *American* classrooms that, in the small-scale studies, originally determined these criteria of effective teaching, the first question that comes to mind is: Why do American teachers so consistently contravene the results of American research, whereas Asian teachers consistently follow its imperatives? In an important study of class-room effectiveness that reported similarly disconcerting findings, W. James Popham, an education professor at UCLA, stated the following about Ameri-can teachers:

*Rarely does one find a teacher who, prior to teaching, establishes clearly stated instructional objectives in terms of learner behavior and then sets out to achieve those objectives. . . . Lest this sound like an unchecked assault on the teaching profession, it should be pointed out that there is little reason to expect that [American] teachers should be skilled goal achievers.* Certainly they have not been trained to be; teacher education institutions rarely foster this kind of competence. Nor is there any premium placed on such instructional skill after the teacher concludes preservice training. *[My emphasis.]*[74]

The very thing which Horace Mann called upon teacher-training schools to do and which the American public assumes that such schools *are* doing—the teaching of effective pedagogy—is a domain of training that, according to both sympathetic and unsympathetic observers, gets short shrift in our education schools.[75] Instead, it is mainly theory, and highly questionable theory at that, which gets more attention in education-school courses. That point should be stated even more strongly: not only do our teacher-training schools decline to put a premium on nuts-and-bolts classroom effectiveness, but they promote ideas that actually run counter to consensus research into teacher effectiveness. In Section 1 of this chapter, I quoted the sorts of things our teachers are being told regarding classroom practice. It will be instructive to recall those things here, from the 1993 book called *Best Practice:*

> *In virtually every school subject, we now have recent summary reports, meta-analyses of instructional research, bulletins from pilot classrooms, and landmark sets of professional recommendations. Today there is a strong consensus definition of Best Practice, of state-of-the-art teaching in every critical field. . . . Whether the recommendations come from the National Council of Teachers of Mathematics, the Center for the Study of Reading, the National Writing Project, the National Council for the Social Studies, the American Association for the Advancement of Science, the National Council of Teachers of English, the National Association for the Education of Young Children, or the International Reading Association, the fundamental insights into teaching and learning are remarkably congruent. Indeed on many key issues, the recommendations from these diverse organizations are unanimous.*[76]

Then, as the reader may remember, the book lists twenty-five "LESS" and "MORE" admonitions on which all these organizations agree. Among them are the following:

> *LESS whole-class teacher-directed instruction*
> *LESS student passivity, sitting, listening, receiving*
> *LESS attempts by teachers to cover large amounts of material*
> *LESS rote memorization of facts and details*
> *LESS stress on competition and grades*

MORE *experiential, inductive, hands-on learning*

MORE *active learning with all the attendant noise of students doing,
 talking, collaborating*

MORE *deep study of a smaller number of topics*

MORE *responsibility transferred to students for their work: goal-setting,
 record-keeping, monitoring, evaluation*

MORE *choice for students; e.g., picking their own books, etc.*

MORE *attention to affective needs and varying cognitive styles of students*

MORE *cooperative, collaborative activity.*[77]

The authors praise the current consensus on these "child-centered" principles for being "progressive, developmentally appropriate, research based, and eminently teachable." These claims are not, however, "research based" in the way the authors imply. Quite the contrary. No studies of children's learning in mainstream science support these generalizations. With respect to effective learning, the consensus in research is that their recommendations are worst practice, not "best practice."

This Alice in Wonderland reversal of reality has been accomplished largely by virtue of the rhetorical device that I have called "premature polarization." Discovery learning is labeled "progressive," and whole-class instruction "traditional." Under such descriptors, one mode is assumed to be active and engaging, the other passive and boring; one holistic and indirect, the other step-by-step and direct. As a result of such terminological polarization, the term "direct instruction," which is the mode advocated by a number of teachers and educational specialists, has come in for some heavy criticism from antitraditionalists. The distinction, however, between direct and indirect instruction is an unfortunate simplification of some complex issues. It overlooks, for instance, the different pedagogical requirements for procedural learning and content learning, and thus neglects the different pedagogical emphases needed at the different ages and stages of learning. Effective procedural learning requires "overlearning," and hence plenty of practice. Content learning is amenable to a diversity of methods that accommodate themselves to students' prior knowledge, habits, and interests.

What the international data show very clearly is that both procedural and content learning are best achieved in a focused environment which preponderantly emphasizes whole-class instruction but which is punctuated by small-group or individualized work. Within that focused context, however, there are many good roads to Rome. The classroom observations of Stevenson and his colleagues bring home the ancient wisdom of integrating both direct and indirect methods, including inquiry learning, which encourages students to think for themselves, and direct informing, which is sometimes the most effective and efficient mode of securing knowledge and skill. A combination of show and tell, omitting neither, is generally the most effective approach in teaching, as it is in writing and speaking.

The only truly general principle that seems to emerge from process-outcome research on pedagogy is that focused and guided instruction is far more effective than naturalistic, discovery, learn-at-your-own-pace instruction. But within the context of focused and guided instruction, almost anything goes, and what works best with one group of students may not work best with another group with similar backgrounds in the very same building. Methods must vary a good deal with different age groups. Within the general context of focused and guided instruction, my own general preference, and one followed by good teachers in many lands, is for what might be called "dramatized instruction." The class period can be formed into a little drama with a beginning, middle and end, well directed but not rigidly scripted by the teacher. The beginning sets up the question to be answered, the knowledge to be mastered, or the skill to be gained; the middle consists of a lot of back-and-forth between student and student, student and teacher; and the end consists of a feeling of closure and accomplishment.

The idea of teaching as drama or as storytelling gains a great deal of credence from its agreement with demonstrably effective classroom teaching and with an ancient and highly effective tradition, particularly in that subtle domain of teaching consensus values and virtues. How do we teach and model such values as independent thinking, toleration, respect, aspiration, civility, resistance to the mob, and at the same time teach subject matters and skills like history and science, reading and writing? From Plato to Sir Philip Sidney to Robert Coles to Kieran Egan, there is general agreement that dramatizing, telling, or implicitly enacting stories, both fictional and factual, is a sound and sure teaching method.[78] In early grades especially, no opportunity should be lost to combine skill instruction, which can itself be dramatized, with virtue-and-knowledge-enhancing stories.

The focused narrative or drama lies midway between narrow drill and practice (which has its place) and the unguided activity of the project method (which may also occasionally have a place). Sir Philip Sidney argued (in 1583!) that stories are better teachers than philosophy or history, because philosophy teaches by dull precept (guided instruction) and history teaches by uncertain example (the project method). The story, however, joins precept and example together, thus teaching and delighting at the same time. Thus Sidney in the sixteenth century:

*The philosopher therefore and the historian are they which would win the goal, the one by precept, the other by example. But both, not having both, do both halt. For the philosopher [sets] down with thorny argument the bare rule. . . . The historian, wanting the precept, his example draweth no necessary consequence. . . . Now doth the peerless poet perform both. . . . With a tale forsooth he cometh unto you, with a tale which holdeth children from play, and old men from the chimney corner. And pretending no more, doth intend the winning of the mind from wickedness to virtue.[79]*

Elsewhere in his essay, Sidney makes it clear that good history can also be a good story which combines precept and example. Excellent classroom teaching has a narrative and dramatic feel even when there is a lot of interaction between the students and the teacher—it has a definite theme, and a beginning, middle, and end. This teaching principle holds even for mathematics and science. When every lesson has a well-developed plot in which the children themselves are participants, teaching is both focused and absorbing. The available research is consistent with this scheme, though it by no means says that thoughtful sequencing, plotting, and dramatizing of learning activities are the exclusive or whole key to good pedagogy. For many elementary learnings, repeated practice has to be an integral part of the plot.

That recent psychological research should yield insights which confirm what Plato and Sidney said about stories should probably make us more, not less, confident in the results of this recent research. Education is as old as humanity. The breathless claim that technology and the information age have radically changed the nature of the education of young children turns out to be, like most breathless claims in education, unsupported by scholarship. Nor should current studies surprise us when they show that a naturalistic approach, lacking a definite story line and a sharp focus, has the defect Sidney saw in history as a teacher of humankind: it "draweth no necessary consequence." There *is* a modest place for discovery learning, just as there is for drill and practice. But research indicates that, most of the time, clearly focused, well-plotted teaching is the best means for "[holding] children from play and old men from the chimney corner."

# 6.

# Test

# Evasion

CLEOPATRA.                          What say you? Hence,
Horrible villain! Or I'll spurn thine eyes
Like balls before me; I'll unhair thy head:
Thou shalt be whipp'd with wire, and stew'd in brine,
Smarting in lingering pickle.
MESSENGER.                          Gracious madam,
I that do bring the news made not the match.
                                    —Shakespeare, *Antony and Cleopatra*

## 1.
## Shooting the Messenger

S ince mistaken ideas have been the root cause of America's educational
problems, the ideas must be changed before the problems can be solved.
That is the main theme of this book. But, in addition, the exposition has been
compelled by the recent history of American education to deal with a corollary
theme: that the reforms currently being proposed are themselves part of the
problem. Hence my epigraph to the book: "Who will reform the reformers?"
To overcome the illness, we first need to abandon the cures. In previous
chapters, I cited research which showed that effective improvement must include precisely those practices which are being caricatured and rejected in old-
line progressivist attacks on factual knowledge, drill and practice, memorization, whole-class instruction, and other badly needed traditional practices.
This chapter will once again illustrate the pattern. The proposed cure—this

time the repudiation of objective tests—is part of the disease. But again, it is the attack rather than the thing attacked that chiefly needs to be repudiated.

The campaign against giving students tests is an integral part of a Romantic progressivism that goes back to the 1920s. Then, as now, tests were repudiated for belonging to a "factory model" of education, for introducing competition where it does not belong, for denying the individuality of students' talents and interests, for degrading education by encouraging passivity, mindlessness, and triviality, and for sending the wrong messages about what is valuable in education and in life. To those former objections have now been added the further ones that objective tests have helped cause our educational decline, that they are unfair to minorities, and that they injure social justice. If testing is to be conducted at all, reformers propose that its drawbacks be avoided by using more humane, performance-based tests that gauge real-world abilities and give each individual his or her due.

In this chapter, I will acknowledge that some of the criticisms of objective tests are valid, but these pertain to specific test abuses that can easily be avoided by watchful educators and an informed public. My main task will be to show that the larger, oft-repeated criticisms of objective tests are *not* valid. In addition, I shall argue that in the American context such tests are necessary to achieve excellence and fairness. They function as achievement incentives for students and teachers, as ways of monitoring students' progress in order to remedy their deficiencies, and as essential helps in the administrative monitoring of classrooms, schools, and districts. Without effective monitoring, neither good teaching nor good educational administration is possible. Finally, and above all, objective tests are needed for academic fairness and social equity— the chief reasons that Americans, to their credit, have been pioneers in developing objective tests.

In the midst of the furious attacks on standardized tests by the educational community, it may preserve perspective to remind ourselves of some different functions of standardized and unstandardized tests. Tests are used for many reasons other than "sorting," "gatekeeping," or "pigeonholing" (just one type of complaint in the attacks). Properly used, tests have an irreplaceably positive effect on learning. In the classroom, for example, they give the teacher feedback to determine whether students have attained a desired learning goal and are ready for a new one. Tests are also effective in determining the adequacy of a teacher's or a school's performance, in gaining students' attention, and in creating an opportunity for further learning while students are reviewing for the test and while they are taking it. Well-conceived and properly used tests, even of the multiple-choice variety, have been employed with great success to motivate students to put forward greater effort. Learning requires effort. Tests that carry high consequences have been shown over and over again to act as spurs to effort—a fact that (to the distress of all Romantics) tends to support the Augustinian view of human nature.

Nonetheless, the furious attack on standardized tests goes on unabated. George Madaus, himself no slouch as an attacker, has excellently summarized the current scene in the following assertions, which he took from thirty-six printed sources published between 1990 and 1992:

> *American testing is in tumult. Traditional, standardized, norm-referenced, multiple choice tests—the policy choice for the past 70 years—are under attack. The most widely touted policy alternative is a national system of examinations which would employ "authentic" assessment techniques. These techniques do not require students to select their answers from given alternatives; rather they require students to construct answers, perform, or produce something for evaluation. Authentic assessments, it is asserted, are worth teaching to; defeat negative test preparation effects associated with multiple choice tests; give teachers clear models of acceptable outcomes; have a positive influence on instruction and learning; measure higher order skills; and lay bare examinees' thinking processes. Proponents of a national examination system argue that such a system will motivate unmotivated students; all students will meet world class standards; our nation's productivity will be increased, and our global competitiveness restored; and [. . . they] will help to improve the academic performance of all students, regardless of race, native language, culture, or gender.[1]*

This summary usefully encapsulates the current push-pull rhetoric on assessment—the push against standardized tests and the pull toward "authentic" ones. But are these "authentic" tests either accurate or fair? Madaus says probably not, and I shall add further arguments to show that he is right. Before our policymakers give way to the chorus of endlessly repeated but inadequately founded assertions in favor of performance-based assessments, the proponents should be required to show that exclusive reliance on performance tests does in fact yield accuracy, fairness, and educational improvement.

The bad educational news began coming in long before 1990–92, when Madaus collected his thirty-six attacks on standardized tests. In the 1970s, when the sharp decline on the SAT and other measures had become alarming, Christopher Jencks published a shrewd analysis of the reasons for the academic decline—principally, he thought, because schools no longer taught and required demanding academic work. Along the way, Jencks quoted several self-serving explanations for the test decline offered by the National Education Association, which, already in the 1970s, was taking the lead in blaming the messenger that was bringing the bad news. Standardized tests, said the NEA, have become outmoded and no longer test what currently needs to be taught. Furthermore, such tests do not measure students' ability to "analyze, synthesize, draw generalizations, and make applications to new phenomena"—a charge Jencks disposed of by simply quoting sample questions that obviously required those very abilities. Jencks also refuted the NEA claim that standardized tests were "biased in favor of white middle-class culture" by pointing out that scores had declined sharply in Iowa, which was

> *98 percent white, and largely "middle class" in values and outlook. It is hard to believe that Iowans' declining performance on their traditional tests is due to the Iowa schools' having made systematic effort to introduce their students to the argot of Harlem or skid row. . . . Rather Iowa students' total vocabulary has almost certainly contracted. It is hard to see how that can be a good thing either in Iowa or elsewhere.*[2]

Jencks also parried the implicitly condescending view that tests are biased because the middle class places more value on cognitive skills than the lower class does. And finally, he repudiated the NEA objection that standardized tests contain "complex language and obscure vocabulary," saying, "If the NEA no longer thinks it is worthwhile to teach students how to read [complex] prose, this may explain why students are less capable of doing so." Jencks's essay was published in 1978. The attacks against standardized tests that Madaus cited from the 1990s have now been going on for so long that repetition alone has given them axiomatic status within the educational community.

The term "standardized test" requires a gloss. It is used promiscuously to characterize several different things. It is used to refer to objective tests, such as fill-in-the-blanks and multiple-choice tests; it is used to refer to norm-referenced tests, which may be of any form and which provide percentile rankings for a pool of test takers; it is used to refer to criterion-referenced tests, which may be of any form and which provide absolute scores. I shall use the term "standardized test" to mean any objective test, or combination of objective and performance tests, that yields the same score for the same performance, no matter who is doing the scoring. The difficulty of standardizing certain kinds of tests in this sense will be a focus of my remarks.

Because good tests properly used, including good standardized ones, are a strong aid to learning, I view the war on standardized tests as mainly a disheartened, scapegoating attempt to shoot the messenger that is bringing the bad news. Educators would hardly be so preoccupied with attacking standardized tests, and blaming them for the ineffectiveness and inequity of American schooling, if those machine-scored messengers were bringing less depressing bulletins, or if educators had workable ideas about how to make the results better. If our children's scores on standard tests were getting significantly higher, or if the spread of scores were more equitably distributed by race, class, and gender, or if American kids were further from the bottom on international rankings, these unceasing attacks on standardized tests would subside.

But perhaps not. Orthodox educational doctrine since the 1920s has been consistently opposed to testing and grading. When William Heard Kilpatrick designed his demonstration school at Teachers College, one of his first innovations, after having dispensed with the subject-matter curriculum, was to abolish tests and grades. In the progressive-Romantic view of education, to give number or letter grades to students in the classroom or on tests is a fundamental educational mistake. It sends an implicit message that one child is better or abler than another, and thus fosters undesirable competition instead of cooperation. It offends against the antihierarchical principle that all children are equally worthy. One simply cannot properly describe complex flesh-and-blood human beings, each of whom is immediate to God, with single letters and numbers. Romantics have always abhorred connecting human beings with numbers. As Blake put it with customary trenchancy: "Bring out number, weight & measure in a year of dearth."

Kilpatrick and his intellectual descendents argue that the use of such measures imposes external rewards and punishments for learning rather than encouraging an inward motivation toward learning for its own sake. According to this orthodoxy, which is contravened by psychological research, what is learned under compulsion or through external incentives is superficial, artificial, and short-lived. It will not lead to deep understanding or to lifelong love of learning. Learning must be natural. And to enhance that naturalness, any evaluation of learning must be lifelike and "authentic." To these earlier educational and psychological objections against grades and tests has been added in recent years a corollary—racial-social objection. Tests and grades discriminate unfairly against minorities and poor people, and sometimes against females— the proof being that on some measures these groups do not receive average marks as high as those of white males. The strength and influence of such objections against grades and tests among educators have not diminished.

Resistance to these antitest criticisms comes from parents and the general public rather than from the educational community.

In *Education Week* for June 14, 1995, there was a long article on a controversy over a "new research-based" idea: abolishing letter grades. In the Rhode Island city of Cranston, an intense controversy between parents and the schools had arisen over yet another attempt to introduce "descriptive" rather than "evaluative" report cards. (Just a few weeks earlier, *Education Week* described an emotional controversy in Massachusetts over a proposal to unbolt classroom desks in a fondly remembered classroom.) Both the desk unbolting and the grading controversies are symbols of the undying influence of progressive orthodoxy, though now dressed up in such modern terminology as "narrative report cards" and "portfolios," and through new-age techniques such as videotapes that can provide parents with "greater insight into what their children are learning." Equally persistent since the 1920s, however, has been the "reactionary" resistance of parents and citizens against ideas that do not seem to them persuasive or practical.

Few teachers who aren't sadists are fond of grades and tests. After more than thirty years of teaching, I still view those parts of my job with a distaste that has grown rather than diminished with the years. Teachers want all of their students to be A students, each in his or her own way. They want them to work hard without the extrinsic motivations of punishment and reward, and to be motivated entirely by intrinsic interest in the subject matter at hand and by the inherent joys of learning and accomplishment. They wish and hope that students' inherent desire to learn and do a good job will be its own reward. Teachers often blame themselves when not every student is intrinsically motivated by schoolwork. Moreover, most teachers strongly dislike disappointing a student with a bad grade. On the other hand, they also dislike the idea of giving everyone the same grade, because doing so, apart from other disadvantages, is egregiously unfair to students who do better work. Consequently, most teachers feel compelled to perform the disagreeable acts of testing and grading because they feel a sense of responsibility not only to honesty and fairness but also—and this is the critical point—to effective teaching.

It has been shown convincingly that tests and grades strongly contribute to effective teaching. This commonsense conjecture was confirmed by research conducted after the antigrade, pass/fail mode of grading had become popular at colleges and universities in the 1960s and '70s. Quite unambiguous analysis showed that students who took courses for a grade studied harder and learned more than students who took the courses for intrinsic interest alone.[3] This scientific confirmation of the common sense of Cranston, Rhode Island, parents runs counter to the claim that "research has shown" that giving marks *inhibits* learning. According to one expert quoted in the *Education Week* article, there are "detrimental aspects" of report cards that give grades because they make

> *learning a highly competitive activity. Students compete against each other for the few scarce rewards—the high grades—that are going to be administered by the teacher. It sets learning up as a win-lose situation for the students, and because the number of high grades is typically limited, most students will be losers.*[4]

Losers in what sense? Since research has clearly shown that students learn more when grades are given, the main issue for this expert is not how much students learn but how much their self-concept may be affected. The antigrade view continues to be associated with its origins in Romantic egalitarianism, which declines to accept any version of the idea that "most students will be losers" (i.e., get less than super grades). But this absolute, Romantic version of egalitarianism is very different from Jeffersonian democratic egalitarianism, which aimed to give rich and poor the same foundations for achievement, but to be quite rigorous in selecting only the better students for subsequent free education through a system of tests and grades.[5] This Jeffersonian version of meritocratic equality has been attacked even by (or especially by) some members of the testing community. In a recent newsletter put out by the UCLA Center for Research on Evaluation, Standards and Student Testing (CRESST), one expert was quoted as saying that "Americans have long supported what she called *procedural* equity that ensures that every one has access to valued goods. But *substantive* equity or equal results has never enjoyed public support." Far from accepting Jeffersonian meritocratic equality, the test expert recommended "re-educating" the public to favor equal results for everyone by appealing to their "self interest for a better society."[6] This improvement is to be accomplished by repudiating standardized tests in favor of more "equitable" nonstandardized kinds which will ensure that every group performs the same.

I do not mean to disparage nonstandardized tests, however. The last chapter of my 1977 book on the teaching of writing was titled "The Valid Assessment of Writing Ability," and it called for what are now labeled "authentic" or "performance-based" assessments.[7] Later on in the 1970s and early '80s, I continued to do research on performance-based writing tests and conducted experiments over a number of years. To my pleasure, the results were published in a refereed scientific book alongside the work of mainstream cognitive psychologists.[8] I mention this history not to project authority but to indicate my bona fides on the subject of performance-based assessment, and to show that my interest in and sympathy for the idea are of long standing. But my own research in performance-based assessment, coupled with the researches of others, caused me after a time to give up hope (for reasons I shall present) that such an approach to large-scale assessment could possibly be accurate, fair, and reasonable in cost. Inconvenient research to that effect by Diederich, Godshalk, Coffman, and others is rarely cited, and seems unknown or unheeded in the present bandwagon atmosphere.[9] For reasons both empirical and theoretical, it is likely that present workers in this vineyard will find that they, too, will have to give up hope of relying uniquely on a performance-based approach to large-scale K–12 testing.

But strict fairness is not essential in all educational contexts. In the classroom, the teacher's monitoring of students' progress does not have to be highly accurate and fair. There remains a strong need in the classroom for nonstandardized tests of all sorts, including performance-based ones. Since the 1960s, specialists have drawn a useful distinction between "formative" assessments, which are made by the teacher for teaching (i.e., formative) purposes, and "summative" assessments, which have more existential consequences and are used for student placement and, not insignificantly, for evaluating teaching methods and abilities. Just because the thirty-six sources that Madaus cited are all singing the same song about the evils of standardized tests and the virtues of performance tests does not mean that those lyrics are true. Indeed, they are probably false. Before proceeding further with this subject, I should like to acquaint the reader with the other side of the research story, which exposes some of the defects of performance tests and some of the very considerable strengths of standardized ones—when properly used.

## 2.
## "Authenticity" vs. Fairness

S tudents have long believed (on good evidence) that if the same paper is submitted to two teachers in two different sections of the same course, the paper is likely to receive two very different grades. In 1961, Paul Diederich and his colleagues proved that this student belief is no myth. When 300 student papers were graded by fifty-three graders (a total of 15,900 readings), more than one third of the papers received *every* possible grade. That is, 101 of the 300 papers received all nine grades: A, A–, B+, B, B–, C+, C, C–, and D. Diederich also reported that

*94 percent [of the papers] received either seven, eight or nine different grades; and no essay received less than five different grades from fifty-three readers. Even when the raters were experienced teachers, the grades given to the papers by the different raters never attained a correlation greater than .40.[10]*

Advocates of performance assessment have argued that professionals can be trained to agree more closely than this. The Educational Testing Service in Princeton has for many decades been training assessors of essays to agree rather well with each other during special grading sessions. But the ETS has also discovered this momentarily achieved agreement to be arbitrary and unstable. Although the various readers in a small group could be socialized to share similar explicit and implicit grading principles, the grades of their group would differ from those of a different group at the same session. During each ETS reading session, the various "table leaders" must confer with each other continually to keep the groups in tune. And even after the lapse of just a weekend, the groups need to engage in recalibration sessions.

Equally disconcerting is the fact that the grade given to a paper in one year in a large-scale session at the ETS will very likely be different from the grade given to that same paper in another year, if the session happens to have a different Chief Reader. The Chief Reader is the god of grade calibrations in any given session. A different grading deity can cause quite different grades to be given to another session's papers. Unless elaborate and expensive (and arbitrary) restrictions are imposed, even the expenditure of a great deal of money and effort by the ETS cannot guarantee that the student whose paper got an A in one year might not get a C in another. In fact, one of the College Board's reasons for instituting multiple-choice testing was the finding that the high-stakes grades given to a student's performance-based test "might well depend more on which year he appeared for the examination, or on which person read his paper, than it would on what he had written."[11]

Taking the trouble and expense to secure accuracy and fairness on performance tests is worthwhile in special, restricted cases, as I shall argue in a moment. But even when fairness is achieved, an inexpungible arbitrariness lies at the heart of grading performance-based assessments. The causes of this arbitrariness have been analyzed and are well understood.[12] Not only do people disagree about what qualities make for good writing, good problem solving, good ice skating, good musicianship, and so on, but more important, even when they agree on the elements that make for high quality, they may disagree about the relative weights that should be awarded to those elements. Should quality of ideas, for instance, count for more in writing than quality of organization? Should style, flavor, and individuality count for more than grammar, spelling, and punctuation? The different weights that graders attach to these different aspects of performance may vary greatly between persons, and even for the same person when grading two different performances.

The second main source of inconsistency in the grading of performance-based assessments is the inconsistency of the performer. I don't refer just to the variations we all exhibit on different days in performing the very same task. (Within a limited range, everybody has good and bad days.) The more important performer inconsistency lies in task variability: some pianists play Liszt a lot better than they do Mozart; some kids write better about snakes than they do about computers. There is just no such thing as equal, across-the-board writing ability any more than there is generalized, homogeneous reading ability. A person's performance varies not just because of temperamental congeniality with a certain task but, mainly, because of his or her level of familiarity with the task. People tend to craft technically superior papers about subjects they happen to be familiar with, and they tend to write technically inferior papers on unfamiliar topics or in unfamiliar genres. Sondra Perl and her colleagues at the City University of New York have shown that even on a measure as objective as spelling and punctuation, quality of performance is higher when the topic is more familiar to the writer.[13]

This task variability is easily accounted for by the skills-related psychological considerations discussed in the preceding chapter. When a task is unfamiliar and requires a great deal of attention in dealing with its middle-level components, the limited capacity of working memory leaves little room for monitoring the various lower- or higher-level components of the task. One writing sample, even when graded by socialized graders, may yield a very misleading inference about a student's average writing ability. If the topic is especially familiar and congenial to a particular student, the performance is likely to be uncharacteristically good. Conversely, if the topic is unfamiliar, it is likely to be uncharacteristically bad. Given these inconsistencies of both the grader and the performer, it is no surprise that a performance-based assessment, graded by a single trained rater or even by a group of trained raters, has a low likelihood of accurately assessing a student's average ability to perform.

In Vermont, a recent large-scale attempt to use performance-based tests was analyzed by Daniel Koretz, who reached the following conclusions, quoted from his 1994 study:

1. *The unreliability of scoring alone was sufficient to preclude most of the intended uses of the scores.*

*2. The system did not differentiate well between best pieces and the rest of the portfolio.*
*3. The rating system failed to discern real differences in quality.*
*4. The rate of exact agreement was 45%, but the rate expected by chance alone was 35%.*
*5. The financial costs appear to be sizeable.*[14]

Since these unreliable and unfair tests are supposed to overcome the unfairness, inaccuracy, and other defects of multiple-choice tests, it will be valuable to summarize research that has correlated the results of a carefully controlled, highly valid (but therefore extremely expensive) performance-based assessment with a short, cheap, intelligently constructed multiple-choice assessment. Data for the study were obtained from 1,300 eleventh- and twelfth-grade students from public and private schools in large and small cities and rural areas in California, Connecticut, Kansas, Maine, Michigan, Minnesota, Mississippi, New Mexico, New York, Pennsylvania, Rhode Island, Tennessee, Washington State, West Virginia, and Wisconsin. Each student completed five different types of essays on required topics (to compensate for topic variability) and also took several batteries of multiple-choice tests. Complete data were obtained for 646 cases.[15]

Each of the five essays was scored independently by five different graders using three ratings—above average, average, and below average. This reduction of possible scores to three (with a well-known tendency to choose the middle score) nonetheless resulted in only about a .40 correlation between raters when just one essay was read. When, however, the ratings for all five essays were averaged out, the correlation among raters increased to .92, and the average correlation among the five scores received by a single student on all five essays increased to .84. Thus, by training the graders and by having five set topics and twenty-five independent readings for each student, it was possible to reach a reasonably sound conclusion about each student's average writing ability. Needless to say, the cost of achieving that degree of accuracy and fairness was very high indeed.

Having performed these labors, and using each student's results as a criterion of that student's actual writing ability, the researchers then investigated how well various sorts and combinations of tests would consistently reflect that reality. If, to keep costs within reasonable bounds, a test were to last one hour, what reliability would be obtained when three twenty-minute papers were assigned, each read by one or two raters? We know from other research that assigning three twenty-minute topics is fairer to the student than assigning a single one-hour paper. With a single paper read once, the score reliability is about .25. If *three* papers are read once, the score reliability is about .454. If the three papers are read twice, the reliability rises to .542; and if three papers are read by three readers, the reliability rises to about .640. Now, suppose we replace the essay task with three types of multiple-choice questions, with each type allotted twenty minutes. The best correlation with the prior criterion (that is, with twenty-five readings of five papers) is .775—an acceptable level of fairness.

In short, much *higher* accuracy and fairness (.775 vs. .640) are obtained by using three multiple-choice sections than by using three essays that are given three readings each. Moreover, the better result is obtained at a fraction of the cost of reading three papers three times. But there is a twist to this story. A combination of multiple-choice items plus one essay was the best and fairest test of all. Godshalk and his colleagues determined that an hour test consisting of two multiple-choice segments plus a writing sample yielded a still higher test validity against the criterion—that is, .784 vs. .775.

It is worth quoting the policy conclusion that Godshalk and his colleagues drew from these results at the end of their impressive study:

> *When essay scores are combined with objective subtest scores, they produce validity coefficients even higher [i.e., .784 vs. .775]. It is doubtful that the slight increase in validity alone can justify the increased cost. Rather, the advantage has to be assessed in terms of the model the essay provides for students and teachers. An essay in the English Composition Test says to the student that skill in actual writing is an important outcome of instruction. It says to the teacher that the ability to answer multiple-choice questions, unless accompanied by the ability to compose answers to essay questions, is not sufficient evidence of effective teaching.*[16]

This seems to me exactly the right policy balance regarding performance-based and multiple-choice tests, at least in testing writing ability. For reasons given by Godshalk and his colleagues, neither type of test should be relinquished for that purpose. By including a performance component, policymakers can ensure that these tests are sending out the right educational messages to students and teachers; but at the same time, by including a generous multiple-choice component, they can ensure accuracy and fairness at a reasonable cost. But this peaceable and prudent conclusion can hardly be translated into thoughtful policy in the present atmosphere, in which the angry attack on multiple-choice tests goes on without surcease. Research has repeatedly shown that fair and accurate performance assessments *cannot* be achieved on a large scale at a reasonable cost. That being so, what will be left if the smear campaign against multiple-choice tests continues without challenge? We will be left with what some people apparently want—a successful discrediting of *all* reliable means of accountability for students and schools.

Both multiple-choice and performance tests have defects and are open to abuses, yet neither form of testing should be abandoned. The shortcomings of multiple-choice tests should be identified and corrected, and there are some rather direct means for doing so. But once the abuses of standardized tests *are* corrected, the remaining complaints against them can be shown to be unjustified and misguided. Before turning to those issues, I shall explain briefly why, for high-stakes, summative assessments, a multiple-choice component contributes enormously to a test's accuracy and fairness. I shall review the main reasons, other than cost-effectiveness, that originally persuaded psychometricians to replace performance assessments with objective tests.

The main consideration was fairness. A test is primarily a sampling device. The principal reason that a good objective test is fairer than a good performance test is that, for a test of any reasonable length, a good objective test can probe a much larger and more representative sample of the domain being sampled. If the domain is a skill, then the objective test will be able to sample a larger and more representative variety of factors that make up the skill. A performance test of writing, for instance, adequately covers just one or two genres of writing, whereas an objective test can sample five or six. If the domain being tested is a field of knowledge, then a good objective test can sample a bigger portion of the whole domain than a performance test of similar length can.

Typically, an objective test of eighty items for a particular domain will have a very high reliability. That implies, for example, that the same person taking a different form of the test will reliably tend to make close to the same score. Adding further items typically improves reliability only very gradually, as the following graph from Ebel illustrates. After that point, the law of diminishing returns sets in dramatically:

In the Godshalk study, discussed above, it was demonstrated that a multiple-choice test is a far more valid and reliable measure of writing ability than a performance-based test of the same length. In that study, researchers experimented with six different types of multiple-choice items. It will be instructive to look at three types of items that proved to be highly informative in sampling a student's writing ability:

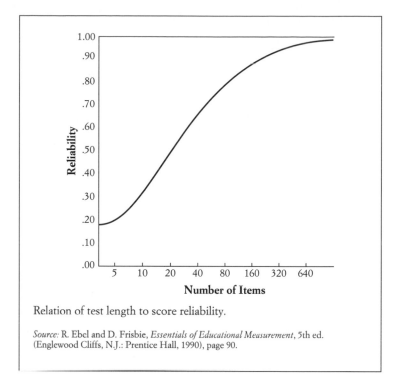

Relation of test length to score reliability.

*Source:* R. Ebel and D. Frisbie, *Essentials of Educational Measurement*, 5th ed.
(Englewood Cliffs, N.J.: Prentice Hall, 1990), page 90.

*Type I. Usage to be corrected or, if correct, to let stand.*
1. *He spoke* bluntly *and* angrily *to* we spectators.
(A) *bluntly*
(B) *angrily*
(C) *we*
(D) *spectators*
(E) *No error*

*Type II. Sentence to be corrected, improved, or, if OK, to let stand.*
2. While waving *goodbye to our friends, the airplane took off, and we
watched it disappear in the sky.*
(A) *While waving*
(B) *Upon waving*
(C) *Having waved*
(D) *Waving*
(E) *While we waved*

*Type III. Forming a new construction.*
*3. Statements such as "this picture is trash," or "the outlook is dark,"* or *"this steak is wonderful,"* are statements not only *about the picture, the outlook, or the steak, but also about the speaker's reaction to them.*

*Directions: In the above sentence, substitute the new phrase "give less information" for the present phrase "are statements not only." Your rewritten sentence will then also need to contain which of the following?:*
*(A) but about*
*(B) as about*
*(C) than about*
*(D) than the*
*(E) and more about*[17]

On the surface, there are several aspects of these items that seem designed to repel a sensitive observer. Antitesters have been quick to exploit these repellent features. First of all, young people are very tired of taking tests like these. Secondly, it is not obvious that what is being tested has much to do with higher levels of writing skill. Thirdly, the items seem not to be testing writing skill at all, only editing skill. As a teacher, I would find such objections alone decisive, and in fact I do not use such tests in my classroom, nor were the tests designed for such use. The reason the psychometric community defends their use for high-stakes, summative tests is that, bad as objective tests might seem to be, they are, as Churchill said of democracy, better than all the other systems.

The early proponents of objective tests did not pause to analyze in minute detail how they work in particular cases. It was enough to show that there was a strong and consistent correlation between the criterion (in this case, the criterion of actual writing ability) and the test. It was deemed sufficient to show that a test discriminated well between levels of ability or achievement, and that the rank ordering of students taking the test would be the same as their rank ordering according to a real-world criterion. More recently, however, thanks to the work of scientists like Cronbach and Messick, test theory has become more sophisticated and demanding.[18] Test makers are being asked to explain and justify the objective correlations between tests and the real world with an adequate and coherent theory of why the correlations exist.

In the Godshalk experiment, that requirement is not really difficult to meet. While the test items reproduced above seem to be sampling editing ability rather than writing ability, that is a superficial description of what the items are actually doing. The distinction between editing ability and writing ability is highly oversimplified—especially under test conditions. The creative, constructive side of writing is not well sampled even in the best performance tests, since no reliable performance test can offer free choice of topics and unlimited time. The quality of real-world writing is much more dependent on editing ability than on facility in initially getting words down on paper. The best writers edit in their minds before they write. Excellence in editing and excellence in writing are inextricable. Godshalk, Swineford, and Coffman, after examining all of their item types in detail, were quite justified in concluding the following:

> *One hypothesis of this study was that the multiple-choice questions were discriminating primarily at the lower levels of skill while the interlinear exercise, involving as it does a total context, would be most suitable at the higher levels. No convincing support for this hypotheis was found. . . . Before concluding that objective English questions focus on only superficial aspects of writing ability, one ought to give serious consideration to the data reported here.*[19]

The more general idea that the form of multiple-choice tests imposes superficiality, rote memorization, and fragmentation upon students and teachers is an exemplary case of judging a book by its cover. Humanists who would be horrified at the stereotyping of people take delight in stereotyping objective tests, allowing their form to belie their substance. Those same humanists would think people uninformed (to put it mildly) if they claimed that the sonnet is a fragmenting and trivializing form of poetry just because it is fourteen lines long and has strict formal limits. A sonnet sequence can accomplish epic ambitions, and a sequence of objective questions can swiftly gauge the depth and breadth of a person's knowledge, sometimes by using a great deal of ingenuity and wit. There is no reason why objective tests have to be dull. Let me close this little excursus on objective tests with an example of the degree to which they manage to probe higher-order skills:

> *If the radius of the earth were increased by 3 feet, its circumference at the equator would be increased by about how much?*

> *(A) 6 feet*
> *(B) 9 feet*
> *(C) 12 feet*

*(D) 19 feet*
*(E) 28 feet*

I shall provide even more challenging examples in Section 4 of this chapter, but I now wish to turn without further delay to some well-founded objections to real abuses of standardized tests.

## 3.
## Overcoming the Abuses

Although good standardized tests should be defended against facile scapegoating, there are two complaints of the antitest movement with which most thoughtful observers would agree. First, the practice of teaching narrowly to high-stakes, continually reused tests, instead of teaching to the subject, often corrupts education in the schools. Second, it is an abuse of these off-the-shelf tests to rely on them as *primary* tools of educational reform—a convenient practice that enables policymakers to evade hard decisions about educational goals and strategies. Legislators and the general public, lacking firsthand knowledge of what is being tested, have tended to use test scores as a blunt (and ineffective) instrument of compulsion, and have neglected the intellectually and politically difficult task of setting forth precise goals. It is hard to make or interpret tests in the absence of clearly defined educational and social goals. The duty to decide on such goals properly belongs to society as a whole—to parents, teachers, and the representatives of the people—not to test makers. Mindlessly legislating to standardized tests is as great an abuse as mindlessly teaching to them. It is the latter abuse, however, that is the more significant and remediable.

It has long been claimed that tests debase educational achievement by fragmenting instruction. Many teachers, it is said, teach to a particular test to enable their students to perform better than they would if they had not been specifically prepped for that test. Multiple-choice tests are particularly vulnerable to this sort of abuse because they probe knowledge and skill at very specific points and in very specific ways. All that a teacher need do to improve performance is to know the test items in advance and then give undue classroom emphasis to the specific topics that are going to appear. Such fragmented and irresponsible teaching *is* practiced, and it *does* enable unskilled students to appear more skilled (and teachers and administrators more competent) than they really are.

Such debasing of education is a significant abuse of testing that lends credence to the complaints of antitesters. I once asked a school superintendent who was proud of having developed a districtwide content-based test why he gave the same test year after year, since it is very easy and relatively cheap to make parallel forms of any test that does not need to be nationally normed. I also asked him whether he realized how open to abuse such repeated use of the same multiple-choice test was. His answer was a silent smile.

The pedagogical abuses of objective tests are prevalent enough to give surface respectability to those who exploit such test abuses as a pretext for avoiding meaningful accountability altogether. One avoidance technique is to recommend a pseudoaccountability (matrix testing) that transcends individual students and teachers, and yields a systemic, no-fault diagnosis that simply determines where more money needs to be spent. California has been a leader in matrix testing, which takes random samples of different sections of tests from individual students and schools and puts them all together in a mathematically valid way to get a sound large-scale result. The design is clever and gives a fairly accurate overall picture, but since individuals are not scored, it provides few incentives or disincentives to individuals, little monitoring, and no real accountability at the classroom level.

An argument can be made for matrix testing for special purposes, but when such individually nonaccountable testing has been coupled with a state policy that favors naturalistic teaching of reading, the result was California's dropping to the bottom in national reading scores. It is hard to decide which is the greater evasion of responsibility—wielding tests as a blunt legislative instrument to substitute for thoughtful policy *or* blurring the interpretation of tests to avoid accountability for individual students, teachers, and schools. When the two kinds of evasion are conjoined, the results can be disheartening and even tragic, as California has shown.

The teaching of reading offers a good example of the absolute need for standardized testing as a tool of accountability for individual teachers and students. I am told by researchers in the area of beginning reading that every child who is not organically impaired can be brought to an appropriate degree of reading competence by the end of first grade.[20] Whether or not that claim can be sustained, we have the means to monitor progress during first grade (and, more important, before first grade) and to provide teachers with necessary tools and guidance for reaching the goal. Ongoing diagnostic tests and a standardized reading test given to each child at the end of first grade are absolute duties of every modern educational system. If reading researchers prove to be right, once a first-grade teacher has been taught how to bring every nonimpaired child to a level of reading competence, failure to accomplish that goal should simply not remain a professional option.

Using reliable tests to gauge the achievement of well-defined and reachable educational goals, while at the same time ensuring that teachers and parents are provided with the tools to meet them, illustrates a proper use of high-stakes standardized tests. If there is to be responsible accountability, there is at the same time a moral imperative to provide sufficient advice and guidance. Not to provide the means for accomplishing the teaching goals on the one hand, and not to hold parents, teachers, and students accountable for achieving them on the other, are equal abandonments of adult responsibility to children. Testing without guidance is as irresponsible as guidance without testing. Neither side of the equation should be neglected.

But even this highly responsible use of standardized reading tests has been criticized on the grounds that such tests do not *really* test reading—a misleading way of saying that some tests are badly constructed and that many reading tests do not replicate real-world reading activities.[21] What this argument fails to disclose, however, is that more "authentic" types of reading tests are not only uncontrolled, hence unfair, but also unable to replicate real-world reading. No "performance" that takes place in school reproduces performance in the real world. Of course, all criticisms of existing tests are valuable if they lead to improvements in standardized tests. But at the present time, even the worst standardized reading tests, with all their faults, correlate well with the best ones—and with real-world reading abilities.

The educational misuse of these tests consists mainly, and in varying degrees, of what can only properly be termed "cheating"—sometimes outright, sometimes subtle. Prior knowledge of what will be tested makes cheating easy. Sampling what students know and can do is a principle of all tests. To know the sample in advance and to prep students for it specifically is a prime example of putting the temporary convenience of adults above the long-range good of children. Instead of colluding in this practice, school boards and administrators should take every precaution to make it unlikely to happen. That is what antitesters are aiming to achieve by abolishing standardized tests. But a more constructive way to achieve the result would be to make it very difficult for current educational misuse to continue, rather than abandoning the most accurate and fair instruments available.

First, how widespread is such misuse? Claims about the baleful influence of tests on teaching have been mainly anecdotal—until recently. Not long ago, Daniel Koretz conducted a well-designed experiment that exposed the breadth of the corruption which had long been suspected. He simply gave to a group of students in an urban public school district an additional set of standardized tests, which happened to be unfamiliar ones, not currently used in the district. Koretz wanted to determine how well the students would fare if both they and their teachers were unfamiliar with the specific tests the children would be taking.

Although the two standardized tests were highly correlated with each other, the children performed much worse on the unexpected test than on the familiar one. This result meant that the district's usual test scores were significantly overstating students' knowledge and skill—a distortion that is undoubtedly widespread. Clearly, the most probable reason for the difference in student performance on the two tests was that teachers were focusing their instruction narrowly on the specific kinds of items that would be tested—precisely in order to help achieve the misleadingly favorable result.[22]

Koretz's experiment is nothing less than a smoking gun that demonstrates the corrupting influence standardized tests can have on teaching in the schools. Notice, however, that standardized tests were the very instruments used in the experiment to demonstrate this baleful influence. It is hard to imagine what other tool could have been so effectively employed for the purpose, which suggests that the root of the problem is not reliance on standardized tests (unstandardized tests, after all, are inherently unfair) but, rather, widespread misuse of standardized tests by teachers and administrators.

Can such misuse be prevented? Yes, easily, and the Koretz experiment indicates the simplest preventive approach. A district should not determine which form of a test will be used until the last possible minute. Providers of the SAT and some other tests ensure this cheating-proof system by creating new questions for each administration of the test. But that is an expensive way to keep teachers and students in the dark. A cheaper way is to make use of several already existing tests, and to choose one at the last minute from a number of tests put out by different companies, or from a large number of parallel forms of the same test. The latter approach has the virtue of enabling year-by-year comparisons of scores. Every maker of tests provides these parallel forms, which are similar in format, in difficulty, and in the domains being sampled, but vary in specific items. Enough of the parallel forms can be assembled to cover a generous portion of the knowledge and skill of each domain. At the last minute, the particular form to be given in a particular year could be randomly chosen. It would be difficult if not impossible to outsmart such a system, since to teach the right answers to all the many forms of the test would be more or less equivalent to teaching the whole domain. In that circumstance, one might as well teach without regard to possible questions on the tests, and teachers would be well advised simply to teach their subject as effectively as possible.

Members of the public are not generally aware that identical tests are used year after year, and assume that an uncorrupt system of testing is already in place. That there exists instead a lot of tacit collusion aimed at keeping test scores inaccurately high, and a lot of silent pressure on teachers to teach narrowly in order to do so, is not widely known. Recently, the press gave a lot of attention to the "Lake Wobegon effect," discovered by Dr. John J. Cannell, which made the scores in every state "above average."[23] But this apparent scandal was interpreted as consisting mainly in a misleading reporting of scores. The press ignored the more subtle corruption of testing and of the entire educational process. Lack of public awareness of this more subtle test misuse is another illustration of the need for savvy and independent probing by the reporters who cover education.

After framing the suggestion about the use of parallel test forms, I asked experts whether such an arrangement would in fact work, or whether there might be technical or financial hindrances I was unaware of. I was told, reassuringly, that exactly such a system had recently been put in place in Chicago. Currently, eight parallel forms of standard tests are available for use in the city's school system each year, and no one knows until the last minute which form will be chosen. The immediate effect of this practice on teaching and scores remains to be seen, but it self-evidently represents an advance in probity. If Chicago also goes on to provide teachers with clearly defined goals and the guidance to achieve them, the likelihood of improvement will be great indeed. The costs of this change in testing practice are not prohibitive. The main expense of standardized testing lies not in printing the test booklets but in grading the tests. Hence, the use of multiple parallel test forms is a solution within the financial reach of any district. One hopes that the Chicago arrangement will become a model for the nation. Should that happen, the chief abuse of standardized tests—the one really convincing educational objection to using them (i.e., teaching narrowly to the specific test)—will have been removed.

## 4.
## Answering the Charges

The specific charges leveled against multiple-choice tests need to be examined with some care to distinguish what is justified from what is wrong and misleading. Some of the complaints concern the unfairness of standardized tests: that, being standardized, they are culturally and racially biased, insensitive to individual differences, and conducive to social inequality. Other objections concern their impact on the quality of education: that standardized tests measure only lower-order skills, encourage passivity and superficiality in learning, and convey a hidden message that there is a simple right answer to every problem, no matter how complex and ambiguous. As one writer summarizes the educational case for the prosecution:

*America's obsession with multiple-choice tests has damaged teaching and learning by*
* *putting too much value on recall and rote learning at the expense of understanding and reflection.*
* *promoting the misleading impression that there is a single right answer for every problem or question.*
* *turning students into passive learners who need only to recognize, not to construct answers and solutions.*
* *forcing teachers to focus more on what can be tested easily than on what is important for students to learn.*
* *trivializing content and skill development by reducing whatever is taught to a fill-in-the-bubble format.*[24]

The effect of such criticism is to suggest that those who oppose standardized tests are the true advocates of greater social equity, more demanding education, higher real-world competencies, and greater independent-mindedness. By contrast, those who favor standardized tests are depicted as supposing that human worth can be rated on a linear scale, as wrongly assuming that the language of test accountability is the language of genuine education, and as entertaining the misguided belief that the world can be purged of its complexity, diversity, and ambiguity. I shall try to identify where these criticisms are plausible and even right, but also where they are wrong and fundamentally confused. It is true that some of the existing multiple-choice tests do encourage superficiality and passivity. But it is also true that some do not. The wholesale indictment of standardized tests is facile and inaccurate. And since the proposed alternatives (i.e., performance tests) are not by themselves reliable or fair, a successful campaign to abolish standardized tests would result in our schools becoming even less equitable and our students less competent than they now are.

The charges I shall quote and examine are that multiple-choice tests

* Don't tap higher-order or real-world skills
* Encourage passivity and rote learning
* Have *caused* the decline in higher-order skills

• Are unfairly biased against certain groups, and indeed have contributed to the inequities they reflect

While most people outside the field of education may be skeptical of these charges, and may feel that answering them is a somewhat tedious enterprise (which, alas, it is), the exercise is important to undertake on the chance that it will help make the half-truths of the antitest movement less likely to be believed.

### Multiple-Choice Tests Don't Tap Higher-Order or Real-World Skills

*Standardized tests cannot distinguish between students who understand underlying concepts and students who are only able to perform procedures by rote and who therefore cannot apply these procedures to new situations.*

*Current research on human learning and performance has suggested that many currently used tests fail to measure students' higher order cognitive abilities or to support their capacities to perform real world tasks.*[25]

It is certainly true that if students are consistently given tests that do not require or measure higher-order skills, then those tests will not encourage the teaching of higher-order skills. This is evident to common sense, no matter what the format of the test, and independent of the fact that it is standardized (i.e., has been normed to a large group and given under standard conditions). A superficial and undemanding test is superficial and undemanding whether in multiple-choice or in essay form. Districts should identify any such inferior tests and discontinue their use. But, so far, complaints like the ones quoted above have not identified any particular inferior tests or *demonstrated that their being put in multiple-choice format causes them to probe only lower-order skills.* What is highly misleading about the quoted statements is the implication that the form of the tests—multiple choice—is the element that causes these defects, and this may be the impression that the words "current research on human learning and performance" are meant to leave us with, though the rhetoric is, on close inspection, rather hedged.

The research on the shortcomings of the multiple-choice format was summarized by the psychometrician Norman Frederiksen in a much-cited article of 1984. This report does not, however, say what antitesters who cite it claim or assume that it says. Frederiksen was indeed concerned that those who make up multiple-choice tests tend to probe information rather than real-world, problem-solving skills, because it is easier to make test items that simply probe information. But he was careful to acknowledge that expediency was not the same as necessity, and conceded that the format itself did not require passivity and mere recall on the part of test takers. What the multiple-choice format cannot test, Frederiksen showed, is *creativity* in solving real-world problems. That is because the form of the test does not allow for the production of new ideas or hypotheses, since each of the choices has already been formed. Frederiksen speculated that it might be highly desirable to make tests that encouraged the teaching of creativity in solving real-world problems—if such skills could in fact be taught. It is certainly desirable to *encourage* creativity, but many believe it cannot be taught. Frederiksen warned that appropriate testing for it does not yet exist:

> *The development of new tests is of course not as simple as the above implies. There are problems of discovering what are the salient aspects of performance in carrying out a particular task and in identifying the cognitive processes that it requires. There are problems of scoring—how to record the raw information and how to count, evaluate, or otherwise transform the information into meaningful scores.*[26]

That these conceptual and practical problems have not been solved, and are not likely to be, was the theme of a recent review article by Swanson and others, which showed that in the area of study where real-world higher-order skills have been most consistently tested—medicine—the decades-long attempt to produce fair and accurate performance tests of productive skills has ended in failure.[27] The article is particularly useful in setting forth the reasons for this failure: that scoring is highly inconsistent; that "generalizability is low"; that "expertise is not a general trait"; that simulations are not the real world, and "examinees do not behave in the same way they would in real life"; "that performance in one context does not predict performance in other contexts"; in short, that Frederiksen's warnings were just as well grounded as his concerns over the potential effects on teaching of the multiple-choice format. Indeed, Swanson and his colleagues concluded that a "consequence of enthusiasm for performance-based assessment in the health professions is, ironically, the improvement of multiple-choice tests."[28] Frederiksen's own recommendation was suitably cautious:

> *Situational tests are not widely used in testing programs because of considerations having to do with cost and efficiency [and reliability!]. It is not likely that costs of such tests can be made competitive with multiple-*

*choice tests even with computers. It might, however, be possible to justify the costs of testing and scoring if the primary purpose is instruction rather than evaluation and assigning course grades.*[29]

As for the notion that the multiple-choice format is condemned to probe only surfaces rather than deep understanding, Frederiksen was quite explicit in stating that research had rejected the claim: "The correlations are generally interpreted to mean that the format does not influence what a test measures. Other investigators have carried out more sophisticated analyses with rather similar results." Investigators in general, and sometimes to their surprise, "have found no evidence of format factors." And "tests of mathematical reasoning measure the same attribute regardless of test format."[30] These clear repudiations of anti-standardized-test claims are being stated not by a defender of multiple-choice tests but, rather, in a research report cited by anti-testers as lending scientific support to their position! With this rejection by researchers of the incorrect charge that multiple-choice items cannot test complex or real-world skills, let's turn to the second, related, criticism.

**Multiple-Choice Tests Encourage Passivity and Rote Learning**   They are said to have this effect because they

> *emphasize the quick recognition of isolated facts not the integration of information and the generation of ideas. [And they] exclude a great many kinds of knowledge and types of performance we expect from students, placing test takers in a passive, reactive role rather than one that engages their capacities to structure tasks, produce ideas, and solve problems.*[31]

Perhaps the best way to deal with this allegation, which according to most researchers is also incorrect, is simply to reproduce or even to invent an example of a multiple-choice question that refutes the objection. Let's see if we can generate one or two test items that do require students to generate ideas and structure tasks. The exercise turns out not to be hard. In fact, it took just a few minutes to create the following question, which, for all its faults, easily refutes the claim that the multiple-choice format imposes passivity and fragmentation of thought:

In 1995, the small town of La Gomma, California, a suburb of Los Angeles, considered means of eliminating smog. The following plans were advanced to accomplish this. Which would be likely to succeed?

(A) Ban all diesel trucks within the town limits.
(B) Reduce the speed limit from 50 to 30 miles per hour.
(C) Require catalytic converters in all cars registered in town.
(D) Create a car-free zone in the downtown area.
(E) None of the above.

In order to answer this question correctly, the students, who might someday be in the position of evaluating such real-world proposals, would have to know the causes of smog and imagine the consequences of each of these recommendations. They would need to engage in productive thought and to possess—as in all real-world problem-solving situations—relevant background knowledge. They would need to engage in the following kinds of problem-solving activities to evaluate each of the proposals:

(A) Banning diesel trucks. What contribution to smog is made by diesel trucks? Very little, since there are very few of them compared to passenger cars, and since the trucks in the area of La Gomma contribute very little to the totality of smog conditions. Moreover, even if the emission contribution were great, could the town continue to function without permitting trucks to deliver? Probably not. Conclusion: This is an impractical proposal that would neither attain the desired goal nor be accepted by the town. It can't be the correct answer.

(B) Reducing the speed limit. If a car moves from point A to point B at a lower rate of speed, does that reduce smog-causing emissions? Yes, but not very much, and certainly not enough to prevent smog. This answer has to be wrong.

(C) Requiring catalytic converters. Since in 1995 catalytic converters were already installed in most cars in California, this could not significantly reduce smog.

(D) Creating a car-free zone downtown. While car emissions in the immediate downtown area would be reduced by 100% under this plan, would that very local air improvement cause a significant reduction in the town's smog—even in the downtown area? Since smog is caused by a combination of weather factors and car emissions over a large area, reduction of emissions in the downtown area of a small town could not abolish the town's smog.

(E) None of the above. This is the correct answer, but it can only be known with confidence if the student thinks productively and critically about the proposed alternatives, and has enough relevant knowledge to recognize that nothing a small suburban town can do by itself will free it from smog. Of course, if the student already knows that fact, without having to figure it out, then much less productive problem-solving will be necessary. But no matter what the test formats, relevant knowledge is always a shortcut in real-world problem solving, and it is hard to see how this type of question could possibly be answered without calling into play the productive problem-solving abilities that critics assert a multiple-choice format inherently discourages.

Nowhere is the accusation of triviality and rote learning more misguided than in the domain of mathematics. Math questions can easily be devised in the multiple-choice format, requiring the student productively to work out multistep problems before being able to make a rational choice among the alternatives. Moreover, it is possible to include a performance component directly in such tests by requiring, as some math tests do, that the student write down all computations in spaces provided near the question. Indeed, in two of the most important kinds of tests given in elementary schools, reading tests and math tests, there is a built-in productive or performance component in the tests themselves. After all, students must productively read and comprehend passages before they can answer multiple-choice questions about them, and they must constructively produce solutions to math problems before deciding upon answers. A well-constructed and designed standardized test of math or reading *is* inherently a performance test which requires the "integration of information and the generation of ideas" and which "engages [students'] capacities to structure tasks, produce ideas, and solve problems."

Here is a simple example:

Apples are distributed one at a time into six baskets. The first apple goes into basket one, the second into basket two, the third into basket three, and so on, until each basket has one apple. If the pattern is repeated beginning each time with basket one, into which basket will the seventy-fourth apple be placed?

(A) Basket two
(B) Basket three
(C) Basket four
(D) Basket five
(E) Basket six[32]

This problem can be solved by tedious simulation of the entire process, which would penalize the student by taking time from other questions and by providing many opportunities for counting errors. The better way is to figure out how a computation can provide a shortcut. Thus, it is not the computation itself that requires productive, problem-solving abilities. Rather, it is figuring out which computation would be applicable. Mere computational skill is not enough.

Here is an equally simple problem that requires an understanding of geometrical relations, a highly productive imagination, and the actual production of a sample figure:

If *j*, *k*, *l*, and *m* are four distinct lines in a plane, such that *j* is perpendicular to *k*, *l* intersects *k* but is not perpendicular to it, and *l* is perpendicular to *m*, which of the following must be true?

I. *j* is parallel to *l*
II. *m* intersects *j* but is not perpendicular to it
III. *m* is perpendicular to *k*

(A) I only
(B) II only
(C) III only
(D) I and II
(E) I and III

These unstrained examples refute the thoughtless, oft-repeated objection that the multiple-choice format encourages passivity and rote learning, and again illustrate an important principle: that many educational doctrines have become axiomatic not by being correct but by being repeated so often that it seems they *must* be correct.

On the other hand, if there were not some truth in the charge that multiple-choice tests encourage superficiality and passivity, it is unlikely that it would be repeated so often. But its validity can only come from the corrupt use of these tests. If a teacher knows that there will be a smog question and an apple-basket question and a perpendicular-line question, then most children in the district *will* probably be able to answer all the above examples by passive recall and rote memorization. In that case, the test and the teaching to it will indeed "emphasize the quick recognition of isolated facts not the integration of information and the generation of ideas," and will indeed place students "in

a passive, reactive role rather than one that engages their capacities to structure tasks, produce ideas, and solve problems." But, as Sidney said in his
eloquent defense of poetry against the charge that it corrupts morals, "What!
Shall the abuse of a thing make the right use odious?"

### Multiple-Choice Tests Have *Caused* the Decline in Higher-Order Skills

*Since about 1970, when standardized tests began to be used for a wider
variety of accountability purposes, basic test scores have been increasing
slightly, while assessments of higher order thinking skills have declined in
virtually all subject areas.*[33]

Clearly implied in this complaint is the proposition that multiple-choice
tests have themselves contributed to educational decline. The premise of this
*post hoc, ergo propter hoc* thinking is that multiple-choice tests can measure
only basic skills. This would explain why they have induced an improvement
in such skills, accompanied by a diminishment in the more desirable higher
skills that they supposedly cannot measure and do not encourage. Conveniently not mentioned in this argument is the fact that we know about this
diminishment through the test-item analysis of the National Assessment of
Educational Progress, which consists of a set of tests that until very recently
were multiple-choice items designed to gauge various levels of both lower- and
higher-order skills. If the NAEP test items could not measure higher skills,
how could they tell us that they had declined?

But while the argument that tests have *caused* the decline is fallacious, and
its premises contradictory, it retains a certain plausibility because the actual
tests used by states and districts have been slanted toward basic skills and have
been corrupted by repeated reuse. It is true that in the 1970s the decline in
basic skills alarmed the states, which then took measures to ensure that these
skills were acquired by a greater percentage of students. That effort was successful. But so long as tests remained focused on lower skills, and so long as
the states provided no incentives for teaching higher ones, the practical effect
of the basic-skills movement was indeed to neglect higher-order skills. The
mistake in the argument lies in the suggestion that the format of the tests
prevents them from testing higher skills, whereas they could in fact help
achieve the same sort of improvement in higher skills as they have accomplished in lower ones—an inference that has been eloquently argued by Bar-
bara Lerner. What is required is not the abolition of standard tests but the
insistence on more demanding ones, on their proper use, and on a higher level

of achievement by students and schools. Basic skills are no bar to higher skills but are in fact their only possible foundation.

## Multiple-Choice Tests Are Unfairly Biased Against Certain Groups, and Indeed Have Contributed to the Inequities They Reflect

*Test makers claim that the lower test scores of racial and ethnic minorities and of students from low-income families simply reflect the biases and inequities that exist in American schools and American society. Biases and inequities certainly exist—but standardized tests do not simply reflect their impact; they compound them.*

*These tests tend to reflect the language, culture, or learning style of middle- to upper-class whites. Thus scores on these tests are as much measures of race or ethnicity or income as they are measures of achievement, ability, or skill.*

*Even if there were no bias in any technical sense, the tests' basis in one particular culture renders them unfair.*[34]

These issues are fundamentally different from the technical ones dealt with so far. Indeed, the *technical* bias of tests against particular groups is not the main burden of these complaints, though antitesters rarely pause to distinguish technical bias from other causes of unequal performance among social, racial, gender, and ethnic groups. The American Psychological Association has described test bias as a consistent difference between the way a definable subgroup of test takers perform on a test and the way they perform on some real-world criterion or construct that the test is meant to measure.[35] If twelve-year-old girls perform worse on math tests, and also perform worse on real-world math problems, then a score differential between the sexes does not in itself reflect technical test bias or unfairness. Similarly, if twelve-year-old boys perform worse on verbal tests, and in fact cannot read and write as well as girls the same age, then a group difference in scores on the test does not in itself denote test bias. Test makers in recent years have taken pains to ensure the absence of bias in this technical sense, and it is unlikely that any significant degree of technical bias exists in present-day high-stakes multiple-choice tests. The issue of fairness, which is a major theme of this book, needs to be addressed separately from the issue of technical test bias, which is a distraction whose chief function is to create a convenient confusion between the technical and the ideological.

## 5.
## The Question of Fairness

The question of fairness in testing and in education generally is not only ideological; it is also practical. One proposal that, in my estimation, does not meet the criterion of practicality is the recommendation to create a compensatory principle of scoring or test making that will simply erase, by Byzantine arrangements, the current inequalities in scores between groups. Consider the following statement written jointly by an education professor and an official of a large foundation:

> *Because of the enormity and pervasiveness of inequity in American educa-tion as reflected by student performance on various types of tests and assessments, [here the ordinary reader might well expect a recommenda-tion for lifting educational* achievement *for these students, but gets in-stead the following inference:] the dual issues of improving the ways student performance is measured, and eliminating the racial and socio-economic gaps on whatever measures are used are enduring ones for policy makers and educators to address in the years ahead.*[36]

This seems to say that since inferior test performance by some groups indicates educational inequity, we should improve the tests by eliminating the score differentials between groups. Technically, the elimination of the differen-tials is not a complex task. One simply takes the scores from each "racial and socio-economic" group that shows a gap, and then one makes a mathematical adjustment for all members of that group. This is called "renorming." It is the exercise that the College Board recently engaged in for the benefit of all the nation's SAT takers, lifting, with the wave of a formula, the mean of the entire country without changing the underlying reality. But it is one thing to renorm for everybody, and quite another to renorm selectively for particular groups. The difficulty in that approach is obviously not technical but political. After technical test bias is removed, many people might not accept and (according to some solid analysis by Linda Gottfredson) should not accept the practice of renorming selectively to remove the score differences between groups.[37]

But surely the gravest objection to attempting to achieve educational equity through adjusting test scores is the practical injustice it commits upon those it proposes to help. Getting a high score on a test is not the ticket to social equality for students whose actual educational competencies are low, no mat-ter what scores or grades have been attached to their performances. Real social justice lies beyond the sheltered halls of school and college—in improving the relative economic condition of groups that have been both economically and educationally depressed. Improvement in one's economic condition depends nowadays more upon one's real-world competencies than upon one's grades or scores, whether adjusted through mathematical renorming or by "improving the ways student performance is measured."

The notion of high-stakes testing as merely a gatekeeping function that prevents members of disadvantaged groups from full participation is a grave oversimplification of the economic realities. These have been well identified by Ronald Ferguson in his work on black-white wage inequality. Ferguson is an economist who decided to probe more deeply into this much-studied subject, which has traditionally made black-white comparisons by matching the nominal educational level of the two groups. But a wage earner's nominal educational level can be a very misleading statistic in an era of social promotion to the next grade for every level of schooling. Instead, Ferguson studied black-white wage inequality in terms of actual educational achievement. Once he made that adjustment, he found that the wage gap between the races closed dramatically.[38]

Ferguson, himself a black, would certainly not claim that this shows the United States to be color-blind. Continued race and class prejudice undoubtedly explains the unacceptable fact that, once real competency is taken into account, there should remain any economic gap at all. But this qualification should not obscure the underlying significance of Ferguson's findings regarding the economic implications of real educational achievement. It is real-world, achieved competency, however gained, that counts for most in the marketplace—for all groups.

In the context of the test debates, it is worth noting that Ferguson based his analyses on unrenormed test scores alone—in this case, scores made on the Armed Forces Qualification Test (AFQT), a multiple-choice test in reading, general knowledge, and math. The AFQT measures academic attainment and achieved competency. Quite aside from the light Ferguson's work throws on the issue of fairness in testing, which I will discuss in a moment, his analysis is important because it confirms the real-world economic implications of the competencies measured by well-made standardized tests. Ferguson's work is thus yet another refutation of the claim that multiple-choice tests do not probe real-world competencies. The AFQT is probably the best single refutation of that claim, since scores on the AFQT have been shown to reliably predict the quality of job performance in the military services.[39]

Ferguson's work also throws light on the issue of fairness and cultural bias in present-day standardized tests. Since scores on these tests correlate highly with actual economic achievement and job performance regardless of race, they are not biased against any group with regard to real-world competency. On the other hand, the antitesters are right to say that tests of proficiency in reading, writing, and math are biased against certain cultural and linguistic groups—not technically biased, since the tests have been demonstrated to correlate with real-world performances, but culturally biased, since certain cultural groups do not score as well as others on the tests. If that result is in itself the mark of cultural bias, then the accusation of bias is correct by definition. But it is of great importance to uncover the implications for educational practice by using the term "bias" in this way. As far as I can see, the accusation is leveled in order to support a policy that will oblige an adjustment in what schools teach and tests test, to ensure that the home cultures of various groups are not discriminated against. If the home cultures happen not to promote reading, writing, and speaking in standard English, and the solving of math problems, it will be up to the schools and the test makers to adjust to the home culture, not the other way round.

This may be a legitimate ideological position. But most parents, including most minority parents, accept the idea that schools should teach mainstream science, mathematics, or language arts. Wherever public schools have offered the choice of truly effective mainstream academic training in reading, writing, and mathematics, minority families have signed up in disproportionate numbers, and their children have responded eagerly and well.[40] These parents clearly recognize the direct connection between economic advancement for their children and the mastery of the culture of the marketplace, which in the United States is mainstream culture.

The marketplace is a commons. It erases ethnic distinctions. It has been the creator of the great lingua francas of the world—Koine (the language of the New Testament), Latin, and, now, English. The standard forms of those written languages are hybrids created in and by the marketplace. The notion that such a hybrid culture, devised to enable communication between strangers, is somebody's essential, identity-defining culture is a historical and an economic mistake.

It is a mistake that, like many other ideas in our intellectual history, must be laid at the door of Romanticism. Where Enlightenment thinkers like Jefferson and his disciple, Horace Mann, saw the common schools as agencies for making everyone a participant in the political and economic marketplace, the Romantics invented the idea that one's home language and culture were central to one's very essence. The Enlightenment held up the ideal of cosmopolitanism, in which everyone not only had a home culture but also adapted to the culture of the cosmopolis (i.e., "world-city"). This cosmopolitanism was regarded by Fichte and other Romantics as an effete, Frenchified concept. No one but a true German, Fichte said, could properly understand and speak German. The home culture was derived from the soil and flowed in the very blood *(Blut und Boden*—blood and soil).⁴¹

This mystical concept is incorrect in every respect except the psychological. Cultural identity is a contingency—an accident, not an essence. But, of course, it *feels* like an essence, especially when Romantics encourage such feelings. And, indeed, so long as the feeling is left to the domain of culture itself and does not deny children the school-acquired ability to put on the public garments of the marketplace, little harm is done by cultural Romanticism. The capacious multicultural cosmopolitanism of the Enlightenment can accommodate itself even to cultural Romanticism, so long as it does not venture to insert itself impractically into the schools and the economic and political marketplace, where a lingua franca is a practical necessity.

The policy difference between the Enlightenment and Romantic versions of multiculturalism were accurately laid out in the following passage in an essay that attacks standardized tests as being culturally biased:

> *The first [Enlightenment version of multiculturalism] is concerned with assimilating minority students to the majority culture—including the excluded on the terms of the majority, not changing the basic practices of the school regarding multiculturalism—so that the ethos of the school remains essentially monocultural. This approach is not only limited, it is also not likely to work given the resistance to schooling exhibited by many low income students and students of color, since their resistance is precisely to being assimilated.*
>
> *The second [Romantic] approach favored by all these authors focuses on reconstructing schooling to adapt to the students and their cultures. In this approach, attention can be paid to issues of race, class, gender, language, and disability, and to their interactions. The core of this process of inclusion should be students, their own lives and backgrounds.*⁴²

What this account fails to state is that effective classroom schooling *has* to be monocultural for the same reason the marketplace has to be—so that all can participate. But it is misleading to suggest that this monocultural school-based culture is not itself a hybrid, as lingua francas always are. In the present-day American school, it is difficult to find any examples of pure-bred "Eurocentric" or "Anglocentric" instruction. One hopes that the lasting legacy of the recent multicultural movement will not be, as it cannot practically be, the Balkanization of the American school but, rather, the hybridization of the American school. To us inheritors of the Enlightenment, that is an excellent legacy which lies squarely in the tradition of cosmopolitanism. Time, experience, and a profounder sense of fairness will, one hopes, repudiate as impractical the idea that Balkanized schooling or testing could lead to social and economic equity.

The debate over making test scores come out the same for all groups reflects a larger debate about egalitarianism in Western democracies that has gathered intensity since World War II. On one side are those who favor meritocracy and who, in the name of fairness and social utility, want schools to separate gifted students from less talented ones so that every child can attain his or her potential without being held back. On the other side are egalitarians or inclusivists who, in opposition to all tracking, especially in early grades, hold that such a policy not only discourages slower and less advantaged students but also deprives abler ones of leadership training and democratic attitudes. In many democracies of the world, and especially in the United States, the debate has focused on whether fairness should be defined as "equality of opportunity" or "equality of result," with both sides pronouncing themselves in favor of "true fairness."[43] Administrators and teachers in many American schools, along with those members of the public who think of themselves as socially progressive, favor equality of result, particularly for large social groups, while those who consider themselves conservative favor individual equality of opportunity. Would that the issue were as manageable as these phrases suggest!

In the United States, some cultural groups have been unfairly deprived of equality of educational opportunity. The reasons for the unfairness are not primarily cultural but historical and economic, making the charge of cultural bias in tests and schooling highly misleading, if not irrelevant. The principal unfairness connected with testing consists in a failure to prepare students adequately for the competencies for which they are to be tested. These competencies usually require a great deal of intellectual capital. The verbal section of the SAT, for instance, is at bottom a vocabulary test.[44] It is easily demonstrated that the public elementary schools of the United States provide neither equality of opportunity nor equality of result. Comparative studies show that our system affords far less equality of educational opportunity than exists in most developed nations.[45] Under such circumstances, it may be premature to choose between equality of opportunity and equality of result, since, for both parties to the debate, the precondition for the possibility of fairness is equality of educational opportunity. That unfinished business must take priority over the scapegoating of tests and the resolution of the dispute between meritocrats and egalitarians.

Fairness in testing cannot be separated from fairness in schooling. Those who place emphasis on achieving equality of test results seem particularly misguided when they focus on tests and neglect the underlying realities denoted by the test results—incompetent students and ineffective schools. The tendency to blame the messenger instead of changing the news itself suggests a state of despair regarding the improvement of students and schools, and regarding substantial compensatory efforts to achieve equality of opportunity. The College Board unwittingly expressed such hopelessness when it justified its renorming of SAT scores with the explanation that many minorities were now taking the test. Such sociological determinism borders on condescension toward minority students and represents the same sort of mindset that anti-testers display when they demand equality of test results whether or not underlying competencies are equalized.

It must be conceded that blaming the messenger has an honorable history in the effort to bring about greater social justice. The journalist and historian of civil rights Nicholas Lemann reports the following incident. In 1974, Supreme Court Justice William O. Douglas wished to rule against a white student, DeFunis, who had been excluded from a law school although his Law School Aptitude Test scores were higher than those of any black who had been admitted to the school. In his first response to the situation, Douglas wrote a preliminary opinion in which he stated (on no evidence) that the LSAT was "by no means objective" and might contain some "hidden bias." Douglas was forced into this position by the fact that he was a fierce believer in meritocracy and had prefaced his draft opinion with an allusion to Jefferson's phrase "aristocracy of virtue and talent." "The democratic ideal as I read the Constitution and Bill of Rights," Douglas wrote, "presupposes an aristocracy of talent, and that all races must be allowed to compete for a position in that hierarchy." But the LSAT was statistically accurate in predicting the grades that both blacks and whites would make in law school. There seemed to be no way out of Douglas's dilemma. Lemann writes:

> *The way Douglas got to this final position [against DeFunis] was by returning to his attack on the L.S.A.T., with greater fury than ever before. It is racially biased, he wrote; its bias justifies reverse bias by the law school; in fact, the L.S.A.T. should be abolished entirely. That Douglas decided to declare the L.S.A.T. biased although he had no evidence that it was is mainly a demonstration that he was intellectually trapped and couldn't find any other way out. He couldn't reconcile his passionate belief in meritocracy with the actual meritocracy's mechanical feeling and its tendency to reward some cultures far more than others.*[46]

Perhaps a way out of Douglas's intellectual dilemma might have been based on the fact that, despite school integration, American public education had then—and continues to have—a differential effect on social classes, and because of that more elemental and decisive fact, a differential effect on ethnic and racial groups who belong disproportionately to disadvantaged classes. The reason for the differential effect is as follows: Students from middle and upper classes, coming from educated homes, learn more in school and become more competent than educationally less advantaged students because the intellectual capital derived from their homes enables them to derive a great deal more from gap-ridden and repetitive schooling than can students who are in no position to fill in the gaps with home-provided knowledge. In a mediocre school system, the competence gap between social classes widens during the school years. In a good, coherent school system with definite year-by-year goals for all students, early, systematic compensation becomes possible, and the competence gap is narrowed. If Justice Douglas had cited this fact, he could have justified compensatory action as late as law school without being false to meritocratic principles, because meritocracy depends upon genuine equality of opportunity. Given the initial differential in intellectual capital between social classes, there can be no equality of educational opportunity without effective compensatory measures—the earlier the better. That is a policy I strongly favor.

In previous pages, I have explained why American efforts at early and continued compensatory education have been unavailing.[47] It is often said in defense of the disappointments of Head Start and of our school results generally that we are a diverse nation with unique problems. Stating this much-exaggerated fact is perhaps meant to imply that it is impossible for us, because of our uniqueness, to achieve equality of educational opportunity, and to suggest that we have nothing to learn from nations that have better solved the problem of equal educational opportunity. But in a recent study of math achievement in three nations—Taiwan, Japan, and the United States—Harold Stevenson and his colleagues produced the following three curves representing the level and distribution of test scores for students of the three countries. The scores for Asian students were, as we have come to expect, much higher than those for our students. But with respect to the debate between meritocrats and egalitarians, the *shapes* of the two Asian curves also tell an important story about the educational consequences for fairness of a good educational system.

Taiwan's curve is meritocratic, Japan's egalitarian. The meritocratic curve is bimodal, with two distinct bumps in the middle, representing a fusion of test results from the regular track and the elite track of schooling. But since both the regular and the elite tracks are coherent systems, driven by specific yearly

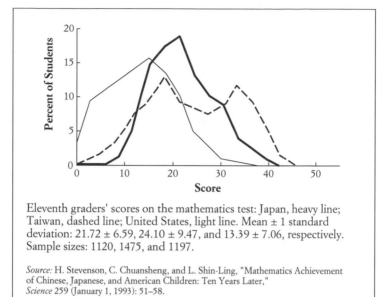

Eleventh graders' scores on the mathematics test: Japan, heavy line; Taiwan, dashed line; United States, light line. Mean ± 1 standard deviation: 21.72 ± 6.59, 24.10 ± 9.47, and 13.39 ± 7.06, respectively. Sample sizes: 1120, 1475, and 1197.

*Source:* H. Stevenson, C. Chuansheng, and L. Shin-Ling, "Mathematics Achievement of Chinese, Japanese, and American Children: Ten Years Later," *Science* 259 (January 1, 1993): 51–58.

requirements that are well taught and well monitored, the average scores from both the Taiwanese tracks are much higher than the U.S. average. The Japanese curve, in contrast to the Taiwanese, is more egalitarian; everybody is on the same track and receives the same high-quality curriculum and instruction. The result is a neat, normal-shaped curve, but one that displays a very high average level of competency. The two curves represent the two different ideological parties with respect to fairness. Both could be defended, but few Americans would view the Taiwanese system as a fair one. But clearly both Asian curves are fairer than the American curve, which leaves behind so many incompetent students, that it could not be called fair on either ideological principle. In the United States, the philosophical debate between egalitarian and meritocratic versions of fairness may be somewhat beside the point until we rationalize and generally improve curriculum and instruction in our public schools.

Fairness in testing cannot be separated from fairness in schooling, but as the graphs also suggest, fairness in schooling cannot be isolated from excellence in schooling. Fairness and excellence invariably go together in national systems of education because the educational principles and arrangements that elicit the best performances and highest competencies from advantaged students also elicit the best from disadvantaged students. If every child in every grade has to meet a high level of achievement, and if the teachers are able professionals who make sure that the goals are met, all students will learn. Extra time must be spent with slower or disadvantaged students both inside and outside of class to bring them up to the required level, but meanwhile, faster students are doing various demanding tasks, including helping with instruction, advancing their own progress, and, by those means, staying challenged and averting boredom. In such systems, all children are brought up to the required high level, enabling the class as a whole to move forward step by step.

This arrangement explains the high average level of achievement in excellent national systems, and it also explains how those systems achieve compensatory equalization of educational opportunity. When there are very explicit requirements that all must meet, every student is assured of gaining from the school essential intellectual capital that was not derived from the home. This compensatory equalization of intellectual capital was implicit in the Jefferson-Mann vision of the democratic common school. It is a sad historical irony that, because of accidents of intellectual and institutional history, their ideal is being realized better in Asia and Europe than in the United States.

The final irony of the antitesting movement is that in the name of social fairness it opposes using high-stakes tests as gatekeepers, monitors, and incentives—functions that are essential to social fairness. Without effective monitoring and high incentives, including high-stakes testing programs, no educational system has achieved or could achieve excellence and equity. Good tests are necessary to instruct, to monitor, and to motivate. John Bishop has shown in great detail the importance of high-stakes tests in motivating students to work hard.[48] The Romantic idea that learning is natural, and that the motivation for academic achievement comes from within, is an illusion that forms one of the greatest barriers to social justice imaginable, since poor and disadvantaged students must be motivated to work even harder than advantaged students in order to achieve equality of educational opportunity. It was Antonio Gramsci, that wise spokesman for the disadvantaged and disenfranchised, who wrote that the gravest disservice to social justice entailed by Romantic theories of education is the delusion that educational achievement comes as naturally as leaves to a tree, without extrinsic motivation, discipline, toil, or sweat.

# 7.

# Summary

# and

# Conclusion

## 1.
## Practical Effectiveness, Not Ideology

This book has covered a multitude of topics, the details of which no reader can be expected to keep steadily in mind. For the sake of clarity, I shall now select, quote, highlight, and condense those parts of the previous discussion that seem to me the most fundamental and important.

To provide historical perspective, the book has devoted a number of pages to showing that the direct origin of our dominant (and ineffectual) educational orientation was the progressive movement of the 1920s that emanated from Teachers College, Columbia University. That is not of course a new observation, as any reader of Laurence Cremin or Diane Ravitch can attest.[1] More broadly, I have placed the progressive movement within the tradition of American Romanticism, which began in the early nineteenth century and has persisted powerfully in our culture ever since. It is this pervasive, deep-dyed Romanticism, not just its one-time expression in the progressive movement, which continues to thwart a balanced educational approach that would emphasize high standards, book learning, and hard work in school. Persistent educational Romanticism is the source of many assumptions about childhood and human nature that still pervade our minds and hearts. These deep-lying assumptions need to be modified—no easy task.

But it would be a grave oversimplification of my theme if the reader inferred that this book merely invites a revival of our Enlightenment educational traditions in order to counterbalance our too-dominant Romantic ones. That is certainly part of my message, but to overstress it would misleadingly suggest that the main issue is philosophical or ideological. On the contrary, the main issue is practical. My discussion of the basic, controlling ideas of the past seven decades is meant to help emancipate the debate, to lead it beyond self-confirming Romantic slogans and toward what is known to be practically effective in schooling. My chief complaint against educational Romanticism is that it fails to conform to educational reality. The strongest case against it lies not in the opinion that it is wrong in its ideology but in the fact that it is wrong in its empirical assumptions, and hence ineffectual in practice. In the sphere of poetry, Romanticism is arguably superior to the Enlightenment, but in the sphere of education, Romantic principles have proved to be much less valid than Enlightenment ones as guides to practice.

By now it is obvious to everyone that the Romantic-progressive approach to learning has not worked in American public schools. But the danger remains that Americans will give credence to the continually repeated claim that the "new" ideas have never been properly tried. In the 1990s, that is the only plausible-sounding argument which could be marshaled in defense of these failed Romantic-progressive ideas. The "never-properly-tried" argument is difficult to counter decisively, because any example of failure can instantly be labeled a flawed, inauthentic attempt, while any anecdotal success can instantly be labeled a triumphant vindication of progressivist theory. *But the research literature offers not one example of successful implementation of progressivist methods in a carefully controlled longitudinal study.* In fact, as I showed in Chapter 4, process-outcome research has consistently shown just the opposite, that the Romantic-progressive approach is always the least effective approach studied.[2] No wonder there is a continual demand by progressivists for new types of assessments that would make these results come out differently! It is incumbent upon the public and the press to reject this "never-properly-tried" argument. We simply cannot afford more decades of "child-centered" credulity.

We cannot afford any more decades dominated by ideas that promote natural, integrated project-learning over focused instruction leading to well-practiced operational skills in reading and mathematics, and well-stocked minds conversant with individual subject matters like history and biology. We need to reject the ill-founded notions that every child learns naturally at his or her own pace and that teaching the child is more important than teaching the subject (whatever that means, beyond failure to teach the subject). We must not accept the claim that knowing how to learn (which is an abstract skill that does not even exist) is more important than having a broad foundation of factual knowledge that really does enable further learning. We must reject the disparagement of verbal learning and the celebration of "hands-on" learning, based on the false Romantic premise that mere words are inauthentic compo-nents of human understanding. We cannot afford still to accept the untrue belief that adequate schooling is natural and painless, and mainly a function of individual talent rather than hard work. We must reject the false claim that delaying learning until the child is "ready" will speed up learning in the long run. We must cease listening to the siren call that learning should be motivated entirely by inward love of the subject and interest in it, without a significant admixture of external incentive. In short, we must cease attending to the Romantic ideas that the reformers of the 1990s, echoing the reformers of the 1920s, '30s, and '40s and all the decades in between, have been pronouncing in chorus. These ideas are emphatically not reforms. They are the long-domi-nant controlling ideas of our failed schools.

Those ideas fall on receptive ears among teachers and Americans generally because of their conformity with our Romantic assumptions about the superi-ority of the natural over the artificial. It is assumed that integrated, lifelike learning is natural, since that is the kind of learning which supposedly takes place in "real life," in a state of nature, outside of school, and it is assumed that this "integrated" approach is therefore the more effective context for human education inside the school as well. To repeat a telling quotation from Emerson:

> *Education! . . . We are shut up in schools and college recitation rooms for ten or fifteen years & come out at last with a bellyfull of words & do not know a thing. We cannot use our hands or our legs or our eyes or our arms. We do not know an edible root in the woods. We cannot tell our course by the stars nor the hour of the day by the sun. It is well if we can swim & skate. We are afraid of a horse, of a cow, of a dog, of a cat, of a spider. Far better was the Roman rule to teach a boy nothing that he could not learn standing. . . . The farm, the farm is the right school. The reason of my deep respect for the farmer is that he is a realist and not a dictionary. The farm is a piece of the world, the School house is not. The farm by training the physical rectifies and invigorates the metaphysical & moral nature.[3]*

Emerson here expresses forthrightly what progressivists continue to assume implicitly, that traditional schooling indoors—at desks, in rows, and largely by means of words and drill and practice—is unnatural and therefore harmful. The natural way of learning is envisioned as taking place in a lifelike setting with a lifelike goal, thus allowing the student to construct or discover what is to be mastered. This mode of schooling, it is claimed, will not only integrate the various kinds of knowledge and skills that need to be learned, but will also interest and motivate the student much more effectively than the artificial incentives of rewards and punishments.

Why did these attractive pedagogical assumptions not in fact work out when they were put into practice in American schools? One reason they failed was that the naturalistic approach turns out not to motivate all students equally. More important, it does not inculcate knowledge and skill effectively, securely, or universally.[4] Using the project method to teach children an understanding of the Underground Railroad, for example, is all too likely to result in something like biscuit-making (complete with butter and jam), designed to give a "hands-on" idea of the food eaten by the escaping slaves. The remembered understandings that young children bring away from such unfocused instruction are not controlled by a benign, invisible, right-tending nature. What children remember remains uncontrolled, contingent, and largely irrelevant to definite and responsible learning goals. Wherever there is an absence of explicit focus and definite goals—that is, wherever there is an absence of "traditional" schooling—there is also an absence of secure and universal learning. Process-outcome research has shown that what children bring away from naturalistic, "integrated" learning is likely to be highly variable and uncertain.

## 2.
## Two Historic Errors: Formalism and Naturalism

It will be useful to restate why the two fundamental tenets of American educational orthodoxy, formalism and naturalism, are incorrect. By "formalism" I mean the belief that the particular content which is learned in school (the content I have called "intellectual capital") is far less important than acquiring the formal tools which will enable a person to learn future content. This tool-providing idea is the source of the dictionary-accessing and critical-thinking exercises that now pervade the schools, in lessons where the *content* of what is being accessed or critically thought about is left up for grabs. I call this approach "formalism" because it considers the main goal of education to consist in giving students formal intellectual tools like "learning to learn," "accessing skills," and "critical-thinking skills" rather than in transmitting knowledge.

By the second term, "naturalism," I mean the belief that education is a natural process with its own inherent forms and rhythms, which may vary with each child, and is most effective when it is connected with natural, real-life goals and settings. Naturalism assumes that the best mode of learning is the one that follows and supports this lifelike and inherent process of development. Schooling which goes against this natural process is believed to be either ineffective or spiritually harmful. Both formalism and naturalism are half-truths—the most pernicious kinds of errors because they appear so plausible.

Educational formalism is in error in purely practical terms, because an emphasis on process and skills rather than on content does not in fact result in significantly improved formal skills for students. The real-life competencies that people need, such as the abilities to read, to write, to communicate, to learn, to analyze, and to grasp and manipulate mathematical symbols, have major components that psychologists have found to be "domain-specific." This means that an ability to think critically about chess does not translate into an ability to think critically about sailing. An ability to read or write effectively about the Civil War does not translate into an ability to read or write effectively about agriculture. It is true that certain operations of reading are the same from one task to another, so that expertness in reading partly depends upon the automation (through a great deal of practice) of those repeated operations, thus freeing the conscious mind for critical thought. But competent reading about the Civil War also depends upon the acquisition of the relevant vocabulary, conventions, and schemas that form the relevant knowledge base for reading and learning about the Civil War. There is no substitute for this requisite domain-specific content knowledge in the performance of reading or any other intellectual skill.

It is a fallacy, then, to claim that the schools should or could teach all-purpose reading, thinking, and learning skills. But paradoxically, adequate attention to the transmission of broad general knowledge actually does lead to general intellectual skills. The paradox is quite stunning. Our emphasis on formal skills has resulted in students who are deficient in formal skills, whereas an appropriate emphasis on transmitting knowledge results in students who actually possess the skills that are sought by American educators—skills such as critical thinking and learning to learn. To explain this paradox, one must grasp the difference between a formal skill and a general skill.

A formal skill is the application of a formal pattern or strategy to a new problem. Psychologists have found that this formalistic model does not work in the real world.[5] It represents the slow, unreliable approach of amateurs and novices rather than the knowledge-informed approach of experts. It is an approach that results in incompetent performance. A *general* skill, by contrast, is based only partly on habituation to the formal, repeated aspects of the skill (such as word recognition in reading); it is also based on wide-ranging general knowledge. A broad base of knowledge enables a well-educated person to apply domain-relevant knowledge to a wide range of new problems and experiences—which is the true meaning of "learning to learn." For instance, having as part of one's general intellectual capital some key factual relationships regarding the Civil War is a much better foundation for skilled, critical reading about the Civil War than an armory of formal procedures. The best foundation for general skill is not the inculcation of abstract strategies but the inculcation of broad knowledge. This important psychological insight about the mixed nature of skills provides the best utilitarian defense of a broad liberal education.

The second fundamental error of the current doctrine, educational naturalism, holds that the progress of learning is like the growth of a tree or flower, a process that should follow its own proper and inherent unfolding—ideally within a context that is like "life itself." The religious and philosophical bases for this naturalism are so widely held that the position usually doesn't need to be argued. We Americans are predisposed to believe in the rightness of the natural and the harmfulness of the artificial. But quite apart from our cultural predisposition in its favor, educational naturalism also gains acceptance from its obvious validity in some learnings that are indeed natural. The most stunning example is the learning of the mother tongue. While this attainment is an immense intellectual feat requiring a great deal of time and effort, it is a feat that all normal children achieve in the natural course of things, in their own good time. Advantaged toddlers, with lots of encouragement and stimulation from their parents, usually become more proficient in language than disadvantaged children, showing that "artificial" interventions are important even in this universal learning. Nonetheless, the basic process *is* natural. Scientific opinion has converged on the view that native-language learning is mediated by dedicated locations in the brain, and is as inexorable and inherent as physical development.

If all school learnings were as innately motivated, as joyful, and as certain as the learning of the mother tongue, effective schools would be Edenically happy places where effort would be joy and learning would be assured. This is in fact the image of the ideal school according to the progressivist tradition. But the adequacy of that naturalistic tradition hinges on the truth or error of the premise that school learnings are analogous to natural processes like physiomotor development and the learning of the mother tongue. If this foundational premise turned out not to be correct, if, on the contrary, many learnings to be gained in school are inherently unnatural attainments, just as Emerson complained, then the naturalistic approach would not be self-evidently the best approach to achieving them. It might be the case that such nonnatural goals are best attained, perhaps *only* to be attained, through nonnatural means.

Reading is a good example, regarding which we now have a great deal of evidence. (It could hardly be objected that the naturalistic approach to reading instruction has not been properly tried; under the rubric "whole language," it has been tried on a massive scale.) The whole-language approach makes the assumption that learning to read is analogous to the original, natural learning of the mother tongue: the child should be exposed to print in meaningful, lifelike contexts and should be encouraged to figure out the oral-written correspondences by the same sort of trial-and-error processes that characterized his or her learning of the mother tongue. Learning to read is to be understood as "a psycholinguistic guessing game" on the analogy of primary language acquisition. If it takes place in real-life settings, with first-rate, interesting literature, this approach will lead inevitably to love and mastery of reading in the same way the child's earlier linguistic guessing led to mastery of oral language.

What is the evidence for or against the premise that learning to read is a natural process analogous to learning to speak? The most striking evidence against the naturalness of reading is the brute fact that alphabetic literacy is extremely rare among the historical cultures of the world, whereas oral language is universal. This is strong prima facie evidence that literacy is not a natural learning analogous to oral language acquisition, but it still leaves open the question whether the most effective approach to gaining literacy is naturalistic or nonnaturalistic. To most researchers in literacy, the answer has now become clear. A nonnaturalistic approach, including direct instruction in letter-sound correspondences, is by far the most effective approach to the teaching of reading. The state of California unwittingly performed a vast confirmation of the research regarding educational naturalism when it insisted that reading instruction be conducted through the whole-language approach. Subsequently, on the next national survey, California had sunk to the bottom in reading scores.

So strong is the naturalistic orthodoxy that even mathematics, where American students score lowest of all subjects in international comparisons, is to be taught by naturalistic methods such as integrative projects and the hands-on discovery method. Just as in the case of reading, where it is considered harmful to submit children to the deadening process of directly learned letter-sound correspondences, it is considered equally harmful to submit children to the "drill and kill" process of learning the number facts of addition, subtraction, and multiplication by heart. No, say American experts, children will learn better if they discover the truths of mathematics for themselves naturally by solving "real-world" math problems when they are developmentally ready to solve them. Professor David Geary, in an important series of studies, has shown that the psychological and developmental assumptions behind these naturalistic dogmas are as incorrect in mathematics as they are in reading, and lead to equally poor results.[6] It is hard to decide which dogma is the more harmful, formalism or naturalism. Together, they are lethal to effective education, and will continue to work their baleful effects until they are challenged frontally and forcefully by an informed public.

### 3.
### Key Findings of Research

Researches into the neurophysiology of learning and the structure of cognitive skills converge on a few fundamental psychological principles. These foundational principles can be actualized in different ways, but they cannot be circumvented. The research findings are especially significant for current educational policy debates, because of the consistent rhetorical use of science by anti-subject-matter progressivists. Ever since William Hearst Kilpatrick justified the unscrewing of student desks from the floor and the abolition of subject matter and grades by citing scientific findings about "neurones," "synapses," and "laws of thought," the rhetoric of educational professionals has bristled with references to "current research." But the references have been selective and have often ignored inconvenient mainstream findings. Progressivism's greatest distortion of the scientific consensus may be the use of scientific-sounding terms like "developmentally appropriate" to justify deferment or neglect of diligence, or derogation of factual knowledge, while the mainstream scientific community has come to very different conclusions.

One of the most useful lines of research in recent years has concerned innate and noninnate learnings, a subject that has much relevance to educational naturalism. A human child is biologically so helpless and vulnerable in its early years, so dependent upon the wider community for survival, that in the course of human evolution, children who lacked the learning instinct would not have been likely to survive.[7] Everyone concedes that young children exhibit a natural eagerness to learn. Steven Pinker has shown that children are born with a "language instinct."[8] Play, which is instinctive and universal in children and also many kinds of animals, helps develop basic cognitive activities into more integrated and complex cognitions involving orientation in space, physical manipulation of objects, representation of objects, social relations, speaking, and elementary counting. These learnings appear to follow a temporal sequence that can reasonably be called "natural" because they have been shown to be transcultural and universal. These natural learnings are based on (though not limited to) primary processes determined by human evolution. These "primary learnings" seem to follow a definite and universal sequence.

Beyond these primary learnings, however, there are secondary learnings that, while necessary within particular cultures, are not universal, such as reading, writing, the base-ten system of counting, multicolumn addition and subtraction, carrying and borrowing, multiplication and division. These secondary learnings do *not* fit the naturalistic scheme of automatic development. It is quite misleading to think of them on the analogy of an acorn developing into an oak. The learnings do not develop at all unless they are taught. The implication of research along these lines is that while the normal tempo of psychomotor and conceptual development makes it inefficient to teach certain aspects of reading, writing, and arithmetic too early (before, say, age four), there is *no* age when a child is developmentally ready by nature to learn reading, writing, and arithmetic. Children's readiness for secondary processes is not a matter of natural development but of *prior relevant learning.* Learning builds on learning. After age five, the plasticity of the young mind makes many secondary learnings easier and more durable at early ages.[9] Jerome Bruner once said that "any subject can be taught effectively in some intellectually honest form to any child at any stage of development."[10] While this famous remark is usually quoted in order to be dismissed, it represents the current thinking of mainstream neurobiology. "Nature" is actually telling us something very different from the message carried by the phrase "developmentally appropriate." What nature is really saying about much learning much of the time is "the earlier the better."

Mainstream research has exploded the idea that natural learning, properly timed and organized, is effortless. Kilpatrick put the standard progressivist view this way: "Our old-type school, with its formal subject matter, remote from life, made us think of the learning process as laborious and repellent. But . . . life's inherent learning comes in fact without effort, comes in fact automatically and stays with us."[11] On the contrary, scientists have found that it takes repeated practice to forge new neural paths in our brains. Learning involves effort, whether through unconscious play or conscious diligence. There is *no* way around this repeated effort, though it need not be in the least unpleasant. Nothing can be reliably stored for recall without repetition. "Once is not enough" is a good operational motto for fixing new learnings in long-term memory. Memory studies indicate that the best approach to achieving retention in long-term memory is "distributed practice," with rehearsal occurring at moderately distant intervals.[12] An overemphasis on effortlessness and naturalness in learning really amounts to an empirical mistake. A child does

not effectively learn the multiplication table by osmosis. If the effort of learning can be made fun, so much the better. But repeated effort there must
usually be, and for many learnings, the sooner and more focused the better.

For higher-level competencies, cognitive science has constructed theoretical models that describe skills and learning processes. The current consensus is
that these competencies are described, at least operationally, by schema theory—a schema being a remembered system of typical traits that are related to
each other in typical but adjustable ways. For example, when I read the word
"ostrich" (assuming I understand it), I activate a schema and select from it a
range of traits and meanings that seem most appropriate in the context. But
there are other components of reading skill that depend less on conscious-
knowledge schemas and more on habitual operations like eye movements and
letter recognitions. These constantly repeated, automated strategies (sometimes called "rules") are learned through practice and repetition. Reading
skill, for example, includes both "rules," that is, mastery of operations continually repeated to the point of automaticity, and schemas consisting of intercon-
nected frames of knowledge.[13] In the case of reading skill, the most important
schemas are represented by particular word meanings and cultural conventions.

That intellectual skills should rest on rules and schemas arises from a fundamental limitation of the mind called "short-term," or "working," memory,
which is capable of retaining and manipulating only a very limited number of
items over a very brief time span before degenerating. This fundamental limitation of thinking and learning is physiological; it applies to novice and expert
alike. Once the very constraining limit of short-term memory is reached, some
elements disappear from awareness. The mind must strike while the iron is
hot; if it doesn't, those vanished elements will cease to be available. For overcoming these limitations of working memory, the mind uses rules and schemas
to achieve automation and chunking. Automation is a technique that enables
the mind to engage rapidly and unconsciously in the subroutines of an activity
without bringing them into working memory at all. Chunking is a means for
rapidly representing a whole range of knowledge elements by a single image,
word, or symbol, so that the whole array need not be present to the mind all at
once.

In the long run, chunking, which is connected with schema development, is
more important for developing very high levels of intellectual skill. For while
the increase in competency available from the automation of repeated operations is immensely important in the early stages of learning, its limits may be
rather quickly reached. Once automaticity of repeated operations has been
attained, higher levels of skill depend mostly upon the continued acquisition,

habituation, and chunking of relevant knowledge. In reading, for example, once a plateau of rule automation has been attained, higher levels of expertise reside almost entirely in developing, expanding, and making accessible a reader's relevant intellectual capital.

The distinction between rule and schema is roughly equivalent to the traditional distinction between skill and content. But the traditional educational parlance assumes that a skill is an all-purpose tool that can apply to new contents and tasks. Cognitive science shows that, on the contrary, intellectual skills consist of *both* formal operations and concrete schemas. People are rarely able to apply formal procedures in appropriate ways to unfamiliar problems that belong to unfamiliar domains.[14] Students who have just finished a one-semester course in logic are only marginally more logical than people who have never taken the subject. The mere learning of formal procedures cannot result in intellectual competencies. This is another way of making the point that children need to learn a lot of factual knowledge as well as a lot of operational know-how. Such a commonsense conclusion would scarcely require the citation of psychological research if the educational community relied less on the formalistic tool metaphor in describing intellectual skills.

Finally, research has confirmed what Euclid told King Ptolemy: there is no royal road to learning. Learning is cumulative, and at first it is slow. Knowledge gradually builds on knowledge; the principle behind intellectual capital is that it takes knowledge to make knowledge. Because of the cumulative character of learning, the educational conditions of early life exercise a very powerful influence on later competencies. Small early deficits tend to become large deficiencies in later life; conversely, small initial advantages tend to grow into large ones later. The causes of this snowball effect are multiple and complex, and include physiological age effects as well as social and motivational factors. But the chief cause is simply the cumulative character of learning itself. The more one knows, the more readily one learns something new. Experts in a subject can learn new things in their domain faster than novices can, though when novices and experts are equally ignorant about an unfamiliar subject, their rates of learning equalize.

The cumulative effects of intellectual capital derive from there being at least two learning advantages in possessing relevant background knowledge. The first advantage is that there are fewer new things which have to be learned. As work on chess expertise has shown, the expert's possession of well-established schemas reduces the number of new elements that the mind must attend to, helping to prevent the overloading of the expert learner's short-term memory. By contrast, the novice, who has to keep many more new elements in mind at once, may quickly overload his short-term memory and experience constant re-trys and slow progress. Beyond this task reduction effected by prior knowledge, there is a second learning advantage in possessing lots of intellectual capital: the broader the base of relevant knowledge, the greater the number of potential analogies or categories available for assimilating new learnings. This increase in cognitive hooks (a kind of mental Velcro) gives educated adults a learning advantage over young children, who, in raw processing ability, may far outshine them.

These few basic principles of learning apply universally: the distinction between primary and secondary learnings, the importance of early beginnings, the need for effort and practice, the need to automate operations and develop relevant intellectual capital to overcome the limitations of short-term memory, and the cumulative nature of learning. These principles apply to everybody—the palace-tutored prince as well as the neglected pauper. There are a great many ways of applying these principles intelligently. That is a good argument for giving teachers a lot of freedom, so long as they get good results. But while there are a lot of ways to skin the cat, there is no way of dispensing with the separation of the cat from his skin. The fundamental principles themselves cannot be circumvented. Moreover, when they are put into practice in teaching large numbers of children in large systems of education, the possible ways of applying them effectively and fairly begin to narrow.

## 4.
## Policy Implications

An outmoded tool-conception of education and a failure to exploit the cumulative nature of learning have contributed to two shortcomings of American K–12 schooling—a low average level of achievement and a too-exact correlation between social class and educational level. No nation has entirely overcome a correlation between social class and educational achievement, and none is likely to, since the home is an important educational institution in its own right. Nonetheless, international analyses have shown that average levels of achievement across social classes are greatly enhanced and the gap between them reduced when educational systems exploit the cumulative character of learning. Nations like France have recognized that unless an early knowledge deficit is quickly overcome, the deficit grows ever larger. Our failure to exploit and compensate for this cumulative principle accounts for the growing achievement gap between our students and those in other lands, and for the fairness gap between social classes that widens at each successive grade level in American schools.

It is this cumulative principle that causes what educational researchers call the "Matthew effect," referring to the Gospel of St. Matthew, which describes the phenomenon of the widening gap: to those that have shall be given, but from those that have not shall be taken even what they have.[15] In American schools, this "taking away" experienced by the have-nots isn't the purely relativistic result of the haves making much larger gains through the snowballing of knowledge upon knowledge. The widening gap is also the result of discouragement in the have-nots as they witness themselves falling behind. Many of the most desperately needed policy reforms in American education need to be based on the principle that small early deficits or advantages in intellectual capital build to insuperable gaps after just a few years of schooling. Any reform that does not explicitly account for and systematically exploit this cumulative principle is unlikely to make much difference in overcoming the two major shortcomings of our K–12 education—the excellence gap and the fairness gap.

To take cumulativeness explicitly into account means that educational policy has to be developed coherently over the whole range of a child's schooling from preschool on, and with particular concern for the very early years, where small efforts and effects yield very large consequences later on. What new policies would be required to achieve greater quality and fairness by exploiting the cumulative principle of learning? One has already been enunciated. The number-one principle set forth by President Bush and forty-nine governors at the education summit of 1989, and confirmed by Congress in 1993, was that all first graders should enter school "ready to learn." This goal implicitly acknowledges that many first graders do not now enter school properly prepared. If taken seriously, the goal would imply a massive effort to create truly effective preschool programs. Also implicit in the ready-to-learn principle is the correct assumption that children cannot keep up in first grade unless they arrive there with the knowledge, vocabulary, and skill that will enable them to participate actively in the class and gain further learnings. They must be able to talk to the teacher and to other children, and they must be able in turn to understand what the teacher and other children are saying to them. In short, being "ready to learn" means, at a minimum, sharing knowledge, vocabulary, and skills with other members of the first-grade community.

This special focus on first graders is understandable if one assumes that an initial readiness to learn will provide the momentum needed to carry the child through subsequent grades. Otherwise, it would be hard to justify such preferential treatment of first graders. But since the underlying assumption that momentum for all will be sustained is demonstrably false in our current educational system, logical consistency requires that we extend the readiness-to-learn principle to second graders and third graders, and so on. The democratic version of the cumulative principle demands that every student who enters a class at the beginning of the year shall be vouchsafed the academic preparation needed to gain the knowledge and skills to be taught during that year. The readiness-to-learn principle cries out for generalization: In a democracy, all students should enter every grade ready to learn. True, the requisite background knowledge, vocabulary, and skills for such readiness are very unequally provided by the child's home environment. But precisely for that reason, it is the duty of schools in a democracy to compensate and to provide each child with the knowledge and skills requisite for academic progress, regardless of home background.

Recently, as part of the so-called "national standards movement," attempts have been made by several official groups to define the knowledge and skills that children should possess in the various subject-matter areas. Perhaps in order to avoid appearing arbitrarily prescriptive, these official groups have defined these standards in multiyear grade units such as K–4, 5–8, and 9–12. This is at best a preliminary step. The readiness-to-learn principle operates grade by grade. Except for the considerable percentage of children who change schools in the middle of the year, whom I will discuss in the last section, children normally change grades, teachers, and classrooms at the beginning of each new school year, when each new grade requires an achieved plateau that constitutes readiness to learn for that grade. From the standpoint of effective policy, the readiness-to-learn principle must be an annual one, requiring some degree of yearly monitoring and compensatory learning for those who may have drifted below the readiness plateau for the upcoming grade.

The policy implication of such grade-by-grade monitoring must be the introduction of grade-by-grade accountability and incentives for everyone concerned with schooling: parents, the children themselves, teachers, schools, districts. Without clear and specific definitions of what, for example, readiness for second grade means, it is not possible to monitor and rectify deficits in a timely way. Under our current arrangements, and under those now implied by multiyear standards, there is never a specific point when a child, a teacher, or any other participant is responsible for a shortcoming. When a deficit does blatantly manifest itself, it is always possible, and usually accurate, for a teacher or a child to complain that the deficit should have been remedied long ago in an earlier grade. The multigrade approach to accountability is essentially an unmonitored system that offers no fair or enforceable incentives for any participant, including the child.

The inference is unavoidable that only a school system which specifically defines the knowledge and skill required to participate effectively in each successive grade can be excellent and fair for all students. An enormous side benefit of such specific standards lies in the selectivity of the knowledge students are required to gain to reach each plateau. This multiyear core of selective content, being carefully sequenced and cumulative, can be much more meaningful and interesting than a fragmented curriculum. A school system should also administer fair and incorruptible tests to monitor whether the requisite plateau has been reached, and should offer all participants rewards for reaching it, as well as sanctions for not doing so. In negotiating these accountability arrangements, the community should be aware that none of the characteristic objections to tests, or to specific year-by-year goals, or to incentives have proved to be valid objections supported by good research. On the contrary, the best research, such as that by John Bishop of Cornell and Harold Stevenson of Michigan, has shown that tests, incentives, and accountability are necessary to a fair and effective system.[16]

Policymakers should be particularly alert to the objection, unfounded in research, that such a system of grade-by-grade accountability would produce cookie-cutter automatons rather than independent-minded students, or that it would prevent each child from "progressing at his or her own pace." The notions that children can progress through school at their own pace and that teachers are in any position to decide what a child's innate pace actually is are egregious fallacies unsupported by research. These naturalistic ideas cannot stand up to common sense, much less experimental investigation. There is no natural pace for gaining the nonnatural learnings of alphabetic literacy and base-ten mathematics. Moreover, it is impossible to conduct an effective classroom when there are attempts to accommodate twenty-five different "paces" of learning. The best classrooms bring all students along at a slow but sure rate, monitoring success for all at each step, providing compensatory instruction as needed, and, in addition, giving talented and eager students challenging extra work to do.

Nor should policymakers heed those who protest that standardized tests defeat the purposes of learning. Unstandardized tests—that is, tests that are scored differently by different people on different occasions—are inherently unfair, and untested students are, ipso facto, not being adequately monitored for the specific learnings they will need in the next grade. In short, grade-by-grade standards and some form of fair grade-by-grade tests are logically necessary for monitoring and attaining grade-by-grade readiness. Without such readiness, an educational system cannot achieve excellence and fairness.

While these community-wide policies follow inexorably from psychological research and comparative studies of different educational systems, the implications are less clear for school-level and classroom-level policies. The complexities of classroom instruction are so great, and the cultural and personal variables so numerous, that it is the better part of wisdom not to advocate highly specific classroom practices. On the other hand, education schools should be doing a better job of exposing teachers to the research about classroom methods that, on average, work best. Few teachers I have spoken to are aware of the existing process-outcome research into pedagogy. The lack of nuts-and-bolts pedagogical training in education schools was exposed by W. James Popham in a highly significant but rarely discussed study.[17] Popham showed that because of the failure to instruct prospective teachers about the best research into effective pedagogical methods (the findings of which happen to contravene the naturalistic approaches that continue to be advocated), uncertified persons, plopped into the classroom without having taken education courses, got results that were as good as those obtained by certified and experienced teachers.

In view of that outcome, the most important policy implication for teachers and schools would be to reconsider the validity of naturalistic principles, such as letting children advance at their own pace or letting knowledge and skills develop automatically through integrated projects and independent discovery. The existing research says that these methods do not work well. The best way to develop a skill or a domain of knowledge in a group of students is to focus (by any number of agreeable and interesting methods) on that skill or that domain, and to monitor whether that skill or that knowledge has in fact been gained. The research also shows that external incentives combined with intrinsic ones work better than intrinsic incentives alone. It shows that skill and knowledge do not come without effort, even to talented students, suggesting that an accomplishment-through-diligence mentality is more productive than a learning-is-easy-and-joyful mentality—more productive for both students and teachers, and in the end, more satisfying.

Education schools currently do not convey to our teachers the results of this firmly established research showing the superior effectiveness of clear focus, definite standards, diligent practice, and continual monitoring through tests and other means. Instead, American education schools derogate such traditional practices in favor of the progressive program of individual pacing, discovery learning, thematic teaching, nonobjective testing, and so on. Their captive audiences, consisting of millions of teachers, are offered no intellectual alternatives to these constantly repeated mistakes, which are, indeed, presented as fruits of the most recent research. The resulting pandemic of mistaken ideas may be the gravest barrier to America's educational improvement. If this disabling indoctrination continues unabated, then something quite revolutionary will have to be done about our system of training and certifying teachers. A beginning can be made by insisting upon more intellectual diversity within education schools. The tenacity and unanimity with which they adhere to the progressive doctrine may be owing to that doctrine's inability to withstand empirical and intellectual challenge in a free and open encounter. If such is the case, as I believe, then perhaps a rather small cadre of maverick professors in every education school might soon make the whole Wizard of Oz apparatus collapse like a punctured balloon.[18]

## 5.
## The Common School and the Common Good

E very nation that manages to achieve universal readiness in the early grades for all its children—a few examples are France, Hungary, Norway, Japan, Korea, Sweden, and Denmark—does so by following grade-by-grade standards. In large, diverse nations as well as small, homogeneous ones, a common core curriculum appears to be the only practical means for achieving universal readiness at each grade level. Universal readiness, in turn, is the only means for achieving universal competence and for combining excellence with fairness. In contrast, no nation that *dispenses* with grade-by-grade standards has managed to achieve universal readiness, excellence, and fairness. The Netherlands, for example, is a non-core-curriculum nation that has managed to attain a high average level of excellence because of very high achievement among the top half of its students, but it has failed to achieve universal competence and fairness. Indeed, the Netherlands, the only non-core-curriculum nation of Northern Europe, exhibits the lowest degree of educational fairness in that region, with some 16 percent of its schools falling below minimum competency, as contrasted with about 2.5 percent among its core-curriculum neighbors. (The United States figure is 30 percent of schools below minimum competency.)[19]

An informative exception to this correlation is found in Switzerland, which lacks a national core curriculum but achieves the best combination of excellence and fairness in the world, having the highest average level of achievement coupled with the smallest standard deviation.[20] But on closer inspection, we find that in fact Switzerland has one of the most detailed and demanding core curriculums in the world, with each canton specifying in detail the minimum knowledge and skill that each child shall achieve in each grade, and an accountability system that ensures the attainment of those universal standards. There is some commonality in standards among the cantons, but equally important, Swiss children rarely move from one canton to another in the course of their schooling. Each child therefore receives a highly coherent, carefully monitored sequence of early learnings such as children receive in countries that have grade-by-grade standards nationwide.

To the reader who may feel that these international data have little relevance to the United States, with its anticentralized educational traditions and its diversity, the Swiss example, in which each state fixes its own core curriculum, may appear to have the greatest affinity with our own tradition of state and local control. That would be the case, however, only if our children did not move so frequently from one school to another, and stayed put as the Swiss do. In the 1930s, William Bagley summarized the problem of American nomadism (which has grown more acute since he wrote):

> *The notion that each community must have a curriculum all its own is not only silly, but tragic. It neglects two important needs. The first, as we have already seen, is the need of a democracy for many common elements in the culture of all the people, to the end that the people may discuss collective problems in terms that will convey common meanings. The second need is extremely practical. It is the need of recognizing the fact that American people simply will not "stay put." They are the most mobile people in the world. . . . Under these conditions, failure to have a goodly measure of uniformity in school subjects and grade placement is a gross injustice to at least ten million school children at the present time.[21]*

The injustice that Bagley identified has intensified for many reasons, and it now extends to many more than ten million children. The average inner-city mobility rates (the percentage of children in a school who transfer in or out during the school year) lie routinely between 45 and 80 percent. Some inner-city schools have mobility rates of over 100 percent.[22] A recent analysis from the United States General Accounting Office reported that one sixth of all third graders attend at least three schools between first and third grade.[23] Given the curricular incoherence of schooling even for those who stay at the same school, the fragmentation and incoherence of the education provided to frequently moving students are heartbreaking.

In sum, the high mobility of our children, especially of those who can least afford educational disruption, makes common learnings *more* needed in the United States than in most other nations. The argument that we are different from others and require different educational arrangements points to more, not less, commonality in our educational standards. It is certainly true that we cannot reasonably be compared to Switzerland, but our children's high mobility rates are all the more reason why we cannot reasonably follow the Swiss principle of isolated localism. Our diversity, size, and nomadism are arguments in favor of, not against, common, grade-by-grade standards. Until very recently, of course, the idea of common standards in the United States has been unthinkable among American educational experts. Localism remains a quasi-sacred principle, despite the fact that few localities actually impose explicit content standards. But many people are coming to feel that, considering the glaring knowledge gaps and boring repetitions that children experience even when they stay in the same school, continuing our educational incoherence, nonaccountability, and inequity would be even more unthinkable.

Bagley's other point, that common learnings are necessary to a functioning democracy, is an educational principle that has been accepted in most democracies of the world, including our own in its earlier years. The institution of the common school, proposed by Jefferson and fostered by Horace Mann, had the goal of giving all children the shared intellectual and social capital that would enable them to participate as autonomous citizens in the economy and policy of the nation. When Jefferson said that if he had to choose between newspapers and government, he would choose newspapers, he went on to say that his remark was premised on each citizen's being able to read and understand the newspapers.[24] It was a prescient addendum. A citizenry cannot read and understand newspapers, much less participate effectively in a modern economy, without sharing the common intellectual capital that makes understanding and communication possible. In a large, diverse nation, the common school is the only institution available for creating a school-based culture that, like a common language, enables everyone to communicate in the public sphere.

The principle that children should enter a new grade already sharing the background knowledge required to understand the teacher and each other is at bottom the principle that enables the functioning of an entire community or nation. People cannot effectively meet in the classroom or in the marketplace unless they can communicate with and learn from each another. It is the duty of a nation's educational system to create this domain of public communicability. It cannot do so without the common school, and the common school cannot be truly such without providing each child the shared intellectual capital that will be needed in each early grade, and needed ultimately in society after graduation. A shared public culture that enables public communicability is essential to an effective community at every age and stage of life, and most emphatically in the early grades, when deficits can be made up. Once out of school, a citizen must continue to share in the common intellectual capital of the nation in order to communicate and learn.

The need to develop and nurture this cultural commons was implicitly understood by the founders, and is consistent with their motivation for having a First Amendment clause that forbids the establishment of a state religion. Divisiveness was to be excluded from the cultural commons. Guided by the principle of public toleration enunciated by John Locke and others after the bloody seventeenth-century wars of religion, the founders desired that the laws and customs of the public sphere should favor no single sect but should promote the general welfare. Customs devisive and dangerous to the internal peace of the nation, chiefly sectarian religions, were to be relegated to the private sphere, enabling all to meet in the public sphere as fellow citizens and equals. The deliberately artificial wall of separation helped create and nurture a public domain of toleration and civility, while leaving everyone as free as possible in their private lives. It was a brilliant Enlightenment political innovation for encouraging internal peace and solidarity in a large nation, and it led to the development of a uniquely American public culture. The development of this cosmopolitan culture was thus no accident. It had been openly discussed in the later Enlightenment, notably in the writings of Immanuel Kant.[25] In the minds of Jefferson, Mann, and other democratic theorists in France and elsewhere, the common school was to be not just the instrument of knowledge, literacy, and equality of opportunity but also the agent of a cosmopolitan culture that would promote universal respect and civility.

In our own day, the chief danger to this ecumenical, cosmopolitan public culture is not a religious but an ethnic sectarianism. The two kinds of sect, religious and ethnic, are highly similar in their divisiveness and their danger to the shared public sphere. Had the idea of ethnic strife been as present in the minds of the Founding Fathers as the idea of religious strife, our founding laws might have included a clause forbidding the establishment of a narrow ethnic culture. Just as the invocations of the Divinity in our public ceremonies are deliberately nonsectarian, hybrid affairs, engaged in by rabbis as well as priests, so our public culture is a hybrid construct that contains heterogeneous elements from various ethnic groups. Recently, Orlando Patterson has spoken of "cross-pollinating our multi-ethnic communities" in order to "promote that precious overarching national culture—the envy of the world—which I call ecumenical America." But Patterson sees a serious danger to that overarching culture in

> *balkanizing America both intellectually and culturally. One has only to walk for a few minutes on any large campus (the unfortunate coalescence of the left separatists and the right republican anti-communitarian indi-*

*vidualists/separatists!) to witness the pervasiveness of ethnic separatism,*
*marked by periodic outbursts of other chauvinisms and hostilities.*

Patterson urges instead a return to the cosmopolitan ideal of the commons:

*Universities and businesses should return to the principle of integration,*
*to the notion that diversity is not something to be celebrated and pro-*
*moted in its own right, but an opportunity for mutual understanding and*
*the furtherance of an ecumenical national culture.*[26]

Patterson and others, notably Arthur Schlesinger, Jr., have been urging that
the principle of multiculturalism should be guided into this ecumenical, cosmopolitan direction for the good of the nation rather than fostering its all-too-
prevalent tendency toward angry separatism and mutual hostility. This book
strongly supports that view. Whether multiculturalism should be given a Romantic, separatist form (in the tradition of Fichte) or an Enlightenment, cosmopolitan form (in the tradition of Kant) has an obvious bearing on the
educational question of common learnings in the early grades.[27] In my view,
the Romantic version of ethnicity is as deleterious to public education as the
Romantic conception of pedagogy. The common learnings taught in school
should promote a cosmopolitan, ecumenical, hybrid public culture in which all
meet on an equal footing—a culture that is as deliberately artificial and nonsectarian as our public invocations of the Divinity. This school-based culture
belongs to everyone and to no one. Its function is analogous to that of the
hybrid lingua francas of the medieval marketplace, which were the antecedents
of the major national languages—themselves hybrid, artificially constructed
affairs, mostly codified by committees.

In the United States, the process of reaching agreement about a sequence
of common learnings in the early grades is likely to be lengthy, conflict-ridden,
and, at the start, unofficial. A highly specific common core of content is still
repellent to many Americans. Gradually, however, general agreement on such
a core might be developed if the public and the educational community became fully persuaded that some degree of grade-by-grade commonality is necessary to educational excellence and equity. (A 50 percent common core has
proved to be acceptable to parents in Core Knowledge schools.) The public
will be all the more likely to reach this conclusion when it becomes more fully
aware that educational formalism has turned the jealously guarded principle of
local curriculum control into a myth. As far as specific content is concerned,
the local curriculum, with few exceptions, does not exist. One cannot reason-

ably endorse something that does not exist, though one can demand that it come into existence. If the public simply insisted upon a true common core of learnings at the local level, that would mark a huge advance in our educational arrangements, and might in time lead to still broader commonalities.

Because this book has been focused mainly on kindergarten through grade eight—decisive grades for determining the excellence and equity of schooling—I have paid scant attention to high school. That is a conscious omission. If the principles of early education advanced here were to be followed, American high schools would change perforce for the better. Their incoming students would have already received the foundational knowledge and skill needed for good citizenship. (In earlier eras, many exemplary citizens-to-be were compelled to leave school by the end of grade eight.) Students would not need to be shepherded into so many elementary courses; they could follow more varied and intensive strands of academic or vocational study according to their interests and abilities. As a consequence, the American high school would become a more interesting and effective place for all types of students.

Beyond urging agreement at the local level, I have not made many suggestions regarding the large-scale policies needed to create more demanding elementary schools. I haven't answered questions like What shall we do tomorrow? and Who shall be in charge? The possible administrative means for accomplishing the task are many, but there can be no substitute for the main elements of the task itself. Schools need to have a coherent, cumulative core curriculum which instills consensus values such as civic duty, honesty, diligence, perseverance, respect, kindness, and independent-mindedness; which gives students step-by-step mastery of *procedural knowledge* in language arts and mathematics; which gives them step-by-step mastery of *content knowledge* in civics, science, the arts, and the humanities; and which holds students, teachers, schools, and parents accountable for acceptable progress in achieving these specific year-by-year goals. Every school, in short, should have the basic characteristics described in an earlier chapter:

> *All teachers at our school have not only pedagogical training but also a detailed knowledge of the subject matter that they teach. We instill in all children an ethic of toleration, civility, orderliness, responsibility, and hard work. Our staff has agreed on a definite core of knowledge and skill that all children will attain in each grade. We make sure that every child learns this core, and gains the specific knowledge and skill needed to prosper at the next grade level, thus enabling knowledge to build upon knowledge. Our teachers continually confer with their colleagues about effective ways of stimulating children to learn and integrate this specific*

*knowledge and skill. The specificity of our goals enables us to monitor children, and give focused attention where necessary. To this end, we provide parents with a detailed outline of the* specific *knowledge and skill goals for each grade, and we stay in constant touch with them regarding the child's progress. Through this knowledge-based approach, we make sure that* all *normal children perform at grade level, while, in addition, the most talented children are challenged to excel. Attaining this specific and well-integrated knowledge and skill gives our students pleasure in learning, as well as self-respect, and it ensures that they will enter the next grade ready and eager to learn more.*

Since this emphasis on content and coherence requires a restructuring of ideas, and because ideas are slow to change, my colleagues and I have been pursuing a school-by-school grassroots effort in which the leadership of one group of parents or teachers, or of a single principal or superintendent, can revolutionize the ideas and practices of an individual school. That school's success then sometimes encourages other schools to rethink their assumptions. This school-by-school effort is slow, but it is at least an avenue that can be taken now, without delay—the kind of initiative greatly facilitated by large-scale policies that consciously liberate individual initiative, policies such as "parental choice" and "charter schools," which give parents and teachers the power to change their own individual schools, so long as their students are trained to high standards of skill and knowledge.

It has taken nearly seventy years for Romantic progressivism to exercise virtually totalitarian intellectual dominion over not just schools of education but a large percentage of policymakers and the general public as well. Nothing truly effective in the way of large-scale policy change—through federal, state, or local mechanisms—can be accomplished, no new power relationships can be forged, until there is a change of mind by the general public—among whom I include two and a half million teachers. Once that occurs, many different public policies could be successful.

The strongest resistance to commonality in schooling may come from a widespread fear of uniformity—the last bastion of misguided Romanticism. It is said that common elements in the curriculum would destroy our American essence, which is diversity. There is no evidence whatever that this fear of uniformity, which is widespread and often expressed, has any real-world foundation, or that a moiety of commonality in the school curriculum will turn everyone into interchangeable automatons. To the extent that this antisameness sentiment has any concrete implication for the curriculum, it would seem to be the current laissez-faire idea that if all schools and teachers do their own thing, then the invisible hand of nature will cause our children to be educated effectively, and thus ensure their individuality and diversity. The foundation for this curricular confidence (which has in fact resulted in huge knowledge gaps, boring repetitions, and glaring inequalities) would seem to be a Romantic faith in the watchful beneficence of nature, which "never did betray the heart that loved her." It is an expression of the same optimistic naturalism which supposes that the pace and quality of each child's scholarly attainments are determined naturally, and will follow an innate course of development which should not be interfered with by external impositions of drills and hard work.

Improving the effectiveness and fairness of education through enhancing both its content and its commonality has a more than educational significance. The improvement would, as everyone knows, diminish the economic inequities within the nation. Nothing could be more important to our national well-being than overcoming those inequities, which have grown ever greater in recent decades. But something equally significant is at stake. Many observers have deplored the decline in civility in our public life, and with it the decline in our sense of community. The interethnic hostilities that have intensified among us recently, the development of an us-versus-them mentality in political life, the astonishing indifference to the condition of our children—all bespeak a decline in the communitarian spirit, which used to be a hallmark of what Patterson calls our "ecumenical national culture." Bringing our children closer to universal competence is important. But an equally important contribution of the truly common school would be the strengthening of universal communicability and a sense of community within the public sphere. In the long run, that could be the common school's most important contribution to preserving the fragile fabric of our democracy.

# Critical Guide to Educational
# Terms and Phrases

## 1.
## Introduction

This critical guide to terms, phrases, and slogans widely used by the American educational community is conceived as a kind of typhoid-tetanus shot, a controlled dose of the pathogen in nontoxic form to inoculate those who become exposed. Prospective teachers and members of the general public are bemused, bullied, and sometimes infected by seductive rhetorical flourishes like "child-centered schooling" or bullying ones like the dismissive words "drill and kill." These terms and phrases pretend to more soundness, humaneness, substance, and scientific authority than they in fact possess. Promulgating this system of rhetoric has been an ongoing function of American schools of education, whose uniformity of language and doctrine ensures that every captive of the teacher-certification process and every professor trained to continue the tradition is imbued with educationally correct phrases. Consensus-through-rhetoric has been one of the main instruments of the Thoughtworld's intellectual dominance.

As an example of this uniformity in teacher preparation, I quoted on pages 129–30 a typical passage from an education-school textbook called *Best Practice*. The authors claimed that a doctrinal consensus exists among the important educational organizations—including the National Council of Teachers of Mathematics, the Center for the Study of Reading, the National Writing Project, the National Council for the Social Studies, the American Association for the Advancement of Science, the National Council of Teachers of English, the

National Association for the Education of Young Children, and the International Reading Association—regarding the best principles of pedagogy. These consensus principles were lauded as "child-centered," "progressive," "developmentally appropriate," and "research-based."

On the authority of this professional consensus, teachers were instructed to de-emphasize and deplore practices represented by bad words like "whole-class instruction," "passive listening," "textbooks," "broad coverage," "rote memorization of facts," "competition," "grades," and "standardized tests," and to accentuate practices represented by good words like "hands-on learning," "discovery learning," "less is more," "student responsibility," "individual learning styles," "cooperative learning," and "nonstandardized assessments." None of this advice is sound. Yet, for any prospective teacher to whom the advice is presented so authoritatively and repeated so often, it would be reasonable to assume that it *must* be true. Repetition and consensus give the phrases a self-evident, not-to-be-questioned quality which induces those who repeat them to believe them earnestly and implicitly.

Almost all the familiar phrases can be grouped under five themes of progressive education, indicating once again the persistence and power of the progressivist doctrines promulgated from Teachers College in the teens and twenties and then replicated in every education school in the nation. Here are the five themes, along with the phrases still used to support them:

- **Tool conception of education:** *"accessing skills," "critical-thinking skills," "higher-order skills," "learning to learn," "lifelong learning," "metacognitive skills," "problem-solving skills," "promise of technology."*
- **Romantic developmentalism:** *"at their own pace," "child-centered schooling," "developmentally appropriate," "factory-model schools," "individual differences," "individualized instruction," "individual learning styles," "multiaged classroom," "multiple intelligences," "one size fits all," "student-centered education," "teach the child, not the subject."*
- **Naturalistic pedagogy:** *"constructivism," "cooperative learning," "discovery learning," "drill and kill," "hands-on learning," "holistic learning," "learning by doing," "open classroom," "multiaged classroom," "project method," "rote learning," "thematic learning," "whole-class instruction," "whole-language instruction."*
- **Antipathy to subject-matter content:** *"banking theory of schooling," "facts, inferior to understanding," "facts are soon outdated," "intellectual capital," "less is more," "mere facts," "rote learning," "textbook learning," "transmission theory of schooling," "teaching for understanding."*

- **Antipathy to testing and ranking:** *"authentic assessment," "competition," "exhibitions," "performance-based assessment," "portfolio assessment."*

So closely interrelated are the topics mentioned under each of the above headings that the following Glossary will largely omit cross-references in order to avoid bombarding the reader with constantly repeated indications like *See also "Accessing skills," "Critical-thinking skills," "Higher-order skills," "Learning to learn," "Lifelong learning," "Metacognitive skills," "Problem-solving skills," "Promise of technology,"* and so on. The family resemblances among these terms may be owing partly to a process of historical transformation. When a phrase like "learning by doing" becomes discredited, the principle may still live on in a protean transformation like "hands-on learning." If the "open classroom" becomes a source of disillusion, it may be reborn as the "multiaged" classroom. A reader wishing to pursue the transformations of these themes may simply refer back to the groupings listed above, and may also consult the Index to find page references to more extended discussions and documentations in the body of the book.

I hope readers will find the Glossary useful. What is valid in the old rhetoric should be left to flourish, but what is false should be dug up and exposed to common sense. Before we Americans can cultivate new educational ideas, the ancient plot of ground must be weeded. Many people in recent years have expressed a sense that something is not quite right about these facile doctrines in all their various guises. For those persons, the following short commentaries are offered as reinforcements for their own insights and experiences.

# 2.
# Glossary

A ccessing skills." A phrase used to define an aspect of "learning to learn." Accessing skills are currently emphasized by our schools on the grounds that today's knowledge is changing so rapidly that it will be irrelevant tomorrow. It is better to learn how to "access information" (i.e., how to look things up, or how to use a library or computer or spell-check program) than to learn a lot of soon-to-be-outmoded facts. The emphasis on accessing skills is an expression of the tool metaphor of education, which opposes itself to the "banking theory" or "transmission theory" of schooling (which see). The tool conception holds that schooling should emphasize instrumental strategies, such as how to *find* knowledge, rather than emphasizing knowledge itself. The dominance of this tool idea, which dates back to the early days of the progressive movement, has led our schools to spend a lot of time teaching such techniques as dictionary- or encyclopedia-accessing skills, which must indeed be taught to children but are not inherently difficult skills that take a long time to acquire. They cannot replace students' ready knowledge of varied subject matters and word meanings. A speaker on the radio or television does not pause for listeners to look up the words they don't know. Even when using an encyclopedia or CD-ROM, students without prior background knowledge cannot understand the things they look up. Preparing students to cope with new knowledge is indeed central to good education. But knowing how to look things up, while important, is not by itself a skill that effectively enables students to learn new things. The skill to learn new things consists of both general tactics like accessing skills and a generous amount of "domain-specific" knowledge. Contrary to the tool metaphor, a general ability to learn new competencies never consists solely of accessing strategies but also entails familiarity with the most important knowledge in mathematics, the sciences, the humanities, and the arts.

**"At their own pace."** A phrase implying that children should develop naturally rather than being forced to learn too rapidly; also called "self-paced learning." The idea is a logical consequence of the individualistic approach taken by Romantic developmentalism. Going at one's own pace would seem to be more natural than going at someone else's, but there is no reliable evidence to support the idea of self-pacing. On the contrary, the data show that the imposition of externally set timelines, goals, and rewards greatly enhances achievement. It is true that different children learn at different rates because of variations in their abilities, energy levels, and motivations. Some able students are lazy, and some less able ones diligent; some pick up subjects rapidly, others with painful slowness. Although teachers are indeed able to judge whether a child's slowness is owing to a lack of preparation in the subject, not even trained psychologists can say with authority how far nature or nurture has predominated in determining the pace of slow children. If an inherently able child is slow because of academic and social disadvantages, is it reasonable to say that his or her "natural" pace is slow? Should schools allow such children to fall further behind, or should compensatory efforts be exerted to bring them up to grade level? By the same token, should fast learners be left to their own devices, or should they be challenged with tasks that take them beyond their "natural" level? A good example of the grave problems raised by "natural" pacing is found in teaching the skill of reading. Some children never learn to decode naturally; others gradually work up the skill of reading on their own, simply after being read to. Yet reading specialists have concluded that nearly all children can be brought to grade level in reading, though greater effort must be put forth for children who are slower. Should this greater effort be denied them on the naturalistic principle? The doctrine of "natural" pace has achieved its most alarming expression in the practice of multiaged grouping, an experimental practice for which there is little empirical support, and much evidence for its unfairness. In the early grades, when no one is in a position to pronounce definitively on a child's "natural" pace, the most effective educational systems in the world try to bring all children up to grade level without holding back the fastest students. On the whole, they succeed.

**"Authentic assessment."** A laudatory term for "performance assessment," where students receive grades for their performances on realistic tasks such as writing a letter, producing a play, and solving a "real-world" mathematics problem. Such performances are also called "exhibitions." The progressive tradition has long advocated teaching and testing through "realistic" projects instead of through separate subject matters, and has long rejected tests that probe isolated knowledge and skills. Realistic performance assessments, it is claimed, have a number of advantages over multiple-choice tests, which include being more informative, more motivational, and fairer to minorities and nonverbal students. These claims are often plausible, particularly when performance tests are used as teaching and monitoring devices in the classroom context; for instance, in a course on writing, it is clearly preferable to use writing tasks as tests rather than to use multiple-choice tests. However, performance tests are only one of many monitoring devices in classroom teaching, and they have been shown to be ineradicably subjective and arbitrary in grading. They are not appropriate for large-scale, high-stakes testing because no one has been able, even in theory, to make such tests fair and accurate at reasonable cost in money and time. To serve democratic ends, American educators have pioneered the creation of fair and accurate multiple-choice tests that probe a wide variety of knowledge and skills. The consensus among psychometricians is that these objective tests, rather than performance tests, are the fairest and most accurate achievement tests available. Performance tests, while important as one tool for classroom use, should not play a decisive role in high-stakes testing, where fairness and accuracy are of paramount importance.

·  ·  ·

**"Banking theory of schooling."** A phrase rejecting the idea that adults transmit wisdom to students and stock students' minds with important knowledge that will be useful in the future. Such knowledge, opponents of the banking theory say, merely indoctrinates students into accepting the social status quo. They recommend that the banking theory be replaced with "critical-thinking skills" (which see), which will develop independent-mindedness and lead to social justice. This ideological attack on the transmission of knowledge in schooling has proved to be no more effective or practical than other expressions of the tool conception of education. While the attack on the banking theory has been favored by some theorists of the political Left, it is not currently accepted by all of them, since historically the alternative theory has failed to improve the condition of disadvantaged students. A positive version of the banking theory developed by other sociologists of the Left is called "intellectual capital" (which see). Under this theory, knowledge functions like money capital in that it enables the accumulation of still more capital—an idea consistent with findings in cognitive psychology. In short, the attack on the banking theory has failed on its own terms both empirically and ideologically. (See also "Transmission theory of schooling.")

**"Break-the-mold schools."** A phrase used by reformers of the 1980s and '90s to encourage school improvement. Some of the proposed break-the-mold changes have given greater governance power to individual schools and to parents. These changes have sometimes been beneficial. Other proposed changes, concerning the goals, contents, and methods of education, have turned out to be already-failed versions of progressive methods, which are now to be enhanced with "technology" (see "Promise of technology"). The rhetoric of breaking the mold implies that novel educational experiments should be tried on children on a large scale. Since there already exist highly effective schools scattered throughout the United States and elsewhere, it is unclear why these successful models should be rejected in favor of novel experiments.

**"Child-centered schooling."** Also formulated as "student-centered schooling," to include the later grades. The phrase is a self-description of progressive education, as in Rugg's *The Child-Centered School* (1928). The idea is epitomized in the injunction "Teach the child, not the subject" (which see). The opposition between child-centered and subject-centered education implies that teaching which focuses on subject matter tends to ignore the feelings, interests, and individuality of the child. Progressivists describe subject-centered instruction as consisting of lecture format, passive listening, mindless drill, and rote learning, and as directed to purely academic problems that have no intrinsic interest for children. The opposition between subject and child implies that focusing on subject matter is equivalent to inhumane and ineffective schooling. This picture is mere caricature. Observation has shown, on the contrary, that children are more interested by good subject-matter teaching than by an affectively oriented, child-centered classroom. The anti-subject-matter position is essentially anti-intellectual. The dichotomy between subject and child has too often resulted in failure to teach children the subjects and the skills they need. Such failure cannot under any principled use of language be described as "child-centered."

**"Competition."** A negative word in the progressive tradition. Progressive educational doctrine advises against graded tests because giving higher and lower grades destroys the spirit of cooperation and of egalitarianism, as well as causing students to work unproductively for grades rather than for the love of learning. It is undoubtedly true that too much emphasis on class rank and too much identification of intrinsic worth with academic grades are both distracting and inhumane. But the spirit of competition has not been eliminated in those progressive classrooms which have tried to abolish it, and what is even more important educationally, effort and learning have declined wherever grades and tests have been abolished. Human nature has proved to be robust. Evolutionary psychologists have argued that all humans retain a residue of competitiveness. Of course, these primal instincts should be moderated and civilized. But the use of grades and of well-devised tests during a course of study has been shown to improve learning. This suggests that instead of trying fruitlessly to abolish competition as an element of human nature, we should try to guide it into educationally productive channels.

**"Constructivism."** A psychological term used by educational specialists to sanction the practice of "self-paced learning" and "discovery learning." The term implies that only constructed knowledge—knowledge which one finds out for one's self—is truly integrated and understood. It is certainly true that such knowledge is very likely to be remembered and understood, but it is not the case, as constructivists imply, that *only* such self-discovered knowledge will be reliably understood and remembered. This incorrect claim plays on an ambiguity between the technical and nontechnical use of the term "construct" in the psychological literature. Many readers may not be interested in the technical details, but those who are may wish to know that the misleading ambiguity arose as follows. Learning is closely associated with memory, since unrecalled experience cannot be said to be learned. For a long time it has been known that most memories are not just mechanical recollections but constructs built on a whole body of relevant prior experiences. (The constructed character of memory accounts for the unreliability of eye witnesses.) Another example of the constructed character of knowledge is the understanding of language. The meaning of what we read or hear is not transferred directly from one person to another but is constructed by the listener, sometimes incorrectly. Since memory and linguistic meaning constitute a lot of school learning, these two examples alone make plausible the idea that school learning is constructed. The misleading extension of the word to pedagogical method arises from the ambiguity between the idea that memories and word meanings are constructed and the idea that the only way to learn things properly is to construct or discover them for one's self rather than being told them. But since being told things is also a constructive, nonpassive process, the quasi-scientific claim that constructivism favors discovery learning is completely unfounded. In fact, experience has shown that "discovery learning" (which see) is the least effective pedagogical method in the teacher's repertory. "Constructivism" is a good example of the way technical terms are sometimes used to give progressive ideas a spurious scientific-sounding authority. For example, some educationists distinguish between "endogenous" and "exogenous" constructivism. "Endogenous constructivism" is a mystifying term denoting learning that is self-induced by the student; "exogenous constructivism," by contrast, denotes learning that is induced from the outside, usually by the teacher. But note that behind the ponderous rhetoric lies the tacit admission that both discovery learning and guided learning are constructed. This means that, in the end, the term "constructivism" adds little or no illumination.

**"Cooperative learning."** A term describing the pedagogical method of breaking up a class into teams of five or so students who cooperate to complete a joint task or project. One of its advantages lies in its use of more advanced students to help and teach less advanced ones, thus promoting the education of both groups, so long as the two groups are not too far apart in academic preparation. The method still retains vestiges of its historical origins in progressivist practices, when group cooperation was elevated above competition and individual achievement. Recently, parents have complained that capable children who want to do more and better work are sometimes discouraged on the grounds of "not cooperating" with the group. The wise and effective orchestration of several groups in a classroom is difficult to do well, needing careful monitoring, clear purposes, and definite incentives. A faith that the method itself will providentially take care of results is not warranted. Cooperative learning, used with restraint, can be an excellent method of instruction when used in conjunction with whole-class instruction. It has not been effective when used as the principal or exclusive means of instruction.

**"Critical-thinking skills."** A phrase that implies an ability to analyze ideas and solve problems while taking a sufficiently independent, "critical" stance toward authority to think things out for one's self. It is an admirable educational goal for citizens of a democracy, and one that has been advocated in the United States since Jefferson. The ability to think critically is a goal that is likely to be accepted by all American educational theorists. But it is a goal that can easily be oversimplified and sloganized. In the progressive tradition that currently dominates our schools, "critical thinking" has come to imply a counterpoise to the teaching of "mere facts," in which, according to the dominant caricature, sheeplike students passively absorb facts from textbooks or lecture-style classrooms. Critical thinking, by contrast, is associated with active, discovery learning and with the autonomous, independent cast of mind that is desirable for the citizens of a democracy. Conceived in this progressive tradition, critical thinking belongs to the formalistic tool conception of education, which assumes that a critical habit of thought, coupled with an ability to read for the main idea and an ability to look things up, is the chief component of critical-thinking skills. This tool conception, however, is an incorrect model of real-world critical thinking. Independent-mindedness is always predicated on relevant knowledge: one cannot think critically unless one has a lot of relevant knowledge about the issue at hand. Critical thinking is not merely giving one's opinion. To oppose "critical thinking" and "mere facts" is a profound empirical mistake. Common sense and cognitive psychology alike support the Jeffersonian view that critical thinking always depends upon factual knowledge.

**"Culturally biased curriculum."** A term current since the 1980s, when the male, European orientation of the school curriculum came under attack. These attacks were successful, and there arose a consensus (with varying degrees of enthusiasm and reluctance in different quarters) that the American public school curriculum should include more about the contributions of women and excluded ethnic groups. At current writing (1995), this accommodative view has come to dominate. The growth of this curricular consensus is fortunate because the function of the common school is to enable all citizens to master, in addition to their home cultures, a shared, school-based culture that allows them to communicate and work together in the public sphere. The changing character of this school-based culture is a continual subject for democratic negotiation. It is true that because the distance between home and school cultures is great for some students, mastery of the school-based culture is more difficult for them than for other students. It is wise to take these cultural conditions into account in trying to gauge the real abilities and achievements of such students. (See also "Culturally biased tests," "Individual differences," and "Intellectual capital.")

**"Culturally biased tests."** A phrase expressing the claim that many standardized tests, such as the SAT, are culturally biased. The claim arises from the fact that different cultural groups perform differently on the tests. The argument for bias is based on the following two correct premises: the innate abilities of the different cultural groups (as with all large groups) are similar; the groups have experienced similar schooling. From these two premises can be derived the conclusion that, since the innate abilities and the schooling of the groups are similar, and since the test results are dissimilar, the tests must contain hidden bias. The argument is reasonable, but it does not exhaust the logical possibilities, or even the probabilities. For instance, different cultural groups might attain different levels of actual achievement from the same schools if their home cultures have not prepared them for mastery of the school-based culture and the subjects taught within it. The differences in group performance on tests raise two distinct questions:

1. Are the tests themselves technically biased? (If so, everyone agrees they must be changed.)
2. If the tests are not technically biased, what policy decisions should be taken in light of the different group performances on the tests?

As described by the American Psychological Association, technical bias is indicated by a consistent difference between the way a group performs on a test and the way it performs on some real-world criterion that the test is meant to measure. Most current standardized tests are free of technical bias in this sense—which leaves open the policy question regarding what to do about different group performances on these tests. Blaming unbiased tests for bias is not a plausible solution. (See also "Culturally biased curriculum," "Individual differences," and "Intellectual capital.")

**"Developmentally appropriate."** The phrase expresses the idea that education is a natural unfolding, and that for each individual child there is a natural and best time for learning certain subjects and skills. The term often accompanies a desire to preserve childhood innocence from adult civilization. Early-child-hood specialists use the term "developmentally inappropriate" to imply that "premature" exposure and early hard work are harmful and time-wasting. Thus, the term "developmentally appropriate" is generally used to discourage schools from teaching certain subjects too soon, but rarely, if ever, to suggest that subjects are not developmentally appropriate because they are being taught too late. Psychologists have found that there is usually a distinct rise in children's "processing capacity" between age three and age five. But they have also found that there is a great amount of individual variation in children's intellectual development. As generally used, the term "developmentally appropriate" is devoid of scientific meaning and lacks scientific authority. It is not scientifically credible, for instance, that learnings which millions of children throughout the world are easily acquiring in second grade should be labeled "developmentally inappropriate" for American second graders. Yet that is precisely what American early-childhood specialists have stated about the teaching of mathematical place value. The consensus among psychologists is that after age six or so, school-based learnings follow a sequence determined not principally by nature or by chronological age but mainly by prior knowledge, practice, and experience. Many advantaged children receive in their homes the early practice and knowledge they need, whereas many disadvantaged children gain these preparatory learnings, if at all, only in school. The learning processes involved in the unnatural skills of reading, writing, and arithmetic are inherently slow at first, then speed up cumulatively and exponentially. Because of the cumulative character of school learning, educationally delayed children rarely catch up. When an elementary school declines to teach demanding knowledge and skills at an early age, the school is unwittingly withholding education differentially from different social classes. As a result, the doctrine of developmental appropriateness, which holds back all students, has had especially deleterious effects on disadvantaged children and on social justice.

· · ·

**"Discovery learning."** The phrase refers to the teaching method which sets up projects or problems so that students can discover knowledge for themselves through hands-on experience and problem solving rather than through textbooks and lectures. Progressivists made discovery learning the chief or exclusive form of teaching starting with the "project method" (which see.) The premise is true that knowledge acquired on one's own, with difficulty and by expending lots of time and effort, is more likely to be retained than knowledge presented verbally. It is also true that knowledge gained in a realistic context as part of an effort to solve a problem is likely to be knowledge that is well understood and integrated. Unquestionably, then, discovery learning is an effective method—when it works. But there are two serious drawbacks to preponderant or exclusive reliance on discovery learning. First, students do not always make on their own the discoveries they are supposed to make; in fact, they sometimes make "discoveries" that aren't true. Hence, it is essential to monitor students to probe whether the desired learning goal has been achieved, and if not, to reach the goal by direct means. Second, discovery learning has proved to be very inefficient. Not only do students sometimes fail to gain the knowledge and know-how they are supposed to gain, but they do not gain it very fast. Research into teaching methods has consistently shown that discovery learning is the least effective method of instruction in the teacher's repertory.

**"Drill and kill."** A disparaging description of the pedagogical tool of drill and practice to teach children skills. Like the term "rote memorization," it is a good illustration of the pugnacious tone of some progressive rhetoric. The phrase implies that drill and practice kills the interest and joy children have in learning. At the same time, it implies that needed learnings will automatically be acquired in the ordinary course of schooling by using naturalistic pedagogy like "discovery learning," "thematic learning," and the "project method" (all of which see). The factual bases for these claims do not exist, and are invariably contradicted by the attitudes schools take toward pedagogy when it comes to athletics, a bizarre inconsistency in American schools. Authoritative scholars have felt it necessary to state that:

> *Development of basic knowledge and skills to the level of automatic and errorless performance will require a great deal of drill and practice. Thus drill and practice activities should not be slighted as "low level." They appear to be just as essential to complex and creative intellectual perfor-*

*mance as they are to the performance of a virtuoso violinist. (See page 219.)*

This view is strongly supported by cognitive psychologists and neurophysiologists, who have shown that many skills require repeated experience and "distributed practice" to be learned. It is true that such practice ought to be made as interesting, as varied, and as motivated as possible through the art of the teacher. But the assumption that repeated practice can be successfully avoided, or that it can be sufficiently ensured by being embedded in naturalistic themes or projects, has been discredited.

**"Exhibitions."** Another term for "performance-based assessments." At the end of a period of study, students are asked to exhibit their achievements by handing in a portfolio, displaying a project, demonstrating a proficiency, or some combination of these. Exhibitions are excellent, though subjective, devices for motivating students at the classroom level. In the classroom, strict fairness and accuracy in the grading of every student effort, while always to be sought, may sometimes be less important values than effective teaching and learning. So exhibitions should not be repudiated simply because the grading of them has proved to be arbitrary and inconsistent. Exhibitions cannot be used, however, for large-scale, high-stakes testing beyond the individual school or classroom without sacrificing economy, accuracy, and fairness.

**"Factory-model schools."** A disparaging term used by progressivists to describe the sort of school system created to accommodate ever greater numbers of students in the early twentieth century. The massive new school system is pictured as a bureaucratic hierarchy topped by a superintendent or factory foreman whose job is to make sure that all the schools in the production line are performing in lockstep. Within classrooms, too, the factory-model school is pictured as imposing uniformity on students. They are described as sitting in rows, passively listening while an authoritative teacher indoctrinates them in what the system wants them to know and how the system wants them to think. For many progressivists, the most important objection to factory-model schools is their association with "traditional" education, that is, with the lectures, the authoritative teacher-boss, the desks in straight rows, and the student passivity, as well as with rote memorization, "regurgitation" of facts, and lack of joy and independent thought. With such a picture as the only available alternative, it would be hard not to prefer the individualistic, joyful picture of the naturalistic classroom painted by progressivists. Both pictures are myths. The historical reality is more confusing. In the early twentieth century, school systems had to enlarge to accommodate a huge growth in the school-attending population. The progressive movement itself presided over the creation of enlarged school systems in the 1920s and '30s, even as it promoted progressive pedagogical reforms; for instance, the authors of the *Cardinal Principles* (1918), the blueprint for the new factory-model schools, were by and large adherents to progressive themes such as "individual differences." No modern industrial nation has been able to avoid some elements of the "factory model" in its efforts simply to educate ever larger percentages of the population. What is really at stake in the polemical use of the term is the association of the factory model with "traditional" pedagogy, as though the two were indissolubly wedded. On the contrary, within a factory-like, hierarchical school system, it is possible to have nontraditional, progressive-style classrooms. That is precisely the arrangement we have today in the United States. Progressive ideas dominate the system's hierarchy. What makes our current system ineffective is the educational ineffectiveness of those ideas. The best hope for improving our "factory" system, which in some form all modern nations are stuck with, is to provide more coherent and focused teaching, with a view to achieving more specific and coherent goals.

**"Facts are inferior to understanding."** The opposition expressed in this and similar phrases between facts and understanding is a hallmark of progressivism. It is true that facts in isolation are less valuable than facts whose interrelations have been understood. But those interrelations are also facts (if they happen to be true), and their existence also depends entirely upon a knowledge of the subordinate facts that are being interrelated. Since understanding depends on facts, it is simply contradictory to praise understanding and to disparage facts.

**"Facts are soon outdated."** Phrased in various ways, this is one of the most frequently stated antifact propositions of the American educational community. From being so often repeated, it has achieved axiomatic status. Its ultimate originator may not have been William Heard Kilpatrick, but in the 1920s he was certainly the doctrine's chief promulgator and popularizer. He taught and spellbound some thirty-five thousand potential professors of education during his brilliant teaching career at Teachers College, Columbia University. He made it a central theme of his book *Education for a Changing Civilization*

(1926). The facts-are-always-changing idea gains what modest plausibility it has from the observation that history and technology are indeed constantly changing. But this truism would seem to be a good argument for teaching the central facts (for instance, the elements of the periodic table) which do not change rapidly, if at all, and which are useful for understanding and coping with the changes that do occur. Facts that quickly lose their educative utility should indeed be cast out of the curriculum in favor of those having a longer shelf life. But a careful case has not yet been made for the transitoriness of significant factual knowledge. Facts are central to "higher-order skills," and therefore need to be strongly emphasized even (or especially) when the goal of education is seen to be the development of "understanding" and of "thinking skills."

**"Hands-on learning."** A phrase that implies the superiority of direct, tactile, lifelike learning to indirect, verbal, rote memorization. Multisensory learning is indeed an excellent method for integrating and fixing what a child learns, for instance, the use of tactile methods to help children learn the letters of the alphabet. (In one version of that method, children run their fingers over bumpy cutouts of the letters, and this hands-on experience, combined with visual perception and with hearing and pronouncing the names of the letters, helps connect the letter shapes to the names by multiple sensory means that reinforce each other.) Apprenticeship teaching, too, is an enormously effective, integrated, hands-on mode of learning a trade or profession. Caution must be expressed, however, regarding the polemical use of the term to support a single kind of teaching. Very often the term "hands-on" is an honorific term used to praise the progressivist "project method" of education and to disparage a "whole-class instruction," which is conducted mainly by visual and verbal means. Experience does not bear out the superiority claimed for the project method in its various manifestations, called variously "discovery learning," "holistic learning," and "thematic learning." The research suggests that such methods are uncertain, unfair (not all children learn from them), and inefficient, and therefore should be used sparingly. Caution is especially required when the phrase "hands-on" is used to imply disdainfully that visual and verbal learning is artificial and unengaging. Antiverbal prejudices spell disaster for disadvantaged students, who have not been exposed to a breadth of verbal learning outside the school. In contemporary life, the verbal has a strong claim to being just as "lifelike" as the tactile.

· · ·

**"Higher-order skills."** A phrase for the superior thinking skills that many current educational reforms aim to achieve. The goal is to produce students who can think and read critically, who can find information, who have mastered metacognitive strategies, and who know how to solve problems. Such students, it is asserted, will be far better prepared to face the challenges of the twenty-first century than those who merely possess a lot of traditional, soon-to-be-outdated, rote-learned information. Behind this contrast between higher-order thinking skills and lower-order information lies the formalistic tool conception of education, which has been repudiated by mainstream cognitive psychology. If in fact the learning of higher-order skills did suffice to produce critical thinkers prepared for the challenges of the twenty-first century, we and our students would be very fortunate indeed and could forgo a great deal of the hard work associated with gaining factual knowledge and well-practiced operational skills in reading, writing, and mathematics. Since, unfortunately, this tool conception is incorrect, the outlook for the effectiveness of such "reforms" is dim. Higher-order skills are invariably and necessarily conjoined with a great deal of relevant, domain-specific information. Hence, there is no way to gain the skills without gaining the associated information. It is mere prejudice to assert that the strategies associated with using domain-specific information are of a "higher order" than the knowledge itself. This fact has led some cognitive scientists to use the more neutral term "associated strategies" rather than "higher-order skills."

**"Holistic learning."** A term for classroom learning organized around integrated, lifelike problems and projects rather than around standard subject-matter disciplines. The holistic teaching of math, for example, integrates it with lifelike situations and with other subject matters. Among the hoped-for advantages of holistic teaching are 1) increased motivation for children on the grounds that they can see the relevance of learnings which are part of larger or more realistic contexts, and 2) a more natural mode of teaching such as might be gained by life experience itself. The holistic organization of teaching is often combined with the method of "discovery learning" (which see). "Holistic learning" has essentially the same meaning as "thematic learning" and "the project method." It is not limited to progressivist-style projects, however. Holistic, contextualized teaching has always been a part of standard subject-matter instruction, as when American history is integrated with American art in order to provide a more vivid sense of the past. The method is less successful when used to teach a specialized subject or skill like mathematics, which requires a lot of practice. The exclusive use of holistic or naturalistic methods has been shown to be less effective than using it sparingly within more focused, goal-directed pedagogies. As with most progressivist methods, it is not the technique itself but its injudicious overuse, in the confidence that naturalistic methods automatically lead to good results, which has made much holistic teaching ineffective.

**"Individual differences."** A phrase reflecting the admirable desire to combine mass schooling with respect for diversity and individuality. An important early use of the phrase was in a manifesto of education, the *Cardinal Principles* of 1918. The individual differences referred to there were mainly differences in academic preparation and ability, and the accommodation of those differences took the form of ability tracking. Currently, a more egalitarian use of the term implies that children differ in temperament, personality, and the kind of talents they have, and that they have different learning styles and different needs. Children are allowed to proceed "at their own pace," sometimes in multiaged classrooms, and are encouraged to develop their special talents. However, because mass education cannot be organized into individual tutorials, the practical result of the current egalitarian terminology has been de facto ability tracking. Too often, the term "individual differences" can become a rationalization for expecting and demanding less from children for whom we need to provide more support—inherently able students from disadvantaged homes.

**"Individualized instruction."** An ideal in education that recognizes individual differences in talent, interest, and preparation. It is universally acknowledged that the individual tutorial is the most effective form of teaching known. Tutorial instruction is not possible, however, in public schools, where the student-teacher ratio is typically 20 to 1. For that reason, an attempt in the public schools to provide individual instruction to some students often results in individual neglect for others, in the form of isolated, silent seatwork. In typical schools, the best results for most individual students are gained not by one-on-one tutorials but by a predominant use of whole-class instruction, in which all students participate. This interactive, whole-class pedagogy is then supplemented by small-group, cooperative learning, by moderate individual seatwork, and by individual coaching.

**"Individual learning styles."** A phrase referring to the well-accepted fact that different students learn in different ways. The phrase is sometimes used to support an emphasis on small class size and individual attention to students, and as a nonjudgmental term for different levels of academic ability. The results of research on learning styles are decidedly mixed. The claims for different styles among different ethnic groups are disputed in the literature. There seems to be solid support for the idea that some students learn better through visual and verbal means than through verbal means alone. Effective teachers have always taught through a diversity of approaches, both in order to avoid boring students through obvious repetition and in the hope that different approaches will stick with different students. Since the only economically feasible and fair system of schooling is one that engages all students in a class most of the time (i.e., a system that employs a generous amount of effective whole-class instruction), one policy implication of different learning styles is that teachers should vary their teaching by using visual aids, concrete examples, and tactile experiences as well as verbal concepts in presenting what is to be learned. The open appeal to different learning styles, like the appeal to "individual differences," has been used as a disparagement of verbal learning and a rationalization for not achieving better results from inherently able but disadvantaged students. (See also "Multiple learning styles," "Multiple intelligences.")

**"Intellectual capital."** A phrase denoting the knowledge and skills a person possesses at a given moment. Studies have shown that the level of a person's intellectual capital is highly correlated with a person's ability to earn still more money and to gain still more knowledge and skill. As with money capital, the more knowledge and skill one already has, the more one can readily acquire. The idea of intellectual capital opposes itself to the tool conception of education, under which a mere store of knowledge is deemed less important than the gaining of learning skills. In the present book, the work of sociologists and cognitive psychologists has been cited to show that the tool conception is much oversimplified, that skills always require domain-specific knowledge. Hence, intellectual capital, repudiated under the tool conception as inert, soon-to-be-outdated baggage, is in reality the main tool of future learning and earning.

**"Learning by doing."** A phrase once used to characterize the progressivist movement but little used today, possibly because the formulation has been the object of much criticism and even ridicule. It is instructive, however, to include the phrase here because it continues to illuminate the progressivist tradition. Terms currently preferred to "learning by doing" are "discovery learning," and "hands-on learning," but it is important to remember that these latter-day phrases are adaptations of the earlier formulation. The idea behind all of the terms is that the most desirable pedagogy is natural in the sense that it resembles the real-life activities for which the particular learning is preparing the student. It is claimed that the best form of learning is that which best allows the student to learn in the natural, apprentice-like way in which humans have always learned. It implicitly opposes itself to education that is primarily verbal, as well as to schooling that is artificially organized around drill and practice. By performing "holistic" activities, the student, it is claimed, will reliably discover the needed learnings. This is an attractive doctrine, but it is also a highly theoretical one that has proved to be false. The value of such a method depends on its actual effectiveness. If by "effective" one means that all students learn reliably and efficiently by this method, then the theory has been entirely discredited in comparative studies. Both the recent history of American education and controlled observations have shown that learning by doing and its adaptations are among the least effective pedagogies available to the teacher.

**"Learning to learn."** A phrase used to denote the principal aim of schooling under the tool conception of education. The idea is that the possession of a lot of knowledge which will soon be outmoded is educationally useless, whereas if one has the ability to learn, that will be a permanent acquisition. The theory is expressed in the proverb "It is better to teach a child to fish than to give a child a fish." Teaching a child how to learn is, using this analogy, better than teaching a child a lot of facts. Everyone agrees that education should provide students with an ability to learn new knowledge and even new professions. But the tool conception, which makes the fish inferior to the hook, line, and sinker, is based upon a gravely inadequate metaphor of the skill of learning. Indeed, even learning how to fish requires a great deal of domain-specific knowledge—not just fishing equipment and a few techniques. As this book explains in some detail, the opposition between learning skills and factual knowledge is an almost totally misleading opposition that has had tragic economic and social consequences.

**"Less is more."** This phrase is meant to imply that depth is preferable to breadth in schooling. In some circumstances, the idea is certainly true, but the catchiness of the paradoxical formulation should not be permitted to mask the doubtfulness of the idea as a general proposition that can reliably guide teaching or curriculum making at different levels of schooling. The motto is generally valid in one limited respect: selectivity of knowledge is important at all levels. But the balance between breadth and depth in schooling is a perennially thorny issue that is not to be disposed of by a simple slogan, especially one that has all too often encouraged both teachers and students to slack off. If less is more, than skipping a subject altogether might begin to seem a virtue—an attitude not altogether foreign either to the progressive tradition or to many teachers who have been influenced by it. In general, contrary to the motto, breadth is preferable to depth in early schooling, where the child should be provided with a conspectus of the various domains of knowledge and experience so that new learnings can be readily integrated into his or her web of understanding and belief. In the later grades of high school and at the university, when a student has already secured a broad enough background to enable future learning in many fields, he or she should be encouraged to focus more narrowly and probe more deeply. In most cases, the balance between depth and breadth is a subject of a complex judgment that takes into account subject matter, the purpose, and the stage of schooling.

**"Lifelong learning."** The phrase reflects a goal shared by almost all educators since antiquity. Today, when new technologies must be mastered and even new professions learned, the task of making everyone competent to learn throughout life is a primary duty of the schools. There exists, however, a disagreement about the nature of the schooling that best promotes a lifelong ability to learn. Under the tool conception of learning, students must be given not only reading, writing, and computational ability but also further abstract competencies such as "accessing skills," "critical-thinking skills," and "higher-order skills," in the belief that these abstract competencies can then be directed to an indefinite number of future tasks. Of course, everyone *should* be provided with the tools to learn and to think critically. But the dominant progressive tradition has made a fundamental empirical mistake in believing that these general competencies do not depend upon the accumulation of knowledge and vocabulary, and in believing that transferable lifelong competencies will arise naturally from "holistic," integrated activities. Lifelong competencies, including reading, writing, and critical thinking, depend upon the domain-specific factual and verbal knowledge spurned by many present-day "reformers."

· · ·

**"Mere facts."** The phrase "rote memorization of mere facts" may be the most vigorous denunciation of "traditional" education to be found in the progressive armory. The phrase describes an activity that compounds deadly pedagogy (i.e., rote memorization) with deadly content (i.e., mere facts). In Romantic progressivism, facts are dead, but hands-on, lived experience is alive; facts are inert and disconnected, but understanding is vital and integrated. The nineteenth-century romantic William Wordsworth once said that we "dwindle as we pore" over facts "in disconnection, dead and spiritless," and he urged us to see facts imaginatively. For his American successors, mere facts are *always* disconnected, dead, and spiritless. Their "mereness" implies their inherent disconnection and artificiality. As soon as real "understanding" occurs, however, mere facts are transcended. There is some validity in this conception, as there usually is in most views that are long and widely held. Understanding does mean connecting facts; isolated facts *are* meaningless. Where the progressive-Romantic indictment of facts falls short is in the exaggerated idea that facts which are not directly and immediately connected with one's life are inherently fragmented and dead. That blanket accusation amounts to an antiverbal, anti-intellectual distortion. Facts are absolutely necessary to understanding. Whether they are dead and fragmented depends upon teachers and students, not upon the facts themselves, which are not only required for understanding but are sometimes immensely vital and interesting in their own right.

**"Metacognitive skills."** A term that, like "constructivism," has a legitimate technical but an illegitimate nontechnical meaning. The illegitimate, broader application of the term identifies it with "accessing skills," "critical-thinking skills," "problem-solving skills," and other expressions of the antiknowledge tool conception of education. The narrower, technical meaning has useful application. Technically, in the scientific literature, "metacognition" means a self-conscious awareness of one's own procedures in performing skilled activities. ("Meta" means "after" or "beyond" in Greek.) For instance, in solving math problems, a skilled mathematician might think, "First I'll estimate the range within which the right answer is going to fall so that I can be more confident I am going at this right and didn't make a clerical error." Or a good reader could silently think, "I wonder what this text is mainly trying to convey. Knowing that will help me fit in the individual parts I am reading." Such self-conscious monitoring of one's own activities is characteristic of expert performance. Children who have learned how to set and meet such study goals for themselves (e.g., how to scan a text for the main meaning, how to decide on what is more or less important in a subject with respect to their own study aims) are students who are better able to work independently. Such study skills should clearly be encouraged where this can be done effectively without displacing or distracting from solid subject-matter knowledge. The teaching of such self-conscious monitoring can speed up the learning of reading and problem-solving skills. But since expert skills are also dependent on domain-specific knowledge, the teaching of metacognition in this narrow sense is recognized as a useful but not sufficient help in learning a skill.

**"Multiaged classrooms."** A phrase referring to the grouping of children by proficiency rather than by age, with the result that children of different ages find themselves grouped together. The recent popularity of this idea may owe more to political and ideological pressures than to the demonstrated effectiveness of the practice. One such pressure is the great diversity of academic preparation of children of the same age in American schools. This preparation gap would be reduced by a more coherent and specific curriculum and by more accountability for definite grade-by-grade standards. Another cause is the egalitarian reaction against ability tracking, which means that tracking, if it is to exist, has to march under the banner of "learning at one's own pace." The most troublesome feature of the multiaged classroom is the disproportionate number of older students in each learning group who come from disadvantaged homes and who belong disproportionately to ethnic minorities. The result of officially sanctioning their slow progress is a perpetuation of social unfairness, as detailed in the entry under "At their own pace."

**"Multiple intelligences."** A phrase popularized by the psychologist and author Howard Gardner. It is meant to replace the concept of IQ (a single general intelligence) with a theory of seven domains of ability under which almost every child can be good at something. The seven domains are linguistic, logical-mathematical, spatial, musical, bodily-kinesthetic, interpersonal, intrapersonal. Neither Gardner's specific taxonomy nor his general interpretation is widely accepted by the psychological community. Nonetheless, specialists and laypersons alike concede Gardner's general point that people are better (more "intelligent") at some activities than at others. Despite the fact that schools are not competent to classify and rank children on these highly speculative psychological measures, the concept has become highly popular, probably because it fits in with the already popular notions of "individual differences," "individual learning styles," "self-paced learning," and so on, not to mention its appeal to our benign hope for all children that they will be good at doing something and happy doing it. The distinguished psychologist George A. Miller has said that Gardner's specific classifications are "almost certainly wrong." Miller gets to the educational heart of the matter when he observes that even if the classifications were right, no descriptive theory of multiple intelligences could tell us what policies and methods schools ought to pursue. Should they accentuate students' strengths, overcome their weaknesses, or both? The common-school tradition of Horace Mann (with which Gardner would probably agree) implies that we should both encourage students' strengths and overcome their weaknesses, especially in those competencies such as literacy, numeracy, and general knowledge which enable their effective participation in the economic and political life of the nation. Once those common goals are agreed upon, psychological classifications would seem to have little function beyond the encouragement of respect and egalitarianism—admirable virtues that do not require the support of psychological speculation.

**"Multiple learning styles."** See "Individual differences," "Individual learning styles," and "Multiple intelligences."

**"One size fits all."** A phrase that disparages the idea of common learning goals for all children regardless of their interests and abilities. The phrase implicitly advocates the individualizing of education as much as possible—a highly defensible view, since individualized tutorial instruction is, by general agreement, the most effective form of schooling. Simply on grounds of educational utility, then, apart from other grounds such as the value of diversity, a sensitivity to each child's individuality is greatly to be desired. But like many such battle slogans in the war of progressivists against traditionalists, subtleties and complexities are obliterated in the heat of battle. The slogan makes no concession to the practical need for commonality in the elementary grades, which is required simply to ensure that each child in a classroom is ready to take the next step in learning. In high school, on the other hand, once the fundamentals of math, reading, writing, art, and science have been learned, it makes a great deal of sense for the good of the child, as well as of society, to stress a child's individual interests and abilities.

**"Open classroom."** A phrase for an ungraded classroom in which children of different ages can learn "at their own pace," and receive individual attention rather than follow in step with the class as a whole. In its pure form, "open" was also an architectural description—no walls between classes. Like all forms of naturalistic pedagogy, the open classroom has proved to be ineffective as a principal technique of schooling. (See also "Multiaged classroom.")

**"Outcomes-based education."** A term of uncertain meaning which during the 1990s became a symbolic cause of verbal war between political liberals and conservatives. It is best understood historically. In the late 1980s and early '90s, in the midst of public discontent with students' test scores in reading and math, some professional educators proposed that schools pay relatively less attention to methods of schooling, such as discovery learning, and more attention to results. They labeled this idea "outcomes-based education." Their goal was to correlate teaching methods more closely with results. The label stuck, but the idea behind it subtly changed in the early 1990s, when committees of teachers and administrators gathered to define what outcomes were to be achieved. Because of the general antipathy in the educational community to an emphasis on facts, subject matter, and content, the outcomes drafted by these committees tended not to emphasize knowledge so much as various tool metaphors for education and virtue in the form of democratic attitudes and emotions. These included respect for all people, including people of diverse races, religions, and sexual orientations. It was this last idea, and similar socially liberal notions, which raised red flags with conservatives. Thus the battle began, with the term "outcomes-based education" being viewed as a left-leaning conspiracy. It could also be viewed as the transformation of a reasonable idea into impractical vagueness through progressivist antipathy to subject-matter knowledge.

**"Passive listening."** A progressivist phrase caricaturing "traditional" education, which makes children sit silently in rows in "factory-model schools," passively listening to what the teacher has to say, then merely memorizing facts through "rote learning," and finally "regurgitating" the facts verbatim. If this picture really did characterize whole-class instruction, progressivists would be right to reject it. But observations of "whole-class instruction" (which see) in the United States and elsewhere provide a very different, far-from-passive picture of what children are actually doing and learning in whole-class instruction. The caricature is another example of the way a valid point gets carried too far through simplistic slogans, causing teachers to become polarized and to reject sensible practices. The implication is that whole-class instruction makes the teacher boss instead of friendly coach, leads children to become docile and unable to think for themselves. Progressivists claim that this docility is just what traditionalists want to achieve, whereas progressive methods will produce independent-minded, active students who think for themselves. To the extent that more "active" methods like "discovery learning" provide children with less factual knowledge on which to base independent judgments, the claim to produce independent-mindedness seems doubtful.

**"Performance-based assessment."** The original term used by specialists in the psychometric literature for what is called variously "authentic assessment," "exhibitions," and "portfolio assessment." It is a form of assessment in which a student is graded for a unified production similar to one that he or she would be called upon to produce in the real world outside the classroom. For instance, a pianist would be asked to perform a piece, a writer would be asked to produce a whole essay, a math student would be asked to solve a realistic math problem. An advantage of performance-based assessment is that it requires the student to integrate the various sublearnings which make up a skill. This encourages both teachers and their students to stress such integration in the course of teaching and learning. Another advantage is said to be heightened student motivation, since such realistic modes of assessment directly exemplify the practical uses to which learnings are to be put. Criticisms of performance-based assessment by psychometricians include the observation that "performances" in a school context do not in fact authentically duplicate real-world performance, and do not reliably predict it. The most important criticism is that when used for high-stakes testing, performance tests are much less fair and reliable than well-constructed objective tests. The best uses of performance tests are as lower-stakes "formative" tests, which help serve the goals of teaching and learning within the context of a single course of study. (See also "Authentic assessment," "Competition," "Exhibitions," and "Portfolio assessment.")

**"Portfolio assessment."** A phrase for a version of performance-based assessment. In portfolio assessment, students preserve in a portfolio all or some of their productions during the course of the semester or year. At the end of the time period, students are graded for the totality of their production. It is a device that has long been used for the teaching of writing and painting. But there its utility ceases. It has proved to be virtually useless for large-scale, high-stakes testing. (See also "Authentic assessment," "Competition," "Exhibitions," and "Performance-based assessment.")

**"Problem-solving skills."** A phrase often used in conjunction with "higher-order skills" and "critical-thinking skills." In a narrow sense, it refers to the ability to solve problems in mathematics or other specialized fields. More broadly, it refers to a general resourcefulness and skill that will enable the student to solve various future problems. The nature of this general problem-solving skill has not been scientifically defined, and it is doubtful that it exists. Work on the problem-solving abilities of specialists like doctors, chess players, and physicists has shown consistently that the ability to solve problems is critically dependent on deep, well-practiced knowledge within the special domain, and that these problem-solving abilities do not readily transfer from one domain to another. In short, there seems to exist no abstract, generalized, teachable ability to solve problems in a diversity of domains. For schools to spend time teaching a general skill that does not exist is clearly a waste of resources, which illustrates the inherent shortcomings of the tool conception of education.

**"Project method."** A phrase used to describe the naturalistic form of teaching devised by W. H. Kilpatrick at the beginning of the progressive education movement. His article called "The Project Method" (1918) was the most widely distributed article on American education that had appeared up to that time. Under the project method, subject-matter classrooms were to be abandoned in favor of "holistic," lifelike projects that would enable students to gain the life skills they needed by working in cooperation with their fellow students. The method presented itself in opposition to traditional subject-matter education. It abolished the lecture-and-recitation format, tests, grades, and drills. The method was based on a Romantic faith in the superiority of a natural to an artificial approach in learning. It claimed, incorrectly, to be based also on the latest findings in psychology. Subsequently, observers found the project method to be the least effective mode of pedagogy in use in American schools. The method came under increasing criticism, and the term "project method" fell out of favor. But terminology shifted, and the practice itself remained in different forms and under different names, such as "discovery learning," "hands-on learning," "holistic learning," "learning by doing," and "thematic learning."

• • •

**"Promise of technology."** The phrase suggests that computers will revolutionize and transform schooling. Caution is called for. Some explanation is needed for the fact that student scores have not significantly risen in schools that have been well supplied with computers. Many reasons for this disappointment have been offered: teachers have not learned how to use these instruments; good software is slow in coming; the school has not become fully computerized. Undoubtedly, computers will be able to enhance pedagogical principles that are already known to work. One fears, however, that the enthusiasm for computers is based upon a confidence in technical solutions that has not been well explained in theory or well documented in experience. Most of all, one fears that enthusiasm for computers will simply reinforce and prolong the now discredited tool conception of education, which claims falsely that education consists ideally in learning the tools that will enable one to learn things in the future—and what better tool for this purpose could there be than the computer? But there is no evidence that its advent has reduced the need for students to have in their minds well-practiced habits and readily available knowledge. Quite the contrary, the more one looks things up via computer, the more often one needs to understand what one is looking up. There is no evidence that a well-stocked and well-equipped mind can be displaced by "accessing skills."

**"Research has shown."** A phrase used to preface and shore up educational claims. Often it is used selectively, even when the preponderant or most reliable research shows no such thing, as in the statement "Research has shown that children learn best with hands-on methods." Educational research varies enormously in quality and reliability. Some research is insecure because its sample sizes tend to be small and a large number of significant variables (social, historical, cultural, and personal) cannot be controlled. If an article describes a "successful" strategy, such as building a pioneer village out of Popsicle sticks instead of reading about pioneers, the success may not be fully documented, and the idea that the method will work for all students and classrooms is simply assumed. There are strong ethical limits on the degree to which research variables can or should be controlled when the subjects of research are children. Many findings of educational research are highly contradictory. Greatest confidence can be placed in refereed journals in mainstream disciplines. (A refereed journal is one whose articles have been checked by respected scientists, or referees, in a particular specialty.) Next in reliability is research that appears in the most prestigious refereed educational journals. Very little confidence can be placed in research published in less prestigious journals and in nonrefereed publications. The most reliable *type* of research in education (as in medicine) tends to be "epidemiological research," that is, studies of definitely observable effects exhibited by large populations of subjects over considerable periods of time. The sample size and the duration of such large-scale studies help to cancel out the misleading influences of uncontrolled variables. An additional degree of confidence can be placed in educational research if it is consistent with well-accepted findings in neighboring fields like psychology and sociology. Educational research that conflicts with such mainstream findings is to be greeted with special skepticism. The moral: Print brings no reliable authority to an educational claim. When in doubt, ask for specific references and check them. Many claims evaporate under such scrutiny.

**"Rote learning."** The phrase "rote learning" is often followed by the phrase "of mere facts." The practice of rote learning dates back to the now-little-used method of asking a whole class to recite in unison set answers to set questions—whether or not the students know what their recitations mean. That practice has all but disappeared. When present-day educators have been asked what they now mean by the phrase "rote learning," they respond variously that it means "spouting words" without understanding their meaning, or memorizing items without understanding them, or learning a lot of isolated facts. They object that rote memorization breeds a passive and uncritical attitude in students, who, as we all hope, will grow up to be independent-minded citizens. All of these objections to rote learning have validity. It is better to encourage the integrated understanding of knowledge over the merely verbal repetition of separate facts. It is better for students to think for themselves than merely to repeat what they have been told. For all of these reasons, rote learning is inferior to learning that is internalized and can be expressed in the student's own words. These valid objections to purely verbal, fragmented, and passive education have, however, been used as a blunt instrument to attack all emphasis on factual knowledge and vocabulary. Some purely rote learning is, for example, indispensable to learning the words of one's own language, since there is rarely a nonarbitrary reason why particular names are attached to particular things in the world. Nor is there any very meaningful reason why English spelling should use "i" before "e" except after "c" or when sounded as "a" as in "neighbor" or "weigh." Or why "thirty days hath September." Yet it is highly useful to rote-learn those and many other helpful facts. The way things have been learned, whether by rote or other means, very often drops entirely out of memory. Psychologists distinguish "episodic" memory, which may be short-lived, and "semantic" memory, which is very durable. The episode of learning is insecurely stored in volatile episodic memory; hence, it often doesn't matter exactly how things are learned, so long as they *are* learned. In the progressive tradition, the attack on rote learning (timely in 1918) has been used to attack factual knowledge and memorization, to the great disadvantage of our children's academic competencies.

**"Self-esteem."** A term denoting a widely accepted psychological aim of education. There is consensus in the psychological literature that a positive sense of one's self is of great value to achievement, happiness, and civility to others, whereas a negative sense of one's self leads to low achievement, discontent, and social bitterness. The critical question for school policy and teaching is how far on average self-esteem can be induced by positive reinforcement on the teacher's part. There is agreement that some degree of positive reinforcement is necessary, and that teachers should be kindly and encouraging to all students. But there is growing agreement among psychologists that verbal and affective reinforcement is not sufficient, and can in fact be counterproductive if the child is not persuaded. There is strong evidence in the mainstream literature that praise in the absence of achievement does not raise achievement. The best enhancements of self-esteem, according to both psychological and process-outcome literature, arise from accurate and matter-of-fact appraisals of a student's work, as well as realistic encouragement toward effort and actual achievement.

**"Student-centered education."** Another phrase for "child-centered education" (which see), but with the word "student" substituted for "child" to bring the principle into the middle school and high school years. It expresses the idea that it is more humane to focus on the well-being of the child than on "mere" academic learning. But schools are not organized, and their staffs are not trained, to reliably secure the spiritual and psychological well-being of students, though good teachers often inspire by example. Schools are organized and instituted primarily to teach subject matters and skills, and it is their first duty to do so as effectively as possible.

·  ·  ·

**"Teaching for understanding."** A phrase that contrasts itself with teaching for "mere facts." It is associated with the motto "Less is more," which implies that depth is preferable to breadth in education, on the claim that depth leads to understanding, whereas breadth leads to superficiality and fragmentation. Few would dissent from the aim of teaching for understanding. Clearly the term needs different interpretations in the different grades. Take the alphabet. A kindergartner should understand the principle that the letters of the alphabet represent sounds. At a later stage, students should understand some peculiarities of English spelling and the differences between vowels and consonants. Still later, students might come to understand the historical uniqueness of the alphabetic system of writing, as contrasted with the various other modes of representing language in visual form such as hieroglyphics and ideograms. From this simple example, it is obvious that the phrase "understanding the alphabet" has very different content in different circumstances, and that the "deeper" understanding becomes, the more "mere facts" are required. A middle-school child does not need to understand what cuneiform is, or the difference between alphabetic and syllabic modes of phonological writing. As understanding of the alphabet advances, the university student may need to learn this additional information. Few would disagree with a general preference for integration over fragmentation of information, but it is hard to get much useful guidance or meaning from the phrase "teaching for understanding."

**"Teach the child, not the subject."** A phrase connoting the principle behind "child-centered schooling" (which see). The benign and reasonable interpretation of this famous battle cry of progressivism is that one should attend to the moral, emotional, and spiritual well-being of the child at the same time that one is providing an excellent grounding in reading, writing, and arithmetic. Only a hard-hearted person would dissent from this goal. Historically, however, the progressive tradition has continued to attack the disciplined teaching of reading, writing, and arithmetic in favor of "holistic" methods, which supposedly engage and educate the whole child. Progressivists have also continued to disparage merely academic learning. Not surprisingly, disparagement of "the subject" has resulted in a diminishment of student competency in subject matters.

**"Teach the whole child."** The third of the original three child-centered phrases of progressivism: "child-centered schooling," "teach the child, not the subject," and "teach the whole child." All three phrases enjoin the schools to take a more humane, less subject-matter-oriented position toward schooling. It is true that the responsibility of the school extends beyond purely academic skills. Not many would dissent from the hope that in addition to providing training in academic skills, schools will nurture the physical and emotional well-being of children, as well as enhance their civic and personal virtue. Progressivists did not, however, explicitly teach these different spheres of education, but claimed that the development of the whole child would automatically arise from holistic instruction, in which children had to work cooperatively in simulations of real life. In this Romantic faith they were wrong. It was understandable that in the teens and twenties of this century, Americans might still entertain such naturalistic, providential hopes. If we wish to inculcate civic and personal virtue, that too needs to be the object of guided instruction, however indirect and subtle, and monitored for uptake. The theory of automatic, holistic learning has proved to be incorrect.

**"Textbook learning."** A phrase disparaging traditional forms of education, symbolized by textbooks, in favor of more "holistic" and lifelike modes of instruction in which knowledge is gained from hands-on experience rather than from verbal statements in textbooks. Often, the objection to teaching by means of textbooks has all too much validity, because many currently available textbooks are unselective and unemphatic, having been designed to pass through textbook-adoption committees in populous states and, therefore, to please everyone. As a consequence, many textbooks tend to be unfocused, ill-written, bland, difficult to learn from, and lacking in discrimination between the more and the less important aspects of a subject matter. But the alternative to textbook instruction, in the form of hands-on, project-style teaching, has been shown to be highly ineffective. One must be careful, therefore, to distinguish between a justified attack on bad textbooks and an attack on the carefully focused teaching of subject matter through good textbooks. The most effective subject-matter learning is often achieved through the use of well-written, well-thought-out textbooks. In the sciences and in professions such as medicine and engineering, well-crafted textbooks have always been a necessity.

**"Thematic learning."** A phrase used to describe the "holistic" teaching of different subject matters across a common theme. For instance, the theme of "The Seasons" might combine a study of history, art, science, and mathematics in a particular classroom, or grade, or throughout an entire school. There is much to be said for integrated learning that contextualizes subjects and reinforces them. As with various forms of the "project method," however, thematic learning has proved to be more successful when used with prudence as an occasional device than when used consistently as the primary mode of instruction. One reason for entering this caution is that some subjects require different amounts of exposure than others in order to be learned. History and literature, for example, generally require fewer reinforcements to achieve a learning goal than do certain aspects of math and science, whose procedures must be often repeated and practiced. The thematic approach may or may not provide these needed reinforcements. As with most pedagogical methods, the key is common sense. If students have been well monitored and are known to have mastered the basic subject matters that are to be dealt with in the thematic project, then the method is an attractive way of encouraging student enthusiasm and further learning.

**"Transmission theory of schooling."** A derogatory phrase used by progressivists to imply that traditional schooling merely transmits an established social order by perpetuating its culture, knowledge, and values. It is contrasted with the more "modern" tool conception of schooling, which aims to produce students capable of thinking independently and of criticizing and improving the established social order. In progressivist writings of the 1920s and '30s, the transmission theory of education was identified with a decadent and static Europe, while the open-ended tool conception was identified with a vibrant, forward-moving United States. John Dewey, despite having been claimed by progressivists as their intellectual leader, stated explicitly in *Democracy and Education* that the transmission theory of education is both sound in itself and an absolutely necessary principle of civilization: "Society not only continues to exist *by* transmission, by communication, but it may fairly be said to exist *in* transmission." Dewey was certainly correct in taking this view, which coincides with common sense and with the view of the general public.

**"Whole-class instruction."** A neutral description that has negative connotations in the progressive tradition, since it is understood to imply "lockstep," "factory-model" education. It is caricatured by an authoritarian teacher droning on at the head of the class, or by passive, bored students, barely conscious and slumping in their seats, or by intimidated, fearful students, sitting upright and willing only to parrot back the teacher's words. These are not accurate descriptions of what effective whole-class instruction is. It is predominantly interactive, with much interchange between students and teacher; it makes frequent use of student performances and student comments on the performances; it involves consistent informal monitoring of the students' understanding; it engages all students by dramatizing learning in various ways. An overwhelming concurrence of reports from process-outcome studies shows that a predominant use of whole-class instruction constitutes the fairest and most effective organization of schooling. The attempt to sidestep whole-class instruction, and to provide individual tutorial attention in classrooms of twenty to thirty students, results in individual neglect. It has also been shown that an interactive mode of dealing with the whole class is the liveliest and most effective approach to teaching, and that it is useful to vary the mix with some amount of individual coaching, cooperative learning, and seatwork. All these other approaches should be used within a well-organized whole-class context in order to achieve the best and fairest results.

**"Whole-language instruction."** A phrase denoting an approach to the teaching of reading that emphasizes the joy of good literature and avoids drill-like instruction in letter sounds. In theory, the method is supposed to motivate children by emphasizing an interest and pleasure in books, and by encouraging students to learn reading holistically, just as they learned their mother tongue—as a "psycholinguistic guessing game." Some children do learn to read under this method, but many do not. "Whole language," like "outcomes-based education," has grown and spread far beyond its initial confined meaning to become a philosophy of life and teaching, muddled by pseudopolitical associations. The term has become so vague, and so colored with non-pedagogical overtones that it could profitably be dropped entirely from use. After large-scale experience with its unsatisfactory results, especially in California, some former adherents of whole language now advocate a "mixed" approach in which some letter-sound correspondences are taught explicitly. No well-regarded scholar in the field of reading now advocates an approach that neglects phonics and phonemic awareness. Many experts believe that with proper instruction nearly every child can read at grade level by the end of first or second grade.

# Notes

## Chapter 1.
## Introduction: Failed Theories, Famished Minds

1. Three recent and authoritative studies are International Association for the Evaluation of Educational Achievement, *Science Achievement in Seventeen Countries*; Lapointe, Mead, and Askew, *Learning Mathematics*; and Lapointe, Mead, and Askew, *Learning Science*.

2. "American children spent the least amount of time actually engaged in academic activities in academic classes. . . . Data such as these led one of our Japanese colleagues to praise American children's academic achievement. Don't American children do remarkably well, he proposed, when one considers how little of their time they spend in academic activities, how little instruction they receive from their teachers, and how few opportunities they have for out-of-classroom practice?" Quoted in Stevenson and Stigler, *The Learning Gap*, 147–48.

3. Keynes, *The General Theory of Employment, Interest, and Money*, final words of the book.

4. Bruner Foundation, *Evaluation of the New York State Education Department's Community Schools Program*. Lazar and Darlington, "Lasting Effects of Early Education." U.S. Department of Health and Human Services, *The Impact of Head Start on Children, Families and Communities*. Boulot and Boyzon-Fradet, *Les Immigrés et l'école*, 54–58. Centre for Educational Research and Innovation, *Immigrants' Children at School*, 178–259. A summary of the findings of several longitudinal studies covering several thousand students is included in Jarousee, Mingat, and Richard, "La Scolarisation maternelle à deux ans," 3–9, 55.

5. A concise account of the way the metastasis occurred can be found in Ravitch, *The Troubled Crusade*, particularly on pages 52–55. It describes the "curriculum revision

movement" that raged through the public schools like wildfire from the mid 1920s to the late '30s. It was this movement, with its hair-raising derogation of subject-matter knowledge and its anti-intellectualism, that set the schools on their present path. That it took another thirty years before the curriculum "revision" and its attendant attitudes destroyed the U.S. public educational system can be explained by the fact that it took about thirty years to retire all the teachers and administrators who persisted in "traditional" goals and modes of education.

6. J. P. Smith and Welch, "Black Economic Progress After Myrdal," 519–64.

7. Williams, "Black Economic Progress," 531–33. Card and Krueger, "School Quality and Black-White Relative Earnings," 151–200. Bound and Freeman, "What Went wrong?" 201–32. James Coleman and his colleagues reported in 1966 that poor schools had a more negative effect on disadvantaged students than on advantaged ones. See Coleman, *Equality of Educational Opportunity*. A discussion of the reasons for differential learning in the same classroom will be found on pages 23–26 in Chapter 2.

8. Ferguson, "Shifting Challenges," 37–76. The "other factors" are oral communication skills not tested by the Armed Forces Qualification Test, which was the instrument used by Ferguson to correlate wages with actual educational achievement. The schools have recently been quite reluctant to teach standard oral grammar or orthoepy, on the mistaken assumption that standard oral speech is "white" speech rather than simply standard educated speech. The additional shortcoming in economic skills—as perceived by employers—could account for most of the remaining 5 percent disparity. I explain in Chapter 2, pages 33 and 36, why inferior schools widen the learning gap between groups.

9. For comments on Gentile's views and for basic insights into Gramsci's ideas about education, I am grateful to Entwistle, *Antonio Gramsci*. Additional commentary may be found in Broccoli, *Antonio Gramsci e l'educazione come egemonia*; Scuderi, *Antonio Gramsci e il problema pedagogico*; and De Robbio, *Antonio Gramsci e la pedagogia dell'impegno*. For modern data showing that Gramsci is right in holding that traditional schooling greatly improves the academic competencies of low achievers, see K. R. Johnson, and Layng, "Breaking the Structuralist Barrier," 1475–90.

10. Gramsci, "Education."

11. Tennenbaum, *William Heard Kilpatrick*, 110–12.

12. No one could say that Maria Montessori was opposed to hands-on education, yet she has been rejected as a "traditionalist" by the Thoughtworld. Her work, according to Theresa and Frank Caplan, has been "shunned by American educators, . . . [who] complained that the Montessori program and materials were too closely structured to academics; that the classroom environment was 'too prepared' and lacking in flexibility; that the method was firmly anchored in reality and left little or no room for spontaneity, fantasy, and play." T. Caplan and F. Caplan, *The Early Childhood Years*, 142.

13. International Association for the Evaluation of Educational Achievement, *Science*

*Achievement in Seventeen Countries.* Another good source for indicating the success of whole-class instruction combined with a knowledge-based curriculum to provide adequate individualized education to every child, despite individual differences, can be found in data for Belgium, France, Germany, Luxembourg, the Netherlands, Sweden, and Switzerland in the publication by the Centre for Educational Research and Innovation, *Immigrants' Children at School.*

14. Direct observation of American classrooms produced the following data provided in Stevenson and Stigler, *The Learning Gap*: A "critical factor in the erosion of instruction was the amount of time American teachers were involved with individuals or small groups. American children spent 10 percent of their time in small groups and 47 percent of their time working individually. Much of the 87 percent of their time American teachers were working with their students was spent with these individual students or small groups rather than with the class as a whole. When teachers provide individual instruction, they must leave the rest of the class unattended, so instructional time for all remaining children is reduced."

15. See Kosmoski, Gay, and Vockell, "Cultural Literacy and Academic Achievement," 265–72; Pentony, "Cultural Literacy: A Concurrent Validation," 967–72; and Pentony, "Cultural Literacy: An Empirical Investigation." Willinsky, "The Vocabulary of Cultural Literacy in a Newspaper of Substance": "A random sample of 424 terms (9% of the total list) was selected. Each term or expression which was searched produced a figure representing the frequency of occurence in the 'Times' over a period of 101 months. . . . Results indicated that any given day's issue of the 'Times' contained approximately 2,700 occurrences of terms from the list. . . . Results suggest that Hirsch has identified a corpus of cultural terms which play a part in the daily commerce of the published language." For relevance to cognitive ability, see Stanovich, West, and Harrison, "Knowledge Growth and Maintenance Across the Life Span," 811–26. The fullest confirmation of the correlation between cultural literacy and median income has been published by Thomas Sticht and his associates in a 1995 monograph: Sticht, C. H. Hofstetter, and C. R. Hofstetter, *Knowledge, Literacy, and Life in San Diego.* The correlations are rather breathtaking. Median household incomes for those scoring high, middle, and low on a cultural literacy test were, respectively, $65,000, $39,000, and $26,000. These data were gathered from 538 respondents selected by random procedures, resulting in a survey sample that is highly similar in ethnicity and all other respects to overall U.S. Census data.

16. Costa and Liebmann, "Process Is as Important as Content," 23–24.

# Chapter 2.
## Intellectual Capital: A Civil Right

1. Jefferson, *The Life and Selected Writings of Thomas Jefferson*, 51.
2. Ibid., 265.
3. Dewey, *Democracy and Education*, 3–4.

4. Bagley, *Education and Emergent Man*, 139.

5. Hernes, *Core Curriculum for Primary, Secondary, and Adult Education in Norway*, 26.

6. Bourdieu, "Le Capital social: notes provisoires," 2–3. See also Coleman, *Parental Involvement in Education*.

7. Walberg and Tsai, "Matthew Effects in Education," 359–73.

8. Thompson, *The Brain*, 299–333. See also Husen, *Talent, Equality, and Meritocracy*.

9. Statistical data on Belgium, France, Germany, Luxembourg, the Netherlands, Sweden, and Switzerland may be found in Centre for Educational Research and Innovation, *Immigrants' Children at School*, 178–259. The French studies have been the fullest. They show that, when all other factors are accounted for, the difference in performance between Third World immigrant students and French students "decreased more or less markedly, although they did not disappear completely." For further details, see Boulot and Boyzon-Fradet, *Les Immigrés et l'école*, 54–58.

10. Hernes, *Core Curriculum for Primary, Secondary, and Adult Education in Norway*, 26.

11. The current state of research on skills is discussed in Chapter 5, pages 143–58.

12. Coleman, *Equality of Educational Opportunity*.

13. See Chall, *Families and Literacy*; and especially, Chall, Jacobs, and Baldwin, *The Reading Crisis*.

14. Bagley, *Determinism in Education*.

15. Ayres, *An Index Number for State School Systems*.

16. Stevenson and Stigler, *The Learning Gap*, 196.

17. Stevenson, Chuansheng, and Shin-Ying, "Mathematics Achievement of Chinese, Japanese, and American Children," 51–58.

18. The work of Loban and Chall is discussed in Chapter 2, pages 44–46.

19. Jones, *Quality and Equity of Education Outcomes*.

20. O'Keeffe, *Truancy in English Secondary Schools*.

21. Pinker, *The Language Instinct*.

22. Geary, "Reflections of Evolution and Culture in Children's Cognition," 24–36.

23. Stevenson and Stigler, *The Learning Gap*, 140.

24. Ravitch, *The Troubled Crusade*, 52–55.

25. National Academy of Education, *Becoming a Nation of Readers*.

26. General Accounting Office, *Elementary School Children*, 1.

27. Ibid., 32.

28. Cohen, "Moving Images," 32–39.

29. Wood, Halfon, and Scarlata, "Impact of Family Relocation on Children's Growth, Development, School Function, and Behavior," 1334–38.

30. Cohen, "Moving Images," 32–39.

31. Ibid.

32. General Accounting Office, *Elementary School Children*, 5.

33. Ibid., 6.

34. Quoted in Cohen, "Frequent Moves Said to Boost Risk of School Problems," 15. See also Wood, Halfon, and Scarlata, "Impact of Family Relocation on Children's

Growth, Development, School Function, and Behavior," 1334–38. For further confirmation on adverse effects of changing schools, see R. Johnson and Lindblad, "Effect of Mobility on Academic Performance of Sixth Grade Students," 547–52; and Ingersoll, Scamman, and Eckerling, "Geographic Mobility and Student Achievement in an Urban Setting," 143–49.

35. Walberg, "Improving Local Control and Learning." Walberg cites Straits, "Residence, Migration, and School Progress," 34–43.

36. Bagley, *Education and Emergent Man*, 145.

37. Elam, Rose, and Gallup, "The 23rd Annual Gallup Poll of the Public's Attitudes Toward the Public Schools," 41–47. In response to the question "Would you favor or oppose requiring the public schools in this community to use a standardized [*sic*!] national curriculum?", the response was 68 percent in favor, 24 percent opposed, and 8 percent undecided. The majority was even greater when the tendentious term "standardized" was omitted, as in this question: "Would you favor or oppose requiring the public schools in this community to conform to national achievement standards and goals?" Here the response was 81 percent in favor, 12 percent opposed, and 7 percent undecided.

38. College Board, *College-Bound Seniors*. The College Board sent me further details showing the breakdown of scores over 600 between 1972 and 1984. With a constant number of about one million students taking the test, the percentage of students who scored over 600 was 7.3 percent in 1984 and 11.4 percent in 1972. The percentage scoring over 650 was 3.0 percent in 1984 and 5.29 percent in 1972. See also Hirsch, *Cultural Literacy*, 4, 5, 217. Still firmer numbers: "In 1972 over 116,000 students scored above 600 on the verbal S.A.T. In 1982 fewer than 71,000 scored that high even though a similar number took the exam" (from an article by David Barulich in *Education Week*, February 15, 1995, page 31).

39. International Association for the Evaluation of Educational Achievement, *Science Achievement in Seventeen Countries*.

40. Ibid., 100.

41. Ibid., 42.

42. The superb Swiss results are found in two highly informative comparative studies: Lapointe, Mead, and Askew, *Learning Mathematics* and *Learning Science*.

43. Data from Boulot and Boyzon-Fradet, *Les Immigrés et l'école*, 54–58; and Centre for Educational Research and Innovation, *Immigrants' Children at School*, 178–259.

44. Ferguson, "Shifting Challenges," 37–76.

45. International Association for the Evaluation of Educational Achievement, *Science Achievement in Seventeen Countries*, 42.

46. Coleman, *Equality of Educational Opportunity*; for strongest effects of poor schools and teachers on disadvantaged children, see pages 22, 316–18. See also Chall, *Families and Literacy*; and especially, Chall, Jacobs, and Baldwin, *The Reading Crisis*.

47. U.S. Department of Health and Human Services, *The Impact of Head Start on Children, Families and Communities*, 1.

48. Zigler and Muenchow, *Head Start*, 145.

49. U.S. Department of Health and Human Services, *The Impact of Head Start*, 2.

50. Statistical data on Belgium, France, Germany, Luxembourg, the Netherlands, Sweden, and Switzerland may be found in Centre for Educational Research and Innovation, *Immigrants' Children at School*, 178–259. The French studies have been the fullest. They show that, when all other factors are accounted for, the difference in performance between Third World immigrant students and French students "decreased more or less markedly, although they did not disappear completely." For further details, see Boulot and Boyzon-Fradet, *Les Immigrés et l'école*, 54–58.

# Chapter 3.
## An Impregnable Fortress

1. Cuban, *How Teachers Taught*. Zilversmit, *Changing Schools*.

2. See Chapter 5.

3. Olson, "Progressive-Era Concept Now Breaks Mold," 6–7.

4. Rugg, *The Child-Centered School*. Quoted in Ravitch, *The Troubled Crusade*, 50. I have put Ravitch's verbs in the present tense.

5. Wiske, "How Teaching for Understanding Changes the Rules in the Classroom," 21.

6. "Better Teaching or 'Just the Facts, Ma'am'?," *Education Week*, March 11, 1982, 30.

7. Ravitch and Finn, *What Do Our 17-Year-Olds Know?*

8. *Westport* (Conn.) *News*, June 3, 1994.

9. Dewey, *The Child and the Curriculum* 2:276. Quoted in Westbrook, *John Dewey and American Democracy*, 99.

10. This was the evaluation most recently of the report issued by Organization for Economic Cooperation and Development, *OECD Economic Surveys, 1993–94: United States*, Chapter IV.

11. See International Association for the Evaluation of Educational Achievement, *Science Achievement in Seventeen Countries*.

12. The dramatic and happily ending story of the Fort Collins school deserves to be memorialized to inspire others.

13. Bestor, *Educational Wastelands*, 102.

14. M. Smith, *And Madly Teach*, 7.

15. Bestor, *Educational Wastelands*, 110.

16. See Chapter 4, Section 7.

17. Adams, *Beginning to Read*. See also Pressley and Rankin, "More About Whole Language Methods of Reading Instruction for Students at Risk for Early Reading Failure," 157–68.

18. *Springfield* (Mass.) *Sunday Republican*, January 2, 1994. I owe this example to John Kelleher.

# Chapter 4.
## Critique of a Thoughtworld

1. See Jaspers, *Psychologie der Weltanschauungen*, 10; and *Wilhelm Diltheys Gesammelte Schriften,* 8:14. See also Spranger, "Zur Theorie des Verstehens und zur geisteswissenschaftlochen Psychologie," 369.
2. Augustine, *Confessions*, Book VI.
3. Jefferson, *The Life and Selected Writings of Thomas Jefferson*, 265.
4. Froebel, *The Student's Froebel*, 5–6.
5. Pestalozzi, *Pestalozzi's Educational Writings*, 18–19.
6. Wordsworth, "Ode: Intimations of Immortality from Recollections of Early Childhood," lines 125–32.
7. Alcott, "Sonnet XIV."
8. Quoted in Cremin, *The Transformation of the School*, 134–5.
9. Kilpatrick, "The Essentials of the Activity Movement." Quoted in Tennenbaum, *William Heard Kilpatrick*.
10. Twain, *Huckleberry Finn*, last words of the book.
11. Coleridge, *Biographia Literaria*, Chapter XIV.
12. Jarousee, Mingat, and Richard, "La Scolarisation maternelle à deux ans," 55.
13. Bruner, *The Process of Education*, 33.
14. *Life*, July 1994, 68.
15. National Association for the Education of Young People, "Guidelines for Appropriate Curriculum Content and Assessment in Programs Serving Children Ages 3 Through 8," 21–38. The disparaging phrase "memorizing meaningless tricks" reveals a characteristic polarization between "deep understanding" and "rote memorization." It is no doubt a meaningless trick to memorize that you have to carry to the left any double digit over nine. Yet, frequent practice in performing the "meaningless trick" is one way, perhaps the best way, to gain an operational and thence a conceptual understanding of place value. The "meaningless trick" of reciting the Pledge of Allegiance every morning leads by degrees to a conceptual understanding of the word "pledge" and the word "allegiance."
16. The lack of harmful psychological effects is documented in both Europe and Asia. For Europe, the most authoritative work, since it comprises data from twenty thousand students, is Duthoit, "L'Enfant et l'école," 3–13. For Asia, see Stevenson, "Adapting to School." For the required mathematical attainments for grades one through three, see, for example, the national curriculum guides for France and Japan. See also Geary, *Children's Mathematical Development*; and Thompson, *The Brain*, 299–333.
17. See the highly informative video of Japanese instruction in mathematics produced by Harold Stevenson and his colleagues. Called "Polished Stones," it is available from the Department of Psychology, University of Michigan, Ann Arbor.
18. S. Johnson, ed., "Preface," *Shakespeare. The Plays*, 327.

19. Pestalozzi, *The Education of Man*, xii.

20. Ibid., 34.

21. Froebel, *The Student's Froebel*, 6.

22. Piaget, *Science of Education and the Psychology of the Child*, 173. See also Mandler, "A New Perspective on Cognitive Development in Infancy," 236–43; and Mandler, "How to Build a Baby," 587–604. An authoritative discussion of the pernicious effects of developmentalism, along with a usefully full bibliography, appeared while this book was in page proof; see Stone, "Developmentalism."

23. Pestalozzi, *Pestalozzi's Educational Writings*, 20.

24. National Association for the Education of Young People, "Guidelines for Appropriate Curriculum Content and Assessment in Programs Serving Children Ages 3 Through 8," 26.

25. Brophy and Good, "Teacher Behavior and Student Achievement," 338. Walberg, "Improving the Productivity of America's Schools," 19–27.

26. Thompson, *The Brain*, 338: "Semantic and motor skill learning have many of the same basic properties. For example, distributed practice—an hour a day for seven days—is much more effective for both types of memory than seven hours in a row of massed practice. . . . If it is new information or a new motor skill and you do not practice it, some of it will be stored in long-term memory, but most will fade away. If you practice enough you can store it in long-term memory, where it may remain essentially forever."

27. Geary, "Reflections of Evolution and Culture in Children's Cognition," 24–36.

28. Ibid., 36.

29. Norvez, *De la naissance à l'école*.

30. National Association for the Education of Young People, "Guidelines for Appropriate Curriculum Content and Assessment in Programs Serving Children Ages 3 Through 8," 26.

31. Thompson, *The Brain*, 299–333.

32. Geary, *Children's Mathematical Development*. See also Thompson, *The Brain*, 299–333.

33. Thompson, *The Brain*, 324.

34. Quoted in Tennenbaum, *William Heard Kilpatrick*, 243.

35. Stevenson and Stigler, *The Learning Gap*, Chapter 5.

36. See Chapter 2, Section 5.

37. Ministère de l'Éducation Nationale, "Les Éleves de nationalité étrangère scolarisés dans le premier et le second degré en 1993–1994."

38. Bracey, "Why Can't They Be Like We Were," 104–17.

39. Hurn, "The Problem With Comparisons," 7–12.

40. Kammen, "The Problem of American Exceptionalism," 1–30.

41. Elson, *Guardians of Tradition*.

42. Kammen, "The Problem of American Exceptionalism," 7.

43. Quoted in Peterson, *Lincoln in American Memory*, 32.

44. Quoted in Tennenbaum, *William Heard Kilpatrick*, 112.

45. Kilpatrick, *Foundations of Method*, 267.

46. Ravitch, *The Troubled Crusade*, 235–36.

47. Stevenson and Stigler, *The Learning Gap*, Chapter 7.

48. Kilpatrick, *Foundations of Method*, 289.

49. Shain, *The Myth of American Individualism*, 114.

50. Young, *Conjectures on Original Composition*.

51. Dawes, *House of Cards*, 229–51. Mecca, Smelser, and Vasconcellos, *The Social Importance of Self Esteem*.

52. Herrnstein and Murray, *The Bell Curve*.

53. Patterson, "Language, Ethnicity, and Change," 70.

54. Hofstadter, *Anti-Intellectualism in American Life*.

55. Whitman, *Leaves of Grass*.

56. Tocqueville, *Democracy in America: Part I*, Chapter 18.

57. Emerson, *Journals*, entry for September 14, 1839.

58. Emerson, "The American Scholar."

59. Kilpatrick, *Foundations of Method*, 253, 277, 357.

60. Quoted in Ravitch, *The Troubled Crusade*, 66.

61. Ibid., 62.

62. Ibid., 63.

63. Beck, Perfetti, and McKeown, "Effects of Long-Term Vocabulary Instruction on Lexical Access and Reading Comprehension, 506–21.

64. Pestalozzi, *Pestalozzi's Educational Writings*, 92.

65. Ibid., 93.

66. Clifford and Guthrie, *Ed School*, 332.

67. Quoted in ibid., 200.

68. Ibid., 139.

69. Ibid., 137.

70. Ibid., 261ff.

71. Ibid., 265.

72. Koerner, *The Miseducation of American Teachers*, 28.

73. Traced in Clifford and Guthrie, *Ed School*, 47–122.

74. Quoted in Ibid., 58.

75. Quoted in Westbrook, *John Dewey and American Democracy*, 104.

76. Quoted in ibid., 94.

77. Woodring, "The Development of Teacher Education."

78. This interpretation of Dewey's influence is shared by both Diane Ravitch and Robert Westbrook. See Ravitch, *The Troubled Crusade*; and Westbrook, *John Dewey and American Democracy*.

79. Tennenbaum, *William Heard Kilpatrick*, 226.

80. Quoted in ibid., 226.

81. Kilpatrick, *Foundations of Method*, 266–67.

82. Dewey, *Democracy and Education*, 2–4.

83. Westbrook, *John Dewey and American Democracy*, 504ff.

84. Bagley, *Education and Emergent Man*, 139.

85. Clifford and Guthrie, *Ed School*, 332.

# Chapter 5.
## Reality's Revenge: Education and Mainstream Research

1. Jarolimek and Foster, *Teaching and Learning in the Elementary School*, 142.

2. Zemelman, Daniels, and Hyde, *Best Practice*, 4–5.

3. Hill, "Math's Angry Man," 27.

4. Ibid.

5. See Chapter 5, pages 159–75.

6. Hill, "Math's Angry Man," 27.

7. Ibid.

8. Beane and Apple, "The Case for Democratic Schools," 3–4.

9. *Chronicle of Higher Education*, April 28, 1995, A-71.

10. Ibid.

11. Larkin, "The Role of Problem Representation in Physics."

12. Resnick and Klopfer, "Toward the Thinking Curriculum."

13. Jungwirth and Dreyfus, "Diagnosing the Attainment of Basic Enquiry Skills," 42–49.

14. Klaczynski and Laipple, "Role of Content Domain, Logic Training, and IQ in Rule Acquisition and Transfer," 653–72.

15. George, "Facilitation in the Wason Selection Task with a Consequent Referring to an Unsatisfactory Outcome," 463–72.

16. See above, page 318.

17. McPeck, *Teaching Critical Thinking*, 54–74.

18. Klaczynski, Gelfand, and Reese, "Transfer of Conditional Reasoning," 208–20.

19. On the positive effects of some reciprocal teaching, see Rosenshine and Meister, "Reciprocal Teaching," 479–530; and Palincsar, "Reciprocal Teaching," 56–58. And for its theoretical basis, see Stanovich and Cunningham, "Reading as Constrained Reasoning," 3–60. For positive benefits of other domain-specific metacognitive teaching, see Geary, *Children's Mathematical Development*, 72–78; Singer and Donlon, "Active Comprehension," 116–86; Dansereau et al., "Development and Evaluation of a Learning Strategy Training Program," 64–73; and Larkin and Reif, "Analysis and Teaching of a General Skill for Studying Scientific Text," 431–40.

20. Jungwirth and Dreyfus, "Diagnosing the Attainment of Basic Enquiry Skills," 42–49.

21. Sternberg, "Criteria for Intellectual Skills Training," 6–12.

22. Rosenshine and Meister, "Reciprocal Teaching," 480.

23. Siegler, "Adaptive and Non-Adaptive Characteristics of Low-Income Children's Mathematical Strategy Use," 341–66.

24. Rosenshine and Meister, "Reciprocal Teaching," 528.

25. Siegler, "Adaptive and Non-Adaptive Characteristics of Low-Income Children's Mathematical Strategy Use," 363.

26. Palincsar and Brown, "Instruction for Self-Regulated Reading," 19–39. More questionable use of strategy instruction might be the isolated instruction outlined in Duffy et al., "The Effects of Explaining the Reasoning Associated with Using Reading Strategies," 347–68; and Paris and Oka, "Children's Reading Strategies, Metacognition and Motivation," 25–56. That comprehension is a skill to be separated from decoding skill is well argued by Stanovich and Cunningham, "Reading as Constrained Reasoning," 3–60. For strong support for use of metacognitive methods in teaching reading comprehension, see Haller, Child, and Walberg, "Can Comprehension Be Taught," 5–8.

27. Pierce, Duncan, and Gholson, "Cognitive Load, Schema Acquisition, and Procedural Adaptation in Nonisomorphic Analogical Transfer," 66–74.

28. Larkin and Chabay, "Research on Teaching Scientific Thinking," 150–72.

29. Whitehead, *An Introduction to Mathematics*, 41.

30. *Washington Post*, Letters to the Editor, April 25, 1995, A16.

31. Jarolimek and Foster, *Teaching and Learning in the Elementary School*, 142.

32. Spiro, "Cognitive Processes in Prose Comprehension and Recall." Anderson and Shifrin, "The Meaning of Words in Context." Beck, Perfetti, and McKeown, "Effects of Long-term Vocabulary Instruction on Lexical Access and Reading Comprehension," 506–21.

33. Kagan, *The Nature of the Child*, 213.

34. M. J. Adams, interviewed in "Failing Grades: Canadian Schooling in a Failing Economy," video produced by Joe Friedman, M.D., Society for Advancing Educational Research, Edmonton, Canada. For confirming data, see also Juel, Griffith, and Gough, "Acquisition of Literacy," 243–55.

35. Chall, *Families and Literacy*; and especially, Chall, Jacobs, and Baldwin, *The Reading Crisis*.

36. Sticht and James, "Listening and Reading," 293–318. See also Sticht et al., *Auding and Reading*.

37. Juel, "Beginning Reading," 759–88. See also Gough and Hillinger, "Learning to Read, an Unnatural Act," 179–96.

38. Geary, "Reflections of Evolution and Culture in Children's Cognition," 24–36.

39. Tierney and Cunningham, "Research on Teaching Reading Comprehension," 609–56. Beck, Perfetti, and McKeown, "Effects of Long-term Vocabulary Instruction on Lexical Access and Reading Comprehension," 506–21.

40. Bransford and Johnson, "Contextual Prerequisites for Understanding," 717–26. Spiro, "Cognitive Processes in Prose Comprehension and Recall."

41. Miller, "The Magical Number Seven, Plus or Minus Two," 81–97.

42. Juel, "Beginning Reading," 759–88. LaBerge and Samuels, "Toward a Theory of Automatic Information Processing in Reading," 293–323. Perfetti and Lesgold, "Discourse Comprehension and Sources of Individual Differences."

43. Britton et al., *The Development of Writing Abilities*. Perl, "The Composing Processes of Unskilled College Writers," 317–36.

44. Geary, *Children's Mathematical Development*.

45. Larkin et al., "Models of Competence in Solving Physics Problems," 317–48. Schoenfeld and Hermann, "Problem Perception and Knowledge Structure in Expert and Novice Mathematical Problem Solvers, 484–94.

46. Some work in this tradition: Tversky and Kahneman, "Availability," 207–32; Collins, *Human Plausible Reasoning*; and Fischoff, "Judgment and Decision Making," 153–87.

47. Larkin and Chabay, "Research on Teaching Scientific Thinking," 158.

48. Ibid., 150–72.

49. Johnson-Laird, *Mental Models*.

50. Kunda and Nisbett, "The Psychometrics of Everyday Life," 195–224.

51. Brown and Siegler, "Metrics and Mappings," 531.

52. Brown and Siegler, "Metrics and Mappings," 531. But see also Scardamalia and Bereiter, "Computer Support for Knowledge-Building Communities," 265–83; and Scardamalia, Bereiter, and Lamon, "CSILE: Trying to Bring Students into World 3," 201–28.

53. Bishop, *Expertise and Excellence*.

54. Pais, *"Subtle Is the Lord,"* 95.

55. The data from the New Zealand study and most other studies cited here are taken from the excellent review by Brophy and Good, who conducted some of the most significant research into effective teaching methods. See Brophy and Good, "Teacher Behavior and Student Achievement," 328–75. Some of the New Zealand work is described in Nuthall and Church, "Experimental Studies of Teaching Behaviour." The importance of this kind of research was well argued by Gilbert T. Sewall in his *Necessary Lessons*, especially pages 131–33. Sewall cites highly similar findings from the British researcher Neville Bennett in N. Bennett, *Teaching Styles and Pupil Progress*. For an explanation why progressive methods like discovery learning have not worked well in teaching science, see Walberg, "Improving School Science in Advanced and Developing Countries," 625–99.

56. Stallings and Kasowitz, *Follow Through Classroom Evaluation Evaluation, 1972–1973*.

57. Brophy and Evertson, *Learning from Teaching*. Anderson, Evertson, and Brophy, *Principles of Small-Group Instruction in Elementary Reading*.

58. Good and Grouws, "Teacher Effects," 49–54.

59. Gage, *The Scientific Basis of the Art of Teaching*.

60. Rosenshine and Stevens, "Teaching Functions," 376–91.

61. Brophy and Good, "Teacher Behavior and Student Achievement," 338.

62. Beck, "Improving Practice Through Understanding Reading," 40–58.

63. Bahrick, "Extending the Life Span of Knowledge," 61–82.

64. Spiro, "Cognitive Processes in Prose Comprehension and Recall"; and Anderson and Shifrin, "The Meaning of Words in Context."

65. Bransford and Johnson, "Contextual Prerequisites for Understanding," 717–26. Spiro, "Cognitive Processes in Prose Comprehension and Recall."

66. Rosenshine and Stevens, "Teaching Functions," 379.

67. Stevenson and Stigler, *The Learning Gap*, 196–98.

68. Ibid., 191.

69. Ibid., 174.

70. Ibid., 194.

71. Ibid., 179, 181–82.

72. Ibid., 190.

73. Ibid., 183.

74. Popham, "Performance Tests of Teaching Proficiency," 105–17.

75. Clifford and Guthrie, *Ed School*. Kramer, *Ed School Follies*.

76. Zemelman, Daniels, and Hyde, *Best Practice*, 4–5.

77. Ibid.

78. Egan, *Teaching as Story Telling*.

79. Sidney, *An Apology for Poetry*.

# Chapter 6.
# Test Evasion

1. Madaus, "A Technological and Historical Consideration of Equity Issues Associated with Proposals to Change Our Nation's Testing Policy," 23–68. A vigorous defense of objective testing having in view many of the same purposes as this chapter was presented in Finn, *We Must Take Charge: Our Schools and Our Future*, Chapter 10.

2. Jencks, "What's Behind the Drop in Test Scores?" 29–41.

3. Melville and Stamm, "The Pass-Fail System and the Change in the Accounting of Grades on Comprehensive Examinations at Knox College." Delohery and McLaughlin, "Pass-Fail Grading." Gold, "Academic Achievement Declines Under Pass-Fail Grading," 17–21. Quann, "Pass/Fail Grading—An Unsuccess Story," 230–35. Suddick and Kelly, "Effects of Transition from Pass/No Credit to Traditional Letter Grade System," 88–90.

4. Olson, "Cards on the Table," 24.

5. Jefferson, "Notes on Virginia," 263.

6. Center for Research in Evaluation, Standards and Student Testing, *Evaluation Comment*, Winter 1994.

7. Hirsch, *The Philosophy of Composition*, 176–200.

8. Hirsch, "Measuring the Communicative Effectiveness of Prose," 189–207.

9. Hopkins, "The Marking System of the College Entrance Examination Board." Noyes, Sale, and Stalnaker, *Report on the First Six Tests in English Composition*. Remondino, "A Factorial Analysis of the Evaluation of Scholastic Compositions in the Mother Tongue," 242–51. Diederich, French, and Carlton, "Factors in Judg-

ments of Writing Ability." Godshalk, Swineford, and Coffman, *The Measurement of Writing Ability*. Fitzpatrick and Morrison, "Performance and Product Evaluation." Coffman, "Essay Examinations," *Educational Measurement*, 237–302. For further studies, the bibliographies of the last three items may also be consulted.

10. Diederich, French, and Carlton, "Factors in Judgments of Writing Ability."

11. Godshalk, Swineford, and Coffman, *The Measurement of Writing Ability*. See also Hopkins, "The Marking System of the College Entrance Examination Board"; and Noyes, Sale, and Stalnaker, *Report on the First Six Tests in English Composition*.

12. Remondino, "A Factorial Analysis of the Evaluation of Scholastic Compositions in the Mother Tongue," 242–51. Diederich, French, and Carlton, "Factors in Judgments of Writing Ability."

13. Perl, "The Composing Processes of Unskilled College Writers," 317–36.

14. Koretz et al., "The Vermont Portfolio Assessment Program," 5–16.

15. Godshalk, Swineford, and Coffman, *The Measurement of Writing Ability*.

16. Ibid., 41.

17. Ibid., 6–8.

18. Cronbach, "Test Validation," 443–507. Cronbach, *Essentials of Psychological Measurement*. Messick, "Validity," 13–104.

19. Godshalk, Swineford, and Coffman, *The Measurement of Writing Ability*, 42.

20. Juel, "Beginning Reading," 759–88.

21. Meier, "Why Reading Tests Don't Test Reading," 457–66.

22. Koretz et al., "The Effects of High-Stakes Testing on Achievement: Preliminary Findings About Generalization Across Tests."

23. Cannell, "Nationally Normed Elementary Achievement Testing in America's Public Schools," 5–9.

24. Hart, *Authentic Assessment*, 7.

25. Neill and Medina, "Standardized Testing," 688–97. Darling-Hammond, "Setting Standards for Students," 14–21.

26. Frederiksen, "The Real Test Bias," 193–202. "The 'real test bias' in my title has to do with the influence of tests on teaching and learning. Efficient tests tend to drive out inefficient tests, leaving many important abilities untested—and untaught" (page 201). Frederiksen's second example of defects in the multiple-choice format was the overemphasis on verbal understanding when the skill is spatial-mechanical, as in the task of "adjusting the oil buffer for maximum rate of fire" on a machine gun.

27. Swanson, Norman, and Linn, "Performance Based Assessment," 5–11, 35.

28. Ibid., 11.

29. Frederiksen, "The Real Test Bias," 200.

30. Ibid., 197.

31. Neill and Medina, "Standardized Testing," 694. Darling-Hammond, "Setting Standards for Students," 15.

32. This and the next example are adapted from College Board, *Test Skills*.

33. Darling-Hammond, "Setting Standards," 15.

34. Neill and Medina, "Standardized Testing," 691. Neill, "Some Prerequisites for the Establishment of Equitable, Inclusive Multicultural Assessment Systems," 121.

35. "Bias is differential validity of a given interpretation of a test score for any definable relevant subgroup of test takers. Validity always refers to the degree to which evidence supports the inferences that are made from the scores. The inferences regarding the specific uses of a test are validated, not the test itself." From American Psychological Association, *Standards for Educational and Psychological Testing*.

36. Nettles and Bernstein, "Introduction: The Pursuit of Equity in Educational Testing and Assessment," 6.

37. Gottfredson, "The Science and Politics of Race-Norming," 955–63.

38. Ferguson, "Shifting Challenges," 1, 37–76.

39. Scribner et al., "Are Smart Tankers Better?" 193–206. Horne, "The Impact of Soldier Quality on Army Performance," 443–45. Fernandez, "Soldier Quality and Job Performance in Team Tasks," 253–65.

40. The direct experiences refer to statements and actions by minority parents in several locations, including the Bronx, New York, and Baltimore, Maryland. A parent-run school of this type in Fort Collins, Colorado, is proportionately greatly oversubscribed by minority families. The claim that minority children resist "assimilation" to school-based culture is not borne out by our experience.

41. See my essay on this subject: Hirsch, "Diversity and the Perils of Romanticism," 27–37.

42. Neill, "Some Prerequisites for the Establishment of Equitable, Inclusive Multicultural Assessment Systems," 126.

43. The researches and writings of Torsten Husen are especially valuable for this subject. See for example, Husen, *Talent, Equality, and Meritocracy* and *The Learning Society Revisited*.

44. Carroll, "Psychometric Approaches to the Study of Language Abilities," 29.

45. See above, pages 38–42.

46. Lemann, "Taking Affirmative Action Apart," 36–66 passim.

47. See above, pages 43–46.

48. See the following by Bishop: "Why U.S. Students Need Incentives to Learn," 15–18; "Impacts of School Organization and Signalling on Incentives to Learn in France, The Netherlands, England, Scotland, and the United States"; and "Impact of Curriculum-Based Examinations on Learning in Canadian Secondary Schools."

# Chapter 7.
## Summary and Conclusion

1. Cremin, *The Transformation of the School*, 134–35. Ravitch, *The Troubled Crusade*, 235–36. For further discussion of the later period, see also Sewall, *Necessary Lessons*.

2. Rosenshine and Stevens, "Teaching Functions," 376–91. See also Brophy and Good, "Teacher Behavior and Student Achievement," 338.

3. Emerson, *Journals*, entry for September 14, 1839.

4. Rosenshine and Stevens, "Teaching Functions," 376–91. Brophy and Good, "Teacher Behavior and Student Achievement," 338.

5. Larkin and Chabay, "Research on Teaching Scientific Thinking," 150–72.

6. Geary, "Reflections of Evolution and Culture in Children's Cognition," 24–36. See also Geary, *Children's Mathematical Development*.

7. Geary, "Reflections of Evolution and Culture in Children's Cognition," 24–36.

8. Pinker, *The Language Instinct*.

9. Thompson, *The Brain*, 299–333.

10. Bruner, *The Process of Education*, 33.

11. Quoted in Tennenbaum, *William Heard Kilpatrick*, 243.

12. Bahrick, "Extending the Life Span of Knowledge," 61–82.

13. Geary, *Children's Mathematical Development*.

14. George, "Facilitation in the Wason Selection Task with a Consequent Referring to an Unsatisfactory Outcome," 463–72.

15. Walberg and Tsai, "Matthew Effects in Education," 359–73.

16. See the following by Bishop: "Why U.S. Students Need Incentives to Learn," 15–18; "Impacts of School Organization and Signalling on Incentives to Learn in France, The Netherlands, England, Scotland, and the United States"; "Impact of Curriculum-Based Examinations on Learning in Canadian Secondary Schools"; and "Expertise and Excellence." See also Stevenson, Chuansheng, and Shin-Ying, "Mathematics Achievement of Chinese, Japanese, and American Children," 51–58; and Stevenson and Stigler, *The Learning Gap*, 196–98.

17. Popham, "Performance Tests of Teaching Proficiency," 105–17.

18. This passage expressing hope that education schools might reform themselves was commented on with a good deal of skepticism by the head of a prestigious education school. Did I really think that a few brave maverick professors could change a powerful sixty-year-old tradition? If such self-induced change were to happen at all, wouldn't it take an unacceptably long time to occur? What concrete steps should be taken right now by reform-minded colleagues to make education schools part of the solution instead of part of the problem?

   I replied by proposing part of an answer for any education-school dean valiant enough to attempt it: *Make teacher certification dependent upon prospective teachers' demonstrating adequate, probing knowledge of the subject matters they will be called upon to teach, as well as adequate knowledge of mainstream research into the most effective pedagogies for imparting those subject matters.*

   To an outsider, the proposal might seem ludicrously self-evident. Within education schools, however, such an innovation might be greeted by a firestorm of protest. It would instantly compel a change in what education schools do, and would implicitly challenge the myth that they provide something deeper and better than mere transitory subject-matter knowledge.

19. International Association for the Evaluation of Educational Achievement, *Science Achievement in Seventeen Countries*.

20. Lapointe, Mead, and Askew, *Learning Mathematics* and *Learning Science*.
21. Bagley, *Education and Emergent Man*, 145.
22. Cohen, "Moving Images," 32–39.
23. General Accounting Office, *Elementary School Children*, 1.
24. Jefferson, *The Life and Selected Writings of Thomas Jefferson*, 126.
25. Kant, "Idea for a Universal History from a Cosmopolitan Point of View."
26. Patterson, "Affirmative Action on the Merit System," A-13.
27. See my essay on this subject: Hirsch, "Diversity and the Perils of Romanticism," 27–37.

# Bibliography

Adams, M. J. *Beginning to Read: Thinking and Learning About Print.* Cambridge, Mass.: MIT Press, 1990.

American Psychological Association. *Standards for Educational and Psychological Testing.* Washington, D.C., 1985.

Anderson, L., Evertson, C., and Brophy, J. *Principles of Small-Group Instruction in Elementary Reading.* Occasional Paper #58. East Lansing, Mich.: Michigan State University, 1982.

Anderson, R. C., and Shifrin, Z. "The Meaning of Words in Context." In *Theoretical Issues in Reading Comprehension,* ed. R. J. Spiro, B. C. Bruce, and W. C. Brewer. Hillsdale, N.J.: Erlbaum, 1981.

Ayres, L. P. *An Index Number for State School Systems.* New York: Warwick and York, 1922.

Bagley, W. C. *Determinism in Education.* Baltimore, 1925; 2nd printing with corrections, 1928.

———. *Education and Emergent Man: A Theory of Education with Particular Application to Public Education in the United States.* New York: Nelson, 1934.

Bahrick, H. P. "Extending the Life Span of Knowledge." In *The Challenge in Mathematics and Science Education: Psychology's Response,* ed. L. Penner et al., 61–82. Washington, D.C.: American Psychological Association, 1993.

Beane, J. A., and Apple, M. W. "The Case for Democratic Schools." In *Democratic Schools.* Alexandria, Va.: Association for Supervision and Curriculum Development, 1995.

Beck, I. L. "Improving Practice Through Understanding Reading." In *Toward the Thinking Curriculum: Current Cognitive Research,* ed. L. Resnick and L. Klopfer, 40–58. Alexandria, Va.: Association for Supervision and Curriculum Development, 1989.

Beck, I. L., Perfetti, C. A., and McKeown, M. G. "Effects of Long-Term Vocabulary Instruction on Lexical Access and Reading Comprehension. *Journal of Educational Psychology* 74 (1982): 506–21.

Bennett, N. *Teaching Styles and Pupil Progress.* Cambridge, Mass.: Harvard University Press, 1976.

Bestor, A. E. *Educational Wastelands: The Retreat from Learning in Our Public Schools.* 2nd ed. Urbana, Ill.: University of Illinois Press, 1985.

Bishop, J. "Why U.S. Students Need Incentives to Learn." *Educational Leadership,* March 1992, 15–18.

———. "Impact of Curriculum-Based Examinations on Learning in Canadian Secondary Schools." Working Paper 94-30. Center for Advanced Human Resource Studies, New York State School of Industrial and Labor Relations, Cornell University, Ithaca, N.Y., 1994.

———. "Impacts of School Organization and Signalling on Incentives to Learn in France, The Netherlands, England, Scotland, and the United States." Working Paper (draft, March 17, 1994). Center on the Educational Quality of the Workforce, Cornell University, Ithaca, N.Y., 1994.

———. "Expertise and Excellence." Working Paper 95-13 (draft, April 28, 1995). Center for Advanced Human Resource Studies, New York State School of Industrial and Labor Relations, Cornell University, Ithaca, N.Y., 1995.

Boulot, S., and Boyzon-Fradet, D. *Les Immigrés et l'école: une course d'obstacles.* Paris: L'Harmattan, 1988.

Bound, J., and Freeman, R. B. "What Went Wrong? The Erosion of Relative Earnings and Employment Among Young Black Men in the 1980s." *Quarterly Journal of Economics* 107 (February 1992): 201–32.

Bourdieu, P. "Le Capital social: notes provisoires." *Actes de la recherche en sciences sociales* 3 (1980): 2–3.

Bracey, G. "Why Can't They Be Like We Were." *Phi Delta Kappan,* October 1991, 104–17.

Bransford, J. D., and Johnson, M. K. "Contextual Prerequisites for Understanding: Some Investigations of Comprehension and Recall." *Journal of Verbal Learning and Verbal Behavior* 11 (1972): 717–26.

Britton, J., et al. *The Development of Writing Abilities.* London: Macmillan Education Ltd., 1975.

Broccoli, A. *Antonio Gramsci e l'educazione come egemonia.* Firenze: La nuova Italia, 1972.

Brophy, J., and Evertson, C. *Learning from Teaching: A Developmental Perspective.* Boston: Allyn and Bacon, 1976.

Brophy, J., and Good, T. L. "Teacher Behavior and Student Achievement." In *Handbook of Research on Teaching.* 3rd ed., ed. M. C. Wittrock, 328–75. New York: Macmillan, 1986.

Brown, R. N., and Siegler, R. S. "Metrics and Mappings: A Framework for Understanding Real-World Quantitative Estimation." *Psychological Review* 100 (1993): 531.

Bruner, J. *The Process of Education.* Cambridge, Mass.: Harvard University Press, 1960.

Bruner Foundation. *Evaluation of the New York State Education Department's Community Schools Program.* New York, 1993.

Cannell, J. J. "Nationally Normed Elementary Achievement Testing in America's Public Schools: How All 50 States Are Above the National Average." *Educational Measurement* 7 (1988): 5–9.

Caplan, T., and Caplan, F. *The Early Childhood Years.* New York: Bantam Books, 1984.

Card, D., and Krueger, A. B. "School Quality and Black-White Relative Earnings: A Direct Assessment." *Quarterly Journal of Economics* 107 (February 1992): 151–200.

Carroll, J. B. "Psychometric Approaches to the Study of Language Abilities." In *Individual Differences in Language Abilities and Language Behavior,* ed. C. J. Fillmore, D. Kemper, and S.-Y. Wang, 29. New York: Academic Press, 1979.

Center for Research in Evaluation, Standards and Student Testing. Graduate School of Education, UCLA. *Evaluation Comment,* Winter 1994.

Centre for Educational Research and Innovation. *Immigrants' Children at School.* Paris: Organisation for Economic Co-operation and Development, 1987.

Chall, J. S. *Families and Literacy: Final Report to the National Institute of Education.* Washington, D.C., 1982.

Chall, J. S., Jacobs, V. A., and Baldwin, L. E. *The Reading Crisis: Why Poor Children Fall Behind.* Cambridge, Mass.: Harvard University Press, 1990.

Clifford, G., and Guthrie, J. *Ed School: A Brief for Professional Education.* Chicago: University of Chicago Press, 1988.

Coffman, W. "Essay Examinations." In *Educational Measurement.* 2nd ed., ed. R. L. Thorndike. Washington, D.C.: American Council on Education, 1971.

Cohen, D. "Moving Images." *Education Week,* August 3, 1994, 32–39.

———. "Frequent Moves Said to Boost Risk of School Problems." *Education Week,* September 22, 1994, 15.

Coleman, J. S. *Equality of Educational Opportunity.* Washington, D.C.: U.S. Department of Health, Education, and Welfare, Office of Education, 1966.

———. *Parental Involvement in Education.* Washington, D.C.: U.S. Department of Education, 1991.

College Board. *College-Bound Seniors: Eleven Years of National Data from the College Board's Admission Testing Program, 1973–83.* New York, 1984.

———. *Test Skills: A Test Preparation Program for the PSAT/NMSQT.* New York, 1992.

Collins, A. M. *Human Plausible Reasoning* (Report No. 3810). Cambridge, Mass.: Bolt, Beranek, and Newman, 1978.

Costa, A. L., and Liebmann, R. "Process Is as Important as Content." *Educational Leadership,* March 1995, 23–24.

Cremin, L. A. *The Transformation of the School: Progressivism in American Education, 1865–1957.* New York: Knopf, 1964.

Cronbach, L. "Test Validation." In *Educational Measurement*. 2nd ed., ed. R. L. Thorndike, 443–507. Washington, D.C.: American Council on Education, 1971.

———. *Essentials of Psychological Measurement*. 5th ed. New York: HarperCollins, 1990.

Cuban, L. *How Teachers Taught: Constancy and Change in American Classrooms, 1890–1990*. 2nd ed. New York: Teachers College Press, 1993.

Dansereau, D., et al. "Development and Evaluation of a Learning Strategy Training Program." *Journal of Educational Psychology* 71:64–73.

Darling-Hammond, L. "Setting Standards for Students: The Case for Authentic Assessment." *The Educational Forum* 59 (Fall 1994): 14–21.

Dawes, R. M. *House of Cards: Psychology and Psychotherapy Built on Myth*. New York: The Free Press, 1994.

Delohery, P., and McLaughlin, G. "Pass-Fail Grading." O.I.R. Report. Vol. 4. Blacksburg, Va.: Virginia Polytechnic Institute and State University, 1971.

De Robbio, A. I. *Antonio Gramsci e la pedagogia dell'impegno*. Napoli: Editrice Ferraro, 1987.

Dewey, J. *Democracy and Education: An Introduction to the Philosophy of Education*. New York: The Free Press/Macmillan, 1916, 1944.

———. *The Child and the Curriculum*. Reprinted in *The Middle Works of John Dewey, 1899–1924*. 15 vols. Carbondale, Ill.: Southern Illinois University Press, 1976–83.

Diederich, P., French, J. W., and Carlton, S. "Factors in Judgments of Writing Ability." *Educational Testing Service Research Bulletin*, Princeton, N.J., 1961.

Dilthey, W. *Wilhelm Diltheys Gesammelte Schriften*, ed. G. Misch et al. 8 vols. Leipzig and Berlin: Teubner, 1921–31.

Duffy, G. G., et al. "The Effects of Explaining the Reasoning Associated with Using Reading Strategies." *Reading Research Quarterly* 22 (1987): 347–68.

Duthoit, M. "L'Enfant et l'école. Aspects synthetiques du suivi d'un enchantillon de 20.000 éleves des écoles." *Education et Formations* 16 (1988): 3–13.

Ebel, R., and Frisbie, D. *Essentials of Educational Measurement*. 5th ed. Englewood Cliffs, N.J.: Prentice Hall, 1990.

Egan, K. *Teaching as Story Telling: An Alternative Approach to Teaching and Curriculum in the Elementary School*. Chicago: University of Chicago Press, 1989.

Elam, S., Rose, L., and Gallup, A. "The 23rd Annual Gallup Poll of the Public's Attitudes Toward the Public Schools." *Phi Delta Kappan*, September 1991, 41–47.

Elson, R. M. *Guardians of Tradition: American Schoolbooks of the Nineteenth Century*. Lincoln, Nebr.: University of Nebraska Press, 1964.

Entwistle, H. *Antonio Gramsci: Conservative Schooling for Radical Politics*. London: Routledge & Kegan Paul, 1979.

Ferguson, R. F. "Shifting Challenges: Fifty Years of Economic Change Towards Black-White Earnings Equality." *Daedalus* 124 (Winter 1995): 1, 37–76.

Fernandez, J. C. "Soldier Quality and Job Performance in Team Tasks." *Social Science Quarterly* 73 (1992): 253–65.

Finn, C. A. *We Must Take Charge: Our Schools and Our Future.* New York: The Free Press, 1991.

Fischoff, B. "Judgment and Decision Making." In *The Psychology of Human Thought,* ed. R. Sternberg and E. Smith, 153–87. Cambridge, England: Cambridge University Press, 1987.

Fitzpatrick, R., and Morrison, E. "Performance and Product Evaluation." In *Educational Measurement.* 2nd ed., ed. R. L. Thorndike. Washington, D.C.: American Council on Education, 1971.

Frederiksen, N. "The Real Test Bias: Influences of Testing on Teaching and Learning." *American Psychologist* 39 (1984): 193–202.

Froebel, F. *The Student's Froebel,* ed. W. H. Herford. Boston: Heath, 1904.

Gage, N. *The Scientific Basis of the Art of Teaching.* New York: Teachers College Press, 1978.

Geary, D. *Children's Mathematical Development: Research and Practical Applications.* Washington, D.C.: American Psychological Association, 1994.

———. "Reflections of Evolution and Culture in Children's Cognition." *American Psychologist,* January 1995, 24–36.

General Accounting Office. *Elementary School Children: Many Change School Frequently, Harming Their Education.* GAO/HEHS-94-45. Washington, D.C., 1994.

George, C. "Facilitation in the Wason Selection Task with a Consequent Referring to an Unsatisfactory Outcome." *British Journal of Psychology* 82 (November 1991): 463–72.

Godshalk, F. I., Swineford, F., and Coffman, W. *The Measurement of Writing Ability.* New York: College Entrance Examination Board, 1966.

Gold, R. M. "Academic Achievement Declines Under Pass-Fail Grading." *Journal of Experimental Education* 39, no. 3 (1972): 17–21.

Good, T., and Grouws, D. "Teacher Effects: A Process-Product Study in Fourth Grade Mathematics Classrooms." *Journal of Teacher Education* 28 (1977): 49–54.

Gottfredson, L. "The Science and Politics of Race-Norming." *American Psychologist* 49, no. 11 (November 1994): 955–63.

Gough, P. B., and Hillinger, M. L. "Learning to Read, an Unnatural Act." *Bulletin of the Orton Society* 30 (1980): 179–96.

Gramsci, A. "Education." In *Selections from the Prison Notebooks of Antonio Gramsci,* ed. Q. Hoare and G. Nowell-Smith. New York: International Publishers, 1971.

Haller, E., Child, D., and Walberg, H. J. "Can Comprehension Be Taught: A Quantitative Synthesis." *Educational Researcher,* December 1988, 5–8.

Hart, D. *Authentic Assessment.* Menlo Park, Calif.: Addison-Wesley, 1994.

Hernes, G. *Core Curriculum for Primary, Secondary, and Adult Education in Norway.* Oslo: Royal Ministry of Church, Education, and Research, 1994.

Herrnstein, R., and Murray, C. *The Bell Curve: The Reshaping of American Life by Differences in Intelligence.* New York: Free Press, 1994.

Hill, D. "Math's Angry Man." *Teacher Magazine,* September 1993, 27.

Hirsch, E. D. *The Philosophy of Composition.* Chicago: University of Chicago Press, 1977; Phoenix paperback edition, 1978.

———. "Measuring the Communicative Effectiveness of Prose." In *Writing,* ed. J. Dominic, C. Fredricksen, and M. Whiteman, 189–207. Hillsdale, N.J.: Erlbaum, 1981.

———. *Cultural Literacy: What Every American Needs to Know.* Boston: Houghton Mifflin, 1987.

———. "Diversity and the Perils of Romanticism." *Tocqueville Review* 16 (1995): 27–37.

Hofstadter, R. *Anti-Intellectualism in American Life.* New York: Knopf, 1963.

Hopkins, L. T. "The Marking System of the College Entrance Examination Board." In *Harvard Monographs in Education.* 1st ser., no. 2. Cambridge, Mass.: Harvard School of Education, 1921.

Horne, D. "The Impact of Soldier Quality on Army Performance." *Armed Forces and Society* 13 (1987): 443–45.

Hurn, G. "The Problem with Comparisons." *Educational Leadership,* October 1983, 7–12.

Husen, T. *Talent, Equality, and Meritocracy: Availability and Utilization of Talent.* The Hague: Nijhoff, 1974.

———. *The Learning Society Revisited.* Oxford: Pergamon, 1986.

Ingersoll, G. M., Scamman, J. P., and Eckerling, W. D. "Geographic Mobility and Student Achievement in an Urban Setting" [Denver public schools]. *Educational Evaluation & Policy Analysis* (Summer 1989): 143–49.

International Association for the Evaluation of Educational Achievement. *Science Achievement in Seventeen Countries: A Preliminary Report.* Elmsford, N.Y.: Pergamon Press, 1988.

Jarolimek, J., and Foster, C. D. *Teaching and Learning in the Elementary School.* New York: Macmillan, 1993.

Jarousee, J. P., Mingat, A., and Richard, M. "La Scolarisation maternelle à deux ans: effets pédagogiques et sociaux." *Éducation & Formations* 31 (April–June, 1992): 3–9, 55.

Jaspers, K. *Psychologie der Weltanschauungen.* 3rd ed. Berlin: Springer, 1925.

Jefferson, T. "Notes on Virginia." In *The Life and Selected Writings of Thomas Jefferson,* ed. A. Koch and W. Peden. New York: Random House, 1944.

———. *The Life and Selected Writings of Thomas Jefferson,* ed. A. Koch and W. Peden. New York: Random House, 1944.

Jencks, C. "What's Behind the Drop in Test Scores?" Working Papers. Department of Sociology, Harvard University, Cambridge, Mass., July–August, 1978.

Johnson, K. R., and Layng, T. V. J. "Breaking the Structuralist Barrier: Literacy and Numeracy with Fluency." *American Psychologist* 47 (1992): 1475–90.

Johnson, R. A., and Lindblad, A. H. "Effect of Mobility on Academic Performance of Sixth Grade Students." *Perceptual and Motor Skills* 72 (April 1991): 547–52.

Johnson, S., ed. "Preface." *Shakespeare. The Plays.* 8 vols. 1765. Reprinted in *Critical Theory Since Plato.* Rev. ed., ed. H. Adams, 327. New York: Harcourt Brace, 1992.

Johnson-Laird, P. N. *Mental Models: Towards a Cognitive Science of Language, Inference, and Consciousness.* Cambridge, Mass.: Harvard University Press, 1983.

Jones, Constance. *Quality and Equity of Education Outcomes: The Effects of School-Wide Content Specificity,* Ph.D. diss., University of South Florida, Tampa, 1993.

Juel, C. "Beginning Reading." In *Handbook of Reading Research,* vol. 2, ed. D. Pearson et al., 759–88. New York: Longman, 1991.

Juel, C., Griffith, P., and Gough, P. "Acquisition of Literacy: A Longitudinal Study of Children in First and Second Grade." *Journal of Educational Psychology* 78 (1986): 243–55.

Jungwirth, E., and Dreyfus, A. "Diagnosing the Attainment of Basic Enquiry Skills: The 100-Year-Old Quest for Critical Thinking." *Journal of Biological Education* 24 (Spring 1990): 42–49.

Kagan, J. *The Nature of the Child.* New York: Basic Books, 1994.

Kammen, M. "The Problem of American Exceptionalism: A Reconsideration." *American Quarterly* 45, no. 1 (March 1993): 1–30.

Kant, I. "Idea for a Universal History from a Cosmopolitan Point of View." In *Philosophical writings,* ed. Ernst Behler. New York: Continuum, 1986.

Keynes, J. M. *The General Theory of Employment, Interest, and Money* (1936). Vol. 7 of *The Collected Writings of John Maynard Keynes.* 30 vols. London: Macmillan/Cambridge University Press, 1971–89.

Kilpatrick, W. H. "The Essentials of the Activity Movement." *Progressive Education,* October 1924.

———. *Foundations of Method.* New York: Longmans, 1925.

Klaczynski, P. A., Gelfand, H., and Reese, H. W. "Transfer of Conditional Reasoning: Effects of Explanations and Initial Problem Types." *Memory & Cognition* 17 (March 1989): 208–20.

Klaczynski, P. A., and Laipple, J. S. "Role of Content Domain, Logic Training, and IQ in Rule Acquisition and Transfer." *Journal of Experimental Psychology. Learning, Memory and Cognition* 19 (May 1993): 653–72.

Koerner, J. *The Miseducation of American Teachers.* Boston: Houghton Mifflin, 1963.

Koretz, D., et al. "The Effects of High-Stakes Testing on Achievement: Preliminary Findings About Generalization Across Tests." Preprint of a paper presented at a symposium called "Effects of High-Stakes Educational Testing on Instruction and Achievement," at a meeting of AERA and NCME, Chicago, April 1991.

———. "The Vermont Portfolio Assessment Program: Findings and Implications." *Educational Measurement Issues and Practice* 13 (1994): 5–16.

Kosmoski, G. J., Gay, G., and Vockell, E. L. "Cultural Literacy and Academic Achievement." *Journal of Experimental Education* 58 (Summer 1990): 265–72.

Kramer, R. *Ed School Follies: The Miseducation of America's Teachers.* New York: The Free Press, 1991.

Kunda, Z., and Nisbett, R. E. "The Psychometrics of Everyday Life." *Cognitive Psychology* 18 (1986): 195–224.

LaBerge, D., and Samuels, S. J. "Toward a Theory of Automatic Information Processing in Reading." *Cognitive Psychology* 6 (1974): 293–323.

Lapointe, A. E., Mead, N. A., and Askew, J. M. *Learning Mathematics.* Princeton, N.J.: International Assessment of Educational Progress and the Educational Testing Service, 1992.

———. *Learning Science.* Princeton, N.J.: International Assessment of Educational Progress and the Educational Testing Service, 1992.

Larkin, J., et al. "Models of Competence in Solving Physics Problems," *Cognitive Science* 4 (1980): 317–48.

Larkin, J. H. "The Role of Problem Representation in Physics." In *Mental Models,* D. Gentner and A. L. Stevens. Hillsdale, N.J.: Erlbaum, 1983.

Larkin, J. H., and Chabay, R. W. "Research on Teaching Scientific Thinking: Implications for Computer-based Instruction." In *Toward the Thinking Curriculum: Current Cognitive Research,* ed. L. B. Resnick and L. E. Klopfer, 150–72. Alexandria, Va.: Association for Supervision and Curriculum Development, 1989.

Larkin, J. H., and Reif, F. "Analysis and Teaching of a General Skill for Studying Scientific Text." *Journal of Educational Psychology* 68:431–40.

Lazar, I., and Darlington, R. B. "Lasting Effects of Early Education: A Report from the Consortium for Longitudinal Studies." Monograph. Chicago: University of Chicago Press [for the Society for Research in Child Development], 1982.

Lemann, N. "Taking Affirmative Action Apart." *New York Times Magazine,* June 11, 1995, 36–66 passim.

Loban, W. *Language Ability: Grades Seven, Eight, and Nine.* Project No. 1131. Berkeley, Calif.: University of California, 1964.

McPeck, J. E. *Teaching Critical Thinking: Dialogue and Dialectic.* New York: Routledge, 1990.

Madaus, G. "A Technological and Historical Consideration of Equity Issues Associated with Proposals to Change Our Nation's Testing Policy." In *Equity and Excellence in Educational Testing and Assessment,* ed. M. T. Nettles and A. L. Nettles. Boston: Kluwer, 1995.

Mandler, J. M. "A New Perspective on Cognitive Development in Infancy. *American Scientist* 78 (May/June 1990): 236–43.

———. "How to Build a Baby: Conceptual Primitives." *Psychological Review* 99 (October 1992): 587–604.

Mecca, M. J., Smelser, N. J., and Vasconcellos, J. *The Social Importance of Self Esteem.* Berkeley, Calif.: University of California Press, 1989.

Medina, N. J., and Neill, M. "Some Prerequisites for the Establishment of Equitable, Inclusive Multicultural Assessment Systems." In *Equity and Excellence in Educational Testing and Assessment,* ed. M. T. Nettles and A. L. Nettles. Boston: Kluwer, 1994.

Meier, D. "Why Reading Tests Don't Test Reading." *Dissent,* Fall 1981, 457–66.

Melville, G. L., and Stamm, E., "The Pass-Fail System and the Change in the Accounting of Grades on Comprehensive Examinations at Knox College," Knox College, Galesburg, Ill., 1967.

Messick, S. "Validity." In *Educational Measurement,* 3rd ed., ed. R. Linn, 13–104. New York: Macmillan, 1989.

Miller, G. A. "The Magical Number Seven, Plus or Minus Two." *Psychological Review* 63 (1956): 81–97.

Ministère de l'Éducation Nationale. "Les Éleves de nationalité étrangère scolarisés dans le premier et le second degré en 1993–1994." *Note d'information 25.03, Ministère de L'Éducation Nationale.* Paris, 1995.

National Academy of Education, Commission on Reading. *Becoming a Nation of Readers: The Report of the Commission on Reading.* Pittsburgh, Pa., 1985.

National Association for the Education of Young Children. "Guidelines for Appropriate Curriculum Content and Assessment in Programs Serving Children Ages 3 Through 8: A Position Statement of the National Association for the Education of Young Children and the National Association for the Education of Early Childhood Specialists in State Departments of Education." Adopted November 1990. *Young Children,* March 1991, 21–38.

Neill, M. "Some Prerequisites for the Establishment of Equitable, Inclusive Multicultural Assessment Systems." In *Equity and Excellence in Educational Testing and Assessment,* ed. M. T. Nettles and A. L. Nettles, 121–26. Boston: Kluwer, 1994.

Neill, M., and Medina, N. J. "Standardized Testing: Harmful to Educational Health." *Phi Delta Kappan,* May 1989, 688–97.

Nettles, M. T., and Bernstein, A. "Introduction: The Pursuit of Equity in Educational Testing and Assessment." In *Equity and Excellence in Educational Testing and Assessment,* ed. M. T. Nettles and A. L. Nettles. Boston: Kluwer, 1994.

Norvez, A. *De la naissance à l'école. Santé, mode de garde, et préscolarité dans la France contemporaine.* Paris: Presses Universitaires de France et Institut National d'Études Demographiques, 1990.

Noyes, E. S., Sale, W. M., and Stalnaker, J. M. *Report on the First Six Tests in English Composition.* New York: College Entrance Examination Board, 1945.

Nuthall, G., and Church, J. "Experimental Studies of Teaching Behaviour." In *Towards a Science of Teaching,* ed. G. Chanan. London: National Foundation for Educational Research, 1973.

O'Keeffe, D. J. *Truancy in English Secondary Schools.* London: Her Majesty's Stationery Office, 1994.

Olson, L. "Progressive Era Concept Now Breaks Mold: NASDC Schools Explore 'Project Learning.'" *Education Week,* February 17, 1993, 6–7.

———. "Cards on the Table." *Education Week,* June 14, 1995, 24.

Organization for Economic Cooperation and Development. *OECD Economic Surveys, 1993–94: United States.* Paris, 1995, Chapter IV.

Pais, A. *"Subtle Is the Lord": The Science and the Life of Albert Einstein.* Oxford: Oxford University Press, 1982.

Palincsar, A. S. "Reciprocal Teaching: Can Student Discussions Boost Comprehension?" *Instructor* 96 (January 1987): 56–58.

Palincsar, A. S., and Brown, A. L. "Instruction for Self-Regulated Reading." In *Toward the Thinking Curriculum: Current Cognitive Research,* ed. L. B. Resnick and L. E. Klopfer, 19–39. Alexandria, Va.: Association for Supervision and Curriculum Development, 1989.

Paris, S. G., and Oka, E. R. "Children's Reading Strategies, Metacognition and Motivation." *Developmental Review* 6 (1986): 25–56.

Patterson, O. "Language, Ethnicity, and Change." *Journal of Basic Writing* 3 (1980): 70.

———. "Affirmative Action on the Merit System." *New York Times,* August 7, 1995, A-13.

Pentony, J. F. "Cultural Literacy: A Concurrent Validation." *Educational and Psychological Measurement* 52 (1992): 967–72.

———. "Cultural Literacy: An Empirical Investigation." Report to the Southwestern Psychological Association, April 1993.

Perfetti, C. A., and Lesgold, A. "Discourse Comprehension and Sources of Individual Differences." In *Cognitive Processes in Comprehension,* ed. M. Just and P. Cartenter. Hillsdale, N.J.: Erlbaum, 1977.

Perfetti, C. A., and McKeown, M. G. "Effects of Long-Term Vocabulary Instruction on Lexical Access and Reading Comprehension." *Journal of Educational Psychology* 74 (1982): 506–21.

Perl, S. "The Composing Processes of Unskilled College Writers." *Research in the Teaching of English* 13 (1979): 317–36.

Pestalozzi, J. *Pestalozzi's Educational Writings,* ed. J. A. Green and F. A. Collie. New York: Longmans, 1912.

———. *The Education of Man: Aphorisms, with an Introduction by W. H. Kilpatrick.* New York: Greenwood, 1951.

Peterson, M. D. *Lincoln in American Memory.* New York: Oxford University Press, 1994.

Piaget, J. *Science of Education and the Psychology of the Child.* New York: Orion Press, 1970.

Pierce, K. A., Duncan, M. K., and Gholson, B. "Cognitive Load, Schema Acquisition, and Procedural Adaptation in Nonisomorphic Analogical Transfer. *Journal of Educational Psychology* 85 (March 1993): 66–74.

Pinker, S. *The Language Instinct.* New York: William Morrow, 1994.

Popham, W. "Performance Tests of Teaching Proficiency: Rationale, Development, and Validation." *American Educational Research Journal* 8:105–17.

Pressley, M., and Rankin, J. "More About Whole Language Methods of Reading Instruction for Students at Risk for Early Reading Failure." *Learning Disabilities Practice* 9 (1994): 157–68.

Quann, C. J. "Pass/Fail Grading—An Unsuccess Story." *College and University* 49, no. 3 (1973): 230–35.

Ravitch, D. *The Troubled Crusade: American Education, 1945–1980.* New York: Basic Books, 1983.

Ravitch, D., and Finn, C. *What Do Our 17-Year-Olds Know? A Report on the First National Assessment of History and Literature.* New York: Harper and Row, 1987.

Remondino, C. "A Factorial Analysis of the Evaluation of Scholastic Compositions in the Mother Tongue." *British Journal of Educational Psychology* 30 (1959): 242–51.

Resnick, L. B., and Klopfer, L. E. "Toward the Thinking Curriculum: An Overview." In *Toward the Thinking Curriculum: Current Cognitive Research,* ed. L. B. Resnick and L. E. Klopfer. Alexandria, Va.: Association for Supervision and Curriculum Development, 1989.

Rosenshine, B., and Meister, C. "Reciprocal Teaching: A Review of the Research." *Review of Educational Research* 64 (Winter 1994): 479–530.

Rosenshine, B., and Stevens, R. "Teaching Functions." In *Handbook of Research on Teaching.* 3rd ed., ed. M. C. Wittrock, 376–41. New York: Macmillan, 1986.

Rugg, H. O. *The Child-Centered School.* Yonkers-on-Hudson, N.Y., and Chicago: World Book Company, 1928.

Scardamalia, M., and Bereiter, C. "Computer Support for Knowledge-Building Communities." *Journal of the Learning Sciences* 3, no. 3 (1994): 265–83.

Scardamalia, M., Bereiter, C., and Lamon, M. "CSILE: Trying to Bring Students into World 3." In *Classroom Lessons: Integrating Cognitive Theory and Classroom Practice,* ed. K. McGilley, 201–28. Cambridge, Mass.: MIT Press, 1994.

Schoenfeld, A. H., and Hermann, D. J. "Problem Perception and Knowledge Structure in Expert and Novice Mathematical Problem Solvers. *Journal of Experimental Psychology: Learning, Memory, and Cognition* 8 (1982): 484–94.

Scribner, B. L. S., et al. "Are Smart Tankers Better? AFQT and Military Productivity." *Armed Forces and Society* 12 (1986): 193–206.

Scuderi, S. G. *Antonio Gramsci e il problema pedagogico.* Catania: C.U.E.C.M., 1985.

Sewall, G. T. *Necessary Lessons: Decline and Renewal in American Schools.* New York: The Free Press, 1983.

Shain, B. *The Myth of American Individualism: The Protestant Origins of American Political Thought.* Princeton, N.J.: Princeton University Press, 1994.

Siegler, R. S. "Adaptive and Non-Adaptive Characteristics of Low-Income Children's Mathematical Strategy Use." In *The Challenge in Mathematics and Science Education: Psychology's Response,* ed. Penner et al., 341–66. Washington, D.C.: American Psychological Association, 1993.

Singer, H., and Donlon, D. "Active Comprehension: Problem-Solving Schema with Question Generation for Comprehension of Complex Short Stories." *Reading Research Quarterly* 17:116–86.

Smith, J. P., and Welch, F. R. "Black Economic Progress After Myrdal." *Journal of Economic Literature* 27 (June 1989): 519–64.

Smith, M. *And Madly Teach.* Chicago: Regnery, 1949.

Spiro, R. J. "Cognitive Processes in Prose Comprehension and Recall." In *Theoretical*

*Issues in Reading Comprehension,* ed. R. J. Spiro, B. C. Bruce, and W. C. Brewer. Hillsdale, N.J.: Erlbaum, 1981.

Spranger, E. "Zur Theorie des Verstehens und zur geisteswissenschaftlichen Psychologie." In *Festschrift Johannes Volkelt zum 70. Geburtstag.* Munich, 1918.

Stallings, J., and Kasowitz, D. *Follow Through Classroom Evaluation Evaluation, 1972–1973.* Stanford, Calif.: Stanford Research Institute, 1974.

Stanovich, K. E., and Cunningham, A. E. "Reading as Constrained Reasoning." In *Complex Problem Solving: Principles and Mechanisms,* ed. R. J. Sternberg and P. A. Frensch, 3–60. Hillsdale, N.J.: Erlbaum, 1991.

Stanovich, K. E., West, R. F., and Harrison, M. R. "Knowledge Growth and Maintenance Across the Life Span: The Role of Print Exposure." *Developmental Psychology* 31 (1995): 811–26.

Sternberg, R. J. "Criteria for Intellectual Skills Training." *Educational Researcher* 12 (1983): 6–12.

Stevenson, H. "Adapting to School: Children in Beijing and Chicago." *Annual Report.* Stanford, Calif.: Center for Advanced Study in Behavioral Sciences.

Stevenson, H., Chuansheng, C., and Shin-Ying, L. "Mathematics Achievement of Chinese, Japanese, and American Children: Ten Years Later." *Science* 259 (January 1, 1993): 51–58.

Stevenson, H., and Stigler, J. *The Learning Gap: Why Our Schools Are Failing and What We Can Learn from Japanese and Chinese Education.* New York: Summit Books, 1992.

Sticht, T. G., Hofstetter, C. H., and Hofstetter, C. R. *Knowledge, Literacy, and Life in San Diego.* San Diego: San Diego Consortium for Workforce Education and Lifelong Learning, 1995.

Sticht, T. G., and James, J. H. "Listening and Reading." In *Handbook of Reading Research,* ed. D. Pearson et al., 293–318. New York: Longman, 1984.

Sticht, T. G., et al. *Auding and Reading. A Developmental Model.* Alexandria, Va.: Human Resources Research Organization, 1974.

Stone, J. E. "Developmentalism: An Obscure but Pervasive Restriction on Educational Improvement." *Educational Policy Analysis Archives* (Electronic). Vol. 4, no. 8. Tempe, Ariz., 1996.

Suddick, D. E., and Kelly, R. E. "Effects of Transition from Pass/No Credit to Traditional Letter Grade System." *Journal of Experimental Education* 50, no. 2 (Winter 1981–82): 88–90.

Swanson, D. B., Norman, G. R., and Linn, R. L. "Performance Based Assessment: Lessons from the Health Professions." *Educational Researcher* 24 (1995): 5–11, 35.

Tennenbaum, S. *William Heard Kilpatrick: Trailblazer in Education.* New York: Harper, 1951.

Thompson, R. F. *The Brain: A Neuroscience Primer.* New York: W. H. Freeman, 1993.

Tierney, R. J., and Cunningham, J. W. "Research on Teaching Reading Comprehension." In *Handbook of Reading Research,* ed. D. Pearson et al., 609–56. New York: Longman, 1984.

Tversky, A., and Kahneman, D. "Availability: A Heuristic for Judging Frequency and Probability." *Cognitive Psychology* 5 (1973): 207–32.

U.S. Department of Health and Human Services. *The Impact of Head Start on Children, Families and Communities: Final Report of the Head Start Evaluation, Synthesis and Utilization Project, Executive Summary.* Washington, D.C., 1985.

Walberg, H. J. "Improving the Productivity of America's Schools." *Educational Leadership* 8 (1984): 19–27.

———. "Improving Local Control and Learning." Typescript, 1994. Walberg cites: Straits, B. C. "Residence, Migration, and School Progress." *Sociology of Education* 60 (1987): 34–43.

———. "Improving School Science in Advanced and Developing Countries." *Review of Education Research* 61 (1991): 625–99.

Walberg, H. J., and Tsai, S. "Matthew Effects in Education." *American Educational Research Journal* 20 (Fall 1983): 359–73.

Westbrook, R. B. *John Dewey and American Democracy.* Ithaca, N.Y.: Cornell University Press, 1991.

Whitehead, A. N. *An Introduction to Mathematics.* New York: Oxford University Press, 1948.

Williams, W. E. "Black Economic Progress: The Rand Corporation Speaks." *Journal of the American Planning Association* 53 (Autumn 1987): 531–33.

Willinsky, J. "The Vocabulary of Cultural Literacy in a Newspaper of Substance." Report, National Reading Conference, Tucson, Ariz., 1988.

Wiske, M. S. "How Teaching for Understanding Changes the Rules in the Classroom." *Educational Leadership,* February 1994, 21.

Wood, D., Halfon, N., and Scarlata, D. "Impact of Family Relocation on Children's Growth, Development, School Function, and Behavior." *Journal of the American Medical Association* 270 (September 15, 1993): 1334–38.

Woodring, P. "The Development of Teacher Education." In *Teacher Education.* 74th Yearbook of the National Society for the Study of Education, ed. K. Ryan. Chicago: University of Chicago Press, 1975.

Zemelman, S., Daniels, H., and Hyde, A. *Best Practice.* Portsmouth, N.H.: Heineman, 1993.

Zigler, E., and Muenchow, S. *Head Start: The Inside Story of America's Most Successful Educational Experiment.* New York: HarperCollins/Basic Books, 1992.

Zilversmit, A. *Changing Schools: Progressive Education Theory and Practice, 1930–1960.* Chicago: University of Chicago Press, 1993.

# Index